The Princeton Review®

DIGITAL SAT®

ADVANCED

D1568126

2nd Edition

The Staff of The Princeton Review

PrincetonReview.com

Penguin Random House

The Princeton Review
110 East 42nd St, 7th Floor
New York, NY 10017

Published in the United States by Penguin Random House, LLC, New York.

ISBN: 978-0-593-51747-5
eBook ISBN: 978-0-593-51748-2
ISSN: 2767-7273

The material in this book is up-to-date at the time of publication. However, changes may have been instituted by the testing body in the test after this book was published.

If there are any important late-breaking developments, changes, or corrections to the materials in this book, we will post that information online in the Student Tools. Register your book and check your Student Tools to see if there are any updates posted there.

Editor: Orion McBean
Production Editor: Kathy Carter and Nina Mozes
Production Artist: Deborah Weber

Printed in the United States of America.

10 9 8 7 6 5 4 3 2 1

2nd Edition

The Princeton Review Publishing Team
Rob Franek, Editor-in-Chief
David Soto, Senior Director, Data Operations
Stephen Koch, Senior Manager, Data Operations
Deborah Weber, Director of Production
Jason Ullmeyer, Production Design Manager
Jennifer Chapman, Senior Production Artist
Selena Coppock, Director of Editorial
Orion McBean, Senior Editor
Aaron Riccio, Senior Editor
Meave Shelton, Senior Editor
Chris Chimera, Editor
Patricia Murphy, Editor
Laura Rose, Editor
Isabelle Appleton, Editorial Assistant

Penguin Random House Publishing Team
Tom Russell, VP, Publisher
Alison Stoltzfus, Senior Director, Publishing
Emily Hoffman, Associate Managing Editor
Patty Collins, Executive Director of Production
Mary Ellen Owens, Assistant Director of Production
Alice Rahaeuser, Associate Production Manager
Maggie Gibson, Associate Production Manager
Suzanne Lee, Senior Designer
Eugenia Lo, Publishing Assistant

For customer service, please contact **editorialsupport@review.com**, and be sure to include:

- full title of the book
- ISBN
- page number

Acknowledgments

Very special thanks to the authors of this title, Kenneth Brenner, Sara Kuperstein, and Scott O'Neal.

Special thanks to the following contributors who assisted with more than one part of this book: Harrison Foster, Beth Hollingsworth, Robert Otey, Gabby Peterson, Kathy Ruppert, and Suzanne Wint.

Thanks as well to the following contributors: Aleksei Alferiev, Tania Capone, Paul Christiansen, Stacey Cowap, Wazhma Daftanai, Adam Keller, Kevin Keogh, Ali Landreau, Aaron Lindh, Jomil London, Sweena Mangal, Sionainn Marcoux, Valerie Meyers, Jason Morgan, Acacia Nawrocik-Madrid, Elizabeth Owens, Denise Pollard, and Jess Thomas.

Content Director of High School Programs
Amy Minster

Contents

Get More (Free) Content
at PrincetonReview.com/prep

As easy as 1·2·3

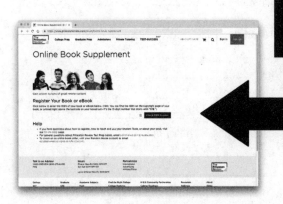

1 Go to PrincetonReview.com/prep or scan the **QR code** and enter the following ISBN for your book: **9780593517475**

2 Answer a few simple questions to set up an exclusive Princeton Review account. *(If you already have one, you can just log in.)*

3 Enjoy access to your **FREE** content!

Once you've registered, you can...

- Access a variety of resources such as summary pages, a chapter guide, and additional Digital SAT Modules with the hardest drill questions and explanations

- Take a full-length Digital SAT

- Get valuable advice about the college application process, including tips for writing a great essay and where to apply for financial aid

- Use our searchable rankings of *The Best 389 Colleges* to find out more information about your dream school

- Check to see if there have been any corrections or updates to this edition

Need to report a potential **content** issue?

Contact **EditorialSupport@review.com** and include:
- full title of the book
- ISBN
- page number

Need to report a **technical** issue?

Contact **TPRStudentTech@review.com** and provide:
- your full name
- email address used to register the book
- full book title and ISBN
- Operating system (Mac/PC) and browser (Chrome, Firefox, Safari, etc.)

Part I
Orientation

Chapter 1
Introduction to the Digital SAT

The pursuit of a perfect or near-perfect SAT score is an impressive goal. Achieving that goal requires a thorough command of the material and strategies specific to the SAT. To begin your quest, learn everything you can about the test. This chapter presents an overview of the Digital SAT, advice about when to take it, information about how SAT scores are used, and a summary of what this book offers.

WELCOME

So, you think you can score a 1450 or better? We're all for it. The Princeton Review supports all students who want to do their best. We've written this book specifically for students who are in a position to score at the very highest levels. This means you are already scoring at a 1350 or above and are looking to fine-tune your approach to get a few more correct answers. We believe that to achieve a perfect or near-perfect score, you have to know as much as possible about the test itself and, more important, about yourself.

You may know all of the basic facts about the Digital SAT already, but even if you think you do, we encourage you to read through this chapter to be sure you know every single thing you can about the test you're going to conquer.

FUN FACTS ABOUT THE DIGITAL SAT

All of the content review and strategies we teach in the following lessons are based on the specific structure and format of the Digital SAT. Before you can beat the test, you have to know how it's built.

Structure

The Digital SAT consists of two main sections: Reading and Writing (RW) and Math. Each section is broken into two modules, so you'll do two RW modules, take a break, and then do two Math modules.

Reading/Writing	Reading/Writing	Break	Math	Math
32 minutes	32 minutes	10 minutes	35 minutes	35 minutes
27 questions*	27 questions*		22 questions*	22 questions*

*Two questions from each module won't be scored. College Board calls these "pre-test questions," but you won't know which two questions are unscored.

Why does College Board break the sections into two modules each? Because the difficulty of the second module actually depends on how you do on the first one. Since you take this test on a computer, the software can go ahead and score your first module of each section instantaneously. Then, it will automatically give you a second module of that section based on the results. Here's how that works:

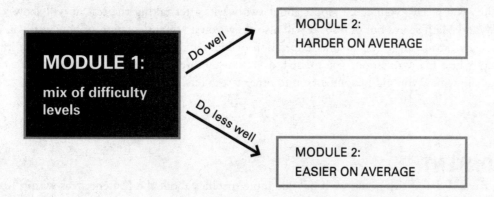

As you can see, if you do pretty well on the first module of either RW or Math, your second module will be a bit (or possibly a lot) harder than the first one. On the other hand, if you don't do as well, you'll get an easier second module. The idea behind this is that you don't waste time with questions that aren't appropriate for your skill level. If someone is very weak on math, that person should be given a greater number of easier questions to do, as there's no point in giving that person a bunch of hard questions that the student is just going to have to guess on. On the other hand, students who are very strong on RW should get to prove their abilities by being given more challenging questions.

Of course, your score is going to be adjusted accordingly. Your second module is going to be weighted more if it is the harder one. That being said, you're reading this book because you are hoping to score at least 1450. In that case, you will need to get the harder second module on both RW and Math, so we won't waste time discussing the easier second module in any greater detail.

You may be wondering what the cutoff is for the harder second module. How many correct answers do you need on the first module to get the harder second module? The answer is a bit complicated. We've found that it differs from test to test, and it may even differ depending on *which* questions you answer correctly—not just *how many*. However, we can confidently say that you need to answer more than half of the questions correctly on the first module to be given the harder second module. If you're reading this book, you should already be answering more than half of the questions right on each first module.

Scoring

The Reading and Writing section and the Math section are each scored on a scale from 200 to 800 and then added together for an overall score between 400 and 1600. How do the two modules together make up that 800-point score? It's hard to say. As you can imagine, there are many combinations of right answers that students can get. College Board hasn't publicized much about the scoring on the Digital SAT. We know that the questions are weighted more on the harder second module and that individual questions are weighted slightly differently depending on factors that College Board hasn't disclosed. Because the scoring on the Digital SAT is so difficult to figure out, it's not worth wasting time trying to determine how many correct answers you need or what your score is going to be with different combinations of right and wrong answers. Our online tests will give you scores, but they should be considered approximate. You're here to score as high as possible, so focus on using the strategies in this book to do just that.

When you receive your score report about two weeks after taking the test, it will show your RW and Math scores out of 800. It will also show you a visual depiction of how well you did in a few broad categories, such as Expression of Ideas and Advanced Math. You won't know exactly how many questions you missed, overall or by category. You will be given a percentile that shows how you did in comparison to other test-takers.

CONTENT

In Parts II–IV of this book, we'll provide more specifics about the content areas within Reading, Writing, and Math. Here's a brief overview of each section.

Reading and Writing

This is one section of the test and one scoring area, but it really consists of two separate subjects (Reading and Writing). Thus, this book covers them separately. Each question on Reading and Writing has a short passage (25–150 words) or occasionally two small passages. Reading questions include vocabulary and reading comprehension, the latter of which will ask you to understand the meaning and/or structure of a text, which could include literature. Writing questions relate to punctuation and grammar rules as well as the composition of sentences. Both Reading and Writing questions have passages on topics such as science, history/culture, and the arts. The Reading and Writing modules are organized in a very specific way, by both topic and difficulty level, which you'll learn more about later.

Math

Most Math questions are multiple-choice, but about 25% are fill-ins in which you type the answer yourself. The Math questions are roughly organized from easiest to hardest, so the most challenging questions will come toward the end of each module. Math subjects include lots of algebra, arithmetic, data and statistics, coordinate geometry, plane geometry, and trigonometry.

TOOLS AND RESOURCES

As the name suggests, the Digital SAT is taken on a computer—but that doesn't mean you can just kick back and click on answers from the comfort of your bed. You'll still need to go in person to take it with a group of students and a proctor, an adult who gives instructions and monitors the test-taking conditions.

Although the test is given on the computer (you'll either take your own device or use one at the testing center), you will be given scratch paper and can take your own pens or pencils. In the Math section of this book, you'll get some advice on how to effectively use the scratch paper. You can also use scratch paper on the RW section if you find it helpful. In addition, you're allowed to take your own basic or graphing calculator.

The computer software that delivers the test does provide you with some extremely helpful tools, though. Let's take a look at what they are:

Tool	Function	Tips
Answer eliminator	Cross off multiple-choice answers on the screen	Use this on both RW and Math anytime you see an answer that definitely isn't right.
Highlight/annotate (RW only)	Highlight any part of the question and/or passage and type an associated note into a box	You can highlight what the question is asking for and any key information in the text. If the answer isn't stated in the text (such as for Purpose questions), annotate what the answer should be in your own words.
Built-in Desmos calculator (Math only)	Perform basic calculations and graph nearly any equation in any format	This calculator is much more powerful and more helpful than a handheld graphing calculator and can help you answer hard questions in seconds.
Reference sheet (Math only)	Provide math formulas (mostly geometry) that may be needed for questions	Make sure you know what formulas are provided so that you'll know to find them on the reference sheet if needed.
Review page	See what questions have been answered, left unanswered, and marked	Instead of clicking the forward and back buttons repeatedly, use the review page to go directly to the question you want to look at.
Mark for review button	Show the question as "marked" on the review page	We recommend using this to indicate questions you started but got stuck on and want to return to later.

Practice with the on-screen tools on your Digital SAT practice tests before test day.

You'll learn much more about how to use these tools effectively later in this book. For now, keep in mind that you want to become fully comfortable with using the on-screen tools before test day. If you don't take advantage of them, you'll really hurt your chances of scoring as high as you'd like.

THE SAT SCHEDULE

The SAT is currently offered in the U.S. and internationally seven times a year: August, October, November, December, March, May, and June. In addition, your school may offer a School Day SAT at other times of the year.

Take the SAT when your schedule best allows. You generally don't need to take the SAT for the first time until at least the fall of your junior year. It's best not to start too early because you want to take advantage of the learning and growth you'll experience leading up to applying for college. Most students end up taking the SAT two or three times. We recommend that you find a 3–4-month window in your schedule that covers at least two SAT tests. Prep first, then take a test, and then continue prepping as needed for a second or third test. This way, you can be finished with the SAT in a relatively short period of time. You'll do better if you concentrate on SAT prep for that shorter window of time rather than dragging out your prep over an extended period. We also encourage you to be finished taking the SAT by the end of your junior year. In your senior year, you'll be busy with college applications as well as all the fun things that come along with your final year of high school. You'll be glad if you're already finished with the SAT at that point!

Here are some example schedules that we recommend:

> **Start prepping:** Summer before 11th grade
> **First test:** August
> **Second test:** October
> **Final test if needed:** November/December

Consider this: The August, October, November, and December tests are close together. You might need to go ahead and register for the next one before you get your scores from the previous one. If you wait to get your scores, you might miss the registration deadline.

> **Start prepping:** Fall of 11th grade
> **First test:** October
> **Second test:** November
> **Final test if needed:** December

Consider this: The October, November, and December tests are close together. You might need to go ahead and register for the next one before you get your scores from the previous one. If you wait to get your scores, you might miss the registration deadline.

> **Start prepping:** Winter of 11th grade
> **First test:** March
> **Second test:** May
> **Final test if needed:** June

Consider this: There are two months between March and May, so you can wait to get your March scores to see whether you need to take the test again. However, if you are taking AP exams, you may not be as focused to take the SAT in May.

REGISTERING FOR THE SAT

Go to collegeboard.org and create a student account. At collegeboard.org, you can view test dates, fees, and registration deadlines. You can research the requirements and processes to apply for extended time or other accommodations, register for the test, view your scores, and order score reports.

You can contact College Board customer service by phone at 866-756-7346 (or at +1 212-713-7789 for international callers), but you cannot sign up for the test by phone if you are taking it for the first time.

> **Test Security**
> As part of the registration process, you have to upload or mail a photograph that will be printed on your admission ticket. On test day, you have to take the ticket and acceptable photo identification with you.

Scores

When you register for the SAT, you'll be given the option to automatically send the scores from that date to four colleges of your choice. If this is your one and only time taking the SAT and you are already in the process of applying to college, go ahead and do this! Most likely, though, that isn't going to be your situation. If you are taking the SAT before your senior year, as we recommend, it'll be too early to send SAT scores to colleges even if you have already solidified your list of schools. Furthermore, you may be considering taking the test again, or you may have already taken it once or twice. In that case, you don't want to automatically send the scores. You might have done better on an earlier test, or you might do better on a future test. So, in most cases you'll want to skip sending scores to colleges until later on when you already have all of your SAT scores across multiple dates and are in the college application process. (There is a fee associated with this.)

So, let's say you end up taking the SAT twice. The second time, you score higher on both RW and Math. In that case, when you apply to college, you'll just go ahead and send the scores from the second date. There's no reason to send the first set of scores since both of them were lower. The only exception to this is if a college says you must send all of your scores, in which case you should be sure to do that.

On the other hand, maybe you take it twice and on the second try you improve your Math but decrease your RW, so your best RW score is from the first date and your best Math score is from the second date. In that case, you'll want to send both sets of scores. Most colleges super-score, which means they'll take your highest RW score and your highest Math score even if you didn't get them on the same test. As a final possibility, some schools ask you to send your single best date. In that case, just send the one with the highest overall score.

It's also worth noting that it's possible to cancel your SAT scores, but only before you actually get the scores. You can cancel your scores at the testing center or within a week of taking the test, but this should be done only in the most extreme circumstances, like if you became violently ill and didn't answer any questions on the test. In any other case, you shouldn't cancel, even if you feel you didn't perform your best, because—remember—you can generally choose which scores you send to colleges. You may not have done as badly as you think, and even if you did, you can simply choose not to send those scores (unless a college asks to see all of your scores, but in that case they are most likely going to take a superscore).

Testing Policies

Colleges will generally accept either the ACT or the SAT, but we're going to focus on the SAT since that's what you've chosen to prepare for.

As you just saw, college admissions policies on test scores can vary in terms of how many scores you need to submit and how they treat those scores. That's why it's crucial that you do some research on colleges you think you might be interested in. Do it now, because you may find that the schools you like don't require you to submit SAT scores—or may not even accept them at all. You definitely want to find out whether you even need to take the SAT before you invest a lot of time into preparing for it. Let's take a look at the different ways colleges can treat SAT scores.

Policy	Description
Test required	You must submit SAT scores in order for your application to be considered.
Test optional	You may submit SAT scores, and they can help your chances of getting in, but scores aren't required.
Test flexible	Instead of submitting SAT scores, you can meet requirements by submitting AP exams, IB exams, or other types of tests or by having a certain GPA or class rank.
Test blind	Even if you submit test scores, they won't be considered as part of your application, so don't waste your time and money submitting them.

It's important to keep in mind that these policies can change from year to year. Many colleges put in place test-optional policies during the COVID-19 pandemic, but some have gone back to requiring test scores and others still may in the future. Make sure to check the admissions website to see what each school's policy is, and call or email the admissions office if you have any questions about the policy.

There are also other reasons to take the SAT besides college admissions. Some schools may not require the test for admissions, but they may still use SAT scores for placement into classes, scholarships, or other uses. And if a school is test-optional, the 1450+ you're aiming for can help you stand out if that's above the average SAT score for that school. It can also help balance out weaker aspects of your application. We'll take a closer look at that in a moment.

THE BIG PICTURE

Ultimately, you're taking the SAT because of college, whether it's for admissions, a scholarship, or something else. So, let's examine what that big picture of applying to college looks like. First, you need to do some research and find schools that are a good fit for your personality and interests and have what you are looking for in a college. For instance, if you want to study Russian literature, you should apply to colleges that offer such a program. We know that high-scorers tend to focus on a small handful of elite, highly selective institutions. There's no harm in considering these schools, but make sure to find out whether they're a good fit for you. Your dream school shouldn't be based solely or even primarily on the name or reputation of the school. There are hundreds of great colleges and universities in the U.S., and just because you may not have heard of one already doesn't mean it couldn't be a good fit for you.

Aside from considering how good of a fit each college is for you, it's also worth looking at how much you're going to have to pay. College is expensive, and it's challenging to have to pay off college loans when you're just starting out in your post-college career. Since you're trying to maximize your SAT score, why not consider a college that will pay you for doing so? There are some colleges that will actually grant you an *automatic* scholarship just for having a high SAT score and a solid GPA. For example, as of 2024, Texas Tech and the University of Oklahoma each offered up to $9,000 per year for a top SAT score and GPA. There are also many colleges that will automatically *consider* you for a scholarship based on your SAT score and GPA. The reality is that neither your near-perfect test score nor your near-perfect GPA is going to make you stand out at an elite college that accepts less than 10% of applicants. Almost everyone applying to those schools has equally good credentials. However, if you're willing to consider schools beyond the ones with the most name recognition, you may find something that is not only a great fit for you but is also significantly more affordable.

Let's also keep in mind that test scores are only one part of the application. When you apply to college, in addition to test scores, you'll submit your high school transcript that includes your courses, final grades, GPA, and class rank; the application with all of your information on it, such as demographics, family data, and extracurriculars; and one or more essays. In addition, you may be submitting a portfolio, other types of test scores (such as those from AP exams), and/or a résumé. Colleges may also consider an audition or interview. All that goes to show that your chances of admission go far beyond the strength of your SAT scores. In fact, for many schools, the test scores are less important than most of these other factors. That's why it's critical not to let test prep consume your life. It's okay to be persistent about improving your score, but it's also important to have other interests and pursue things you're passionate about. Colleges want to accept students who are well-rounded and have activities beyond preparing to apply to college. And as obsessive as The Princeton Review may be about this test, we'd like for you to find some more useful hobbies.

SETTING REASONABLE GOALS

If your last SAT score was a 1400 and your test is in three days, it's not realistic to think that you can improve to a 1550 in that short amount of time (no matter how good the advice in this book is!). Unfortunately, there's no single way to predict how much a student's score can improve. It all depends on how much time you put into it, your willingness to try out and work on new methods, and how quickly you learn. If you take the time to carefully read through this book and work through the exercises it contains, using the new techniques you've learned, we think you'll see a real improvement.

But it's important to keep in mind what improvements look like when you're scoring above a 700 in a given section. As we mentioned earlier, the Digital SAT's scoring looks different from test to test. On previous versions of the SAT, we've seen tests on which you could miss a couple of questions and still get a perfect 800 as well as tests on which missing two questions could bring your score down to a 760. These fluctuations are impossible to predict and relate to how easy or hard the test happened to be on a particular day. According to College Board, a score of 1400 puts you at the 93rd percentile, meaning you're in the top 7% of students who take the SAT. There's nothing wrong with wanting to score even higher, especially if you find it fun to try to maximize your SAT score (yes, we know there are some of you out there!). The better prepared you are, the better your odds of hitting your goal, but it's not a bad idea to come up with a goal you can live with as well as a dream goal. If you happen to have a great test day and get a version of the test that plays perfectly to your strengths, then you may hit your ultimate goal, but otherwise you can at least get to a score you're satisfied with. In this book, we'll give you all the tips and strategies we can come up with to get you as high a score as possible. But admissions officers know just as well as you do that the difference between a 700 and an 800 is a matter of a handful of questions. Do your best to prepare, but don't put too much pressure on yourself. There's more to life (and college admissions) than the SAT!

THIS BOOK AND YOU

As we mentioned at the beginning of the chapter, this book is designed for students who are already consistently scoring at a 1350 or above. If you haven't yet reached this threshold, we would encourage you to pick up a copy of *Digital SAT Premium Prep* first. That book covers virtually every single topic on the SAT and will provide you with great strategies that should help you to correctly answer the majority of the questions on the test. It also includes several practice tests that you can use to work on your overall technique using the strategies from the book. Even if you are a very smart person and do well in advanced classes in school, if you're not already scoring at a high level, you're better off starting with *SAT Premium Prep* because it will help you improve in the areas that affect your score the most.

This book does *not* cover every topic on the test. In fact, it doesn't even cover all of the most common topics. We've chosen topics for this book based on what College Board considers hard questions, the common mistakes higher-scorers make, and smaller strategies that can help with those last few points. Before learning these topics, you need to have mastered the most commonly tested areas and need to have a solid pacing strategy. If you tend to do well on standardized tests but haven't become familiar with the SAT yet, try taking a free practice test either from College Board via its Bluebook app or on our website, princetonreview.com. The resulting score will help you decide whether this book will meet your needs or whether you should start with *Digital SAT Premium Prep*.

If you're ready to proceed, welcome! This book begins with some information on overall strategies and how to find what you need to work on, which we think will be an extremely helpful place to start. After that, you'll find chapters on Reading, Writing, and Math in that order. Chances are, you won't need every chapter in this book. For instance, if you have a strong vocabulary and never miss a vocab question, you may be able to skip the chapter dealing with vocabulary. You have our permission to choose the chapters that are going to be most helpful for you, but be sure to read the introduction for each section before diving in to any chapters from that section.

> Once you've read through Chapters 1 through 3, you will have done some self-analysis and will have a better idea of where to start. You'll also get information on how to find a chapter guide in your online student tools.

Once you feel that you've mastered the content and strategies for each section of the test, you can put all your new skills into practice on the test modules in Part V. There is one for Reading and Writing and one for Math. These represent the mix of topics and difficulty levels you are likely to see on the harder second module in each section. You can go through each one selectively to find more questions on a given topic that you'd like to practice, or you can take the full module, timed, to practice your pacing while applying your new SAT mastery. The choice is yours.

So, what are you waiting for? Let's get started!

Chapter 2
Digital SAT Overall Strategies and Pacing

To earn a perfect or near-perfect SAT score, you need strategies specific to the SAT. In this chapter, we'll provide an overview of the universal strategies. Each section of the SAT demands a specific approach, and even the most universal strategies vary in their applications. In Parts II–IV, we'll discuss these strategies in greater detail customized to the Reading, Writing, and Math portions of the test.

If you are currently scoring at a 1350 or higher, you already have a decent overall strategy. It's probably not a good idea to completely abandon your current techniques, especially if you don't have much time before you plan to take the Digital SAT. In this chapter, we'll go over what we think are the best ways to approach the test as a whole. Chances are, you've already been using some of these methods on your own. If not, and if you have some time, try them out on a practice test or a practice section to see how they work for you.

SLOW DOWN, SCORE MORE

One of the biggest challenges on the SAT is that you have a limited amount of time to answer the questions in each module. The obvious solution is to simply go faster. Of course, this isn't as simple as it sounds. Moving through the module more quickly comes with major trade-offs, namely that you're going to miss a lot of questions that you would have gotten right otherwise. Don't get us wrong: there *are* ways to save time (and we'll tell you all about them in this book). But rushing, skimming, skipping steps, and all of the other ways to "go faster" are only going to hurt your score. So, we're actually going to tell you the opposite of the "obvious" solution to the time limit: you may actually need to slow down in order to score higher.

This isn't true for everyone. If you find that you don't tend to run out of time and you know that you wouldn't have gotten more right answers even with unlimited time, then feel free to move on to the next point in this chapter. However, if you are making any careless errors or if you find yourself panicking about time and rushing, then slowing down can actually help. The goal is to get every single question right that you are able to get right. If you understand a question and know how to do it, you should be getting it right. Take the time that you need in order to do so. Instead of spending one minute on a question and getting it wrong, spend a minute and fifteen seconds and get it right. Otherwise, you've literally wasted that minute because you got the question wrong. You might as well have skipped it and not spent any time.

Going along with this, you don't want to hurry to answer the questions and then end up having five minutes or more left at the end. You might think it would be beneficial to have extra time to check your work, but in our experience, this isn't the best method. Usually, students don't spot and correct their errors when they go back and check their work, so that extra time doesn't really help. Instead, keep an eye on the clock and try to pace yourself so that you can finish close to when time runs out, not early. The additional time you spend on the questions will make much more of a difference than any "go back and check" time at the end. Plus, if you've applied the strategies in this book, you can be confident that you did the question right the first time. The more you practice full sections and tests, the better you'll get at knowing what the 32 minutes on an RW module or the 35 minutes on a Math module feels like and how quickly or slowly you should be moving through the module.

PERSONAL ORDER OF DIFFICULTY

Hand-in-hand with slowing down on questions is the order in which you attempt the questions, which we call your Personal Order of Difficulty (POOD). As we touched on in the Introduction chapter, both the RW and the Math modules are organized to some extent in an order of difficulty. However, that's based on College Board's opinion of difficulty level. Just because the test-writers think a question is hard doesn't mean it will be hard for you, and just because they think it's easy doesn't mean it will be easy for you. Take a look at the following example:

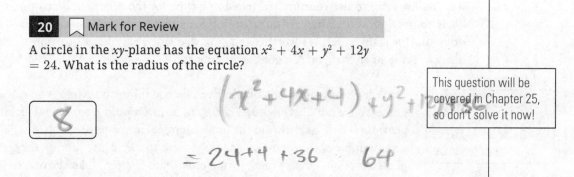

| 20 | 🔖 Mark for Review |

A circle in the xy-plane has the equation $x^2 + 4x + y^2 + 12y = 24$. What is the radius of the circle?

8

> This question will be covered in Chapter 25, so don't solve it now!

College Board has put questions like this near the very end of a harder second module. According to College Board (and your math teacher), in order to solve this problem, you need to be familiar with the standard form equation of a circle, complete the square to get this equation into standard form, and then find the radius using standard form. It's not difficult to see why that would be considered hard. There's a lot you would need to know and be able to do in order to solve this problem College Board's way. Plus, it's going to be fairly time-consuming, especially if completing the square isn't something you do regularly, and there are a few tricky aspects to this problem that could cause you to make a mistake even if you know what to do. However, as you will find out much more about later in this book, you can actually just type this equation exactly as it is into the built-in calculator, see the circle with two endpoints for the diameter, and use that to easily find the radius. For you, this actually becomes an easy question that should take less than a minute to solve, and it's not one you would want to save for the very end even though that's where it appears.

That's exactly why we would always advise you to follow your *Personal* Order of Difficulty. That means you should do whatever questions are easiest for you first, regardless of where they appear in the module. (We'll talk more about what that means for RW later on, since the RW has specific groupings of questions.) There are several benefits to the POOD strategy. First off, you get the easy stuff out of the way. If a question doesn't take much time and you know you can get it right, you might as well go ahead and do it. Although we know College Board does weigh individual questions slightly differently, overall, your score is based on how many correct answers you get. In the interest of getting as many correct answers as possible, you want to make sure you get all of those easy questions and don't run out of time before you get to them. By doing the easier questions first, you'll also start the module more confidently and you won't have to stress about how much time you're spending on harder questions early on.

The other part of this strategy entails skipping harder questions until you've gotten all of the easy ones out of the way. If a question looks like it might take a while or it's on a topic you feel less confident with, just save it for later. Try to think of every question as a point. Your goal is to collect as many points as you can throughout the module. Get the easy points first, and save the harder points for later. You'll find it much easier to pace yourself toward the end of the time limit if you know that you have only the harder questions left. Lastly, don't be stubborn. Your goal is to collect as many points as possible. Be willing to take a break from a question and come back to it if you're not close to getting an answer.

> Remember, if you start a question and get stuck, use the Mark for Review button and come back later.

SKIPPING, GUESSING, AND POE

It might happen that you have a few minutes remaining on the timer and a few hard questions left to do. In some cases, it may actually be strategic to just take a random guess on a question if that allows you to use your limited remaining time for the other questions that you're more likely to get right. Of course, if you're aiming for a top score, you can't guess on many questions. But in many cases, it's worth sacrificing that one really hard question that you're not likely to get right so that you can get the other ones.

> There's no penalty for guessing on the Digital SAT, so don't leave any questions blank.

Don't leave any questions blank. Even on the fill-ins on Math, you can still take a guess. You're not likely to guess correctly, but we would recommend picking an integer from 0 to 5, as these are the most common correct answers. If you have to guess on a multiple-choice question and don't want to spend any time on the question, just guess a random letter—there isn't a letter that's "better" than the others.

On the other hand, if you want to spend a little time on the question, you may be able to improve your odds when guessing. Perhaps you really don't understand a reading passage, but you see an answer that just doesn't seem likely. You don't know for sure that it's wrong, but you want to take a good guess, instead of a random guess. Here's an example:

---

15 🔖 Mark for Review

Which choice most logically completes the text?

(A) Arizona's allocated share of water from the Colorado River is too low in comparison with Colorado's share.

(B) during normal or low rainfall years, the river may have less water than is required for municipal use.

(C) the state of Colorado is able to exercise dictatorial control over the current water allocation system.

(D) Arizona will be subject to catastrophic flood risks due to the existing imbalance of water resources.

Once you have read the Reading chapters in this book, you'll know that answers with strong—or, as we would say, extreme—language are often trap answers. Thus, if we had to guess on this question and didn't have time (or chose not to spend the time) to check the answers against the passage, we probably wouldn't guess (C) because it uses the strong phrase *dictatorial control*. That doesn't mean that (C) couldn't be correct, but if we have to guess, we won't pick it.

Again, guessing isn't going to be a key strategy for anyone aiming to score above a 1400. What will be an extremely helpful strategy, though, is Process of Elimination. In school, you usually have to know the answers to the questions you're asked in order to get them correct. Seems pretty obvious, right? But that's not the case for the vast majority of questions on the Digital SAT. You don't necessarily need to know what the answer is, as long as you know what it isn't. In other words, if you can eliminate three wrong answers, you'll be left with the one right answer. What's more, it's often easier to spot the wrong answers than the right ones, especially on RW.

We'll talk much more about Process of Elimination, or POE, as it relates to specific topics later in this book. But let's go ahead and see an example of how helpful this strategy can be:

---

18 ▢ Mark for Review

In function f, the value of $f(x)$ decreases by a factor of 5 for every increase of 1 in the value of x. If $f(0) = 100$, which of the following equations defines function f?

Ⓐ $f(x) = \frac{1}{5}(100)^x$

Ⓑ $f(x) = x^{100}$

Ⓒ $f(x) = 100\left(\frac{1}{5}\right)^x$

Ⓓ $f(x) = 100(x)^{\frac{1}{5}}$

This is another Math question that College Board considers hard. And we're sure you can see why. The four answers look very similar—they all have the same numbers and variables but in different spots. It's very easy to convince yourself that one of the answers "makes sense," but that's an extremely risky strategy. You might also be tempted to construct the equation yourself the way you would in school, but there's an easier way. Instead, take advantage of the fact that this is a multiple-choice question. The question gives you values for x and $f(x)$, so why not plug those numbers into the equations in the answer choices and eliminate the ones that don't work? This way, you avoid wasting time writing your own equation and there's very little risk of making a mistake.

That's only one way that POE can be useful on Math. You'll also be able to eliminate partial answers, ones that are too big or too small, ones that don't match the information in the problem, and so on. And on RW, POE will be even more fundamental to your strategy since you usually won't know exactly how the correct answer will look. So, try to let go of doing all of the work yourself in order to get the answer. If you can *find* the answer instead of solving for it, all the better! You'll save yourself a good deal of time and effort in doing so.

WHAT TO WORK ON

There's a good chance that you picked up this book hoping to improve in some specific areas. Before you go ahead and focus on those areas, though, we want to offer you some advice on what you should be working on because it may not be what you think. Let's say you are scoring 750 on Math and 680 on RW. In that case, most students are going to say that they want to work on RW (perhaps exclusively). Of course, you should work on RW, and you do have more points to gain there. But you still have 50 more points available in Math, and it's your stronger area. Not only that, but you do extremely well on Math. Chances are it won't be that hard for you to improve on a few small areas where you might be missing questions.

The moral of the story? Don't neglect your stronger area in favor of your weaker area. If there's still room for improvement in your stronger area, especially if you have 50 points or more to gain, keep working at it. You may be able to get closer to perfect without too much effort.

It's also okay to focus on the area that you enjoy more. Perhaps you have about a 700 in both RW and Math, but you really enjoy the RW section more. Any points are good points, so it's fine to focus your time on RW. You also want to consider what areas are easiest to improve on. If you can identify any specific topics you tend to miss, it may be easier to work on those topics than to work on a section of the test where your missed questions seem more random. Of course, if you are applying to a program in which either your math or your verbal skills are emphasized, that may also guide which area of the test you focus on improving. We'll talk much more about specific topics to work on in the next chapter.

HOW TO PLAN YOUR STUDY TIME

This book contains lessons that go over specific topics and strategies, exercises and drills on those topics, and two full hard modules. You also have a full online practice test, and you can find additional practice tests through the Bluebook app. When should you use each of these materials? See the chart below.

Material	When to use it
Lesson content	When you are looking to learn better strategies or master the rules for a topic
Topic-specific drills	When you have learned more about a topic or have learned new strategies and are ready to practice them
Timed practice tests	When you want to try out or practice a new pacing strategy or when you have worked on a bunch of topics
Untimed practice tests or individual modules	When you want to do mixed practice, work on the order you attempt questions in without time pressure, or identify questions that you wouldn't be able to get right even with unlimited time

Just as completing the test too quickly can harm your performance, so too can rushing through this book. It takes time to learn, practice, and master new techniques. If your schedule allows, try to do no more than one chapter per day. It's a good idea to complete the exercises and drills associated with the lessons as you do each lesson so that you can test what you've learned and practice any new techniques. Once you've worked on a good deal of the content, take a practice test to continue to fine-tune your pacing and assess how you're doing on the topics you've been working on.

In the next chapter, you'll learn how to use the results of your drills and practice tests to improve further.

Chapter 3
Common Mistakes and How to Fix Them

You probably have some idea about what types of questions tend to give you trouble. But what about the mistakes that seem a bit more random and unpredictable? In this chapter, we'll take a look at the most common reasons students miss questions on the SAT, how you can identify when you're making those mistakes, and what you can do to avoid those errors in the future.

If you are already scoring at a 1350 or above, you aren't missing that many questions in each section, which can be frustrating because it may be hard to identify the source of your errors. There are actually many reasons you might miss a question, so let's take a look at what they are. If any of these mistakes sound familiar, you may want to circle or star them so you'll know what to look for in the next part of this chapter, when we go over how to fix these mistakes.

Mistake	Description	Examples
Lack of content knowledge	This is probably the most obvious mistake. You didn't know or had a misconception about some aspect of the concept.	**Reading**—You didn't know enough of the vocabulary words and had to guess. **Writing**—You forgot the difference between a semicolon and a colon. **Math**—You thought $(x^2)(x^3)$ equaled x^6.
Not reading the question	You answered for something other than what the question was asking.	**Reading**—You picked an answer that was stated by the text, but the question was asking *why* the author said something. **Writing**—You chose a Rhetorical Synthesis answer that you personally liked but that didn't fulfill the goal in the question. **Math**—You picked the value of *x*, but the question asked for *x* + 5.
Going too quickly	You were rushing due to the time limit or were overly confident and didn't take the time to check what you were doing.	**Reading**—You skimmed the passage and misunderstood what it said or skipped over a critical word or phrase within the argument. **Writing**—You read the sentence too quickly and didn't realize that it contained two independent clauses. **Math**—You missed a step or misunderstood the meaning of part of a word problem.
Poor pacing	If you're not comfortable with what the time limit feels like or you panic, you may spend too much time on some questions and not enough on others.	You spent too much time on one hard question and then didn't have enough time for other questions that would have been faster and easier.

Mistake	Description	Examples
Looking at the answers too soon	Sometimes an answer can catch your eye and make you want to pick it, and instead of figuring out the answer yourself, you try to interpret the passage in a way that will match the answer you latched onto.	**Reading**—You looked at the answers before understanding the passage and picked an answer that you really wanted to pick even though it wasn't fully supported by the text.
Using your ear instead of the rules	You picked an answer based on how a sentence sounded or looked instead of following the rules.	**Writing**—You picked an answer with a comma because it felt right even though there wasn't a reason for the comma based on the punctuation rules.
Not writing down steps	You did the work in your head or did a series of steps on the calculator without writing anything down on scratch paper.	**Math**—You did a bunch of work on the calculator or in your head without writing down your steps and accidentally did an operation twice. You solved for the wrong thing because you didn't write down and label what you were finding.
Stubbornly using a harder strategy	The strategies you've learned and perfected in school may be your default methods, but they may not be the most efficient on the SAT. If you're stubborn about solving problems the "right way," you may waste time and energy or risk making mistakes unnecessarily.	**Math**—Even though you learned how to plug in the answers and it would have been easy and low-risk, you chose to solve using algebra, which led to making a mistake.

Before we talk about fixing these mistakes, it's worth considering how easy or hard they are to fix. Generally, content errors can be easy to fix if you can establish what content area you're struggling with. It's fairly straightforward to learn more vocabulary (or math vocabulary) words, practice working with exponents, or memorize the acceptable uses of different punctuation marks. On the other hand, if you never took Geometry, learning all of the terms, rules, and formulas might be a much larger undertaking. You'll need to weigh your content gaps against how much time you have and how likely it is that those content areas will appear on the test. No matter how good your test-taking strategies are, though, you simply won't be able to score 1450 or higher without a near-perfect understanding of the content on the test.

The more strategy-based errors, like going too quickly or not pacing through the module well, can yield big results when you fix them, and you don't even have to learn any obscure trig rules or anything like that. They do require some time commitment to address, though, because you'll need to practice with full tests or at least full modules under realistic timed conditions in order to improve your skills in these areas.

In the chart below, you can see some ways to fix the errors we just went over.

Mistake	How to fix it
Lack of content knowledge	Learn the rules, formulas, and/or terms that you don't already know. Correct the misconceptions that are causing you to miss questions.
Not reading the question	Make it a habit to read the question *before* you read the passage or start doing any math. Then, double-check what the question is asking before choosing your answer.
Going too quickly	Try practicing untimed without rushing and see if you can get every question right. This will give you an idea of how much time you should be spending on the questions.
Poor pacing	Practice with full tests or modules to get more comfortable with the amount of time given. Remind yourself to do the easier questions first and save the harder ones for later. Consider strategically skipping one or two of the hardest, most time-consuming questions if the extra time allows you to get the remaining questions right. Work to identify strategies that will help you get questions right more efficiently.
Looking at the answers too soon	On Reading questions, don't look at the answers until you have read the passage and highlighted/annotated where applicable.
Using your ear instead of rules	Even if you tend to get most Writing answers right using your ear, work to learn the rules instead. They're more reliable than your ear. Remember that the right answer can sound wrong and wrong answers can sound right.
Not writing down steps	When you practice Math, use scratch paper, even if you're using a physical book. Get in the habit of automatically writing down the question number for every question as soon as you start looking at it so that you have a designated place to write down your work, even if you don't need scratch paper for every single question. Write down the steps as you go, even if you do the operations on the calculator or in your head.
Stubbornly using a harder strategy	Open your mind to the fact that your goal is to score as high as possible, which doesn't mean you have to solve problems the "right" way. When you apply to college, the admissions officers won't know whether you used algebra or a "shortcut" strategy—they'll just know that you have a great score. Trust us that our strategies are proven and that they can be more efficient, easier, and less risky than what you're used to doing. But you'll need to practice those strategies before you take the test or they won't be useful for you. It will take a concerted effort to change your mindset.

HOW YOUR SCORE REPORT CAN HELP

If you've taken an official Digital SAT exam through College Board (not a practice test), you've seen that the score reports College Board provides aren't super helpful. They break the RW and Math into only four broad categories each, and the graphic showing you how you did on those categories doesn't even tell you exactly how many questions you missed in each one. You'll never be told the correct answers (which can be frustrating when there was a question you really struggled with) or even get to see the questions again.

The College Board practice tests on the Bluebook app are a little more helpful. Those score reports let you view the questions over again, and you'll be able to access explanations as well. However, those explanations were written by College Board. If you've spent any time looking at them, you might have noticed they're not the most helpful. While College Board's RW explanations are okay, they explain only why answers are right and wrong—they don't help you with any strategies, so you still need to figure those out on your own. When it comes to Math explanations, though, College Board tends to suggest the most complicated methods. You'll rarely, if ever, see a suggestion to graph on the built-in graphing calculator or to use Process of Elimination. If you spend a lot of time reading College Board's explanations, you may learn how to solve problems, but you'll be learning to do them in ways that take far more time than they should.

You don't necessarily want to get your test-taking advice from the people who make the test. After all, they claimed for decades that it wasn't possible to prepare for the SAT, and after years of Princeton Review students proving them wrong, they've finally started admitting that it helps to prepare.

So, we've established that the College Board score reports, for practice tests and real tests, aren't going to help you out a whole lot. Luckily for you, our score reports will. The data provided on Princeton Review Digital SAT score reports will be invaluable in determining your strengths and weaknesses and what you need to work on. They're particularly useful for higher-scorers because you may not be sure exactly where you tend to miss questions. In this section, we'll go over all of the data you can get from your score report. If you haven't taken a practice test on our website yet, come back when you have a score report to refer to!

> Check out *Digital SAT Premium Prep* or one of our other SAT titles for additional online practice tests.

Pacing

Your score report shows the time spent on each question. Look to see if there are any questions you spent 4 minutes or more on. Then look to see if you got those questions right. If you spent 4 minutes on a question and you still got it wrong, that's a question you should have just skipped and guessed on (unless it was the only question you missed in the module, in which case it's fine if you saved it for the end and spent all of the remaining time on it). Being able to recognize questions that will take you a lot of time and that you don't have a great shot at getting right can really help you improve your pacing. At the very least, you should be saving them for the end and/or marking them if you start them and get stuck.

If you spent a lot of time on a question and got it right, you'll have to decide for yourself whether that time was worth it. If you missed several other questions that you think you could have gotten with a little more time, you might decide that you should have skipped the time-consuming question in favor of those other ones. Ultimately, if you feel like you ran out of time on a module, there's a very good chance that you can find at least one or two questions that received more time than they should have. Determining why those questions took as long as they did and whether they should have been skipped is a crucial part of improving your pacing.

Another thing to watch out for is if you spent too little time on any questions, especially toward the end of the module. This could mean that you didn't pace yourself well because you ran out of time before seeing the questions near the end, and they actually could have been easier ones. The score report shows the time spent on the first visit, so you can see if you made a quick decision about the "later" questions, and the column showing the number of times you viewed a question can confirm whether you effectively came back to harder questions later on.

Use of RW Tools

If you used the highlighter and/or annotation tool, you'll see that indicated in a column on the far right when you're looking at the RW modules. This will allow you to see quickly if there are questions for which you should have been using these tools but didn't.

Category Breakdowns

The top of each tab for RW and Math break down the sections into broad topic areas (Reading, Rules, and Rhetoric for RW and Algebra, Problem-Solving and Data Analysis, Geometry and Trigonometry, and Strategies for Math). These breakdowns can help you see broader trends in the types of questions you missed. To look at more specific categories, you have several options. You can simply look at "topic area" next to the questions you missed to see what topics they were from. Alternatively, you can click the "topic area" header to group the questions by topic. Finally, you can click to view by topic area near the upper right of each tab to see all the questions in a given area, as shown below. This is a great way to determine whether you tend to miss questions on specific topics.

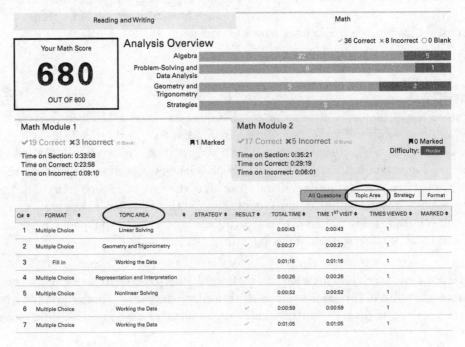

Additional Missed Question Categories

There are some additional categories that don't appear on the score report that you might find it helpful to look for. On RW, did you tend to miss questions on certain genres of passages? For example, if you really struggle with science, perhaps you tended to miss questions with science passages, regardless of the question type. Or perhaps you tended to miss literature, or specifically poetry, reading comp questions. You'll need to click the question numbers of the ones you missed to look back at the actual questions and determine this. On Writing, the Rules questions are broken down into specific topics, but Rules can also be grouped based on punctuation versus grammar. Look to see if you missed several punctuation questions, in which case you'll need to work on that topic. On Math, it's possible you tended to miss word problems or problems with multiple equations, for example. Try to see if the questions you're missing have anything in common besides the categories that appear on the score report.

It can also help to look at these features across multiple tests you've taken. Even if you don't have a Princeton Review score report, you can write down characteristics of the questions you've missed on other drills and tests you've taken and compare them to look for patterns.

Location of Missed Questions

Look to see whether you had groupings of missed questions, such as missing three in a row. If you find that, try to determine the cause. It could be that you were briefly distracted or you were rushing at the beginning or end. Of course, it could also just be a coincidence, but it's worth considering whether there is a reason.

Explanations

The explanations on the score report, which you can find by clicking the question numbers on the left side, should be extremely helpful. The most obvious benefit is that they'll help you understand why the right answer is right, why the wrong answers are wrong, and what strategy you should have used. Beyond that, though, the explanations can help you determine what you can improve on—even on questions you got right. You may realize that there was a more efficient method or that you just had a lucky guess.

Of course, the explanations will also help you determine what you did wrong on questions you missed. Did you go too quickly and skip a step? Did you misread the question? The explanation won't tell you this, so you'll need to analyze your own performance and determine what your reason for missing the question was. On RW, you'll be able to see what you highlighted and/or annotated, so those notes can help you determine where you went wrong. On Math, look back at your scratch paper to try to find your mistake. That's another reason it's helpful to be in the habit of writing down all your work.

We recommend making a chart or spreadsheet for those questions you missed or struggled to get right. On the spreadsheet, you can fill in its features (poetry passage, word problem, punctuation question, etc.) and what your reason for missing it was. See if you notice any patterns. This is especially helpful if you're scoring very high and tend to miss just a few questions here and there. Chances are, there is a pattern—you just need to figure out what it is. Once you've established why you tend to miss questions, try to determine what you can work on or do differently moving forward in order to stop making those mistakes.

The time you spend analyzing your work like this will save you tons of time in your SAT prep. Most high-scorers think that if they take more and more practice tests and complete more and more drills, their scores will automatically improve. This brute force approach is a slow way of making progress, and worse yet, it can actually reinforce bad habits if you continue working problems in a way that isn't the most effective. If you want to use your time efficiently, carefully analyze what you did well and not so well for all of the SAT questions you attempt. Then, determine how you can do better on your next drill or practice test. You'll see improvements *much* faster this way. It'll also keep you from having to continually find more and more materials.

Where To Start
Pages 19 and 20 have some information on What to Work On and How to Plan Your Study Time. After you complete the analysis here, if you'd like even more guidance on the content of this book and what each chapter can help you to achieve, see the Chapter Guide in your online student tools.

DIGITAL SAT SELF-ANALYSIS

Before you go on to the more specific content and strategy chapters, fill out this analysis of how you are doing right now. It will help you figure out what you need to prioritize and what chapters in this book to focus on. You may need to go through your most recent practice tests and drills, as we described earlier, to find your wrong-answer patterns before filling in some of the sections of this chart.

My current score is…	**Total:** **RW:** **Math:**
My goal score is…	**Total:** **RW:** **Math:**
This is my goal score because… (*Do you need to hit this score for a scholarship? Are you trying to stand out at a school with a high average SAT score? Do you need to balance out a weaker GPA? What other reasons do you have for choosing this goal?*)	
If I don't hit my goal score, I'll be happy with this score:	
This is how much time I have to prepare for the Digital SAT:	
I want to work on… (*Circle one and explain why. Remember not to neglect your stronger area if you still have points to gain there.*)	Mainly RW Mainly Math Both equally Because…

Here are the features of the RW questions I tend to miss: (*Examples: Purpose questions, poems, longer passages, punctuation questions, ones with a lot of science vocab*)	
Here are the features of the Math questions I tend to miss: (*Examples: ones at the end of the module, word problems, standard deviation, geometry, the ones with tables of numbers*)	
Here are the reasons I tend to miss RW questions: (*Examples: not reading the passage carefully, using my ear instead of knowing the punctuation and grammar rules, not looking at all four answers, having trouble understanding the passage*)	
Here are the reasons I tend to miss Math questions: (*Examples: going too quickly and making silly math errors, using algebra instead of an easier method, not remembering the geometry rules, not knowing where to start on hard questions*)	

I need to work on these content areas: (*Examples: vocabulary, transitions, exponent rules*)	
I need to practice these overall strategies: (*Circle all that apply and add any additional ones.*)	Slowing down Doing easy questions first Saving harder, more time-consuming questions for later Marking questions I get stuck on to come back to later Skipping and guessing on one or two really hard questions Using Process of Elimination Taking better guesses when I have to guess on questions
I need to learn better strategies for these areas: (*Circle all that apply and add any additional ones.*)	Using the highlighter/annotation tool Vocabulary Reading Comprehension Punctuation Grammar Transitions Rhetorical Synthesis Algebra shortcuts Word problems Geometry Using the built-in calculator Avoiding trap answers Saving time on RW Saving time on Math

Chapter 4
Mastering the
Reading and
Writing Section

Regardless of how well you do on Reading and Writing questions, if there's still room for improvement, we think you may be able to help your score significantly by adjusting your pacing strategy. Most people tend to work the RW section from beginning to end—especially high-scorers who know that they are going to be attempting every single question. You might assume that if you know you're going to be able to do all of the questions, it doesn't matter what order you do them in. However, in our experience, getting the easier stuff out of the way first can really help with your pacing so that you have as much time as possible for the stuff you struggle with a bit more. We already discussed Personal Order of Difficulty earlier in this book, so we won't belabor the point, but the pacing strategy we recommend for RW is a little more complicated and less intuitive than the Math pacing strategy, for which you just do whichever questions are easier for you first.

That's because of the structure of the RW modules. Instead of going from beginning to end by difficulty level, the way Math does, the RW modules are organized by question type. Here's the broadest way of looking at an RW module:

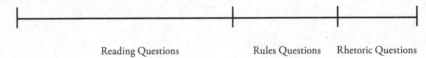

The first (slightly more than) half of the module consists of Reading questions. After that are all of the Writing questions, specifically the Rules questions (the ones that test punctuation and grammar rules) followed by the Rhetoric questions (transitions and then Rhetorical Synthesis). Let's break that down a little more.

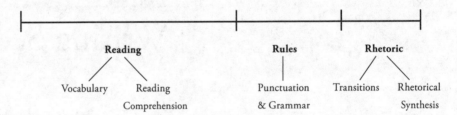

As you may recall, the very first questions on each RW module are Vocabulary questions. Then you have a bunch of different types of reading comprehension questions (such as Purpose, Claims, and Main Idea). After that are the Writing categories that we just went over. Altogether, this turns the module into five basic categories. The module will *always* come in this same order. If you know this, you can use it to your advantage. Since you know roughly where each type of question is going to be, you can choose the order in which you do these topics. If you prefer Writing over Reading, for example, why start at the beginning of the module? You might as well start with the questions you like more, are better at, and/or can do in less time.

RW Pacing Self-Assessment

Use your score report(s) and your recollection of your RW practice to answer the following questions.

Out of the 5 areas on the graphic on the previous page, which ones...

...take the least time for you?_____

...are the most time-consuming for you?_____

...are the easiest for you?_____

...are the hardest for you?_____

...do you tend to get right the most?_____

...do you tend to miss the most?_____

Based on your responses to the questions above, write down the order you think you should do the 5 categories in. Remember, the fastest, easiest, and most accurate categories should come first.

First: _____

Second: _____

Third: _____

Fourth:_____

Last: _____

One more thing to consider is that College Board puts the RW questions in an order of difficulty—by *topic*. So, the Vocabulary questions will go from easy to hard, the specific types of reading comprehension questions will each go from easy to hard, Rules questions will go from easy to hard, transition questions will go from easy to hard, and then Rhetorical Synthesis questions will go from easy to hard. Of course, with only 27 questions in each module and all these categories, you aren't going to notice the changes in difficulty level a whole lot, but it's another thing to keep in mind as you plan out your RW approach.

As you may be able to infer, with our advice, you're doing one category of questions at a time. While doing the easy questions first is always a good thing, doing all the individual easy questions throughout the RW section first would mean switching back and forth between very different tasks. By finishing a question category before going on to your next one, you'll be able to concentrate on one type of question and one set of strategies at a time.

Identifying the Categories

To some extent, you can tell by the graphics on page 32 roughly where each category will appear. We'll give you a little more specific guidance here:

Category	Where it starts
Vocabulary	Beginning of the module
Reading comprehension	Anywhere from question 3 to question 9
Rules	A little over halfway—question 14 or later
Transitions	Around question 20
Rhetorical Synthesis	Around question 22 or later

These estimates will help you follow the 5-category order you wrote down earlier. Remember, at the bottom of the screen you can skip to any question you want, so if you want to start with Rules, for example, begin by clicking to go to question 13 and then advance to the right until you get to Rules. It's very easy to tell what category of question you're dealing with.

The following chart shows you how:

Category	How to spot it
Vocabulary	• Appears at the very beginning of the module, before reading comp questions • Answers have only vocabulary words in them • Question asks about a "logical and precise word or phrase" or what something most nearly means
Reading Comprehension	• Comes after Vocabulary but before Rules • Any literature passage or question with a graph falls into this category • The questions vary, but you'll see examples in the Reading chapters of this book
Rules	• Asks the following question: *Which choice completes the text so that it conforms to the conventions of Standard English?* • After reading comp but before transitions
Transitions	• Asks the following question: *Which choice completes the text with the most logical transition?* • The answers have only transition words • After Rules but before rhetorical synthesis
Rhetorical Synthesis	• After all the transition questions • The passage has bullet points

As you can see, there are lots of ways to quickly identify what type of question you're looking at. Just one of these bullet points is enough for each category, since each of them has something unique.

The following chapters will give you specific advice for Reading questions and then for Writing questions. Make sure to read the first Reading chapter and the first Writing chapter, since they go over some important basic information and strategies. From there, you can choose to work through the chapters that will be most helpful for you, depending on how much time you have to prepare for the test. In addition to working on the areas that you are missing the most questions on, it's also worth considering what is the easiest for you to improve on, especially if you have limited time. If you are more math- or rule-oriented, you might find Rules questions easier to improve on since they require less reading, mostly don't require comprehension, and are based around a set of rules that you can learn. On the other hand, vocabulary may not be a great category to focus on if you have only a week before your test, as you can do only so well on these questions without learning more words, which takes time. Lastly, remember that improvements in your stronger areas can often be achieved more easily than improvements in your weaker areas, so don't neglect your stronger areas if you still aren't consistently achieving 100% in them.

When you are ready to take a practice test or complete a full module, come back to this chapter to revisit the pacing concepts we went over. Try out the order of the 5 categories that you wrote down and see how it works for you. Then, you can alter it as needed until you find the order that's most effective for you.

Part II
SAT Advanced Reading Strategies

Chapter 5
Reading
Introduction

As you already know, the first half of each Reading and Writing module contains questions rooted in vocabulary and reading comprehension. The latter of these includes a wide variety of tasks, from determining the function of a sentence within a passage to supporting an argument using data from a chart. Since Reading questions will quite literally be the first thing you encounter on the Digital SAT, having a game plan for these questions as a whole is critical to achieving the highest scores. Not just to achieve access to the harder second Reading and Writing module, but also to establish a consistent level of accuracy and pacing that you'll need to keep up throughout the exam as a whole.

WHAT MAKES SAT READING DIFFICULT

Reading on the SAT is very different from the reading you do in school. In English class, you are often asked to give your own opinion and support it with evidence from a text. You might have to explain how Pip and Estelle influence each other's growth in *Great Expectations*. Or you might be asked to explain the central conflicts that drive the plot of *Macbeth*. On the SAT, however, there is no chance to give an explanation or offer your own opinion. You don't have the opportunity to justify why your answer is the right one. This can be extremely frustrating, because it can sometimes feel that if you had someone to argue with, you might be able to convince them that the right answer is C and not B as indicated by the answer key. However, consider this: if you are given no such chance to justify your answer, the test-writers must believe that there is a way to demonstrate that one of the four answers can be supported as correct. Consider College Board's own instructions, given at the start of each Reading and Writing module:

DIRECTIONS

The questions in this section address a number of important reading and writing skills. Each question includes one or more passages, which may include a table or graph. Read each passage and question carefully, and then choose the best answer to the question based on the passage(s).

All questions in the section are multiple-choice with four answer choices. Each question has a single best answer.

> You get points for answering questions based on a passage, *not* for understanding the passage itself.

Because there is a *single best answer* and that best answer is *based on the passage(s)*, this is an **open book-test**. This means that you are NOT being tested on whether you have read, studied, and become an expert on ancient Māori musical instruments, the motivations behind the writing of *Catcher in the Rye*, or the wattage of electricity generated by industrial wind turbines. In fact, the more you try to apply your outside knowledge or opinion, the more likely you will argue yourself away from that correct answer. All the test-writers care about is whether or not you can read a passage and understand it well enough to correctly answer a question about it. No matter what strategy you have or will use on these questions, your mission is this:

> Identify what task you have been assigned by the question and find the evidence in the passage that addresses that task.

WHAT CAN MAKE SAT READING EASIER

Before we get to our specific advice on exactly how we recommend someone might find evidence in the passage to address specific tasks, let's check in with how the overall strategies discussed in this book's introduction might apply to the Reading questions.

Slow Down, Score More

On average, you have 1 minute and 11 seconds for each question on the Reading and Writing modules, including, of course, the Reading questions. This doesn't seem like a lot of time, especially given the length of some of the passages. However, even if you can't afford to spare that many seconds to take your time, rushing through the first half of the module to get to the Writing questions is going to cost you precious points. You may get a significant number of the Reading questions correct because your vocabulary is strong or your own opinion seems to sync up with what College Board considers a supported response, but inevitably, at least a few points will be lost because your ear led you to choose the wrong vocabulary word or your speed caused you to miss a small exception to the author's argument that's accounted for in the correct answer.

If you've ever looked at a correct answer when checking over a Reading and Writing module and said "Oh, I just misread that," or "Oops, that's a silly mistake," the first thing you must ask yourself is, "Am I going too fast? Is there a question I would have been better off coming back to later or skipping altogether so I could have slowed down on the two or three questions that I missed?" Throughout the Reading chapters, we've arranged our drills as close to the official test pace as possible to help you get accustomed to using just the right amount of time. Use these drills to practice appropriate pacing: the highest scores come from using every last second available to you and avoiding going either too fast or too slow.

> When reviewing Reading questions you missed, it's just as important to ask, "How will I avoid this error in the future?" as it is to ask, "Why did I get this wrong?

Personal Order of Difficulty

The higher your current score, the more specific the types of questions or scenarios that you find challenging will be. Someone scoring at 1300 may need to work on generally improving their vocabulary or questions involving claims, but someone scoring at 1500 may need to work specifically on Main Idea questions based on a poem. While this book has you covered either way, you need to first assess where your strengths and weaknesses in Reading lie. Look over past exams (there's also a diagnostic drill at the end of this chapter to help with this) and determine what you've handled both efficiently and accurately as well as what has been either time-consuming for you or led you to incorrect answers. Question types or scenarios you've handled both efficiently and accurately should be done as soon as you encounter them, or even actively sought out, while time-consuming questions should be saved for later, which in turn improves your overall pacing.

If you're uncertain as to whether a question will be time-consuming or not, skip it for now—it's better to be pleasantly surprised later on that the question was easier than expected than to have spent a lot of your time on something you should have skipped.

Lastly, question types or scenarios with which you've struggled should be explored more in their corresponding Reading chapters, so you can work on your accuracy. For anything you frequently get wrong, it's generally good advice to first show you can get that question type correct while working untimed and then show you can do it again under the clock. For most situations in these chapters, we've tried to provide at least two examples of each question type or scenario so you can try exactly that.

Skipping, Guessing, and POE

Any answers that you've eliminated using the Answer Eliminator tool will remain crossed out when you return to a question later, so you can pick up right where you left off!

During drills and full-length exams, time-consuming questions and question types or scenarios that cause you trouble should be skipped and saved for later, as mentioned above. Sometimes, you won't realize a question is time-consuming until you've started it (perhaps the question and passage looked fine, but upon reviewing the answers, all four of them seem to be saying identical things, as an example). In these cases, make use of the Mark for Review tool (circle it instead of clicking it if you are working on paper). It's far better to say, "I'll come back to this again when I have time" than to say "Man, I spent WAY too long here and now I need to rush." You can always spend more time later if you skipped a lot of questions, but you can never make up time you've lost on questions you should have skipped.

With no Writing rules or Math formulas to fall back on for the Reading questions, POE becomes that much more important. You're not going to just "know" something is right based on outside knowledge, so it's far more effective to eliminate what cannot be supported from the text.

Since every point matters for the highest scores, guessing aggressively and using Process of Elimination are as paramount on Reading as they are throughout the rest of the exam. The Reading answer choices are the longest you'll encounter on the exam, so they are more prone to second-guessing or incorrect interpretation than the Writing or Math answers. You need to focus on eliminating clearly wrong answers over finding the one perfect correct answer; otherwise, you can go down a deep, dark rabbit hole with the Reading answer choices. No matter what strategy you have or adopt, you should first compare the answers to the passage and then to each other—what you should never do is try to justify or debate answers in your head.

Lastly, remember that every answer eliminated improves your odds of a correct guess dramatically. We've already told you to never leave any questions blank and be willing to enter in a random letter on an overly difficult or time-consuming question, but we understand that if you're reading this book, you probably have a goal of answering everything definitively. Don't let this goal prevent you from taking that fifty-fifty shot if you get down to two answers on a Reading question—it's so much more important that you see all of the questions in the module and have time to work them than it is to debate two remaining answers for more than a minute or so.

THE READING QUESTION TYPES

An important weapon for developing your Personal Order of Difficulty is to understand the eight main types of Reading questions. College Board groups the Reading questions into "Craft and Structure" followed by "Information and Ideas," but these general labels won't help you when there's something specific you need to target. Therefore, we've broken "Craft and Structure" into Vocabulary, Purpose, and Dual Texts questions. "Information and Ideas" can be broken down into Retrieval, Main Idea, Claims, Charts, and Conclusions questions.

We'll be referring to these question types by these names throughout the Reading chapters, so here's a brief snapshot of what each question type typically asks for:

Question Type	Your Job, in 20 Words or Less
Vocabulary	Select a good vocabulary word for a blank in the passage or define an existing word in context.
Purpose	Determine why the author wrote the passage, why a sentence was included, or how the author structured the passage.
Dual Texts	Determine the relationship between people, ideas, or arguments in two different passages.
Retrieval	Select which statement could be made about a person, place, or idea based on details in the passage.
Main Idea	Select an answer that best summarizes the main focus of the passage overall.
Claims	Choose an answer that best illustrates, strengthens, or weakens a claim from the passage.
Charts	Choose information from a chart that illustrates a concept, strengthens or weakens a claim, or completes an example.
Conclusions	Choose the most logical concluding phrase or sentence to a passage.

For the most part, the question types will appear in the order seen on this chart. However, Retrieval and Main Idea questions can be mixed together, as can Claims and Charts questions. In College Board's eyes, these question types test similar enough skills to be grouped together, but we separate them in our materials because each has its own note-worthy quirks.

Not every question type appears on every Reading and Writing module, but with rare exceptions, any question type that doesn't appear on the first module will appear on the second. So, you must be comfortable with all eight question types!

ACTIVE READING

You'll notice that, regardless of question type, we keep using very active words such as "select," "determine," and "choose" in our descriptions above. This is no accident: as we said before, the questions may *seem* as if they can be handled like high school English questions, but in actuality, you are being given extremely specific tasks that require an equally specific piece of information to be found in the passage. This means you need to master the concept of reading actively rather than passively.

A passive reader attempts to be a sponge and understand the passage deeply—because a passive reader has no particular goal, everything gets treated as equally important. The danger with treating every word as equally important is that critical words or phrases can be misinterpreted or glossed over. A further danger is that attempting to understand the passage deeply leads to attempting to interpret the answers or debate them internally, which we've already explained leads to errors.

> Active reading is essentially reading with a purpose—you shouldn't read a single word of a passage until you know exactly what you are trying to find.

An active reader is like a laser beam rather than a sponge—the focus is only on what's needed to answer the question. While an active reader still reads all the words, there is no attempt to focus on deeper meanings. Instead, an active reader takes the words at face value and looks for answers that express the same idea, albeit with slightly different language. It's not that active reading is necessarily faster—you'll still be using all of the available time as an active reader, but you'll be using it more efficiently. And the best way to be efficient on the Reading questions is to use the same approach, every single time.

THE READING BASIC APPROACH

> Consider the Basic Approach a recipe for Reading on the SAT: it needs to be practiced repeatedly at first, but once perfected, it becomes a permanent tool in your repertoire. So, get cooking!

Active reading will work best for you if you follow a step-by-step approach that can be applied consistently throughout the exam, regardless of question type. Because the SAT is a standardized test, the questions are difficult not necessarily because of the content they test (especially in Reading, in which we've already established that you're not being tested on content at all except for vocabulary) but because of the way the questions and answers are structured. Therefore, if you have a consistent strategy to avoid the traps created by that structure, your accuracy will improve accordingly. While we won't ask you to abandon what's already working for you, consider utilizing the below strategy on any question types or scenarios you find challenging (we'll explain the specifics of how this strategy is applied during the drill explanations at the end of this chapter).

Step 1: Read the Question. While the passage is certainly important, part of being an active reader is learning what you're being asked to find first—journey before destination.

Step 2: Identify the Question Type. Identifying the question type and applying the same steps for that type the same way every single time help you avoid the mistakes that can come from passive reading.

Step 3: Read the Passage(s). Read the passage(s) thoroughly, keeping the question task in mind. Remember: you are actively looking for an answer to the question, or at the very least, evidence that can help answer the question. You don't need to memorize, or even understand, every detail.

Step 4: Highlight What Can Help (and Annotate if Needed). Within the passage, you'll want to highlight a phrase or sentence that can help answer the question. It could be a direct answer to the question or a piece of information that the question wants you to do something with. On Vocabulary, Purpose, and Dual Texts questions, creating an annotation to go along with your highlighting can help you remember what word should go in the blank, the function of something in the passage, or the relationship between the passages. However, we encourage you to annotate on any question type, not just those three, on which you believe an annotation will help. Both of these actions help you engage with the passage more than simply reading it.

Step 5: Use POE (Process of Elimination). Aggressively eliminate anything that isn't consistent with what you highlighted and/or annotated. Don't necessarily try to find the correct answer immediately, because this opens the door for you to start interpreting answers and moves you away from actively reading and more towards being stuck in your own head. If you can eliminate answers that you know are wrong, though, you'll be closer to the right answer. If you can't eliminate three answers with your highlights and annotation, it comes down to understanding which answer is correct and which is a trap, which we'll discuss momentarily.

The Dual Texts Basic Approach

The above steps work for most question types. However, one particular area that causes trouble for many students is the Dual Texts questions. The reasons for this are pretty straightforward—twice as many passages to read is twice as much information to keep track of and therefore it's more likely something important can be missed. Additionally, determining the relationship between passages or upon which point two groups within the passages agree or disagree is simply a more involved task than choosing an appropriate vocabulary word. Because it will be fairly obvious when you're confronted with Dual Texts, we modify the Reading Basic Approach into the following.

You'll see the approaches for Dual Texts and Charts applied in the explanations for Questions 3 and 7, respectively, of this chapter's drill.

> Step 1: Read and understand the question.
>
> Step 2: Read the first passage and highlight the claim or a main idea.
>
> Step 3: Read the second passage and highlight what is said about the same idea.
>
> Step 4: Determine and annotate the relationship between the passages.
>
> Step 5: Use POE and eliminate answers that are inconsistent with one or both passages.

The Charts Basic Approach

Charts questions introduce a visual component that may present its own difficulty, especially if you are not a visual learner. Again, these questions provide more opportunities for mistakes to be made, as not only can a wrong answer be inconsistent with the data in the chart, but also a wrong answer can actually be perfectly consistent with the chart but contradictory or even irrelevant to the claim or statement made in the passage. Again, since it's pretty clear when you're dealing with a Charts question, we suggest modifying the Basic Approach as follows:

> Step 1: Read and understand the question.
>
> Step 2: Read the title, key/legend, variables, and/or units in the chart.
>
> Step 3: Read the passage and look for the same information you saw in the chart.
>
> Step 4: Highlight the claim or conclusion in the passage regarding that same information.
>
> Step 5: Use POE and eliminate answers that are inconsistent with the chart, the passage, or both.

POE AND TRAP ANSWERS

If you constantly find yourself down to two or three answers and want to work more on trap answers specifically, explore Chapter 9: Mastering Process of Elimination.

We've already mentioned Process of Elimination in this chapter, and you've seen it mentioned as the final step of each approach we've discussed. Normally, you'll be comparing the answers to what you highlighted/annotated, and for many questions, you'll be able to eliminate all three of the incorrect answers this way. However, you may find yourself down to two or three choices that seem equally supported by what you found. In these cases, asking yourself "What answer do I like more?" opens the door to interpretation and assumption. The only way to remain an active reader at this stage is to instead ask "Which answers are traps constructed by College Board to be attractive to the average test-taker?"

> While trap answers will be useful if you are down to two or three choices, the *best* reason to eliminate any answer is that it doesn't match what you see in the passage.

Below is a list of the six most common traps we've seen consistently appear on the SAT.

Trap Name	Description	Examples
Opposite	These trap answers use a single word or phrase that makes the answer convey a tone, viewpoint, or meaning contradictory to what was intended by the author.	On a Vocabulary question, an answer takes a negative tone toward something the passage is positive toward. On a Dual Texts question, the answer claims that the author of Text 2 would agree with something stated in Text 1, while the passage itself supports a disagreement.
Extreme Language	These trap answers include a word or phrase that takes a stated opinion or viewpoint in the passage too far in a certain direction.	On a Vocabulary question, an answer says "worships" regarding something the author only "approves" of. On a Claims question, a piece of evidence is said to "prove" a theory rather than just "support" the theory.
Recycled Language	These trap answers repeat exact words and phrases from the passage but use those words and phrases incorrectly.	On a Retrieval question, the answer has taken words and phrases from completely different parts of the passage and assembled them into a seemingly cohesive statement. On a Conclusions question, the answer has misused a reference to "the dawn of conflict" to assume the author wanted to discuss day and night cycles.
Right Answer, Wrong Question	These trap answers are actually true based on the passage, but they don't answer the question asked.	On a Purpose question, the answer offers the function of a sentence other than the one that's underlined. On a Main Idea question, the answer offers only a single detail from the passage rather than the overall focus.
Beyond the Text	These trap answers depend on logical assumptions or outside reasoning but lack actual support in the passage.	On a Purpose question, the answer offers a reason why the author might have discussed someone's negative qualities (for example, to discredit them), but no such motivation is actually given in the passage. On a Claims question, a piece of accurate scientific knowledge is included in an answer, but that specific topic was not referenced in the passage itself.
Half-Right	These trap answers address only part of a question task or are longer answers divided into one supported half and one unsupported half.	On a Claims question, a quotation should demonstrate both a physical and an emotional reaction but only displays a physical reaction. On a Charts question, the data is consistent with the chart but would actually weaken rather than support the argument in the passage.

Diagnostic Drill

Now that we've covered the basics, it's time to put our advice to this point into practice. On the following drill, we encourage you to try out the Basic Approach and its variations on each of the eight questions (one of each type). Trying the Basic Approach here doesn't mean you need to stop doing what you're doing on the official exam, but achieving the highest scores means making use of every tool available to you. You may find the Basic Approach useful for all the questions, or you may pick and choose when to apply it. Either way, it's incredibly likely it will be helpful to you somewhere throughout the Reading questions. At the end of this drill, the explanations will take you through the Basic Approach to demonstrate how you would use it in the future. Answers and explanations can be found in Chapter 12.

Time: 10 minutes

1 🔖 Mark for Review

The Bohr Effect illuminates the _____ correlation between hemoglobin's oxygen-binding affinity and the concurrent levels of acidity and carbon dioxide concentration in the blood. Elevated physical activity, prompting increased carbon dioxide production, results in a subsequent increase in acidity. Consequently, hemoglobin exhibits a decreased propensity to bind with additional oxygen molecules under these conditions.

Which choice completes the text with the most logical and precise word or phrase?

(A) inverse

(B) direct

(C) present

(D) alternating

2 🔖 Mark for Review

The supercontinental cycle details a possible series of continental formations and separations, beginning 3.6 billion years ago and culminating in the formation of the supercontinent Pangaea 300 million years ago. This viewpoint has not been universally accepted, however, as a dissenting theory claims that all continental activity is the result of one single breakup: that of the supercontinent Protopangea-Paleopangea approximately 600 million years ago. Researcher Zhang-Xiang Li and colleagues published a paper considering the veracity of this second theory but concluded that it does not account for evidence suggesting more frequent continental activity, such as the oldest crust material on ocean floors being only 170 million years old.

Which choice best describes the function of the second sentence in the overall structure of the text?

(A) It reveals how new parameters yield discoveries that question the premise and proof of an accepted theory.

(B) It explains why previously cited evidence is not relevant to an accepted theory.

(C) It corrects an error in the accumulation of evidence to support a theory by utilizing new technological advances.

 It introduces a hypothesis that Li and colleagues examined but did not find satisfactory.

3 🏳 Mark for Review

Text 1

The Giant Impact Hypothesis states that the Moon formed 4.5 billion years ago when a planetary-sized body, Theia, crashed into Earth, and resulting debris gradually coalesced into orbit around Earth. When astronauts landed on the Moon, samples they collected did not appear to support the theory. Moon rocks were so similar in isotopic composition to rocks on Earth that they link the moon only to Earth and negate any trace of a foreign entity.

Text 2

Scientists at Durham University's Institute for Computational Cosmology have created highly detailed simulations of the Giant Impact Hypothesis. New models reveal plausible scenarios in which the moon formed in a mere few hours after Earth's impact with Theia. This altered timeline could explain why the new moon retained material from Earth in its crust and lost vestiges from other parts of the solar system.

Based on the text, how would the author of Text 2 most likely respond to the underlined claim in Text 1?

(A) By acknowledging that new simulations don't prove the Giant Impact Hypothesis correct, but they may account for previous unexplained inconsistencies

(B) By effectively agreeing with the claim but insisting that new evidence may compel them to reevaluate findings of isotopic similarity

(C) By insisting that material from other parts of the solar system could not have been present when Earth was impacted by Theia

(D) By criticizing the assertion for not allowing for the possibilities suggested by the new timeline revealed by the new modeling simulations

4 🏳 Mark for Review

The following text was adapted from René Bazin's 1910 short story *The Birds in the Letter-box.* An old abbé (monk) has made a discovery near the garden at his residence.

The abbé went hastily through the garden, the house, the court planted with asparagus, till he came to the wall which separated the parsonage from the public road, and there he carefully opened the letter-box, in which there would have been room enough for all the mail received in a year by all the inhabitants of the village.

Sure enough, he was not mistaken. The shape of the nest, like a pine-cone, its color and texture, and the lining, which showed through, made him smile. He heard the hiss of the brooding bird inside and replied:

"Rest easy, little one, I know you. Twenty-one days to hatch your eggs and three weeks to raise your family; that is what you want? You shall have it. I'll take away the key."

Based on the text, how does the abbé react when he sees a bird's nest in the mailbox?

(A) He questions the wisdom of the bird's nesting location, even though he claims to understand the bird's need for safety.

(B) He promises to protect the birds, even though the birds have chosen an unusual location for their nest.

(C) He desires to have the birds removed, even though the birds will be negatively impacted by such a move.

(D) He expresses amusement at the birds' presence, even though the situation is clearly quite serious.

5 🔖 Mark for Review

The following text is adapted from John Gould Fletcher's 1918 poem "In Exile."

> My heart is mournful as thunder moving
> Through distant hills
> Late on a long still night of autumn.
>
> My heart is broken and mournful
> As rain heard beating
> Far off in the distance
> While earth is parched more near.
>
> On my heart is the black badge of exile;
> I droop over it,
> I accept its shame.

What is the main idea of the text?

(A) The speaker is unhappy because he has been left alone.

(B) The speaker is dismayed about being separated from a particular location.

(C) The speaker is anxious about bad weather that is approaching.

(D) The speaker is eager to leave his home for another country.

6 🔖 Mark for Review

Recently, meetings via video conferencing applications such as Zoom have supplanted many in-person interactions. Communicating through a camera and a screen can decrease sensory engagement, such as attention to facial cues and subtle variations in speaking tones that are key to clear exchanges, as well as other neural signaling cues that are linked to healthy communication. Yale University neuroscientist Joy Hirsch used imaging tools to monitor the brain activity of pairs of people in Zoom meetings and in-person meetings. She concluded that in-person meetings were more dynamic interactions than Zoom meetings.

Which finding from Hirsch's research, if true, would most directly support her claim?

(A) Interactions in Zoom meetings registered a greater variety of vocal intonation than the dialogues in the in-person meetings did.

(B) Imaging tools recorded more overall neural activity at the middle of the Zoom meetings than at the beginning or end of in-person meetings.

(C) Neural signaling cues during Zoom exchanges appeared less frequently compared to activity observed in those having face-to-face conversations.

(D) Participants in both Zoom and in-person meetings were able to receive and acknowledge facial expressions with relatively equal discrimination.

7 ▢ Mark for Review

Cytotoxic Reduction Percentages by Cell and Concentration per μg/mL

Cancer Cell	Cisplatin	Tarragon Concentration		
		100mg	500mg	1,000mg
MCF-7	37%	94%	74%	53%
MKN-45	48%	89%	72%	43%
HT-29	53%	87%	56%	40%

Cytotoxic treatments such as chemotherapy are utilized to break down cancer cells. Natural alternatives, such as herbs with strong antioxidant qualities, may also demonstrate cytotoxic qualities. Faranzaneh Motafeghi and colleagues at the University of Mazandaran examined the potential for *Artemisia dracunculus*, commonly known as tarragon, to break down cancer cells. They measured the cytotoxicity of tarragon mixed with three types of cancer cells: MCF-7, MKN-45, and HT-29. They compared the results with a mixture that contained cisplatin, a cytotoxic used for chemotherapy, and confirmed that as the tarragon's concentration increased, the cytotoxic reduction percentage decreased. For example, an MCF-7 cancer cell had a cytotoxic reduction percentage of 53% with a tarragon concentration of 1,000 mg, but _____

Which choice most effectively uses data from the table to complete the example?

(A) an HT-29 cancer cell had a reduction rate of 53% with cisplatin.

(B) an MKN-45 cancer cell had a reduction rate of 43% with a tarragon concentration of 1,000 mg.

(C) an MCF-7 cancer cell had a reduction rate of 37% with cisplatin.

(D) an MCF-7 cancer cell had a reduction rate of 94% with a tarragon concentration of 100 mg.

8 ▢ Mark for Review

If agricultural evidence from an archaeological survey of Easter Island, in the South Pacific, demonstrates that the sweet potato crop arrived at the island during the twelfth century CE, this would lend support to those who believe the crop was brought to the island by Polynesian explorers who were active at the time. An alternate theory, however, claims that the sweet potato arrived at the island thousands of years earlier and by more natural means, such as seed dispersal from migratory seabirds. If the survey reveals that sweet potato seeds arrived both through twelfth-century human visitors and seed dispersal via seabirds that had lived thousands of years ago, that would imply that _____

Which choice most logically completes the text?

(A) surveys of Easter Island may have accidentally disrupted archaeological evidence dating to the twelfth century CE.

(B) seeds carried by Polynesian explorers are easier to study than are seeds dispersed by migratory seabirds.

(C) the sweet potato crop originated elsewhere and eventually arrived at Easter Island through natural, and then human, means.

(D) the Easter Island settlement was founded at a different time than was previously believed.

Chapter 6
Exploring Advanced Vocabulary

First among the Reading questions will be questions that explicitly test your knowledge of vocabulary words. Not only will these be the very first questions you'll see on the Digital SAT, but they are also the ones many students choose to start with due to their shorter length and more straightforward task. Therefore, your performance on these questions will often set the tone for your performance on the rest of the exam. This chapter will examine some of the skills you can apply to increase your odds of getting each Vocabulary question correct.

THE IMPORTANCE OF VOCABULARY

If we could sum up why vocabulary on the Digital SAT matters in just three words, it would come down to **frequency**, **difficulty**, and **versatility.** Since you're reading this book for an in-depth look at what's needed to achieve the highest scores on the exam, let's look at each of these a bit more closely.

Frequency

If you've taken at least one Digital SAT already, you have probably noticed that Vocabulary is the most frequently tested question type among Reading questions. You're confronted with them right at the start of the exam, so they're a bit hard to miss, and you get several of them in a row. In fact, it's rare to see fewer than four Vocabulary questions at the start of any given module, and we've seen as many as eight of them on some of the released modules. On average, Vocabulary questions account for 12 of the questions a student will see on the exam. That would be significant on any exam, but with only 98 questions, it's extremely significant on the Digital SAT. This is doubly true for a student who, like yourself, is looking for a very high score and wants to limit how many questions need to be guessed on.

Difficulty

As mentioned in the last chapter, Reading questions increase in difficulty within each question type. Now, if you get only a single Retrieval question when the Retrieval/Main Idea questions come up, it will be quite difficult to "feel" an increase in that set's difficulty. But with the frequency of Vocabulary questions, you're going to notice the words becoming more difficult. So, even if you're prepared for the number of questions, your confidence can be affected if you start getting bogged down with words you don't know. This increase can also affect your pacing: because Vocabulary questions are accompanied by some of the shortest passages in the Reading and Writing module, students anticipate getting off to a running start. They become accustomed to doing these questions quickly, and when they do hit a wall, two unfortunate things can happen. Time can be lost due to a student trying to remember definitions for unfamiliar words, or accuracy can be affected due to a student taking a random guess or using an incorrect definition for the word.

> While we don't encourage you to do these questions *too* quickly, working them efficiently and accurately is critical for having more time for question types in the module that come with longer passages or more involved tasks.

Versatility

Even if difficult vocabulary words were confined only to their question type, you would already have enough of a reason to study them. However, these words can also be found in many of the passages through the Reading and Writing modules, and even in some of the answers to Reading and Writing questions. This can be difficult for two reasons. Occasionally, an entire answer can hinge on the knowledge of a single word: conflating *underscore* with *undermine* would cause someone to view the answer in precisely the opposite light of how it should be interpreted. More generally, a difficult word or two in a passage can break someone's momentum in a passage, and all of a sudden, the focus becomes defining the word rather than answering the question. While almost any question can still be answered correctly without knowing the definition of one particular word from the passage, the absolute most efficient solution is to know the word itself rather than have to work around it.

YOUR VOCAB STUDY PLAN

Many students want to improve on the SAT by doing endless practice questions and tests. Hopefully by now you are convinced that doing practice questions needs to be supplemented with independent vocabulary review. While there are many ways to study vocabulary, we've provided three of them below and encourage you to incorporate as many of them as you require to achieve the highest possible score.

> Study vocabulary for at least 5–10 minutes each day in addition to any other prep you do.

Method 1: Use the Advanced Word Bank.

After the explanations to this chapter's drill, you'll find a list of the most difficult words we've seen tested on the exam, along with parts of speech, definitions, and examples for the words. While there is no guarantee that any of the words on this list will appear on your specific modules, the bank will serve as both a starting point for your own review and a reference point for just how difficult the words can get. Reviewing this list may help your performance throughout the Reading chapters, allowing you to focus more on other skills you hope to improve.

Method 2: Create Your Own Word Bank.

Throughout these chapters and any practice tests you do, you'll come across words in the passage and answers that you may not know. Create a physical or digital document to track these words. Whenever you encounter a word you're unfamiliar with, add it to the list, along with a definition for how it was used on that question, and, optionally, a mnemonic device to help you remember that word. For example, the word *paucity,* which means scarcity or a lack of something, could be remembered by thinking of a *pauper*, or beggar. You may also want to write your own example sentence using the word in context.

Method 3: Read One Challenging Article/Short Story Per Day.

Publications such as *Forbes, National Geographic, The Economist,* and *The New Yorker* typically publish articles with reading levels equal to and, in many cases, higher than those of the Digital SAT's passages. Additionally, many Digital SAT passages are excerpts from novels, poems, and short stories written in the 1800s and early 1900s. The *Century Past Free Online Library* is a great website to find such passages. By reading one such article or story per day as often as your schedule allows, you'll not only be exposed to difficult words that are often understandable through context, but you'll also train yourself to better sort through some of the more sophisticated Digital SAT passages as you look for the correct evidence to answer the question.

APPLYING THE BASIC APPROACH TO VOCABULARY

Most of the Vocabulary questions you see on the Digital SAT will be accompanied by a blank along with four potential words or phrases that could fit inside that blank. Before we get into the finer points of vocabulary skill-building, let's first review the Reading Basic Approach:

> **Step 1: Read the Question.**
>
> **Step 2: Identify the Question Type.**
>
> **Step 3: Read the Passage(s).**
>
> **Step 4: Highlight What Can Help (and Annotate if Needed).**
>
> **Step 5: Use POE (Process of Elimination).**

While all the steps of the Basic Approach will help you on Vocabulary questions, there are some very specific things you should do during these steps to get the most out of the Approach. First, during **Step 3**, identify **who or what** the blank is supposed to be describing—this could be a noun such as a person, place, or thing; a verb; or even an adjective or adverb. Then, for **Step 4**, highlight the **clue** in the passage—the clue is the textual evidence that must be included by College Board to be able to justify one answer being demonstrably correct and the other three being wrong. Continuing in **Step 4**, make an **annotation** of your own word or phrase for the blank. Your **annotation** should be entirely based on the **clue** and consistent with the **who or what** that the blank is supposed to be describing.

Let's see an example of how this may work. You are welcome to try the example on your own or just read through the passage and then read the **Here's How to Ace It** section below to learn our method for applying the Approach to these questions.

Nuts have long been recognized as _____ sources of protein for active people, such as hikers and distance athletes, and a recent study revealed that walnuts, rich in omega-3 vitamins, may offer a further advantage: people who consume walnuts regularly are at significantly less risk of suffering from heart disease.

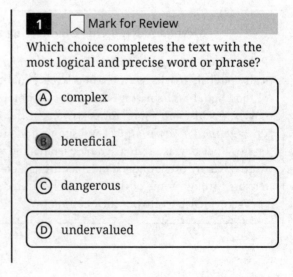

1 ◻ Mark for Review

Which choice completes the text with the most logical and precise word or phrase?

Ⓐ complex

Ⓑ beneficial

Ⓒ dangerous

Ⓓ undervalued

Here's How to Ace It

After you read the question and identify the question type, you'll then read the passage and look for the **who or what**. Note that the blank should be an adjective describing the type of sources of protein that nuts are recognized as. The passage offers two **clues** to highlight that offer such descriptions. First, the text states that *walnuts, rich in omega-3 vitamins, may offer a further advantage*. The passage further goes on to state that *people who consume walnuts regularly are at significantly less risk of suffering from heart disease*. You don't need to find both of these clues, as either one would suggest that nuts are "positive" or "helpful" sources of protein. With either of these **annotations** entered, you can eliminate (A) and (C) because neither matches "positive" or "helpful." Keep (B) because *beneficial* is a great match for "positive." Eliminate (D) because while *undervalued* indicates that something is valuable, or positive, the text states that nuts *have long been recognized*, meaning that they haven't been undervalued or neglected as a source of protein. The correct answer is (B).

Throughout the Vocabulary chapter, you'll receive the core of our explanations presented as a chart to help you keep track of the **who/what** that you should have found, the **clue** you should have highlighted, and a suggested **annotation** you could have made. Here's what that chart would have looked like for this question:

Who/What	the type of sources of protein that nuts have been recognized as
Clue	*walnuts, rich in omega-3 vitamins, may offer a further advantage*
Annotation	"positive" or "helpful"

Accounting for Transitions

The first example was a fairly straightforward one by design. However, many of the more difficult questions on the Digital SAT will contain transitional words in the text that can cause the correct answer to go in the opposite direction of the clue given. It's no coincidence that **Opposite** is one of our named trap answers then, as questions with transitional words will usually feature at least one answer that doesn't account for the transition.

Not every question has a transition, but those that do almost always have an answer or two that fails to account for the transition.

Consider the next example.

In contrast to neighboring wine regions in California that contain loam, a nutrient-rich blend of soil and clay that produces ideal conditions for cultivating grape vines, the Paso Robles region of California contains soil that is mostly derived from calcareous, or calcium-dense, bedrock, which caused winemakers in this region to initially _____ to infuse the soil with adequate nutrients.

2 ☐ Mark for Review

Which choice completes the text with the most logical and precise word or phrase?

Ⓐ neglect

Ⓑ request

Ⓒ labor

Ⓓ cooperate

Here's How to Ace It

If someone fails to highlight and account for the transition at the beginning of the passage, that student could easily arrive at a conclusion such as the following.

Who/What	winemakers' interaction with infusing the soil with adequate nutrients
Clue	*a nutrient-rich blend of soil and clay that produces ideal conditions for cultivating grape vines*
Annotation	"ignore" or "thought it was redundant"

After all, if the soil already contains a nutrient-rich blend, infusing it with more nutrients does seem redundant. However, the transitional phrase **in contrast to** changes the direction of the sentence, explaining that what is true of the *neighboring* wine regions in California is not true of the Paso Robles region. The opposite direction of something being ideal for wine-growing is that it would not be ideal for wine-growing at all, leading to the corrected chart below.

Highlight the transition just as you would a clue.

Who/What	how the bedrock in the Paso Robles region affected winemakers in the area
Clue	*a nutrient-rich blend of soil and clay that produces ideal conditions for cultivating grape vines*
Transition	*in contrast to*
Annotation	"struggle" or "have to work hard"

Choice (A) is wrong because *neglect* is the **Opposite** of "struggle"—this was not something the farmers could ignore, but rather something they had to work quite hard at. Choices (B) and (D) are wrong because they don't match "struggle." Keep (C) because "struggle" matches *labor* (work hard at). The correct answer is (C).

Reuse the Clue for Efficiency

At first, it can feel like highlighting clues and transitions and making annotations will slow you down, but over time, the process will actually help your pacing as you'll spend less time debating between two or three answers. You'll also naturally increase the speed at which you can apply the steps through familiarity, just as with any other new skill. To help improve your efficiency, don't spend too much time thinking about the "perfect" word or phrase for your annotation: if the clue offers a perfectly good word or phrase to plug into the blank, use it and move right on to using POE!

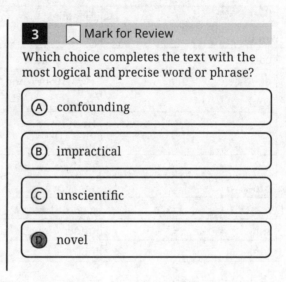

As _____ as it may seem, the Mpemba effect, which states that hot water freezes more quickly than cool water does, is not a new belief. This phenomenon was first noted by Aristotle and has intrigued philosophers throughout history, including Francis Bacon and René Descartes.

3 🔖 Mark for Review

Which choice completes the text with the most logical and precise word or phrase?

(A) confounding

(B) impractical

(C) unscientific

(D) novel

Here's How to Ace It

Who/What	The Mpemba effect
Clue	*not a new belief*
Transition	*may seem*
Annotation	"new"

> While *may seem* is not a transition word by grammatical definition, it still performs the job of changing the direction of the sentence.

Choices (A), (B), and (D) are wrong because *confounding* (confusing), *impractical*, and *unscientific* don't match "new." Keep (D) because *novel* matches *new*. The correct answer is (D).

Using Prefixes and Context

Should you happen to know the definitions of four of the answer choices, the above method will work for you on virtually any Vocabulary question. However, you may be in a situation with one or more answers that you don't know the definition for but still want to attempt the question to improve your score. The first thing you should consider is if any of the answers contain a **prefix** that can help you approximate the meaning of the word.

Below, let's examine the common prefixes we've seen on Digital SAT vocabulary words:

Prefix	Meaning	Example
ambi-	both	ambivalence
co/con-	with / jointly	consensus
de-/dis-	away from / not	degrade
equ-	equal	equity
ex-	from / out	exert
il-/im-/in-	not	inevitable
ob-	in the way / against	obstruct
pro-	for / forward	proponent
re-	again / back	reciprocate
sub-	under / lower than	subsume
un-	not	unobtrusive

Along with these prefixes, you may or may have seen part or all of a word used in **context** previously. For example, someone may not know the word *deleterious,* but because "deleting" something is usually bad, they may be able to approximate the word's definition as "harmful." Now, try the following example, using prefixes and context to understand the words in the answer choices. Remember, if you know all four of the words in the answers, you should work the question as normal and move on to the next skill.

Jordanian sound artist Lawrence Abu Hamdan has been asked to testify as a witness in asylum hearings in the United Kingdom, largely due to his experience with using audio files extracted from cell phones and video cameras to examine the impact of listening and speech on human rights and political law. Organizations such as Amnesty International have cited Hamdan's work as a critical component of modernizing the asylum process, which has been criticized for its _____ and often laborious nature.

4 ☐ Mark for Review

Which choice completes the text with the most logical and precise word or phrase?

(A) unobtrusive

(B) inequitable

(C) antiquated

(D) subversive

Here's How to Ace It

Who/What	the asylum process
Clue	Hamdan's work helps with *modernizing the asylum process*
Transition	*criticized* indicates a negative, but the clue states a positive
Annotation	"outdated" or "not modern"

Once you get to the answers, use prefixes and context for any words you don't know. For (A), un- means *not* and ob- means *in the way*, so *unobtrusive* may mean something like "not in the way." Since this doesn't match "outdated," eliminate (A). For (B), in- means *not* and equ- means *equal*, so inequitable may mean something like "unequal." Since this doesn't match "outdated," eliminate (B). For (C), you may know the word "antique" from context and be able to determine that *antiquated* probably means "old," making it a good match for "outdated." Keep (C). For (D), sub- means *under* and you may know from context that *ver-* means truth. So, *subversive* could then mean something like "under the truth" or "weakening the truth." Since this doesn't match "outdated," eliminate (D). The correct answer is (C).

Using Tone

Sometimes, not only will the answers contain difficult words, but it will be hard to come up with a particularly good word or phrase for the annotation. In these cases, make your annotation all about tone. If you can determine from the clue, transition, and context that the word or phrase for the blank should be positive, negative, or neutral, you may be able to use POE heavily to assist you in getting the question correct, or at least increasing your odds of a successful guess.

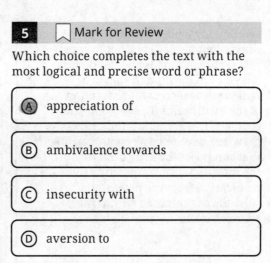

When interviewed about writing in multiple languages, Zimbabwean novelist Solomon Mutswairo, who wrote the first novel in the Shona language, expressed his _____ the fluidity of expression he fortuitously discovered upon beginning to write poetry in English.

5 ☐ Mark for Review

Which choice completes the text with the most logical and precise word or phrase?

(A) appreciation of

(B) ambivalence towards

(C) insecurity with

(D) aversion to

Here's How to Ace It

Who/What	Mutswairo's opinion of the fluidity of expression when writing in English
Clue	*fortuitously discovered*
Annotation	"positive"

While it's difficult to know from the passage the exact way in which Mutswairo would describe the fluidity of expression when writing in English, since *fortuitously* means "fortunately," Mutswairo would at least describe himself as "positive" towards it. Keep (A) as *appreciation* is definitely positive. Choice (B) is wrong because *ambivalence* (uncertainty) is either negative or neutral depending on the context, but it's definitely not positive. Choices (C) and (D) are wrong because *insecurity* and *aversion* (dislike) are both negative. The correct answer is (A).

Defining Difficult Words in the Passage

While most of the difficult words you'll see on the Digital SAT come in the answers to Vocabulary questions, these words can also show up in the passages to Vocabulary questions and both the passage and answers to each of the other seven question types as well. Don't be intimidated if a piece of the passage on which you need to answer a question contains a difficult word. When authors, including College Board authors, write passages, it's nearly impossible to avoid providing context clues to help the reader understand the topic. If too many such clues are stripped away for the sake of making the passage more difficult, the connection between ideas in the passage will start to become unclear, thus affecting the quality and usability of the passages. So, if you can find those context clues, you can define those difficult words and press on with your approach.

Swallowing a pill or capsule is convenient for patients, but in some cases, abrasive acids and degradative enzymes in the human stomach will prevent successful absorption of the medication. To overcome this obstacle, researchers at the University of Parma developed a robotic capsule that can inject the drug directly into the intestinal tract, protecting the medication from the potentially _____ substances contained within the stomach itself.

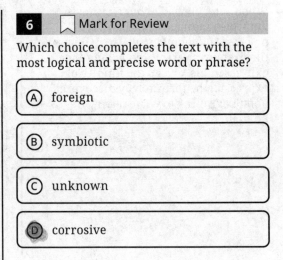

6 ☐ Mark for Review

Which choice completes the text with the most logical and precise word or phrase?

(A) foreign

(B) symbiotic

(C) unknown

(D) corrosive

Here's How to Ace It

Who/What	substances contained within the stomach
Clue	*abrasive acids and degradative enzymes*

After finding the clue, you may or may not know the definitions of *abrasive* or *degradative* at all, or at least you may not know them in the context of this question. Ultimately, it's not necessary to be able to perfectly define them. Since these substances *will prevent successful absorption of the medication* and the robotic capsule is responsible for *protecting the medication* from these substances, you know that these substances are potentially "harmful" or "negative." With this as your annotation, use POE. Choices (A), (B), and (C) are wrong because *foreign*, *symbiotic* (denoting a mutually beneficial relationship), and *unknown* don't match "harmful." Keep (D) because *corrosive* (harsh) matches "negative." Even if you don't know the exact definition of corrosive in this context, you probably know it's a negative thing. Either way, the correct answer is (D).

> Vocabulary questions can also ask what an underlined word in context "most nearly means." All you need to do is treat the underlined word in the passage as if it were a blank, and you've effectively turned the question into a regular Vocabulary question.

We've included a "most nearly means" question at the end of this chapter's drill.

Advanced Vocabulary Drill

While you do typically have about 1 minute and 11 seconds for each Reading and Writing question, you should practice working Vocabulary questions a bit more efficiently if you're going to have enough time for the more involved tasks later in the module. So, we've adjusted this drill timing to reflect this. Try using all of the skills you learned in this chapter on the drill and review the explanations afterward. Answers and explanations can be found in Chapter 12.

Time: 6 minutes

---

1 ⬜ Mark for Review

While cultural observers and educators often _____ that it's difficult to engage younger generations with historical content, Joseph Erb defies that thinking in his work: the Native American artist collaborates with Muscogee Creek and Cherokee students to create animations that portray vital cultural touchstones of traditional tribal legends.

Which choice completes the text with the most logical and precise word or phrase?

(A) suppose

(B) empathize

(C) understand

(D) deny

---

2 ⬜ Mark for Review

As concern for the world's environment increases, the concept of "virtual water," which is that commodities traded internationally can be measured in terms of the water required to produce them, has gained traction. Its support is not _____, however. Certain countries, such as Australia, dismiss it for being too simplistic to be relevant.

Which choice completes the text with the most logical and precise word or phrase?

(A) determined

(B) isolated

(C) universal

(D) waning

3 | Mark for Review

Currently the Chickasaw Nation's writer-in-residence, American writer Linda Hogan _____ many different writing genres throughout her career. She wrote novels and poetry, penned a script for a PBS documentary about Native American freedom of religion, and collaborated with other authors for *National Geographic* non-fiction books.

Which choice completes the text with the most logical and precise word or phrase?

(A) settled for

(B) contributed to

(C) recommended against

(D) agonized over

4 | Mark for Review

Filipina pediatrician Fe del Mundo is recognized for several innovations, including founding the first Filipino hospital specializing in pediatrics and for _____ the first modern pediatric healthcare system in the Philippines. Her career started with the American Red Cross, where she agreed to care for children held at the University of Santo Tomas internment camp in 1943.

Which choice completes the text with the most logical and precise word or phrase?

(A) revitalizing

(B) pioneering

(C) repudiating

(D) monetizing

5 | Mark for Review

Muslim polymath Ismail al-Jazari contributed to the field of mathematics in both informational and _____ ways: he wrote a book about mechanical devices and how to build them, and he invented the elephant clock, a clock that uses water to maintain time.

Which choice completes the text with the most logical and precise word or phrase?

(A) whimsical

(B) debatable

(C) incendiary

(D) innovative

6 | Mark for Review

The following text is adapted from Guðmundur Friðjónsson's short story "The Old Hay."

During the latter part of the reign of King Christian the Ninth, there lived at Holl in the Tunga District a farmer named Brandur. By the time the events narrated here transpired, Brandur had grown prosperous and very old—old in years and old in ways. The neighbours thought he must have money hidden away somewhere. But no one knew anything definitely, for Brandur had always been reserved and uncommunicative, and permitted no prying in his house or on his possessions. There was, however, one thing every settler in those parts knew: Brandur had accumulated large stores of various kinds.

As used in the text, what does the word "prosperous" most nearly mean?

(A) sumptuous

(B) opulent

(C) thunderous

(D) affluent

ADVANCED WORD BANK

Below, you'll find a list of some of the most difficult words you may see on the Digital SAT. As mentioned earlier in the chapter, while these primarily show up on Vocabulary questions, they can also appear in the passages and answer choices—so studying the Word Bank is one of the most straightforward ways to boost your SAT score!

Word	Part of Speech	Definition
ambivalence	**noun**	the state of having mixed feelings or contradictory ideas about something or someone

Example: Understandably, Jillian struggled with *ambivalence* regarding the group project: she loved working with her friends but felt that the work was never divided evenly.

arbitrary	**adjective**	based on random choice or personal whim, rather than any reason or system

Example: The town's enforcement of parking rules felt *arbitrary*, as some days the rules would be strictly enforced and other days it seemed impossible to get a ticket no matter how severe the infraction.

buttress	**verb**	to increase the strength of or justification for; to reinforce

Example: The commissioner has promised to train 30 new recruits by the end of the year in order to *buttress* the police force as the city's needs expand.

circumvent	**verb**	to find a way around

Example: Having forgotten the password to his email account, Aiden was able to *circumvent* the login screen by having a code sent to his phone.

concede	**verb**	to admit that something is true or valid after first denying or resisting it

Example: After an intense debate, I was forced to *concede* that my opponent had a strong argument regarding the need for district-wide budget reallocation.

congenial	**adjective**	pleasant, friendly, or agreeable

Example: Known as quite the *congenial* host, Davante made sure the atmosphere of his game nights was welcoming to friends both old and new.

culpable	**adjective**	guilty or worthy of blame

Example: Though he insisted upon his innocence, it was clear from video evidence and eyewitness testimony that the bank thief was indeed *culpable* for the robbery.

Word	Part of Speech	Definition
curtail	**verb**	to reduce in extent or quantity

Example: The new office time card system was designed to *curtail* unauthorized extensions of lunch and break times.

deference	**noun**	humble submission and respect

Example: The student spoke with *deference* to his instructor when discussing the proper application of a mixed martial arts technique.

divergent	**adjective**	tending to be different or develop in different directions

Example: Due to the unclear instructions, students took *divergent* paths in their papers, with some arguing multiple perspectives and some switching topics altogether.

dormant	**adjective**	having normal physical functions suspended or slowed down for a period of time; in or as if in a deep sleep

Example: Though the volcano once erupted randomly and violently for decades, it now lies *dormant* and is a popular tourist attraction.

elicit	**verb**	to draw out a response or fact from someone

Example: Through a series of carefully crafted questions, the professor hoped to *elicit* the answer to the geography question from her students, which would prove that they already knew the correct information.

epitome	**noun**	a perfect example of something

Example: The three sisters were the *epitome* of the spirit of entrepreneurship: through their hard work, their baking business had begun as a roadside stand and blossomed into a multi-million-dollar brand.

evince	**verb**	to reveal the presence of a quality or feeling

Example: Benjamin's numerous social media posts within just one day of returning from his vacation were clearly meant to *evince* the enjoyment he had felt during his trip.

evoke	**verb**	to bring or recall to the conscious mind

Example: A country's national anthem is meant to *evoke* feelings of pride in its citizens.

explicit	**adjective**	stated clearly and in detail, leaving no room for confusion or doubt

Example: The teacher's classroom rules were *explicit*; they were written on a poster right above her desk.

Word	Part of Speech	Definition
implicit	**adjective**	implied but not plainly expressed

Example: The teacher's classroom rules were *implicit*; although the rules were not openly stated anywhere, all of the students knew what they should and should not do.

juxtapose	**verb**	to place close together for contrasting effect

Example: Video production teams working on horror movies will often *juxtapose* darker scenes with livelier music to create a deeper sense of tension and discomfort within the viewer.

latent	**adjective**	existing but not yet developed or manifest

Example: From the moment his fingers began dancing over the keys as if he'd been playing his whole life, it was obvious that Nikolai had a *latent* talent for the piano that had hitherto gone unnoticed.

meticulous	**adjective**	showing great attention to detail; very careful and precise

Example: Ruchi was incredibly *meticulous* in the production of her photos on her social media page: the lighting, filter, and exposure were each precisely adjusted to enhance the visual quality of her subjects.

palpable	**adjective**	easily noticeable

Example: The excitement in the air prior to the start of the concert was *palpable*: you could practically see the energy emanating from the crowd before the band even stepped on stage.

pervasive	**adjective**	spreading widely throughout an area or a group of people, especially in an unpleasant way

Example: The aging boat had holes in its hull and a *pervasive* smell of rotting wood.

repudiate	**verb**	to refuse to accept or be associated with

Example: Any time one of her friends advised her to try online dating, Becky would *repudiate* the suggestion completely, as she had been deceived by inaccurate photos or descriptions too many times.

subsumed	**verb**	included or absorbed into something else

Example: Literature texts can be *subsumed* under two general categories: poetry and prose.

tenuous	**adjective**	very weak or slight

Example: With just seconds to go in the game, the team clung to a *tenuous* one-point lead.

Word	Part of Speech	Definition
undermine	**verb**	to lessen the effectiveness, power, or ability of a person or idea

Example: Michael practically ran on his way to school, worried that a mark of tardy would *undermine* his perfect attendance record.

underscore	**verb**	to emphasize or draw attention to

Example: Margaux came to her presentation with a series of handouts for her colleagues, hoping this would *underscore* the amount of work she had put into her project.

unobtrusive	**adjective**	not conspicuous or attracting attention

Example: Garbage cans at the theme park are painted to be as *unobtrusive* as possible, often blending into their surroundings.

verisimilitude	**noun**	the appearance of being true or real

Example: Despite being a work of fiction, the movie possessed such authentic characters and believable dialogue that critics praised it for its *verisimilitude*.

vexation	**noun**	the state of being annoyed, frustrated, or worried

Example: Carla could not hide her *vexation* at her son for arriving home two hours past curfew without telling her ahead of time.

vindicate	**verb**	to clear someone of blame or suspicion

Example: Upset that he had been accused of staying home sick to avoid an exam, Xander hoped that a formal doctor's note would *vindicate* him in his teacher's eyes.

Chapter 7
Identifying Structural Words

Across all eight Reading question types, you'll come across passages written by a variety of authors. The social science, natural science, and cultural texts will all be written by College Board, while passages from literature will be written by a whole host of authors from the 18th, 19th, and early 20th centuries. However, all authors, regardless of background, use certain words when constructing their works that can help you keep track of the structure of the text, improving your odds of locating the right evidence. This chapter will explore seven of the most common types of structural words you'll encounter on the Digital SAT.

THE IMPORTANCE OF STRUCTURE

As far as we know, you can't speak to the author of each passage during the Digital SAT. If you could, the questions would be a lot easier, or at least, you would have someone to argue with regarding a specific answer. However, in a way, the author of each passage does speak to you. Authors organize their texts in a certain way and chooses specific words and phrases to communicate ideas. While some of these words and phrases are just informational and descriptive in nature, meant to convey the actual details of the author's chosen topic, many of them help you understand the relevance of the sentence you are about to read or even understand why a previous sentence was included. Before we dive in, here's a list of the seven types of structural words you'll see on the Digital SAT.

- Pivotal Words
- Continuation Words
- Concluding Words
- Comparing and Contrasting Words
- Emphasizers
- List Indicators
- Example Indicators

PIVOTAL WORDS

By a long shot, the most important structural words you want to find on the SAT passages are pivotal words. These words indicate a shift in the direction of the argument, and almost every correct answer to a Reading question will account for this shift, when present. If this concept sounds familiar to you, it should! In the Vocabulary chapter, we looked at transitions, which are pivotal words. You've already seen how transitions affect the type of word you want to annotate, but below, you'll see a more comprehensive list of these words. Review the list, and then see if you can catch the pivot in the Vocabulary example that follows.

Common Pivotal Words

but	however	although
nevertheless	nonetheless	even though
despite	yet	still

time change words such as previously *and* now

Traditionally, most Taiwanese art was either a portrait of a Taiwanese leader or a glimpse into the lives of ordinary Taiwanese citizens. However, Taiwanese artist Wu Tien-chang _____ these disparate foci when he released a series of four large oil paintings of Taiwanese political figures but depicted within each figure the struggles of the common citizen against oppression. Contrasting the leaders and the citizens in the same images prompted discussions about methods to improve social and political conditions in Taiwanese society.

1 ☐ Mark for Review

Which choice completes the text with the most logical and precise word or phrase?

(A) celebrated

(B) chastised

(C) ridiculed

(D) synthesized

Why This Question is Hard

Each of the answer choices to this Vocabulary question seems like a reasonable action for an artist to take. Artists are known to celebrate their subjects or synthesize multiple art forms together, and in the realm of political art, chastising and ridiculing those who would oppress others seems quite logical for a socially oriented artist. Furthermore, the passage offers information about the effects of Wu Tien-chang's art, which could distract from his choice of subject, which is the true focus of the blank.

Here's How to Ace It

Note the **pivotal word** *However* at the start of the second sentence. Because the blank is in the second sentence, the only thing you care about is how the first and second sentences interact. The word *However* serves to literally **pivot** the flow of ideas, switching the direction in which the passage was going. If you read the previous chapter, your thoughts, highlighting, and annotation might look something like this:

Who/What	What Wu Tien-chang does with the two disparate (different) foci (focuses), those being the Taiwanese leaders and the lives of ordinary citizens
Clue	*most Taiwanese art was either a portrait of a Taiwanese leader or a glimpse into the lives of ordinary Taiwanese citizens*
Transition	*However*
Annotation	"combined" or "blended"

Only (D), *synthesized*, matches that annotation. The other three answers go **Beyond the Text**— they are all logical but unsupported assumptions about what an artist might do. The correct answer is (D).

> Pivotal words shift the direction of a passage or an argument and are the most critical words to catch.

CONTINUATION WORDS

Exactly as the name implies, continuation words are the opposite of pivotal words: they keep the passage or argument headed the same direction. This doesn't mean they don't matter. After a continuation, the author will further develop or explain a point that was just made. If you're asked how one sentence relates to another, catching a continuation word could answer that question for you almost automatically. Below is a list of common continuation words, followed by a Purpose question for you to try.

Common Continuation Words		
additionally	despite	also
moreover	furthermore	

For many years, proteins were believed to be the key storage unit of genetic information inside of bacteria. <u>Furthermore, it had been posited that the genetic information inside the proteins of a deceased bacterium could not be passed on to living specimens.</u> In 1944, Oswald Avery, Colin MacLeod, and Maclyn McCarty demonstrated that DNA, not protein, stored genetic data within bacteria. The team introduced deceased samples of *Streptococcus pneumoniae* into samples of living, benign pneumococci bacteria. The living pneumococci bacteria incorporated the DNA from the *S. pneumoniae* samples into their own DNA and became virulent, or potentially hostile to host organisms.

2 ⬗ Mark for Review

Which choice best describes the function of the second sentence in the overall structure of the text?

(A) It postulates background knowledge that explains why the *S. pneumoniae* DNA was incorporated into the living bacteria.

(B) It outlines the hypothesis that Avery, MacLeod, and McCarty verified using two species of bacteria.

(C) It elaborates upon a hypothesis that was contradicted by the results of the Avery-MacLeod-McCarty experiment.

(D) It states an alternate justification for the results of the Avery-MacLeod-McCarty experiment.

Why This Question is Hard

This passage is science-heavy, which may or may not pose a difficulty for students depending on their background. Science topics can cause students to become distracted by the science, sometimes focusing too much on understanding the experiment and jargon and not focusing enough on finding the answer to the question. Lastly, the passage asks students to keep track of two different and contradictory conclusions, and the wrong answers are based on students losing track of which conclusion is being discussed.

Here's How to Ace It

The word *Furthermore* at the beginning of the underlined sentence is a **continuation word**, which means it's further explaining the first sentence. Together, these sentences form what scientists believed regarding proteins and their ability to pass on genetic data. In order to fully understand the function of the sentence, you also need to examine what happens later—both of the beliefs regarding proteins were soundly contradicted by the Avery-MacLeod-McCarty experiment. Therefore, after highlighting the first two sentences, you can enter into the annotation box something like, "further explain the old theory, which has been contradicted."

Choice (A) is wrong because it's **Half-Right**. While the sentence does contain background knowledge, it has nothing to do with the reasons for or process used in the later DNA experiment. Choice (B) is wrong because it's the **Opposite** of what the Avery-MacLeod-McCarty experiment did. It *contradicted* the previous hypothesis rather than *verified* it. Keep (C) because it accounts for both the continuation and the contradiction from the experiment later in the text. Choice (D) is wrong because the second sentence does not focus on the later experiment at all, similar to the flaw in (A). The correct answer is (C).

> Continuation words indicate that a point from the previous sentence is being further explained.

CONCLUDING WORDS

Authors use conclusions to sum up their main points or to articulate an argument made by someone else in the text. Finding these words, when present, can be a big deal because many question types on the Digital SAT are concerned with the arguments in the passage. While it's common for these words to appear at the end of a passage, it's also possible for a conclusion to exist earlier in the passage, only to be further supported or even contradicted later on. Below is a list of common concluding words, followed by a Dual Texts question for you to try.

Although *claim, assert,* and *conclude* may be different parts of speech from *therefore, thus,* and *hence,* they still perform the same role on the Digital SAT and are incredibly helpful for finding main arguments quickly.

Common Concluding Words		
therefore	thus	hence
claim	assert	conclude

Text 1

Sooam Biotech, a company based out of Korea, obtained muscle and blood samples from a preserved mammoth specimen discovered in Siberia in 2013. The company hopes to use the samples to clone the mammoth and complete a "de-extinction." The company claims that bringing the mammoth back to life through cloning could have a positive impact on the environment, as the creature's traditional diet includes plants that retain heat and therefore contribute to global warming.

Text 2

In order to clone a deceased animal, a cell is extracted from the deceased being and implanted into the egg of a similar living organism. The embryo is then implanted into a female individual to act as a surrogate mother to the potential clone. The cloned animal will contain the DNA of both its deceased forebearer and its living surrogate mother. Therefore, English paleobiologist Tori Herridge believes any cloned animal would not actually be an individual of the desired species, as certain special traits expected of the clone may be altered or absent entirely.

---

3   ⬜ Mark for Review

Based on the texts, how would Tori Herridge (Text 2) most likely respond to the "de-extinction" plan presented in Text 1?

(A) By challenging the conjecture that mammoths are a scientifically significant species to attempt to bring back from extinction

(B) By recognizing that bringing back extinct animals is more important than any potential negative effects of the procedure

(C) By conceding that the use of a biologically similar animal as a surrogate mother for the cloning process is acceptable

(D) By arguing that the clone of an animal from an extinct species may not represent a de-extinction of that species

---

Why This Question is Hard

Besides the choice of topic, Dual Texts always have an inherent difficulty of needing to keep track of two different sets of arguments at once. Additionally, the link between the passages is not obvious at first, as the first passage discusses a plan put forward by a company, while the second passage focuses on an extremely specific science argument that does not directly address the company's plan, but rather, a feature of cloning in general.

Here's How to Ace It

The question focuses on the "de-extinction" plan of cloning the mammoth, and the **concluding word** *claims* helps you find why Sooam Biotech is pushing for this plan: it hopes to *clone the mammoth and complete a "de-extinction."* In the second passage, the **concluding word** *Therefore* helps you find Herridge's view quickly; she believes that *any cloned animal would not actually be an individual of the desired species.* Therefore, after highlighting these two conclusions, you can enter something like, "argue that Sooam won't be bringing back the mammoth, but a hybrid."

Choice (A) is wrong because Herridge's objection has nothing to do with which species is being brought back, but with the results of cloning in general. Choice (B) is wrong because Herridge doesn't make any comparisons as to which of these two things she finds *more important*. Choice (C) is wrong because Herridge is not *compromising* or expressing that she wishes cloning could be done differently—she is pointing out a science truth that could affect the company's cloning plan. Keep (D) because Herridge states that because of the hybrid DNA, *certain special traits expected of the clone may be altered or absent entirely*. The correct answer is (D).

> Concluding words indicate a main point or argument within the text and will almost always be reflected in the correct answer.

COMPARING AND CONTRASTING WORDS

Authors often make comparisons and contrasts as part of their arguments. It can be helpful for readers to be presented with a concept they are likely to know to help them have a reference point for a concept that would be less familiar to them. Producing a second example similar to the first can also strengthen the weight of an argument. Similarly, contrasts help readers understand the various sides of a debate or grasp more complex issues that don't necessarily fall into a single category. Sometimes, comparisons and contrasts can actually be the entire point of the text in the first place. Below is a list of common comparison and contrast words, followed by a Retrieval question for you to try.

Common Comparing and Contrasting Words		
similarly	like	in contrast
difference	unlike	anything indicating a passage of time

You may remember seeing *in contrast* on the Pivotal Words list. When moving between arguments, *in contrast* is a pivotal phrase that shifts the argument. When moving between details or evidence, *in contrast* is used to establish a contrast between two different things. Either way, it's likely to be accounted for by the correct answer, so be on the lookout for it.

Consumers are negatively motivated by perceived "bad luck" days, such as Friday the 13th, because they feel as though events that occur on these days are out of their control. This belief contributes to approximately $900 million annually in lost worker productivity and similarly poor company sales in the United States alone. According to a team of researchers at the University of Cincinnati aiming to understand this phenomenon, incidental unluckiness, or unluckiness that happens to fall on a perceived "bad luck" day, briefly incapacitates consumers, causing them to feel less capable of taking actions that will lead to optimistic results. In contrast, when the same percentage of unfortunate events happens to consumers on perceived "normal" days, the consumer avoids any such incapacitation and is able to often choose the action with the highest possible benefit more readily.

 4 🔖 Mark for Review

According to the text, what was the conclusion reached by the University of Cincinnati researchers?

(A) Consumers feel less able to control their outcomes and avoid negative situations on "bad luck" days, affecting the consumers' responses to unfortunate events.

(B) Consumers are able to avoid negative outcomes by taking coordinated steps to ensure their days are positive on "bad luck" days.

(C) Consumers are not actually affected by "bad luck" days, and the perceived loss in productivity and sales is just a coincidence.

(D) Consumers are capable of choosing whether or not a "bad luck" day will affect them and do not experience a pressure to act a certain way on those days.

Why This Question is Hard

Lengthwise, this question is associated with one of the longer passages you'll see. Additionally, the passage covers a wide swath of subjects, from economics to superstition to psychology and human behavior. The answers are also on the longer side, with two distinct parts. In general, the longer the answer, the easier it is to miss the single word or phrase that may invalidate that answer.

Here's How to Ace It

The first **comparing word** you see is *similarly*, which helps you quickly understand that several bad things tend to happen on these perceived "bad luck" days. The far more important one to catch is the **contrasting phrase** *in contrast*, which helps you see that while unfortunate or unlucky things happen to people on both "bad luck" and "normal days," on normal days consumers are able to *often choose the action with the highest possible benefit more readily*. With the last two sentences highlighted, you're ready to evaluate the answers.

Keep (A) because it's consistent with the statements made by the research team—people react worse to unfortunate events on days they thought would be "bad luck" days in the first place. Choice (B) is wrong because the team does not offer any method for feeling positive on "bad luck" days. Choice (C) is wrong because it's the **Opposite** of the team's claim, which is that people are most certainly *affected by "bad luck" days* according to the second to last sentence. Choice (D) is wrong because it goes **Beyond the Text**—whether or not a consumer could choose to not be affected by a "bad luck" day or avoid *pressure to act a certain way* is unknown from the passage, which focuses more on the fact that people are indeed affected by these days. The correct answer is (A).

> Comparing and contrasting words help you keep track of how authors use evidence as part of their arguments.

EMPHASIZERS

Emphasizers, or emphasis words, are used to draw attention to things that the author, or people within the passage, believe to be especially important. Generally, if you catch an emphasizer, it is probably pointing you to a main idea, like a conclusion does. At a minimum, an emphasizer points you to a detail that is likely more important for understanding the main idea than are most of the other details. Below is a list of common emphasizers, followed by a Main Idea question for you to try.

Common Emphasizers	
most important	must
crucial	chiefly
primarily	critical

Occasionally, the passage may include adverbs like *sadly, fortunately,* and *thankfully* to express an opinion. We don't formally include these Opinion Indicators in this chapter as it's extremely rare for SAT authors to make such a judgment on any aspect of their chosen topic, but it can happen. If these words do show up, they function in a similar way to Emphasizers in that the author is calling attention to something worth commenting on.

In 1946, British-American philosopher Max Black proposed the mutilated chessboard problem, a tiling puzzle that asks whether it is possible to place 31 traditional dominoes to cover an entire 8 × 8 chessboard if two diagonally opposite corners are removed from the board. The problem is impossible to solve, as once the corners are removed, the chessboard contains 32 squares of one color and 30 of the other, but the dominoes must cover an equal number of squares of each color.

5   🔖 Mark for Review

Which choice best states the main idea of the text?

A) Chessboards are made up of two different colors, each with an equal number of squares.

B) Specific features of the components used made a proposed puzzle unsolvable.

C) The puzzle is used to assess people's creative thinking and problem-solving skills.

D) Dominoes are useful for understanding models with two distinct color complexes.

Why This Question is Hard

The complexity of this passage is relatively low, but the trick here is in the answers. All of the answers seem either justified by or implied by the passage, but only one of them can actually serve as the main idea of the passage. It's very common for students under a great deal of stress to start looking for "matching" statements in the passage and answers and accidentally neglect the task given by the question.

Here's How to Ace It

While the passage contains only two sentences, the **emphasizer** word *must* as well as the word *impossible* (which, really, also serves as an **emphasizer** of level of difficulty) should draw your attention to the second sentence. While the features of a chessboard and a domino are certainly interesting to some, all that matters is catching that *the problem is impossible to solve* because *dominoes must cover an equal number of squares of each color.* This final sentence serves as the main idea, as the first sentence only offers background detail to better understand the puzzle itself.

Choices (A), (C), and (D) are all answers that go **Beyond the Text**—all of these answers seem logical and, in fact, are true in the real world. However, all of them fail to account for what the author is focusing on through the emphasizer words—the difficulty of the puzzle itself and the precise reason that it's impossible to solve. Keep (B) because it essentially paraphrases the final sentence, which, by the way, most correct SAT answers do rather than repeating exact language from the passage. The correct answer is (B).

Emphasizers are used to draw attention to concepts that the author feels are particularly significant and therefore are useful for finding main ideas or arguments.

LIST INDICATORS

These words indicate that the author is going to mention several components of an argument or include a series of chronological events that relate to each other. While the list indicators won't indicate an argument themselves, asking what argument or idea the list is related to will help you hone in on the most important sentence within the passage. Wrong answers to questions with list indicators typically combine elements from two different parts of the list or include a single word that misinterprets the information contained in the list, so keep your sets of details separate and carefully reread your highlighting when applying POE. Below are some common list indicators, followed by a Claims question for you to try.

Common List Indicators		
first	second	third
number of reasons	multiple causes	several factors

The Anastenaria is a Greek and Bulgarian ritual that combines fire-walking with enthusiastic dance techniques, and according to the theory endorsed by many prominent scholars, its development can be traced to several key events. First, during the Middle Ages, a church in Saint Augustine caught fire in Kosti, a Bulgarian village. People living in the village helped combat the flames and rescue those trapped inside the church. These acts helped inspire the early versions of the ritual. Second, during the Balkan Wars of 1911 and 1912, refugees from Greece and Bulgaria fled their war-torn lands, bringing the ritual with them to their new villages. For these refugees and their descendants, the ritual took on an even greater significance as a means of hopefully improving their fortunes.

6 Mark for Review

Which finding, if true, would most directly support the scholars' theory?

(A) Bulgarian sculptures dating back to the Middle Ages memorialize the Saint Augustine rescue through a depiction of the Anastenaria.

(B) Written records that mention the Anastenaria prior to the twentieth century exist only outside of Greece and Bulgaria.

(C) Interviews with the descendants of Balkan War refugees reveal that the village to which their family arrived already performed the Anastenaria.

(D) Archaeological evidence reveals that Saint Augustine's Church was most likely empty at the time of the fire.

Why This Question is Hard

The passage itself requires keeping track of two fairly unrelated events which together make up the scholars' theory. Additionally, each wrong answer here contains a single word that truly invalidates it, and it could be easy to miss that word under time pressure.

Here's How to Ace It

The **list indicator** *several key events* tells you right away that you need to keep track of multiple components to the scholars' theory, and you can use the **list indicators** *First* and *Second* to quickly find the events themselves. While you should highlight the main component of each event, it's going to be better to compare the answers back to the passage here rather than highlight everything and look for an answer that matches your highlighting, as you don't know which event the correct answer will focus on.

Keep (A) as it would strengthen the first event, the church fire, as a possible inspiration for the Anastenaria. Choices (B), (C), and (D) are wrong as each would weaken, not support, the scholar's theory. If records exist *only* outside of Greece and Bulgaria or the villages that accepted the refugees *already* performed the Anastenaria, this would weaken the second event's influence. If the church was most likely *empty* at the time of the fire, this would weaken the first event's influence. The correct answer is (A).

> List Indicators help you keep track of a series of items that are relevant to understanding a main point or argument.

EXAMPLE INDICATORS

These words tell you that what follows is an illustration of some larger, more important point within the passage. Oftentimes, when you find an example indicator, it is the sentence before it you should be focusing on, as that sentence is the main claim or argument on which the passage is centered. Even if the question task is entirely about the example itself, you're still going to want to find what point the example demonstrates, as that point is likely to influence the answer that you are looking for. Below is a list of common example indicators, followed by a Charts question for you to try.

Common Example Indicators		
for example	for instance	such as

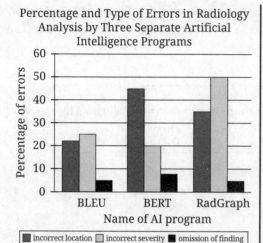

Percentage and Type of Errors in Radiology Analysis by Three Separate Artificial Intelligence Programs

Legend: incorrect location | incorrect severity | omission of finding

If artificial intelligence could be used to analyze medical images, it could revolutionize the accuracy with which doctors could catch cancerous and pre-cancerous cells. While AI-generated radiology reports continue to provide analyses ever closer to the ones generated by human radiologists, limitations in the quality of video equipment utilized by these programs have nevertheless prevented AI-generated reports from matching the quality and thoroughness of human reports. Yu et al. analyzed three different artificial intelligence programs and the errors they made to identify how reliable they are. For example, _____

7 ☐ Mark for Review

Which choice most effectively uses data from the graph to complete the example?

(A) BLEU artificial intelligence is the most likely of the three programs to make errors in severity, while BERT artificial intelligence is the most likely of the three programs to make errors in location.

(B) all three types of artificial intelligence make errors regarding the location and severity of medical issues, and each AI program will occasionally omit findings entirely.

(C) RadGraph artificial intelligence is the most likely to omit a finding entirely, while BLEU artificial intelligence is the least likely to do so.

(D) RadGraph artificial intelligence is just as likely to omit a finding as a human radiologist is.

Why This Question is Hard

With three different programs, three different types of errors, and a science-based topic, it can seem like one has to keep track of a lot of different information and understand what each type of error means in order to decipher which example would be correct. The answers also involve some tedious double checking of the data contained in the graph.

Here's How to Ace It

The **example indicator** *For example* tells you to check the sentence before it, which states that *Yu et al. analyzed three different artificial intelligence programs and the errors they made to identify how reliable they are.* So, as long as the example is consistent with the results reported in the graph, you don't really need to consider the rest of the passage beyond the initial read of it.

Choice (A) is wrong because it's **Half-Right**—the first half does not describe BLEU accurately, but the second half describes BERT accurately. Keep (B) because it accurately describes the graph. Choice (C) is wrong because RadGraph was not the AI program *most likely* to omit a finding, BERT was. Choice (D) is wrong because it goes **Beyond the Text**—no information is given from either the passage or the graph as to the actual percentages of human errors. The correct answer is (B).

> Example Indicators direct your attention to the sentence before, which likely contains a main point or argument.

IN CONCLUSION

Each of these seven categories of words can appear on virtually any question type, and as you may have noticed, passages can use multiple types of words within a single paragraph. For example, the previous question contained the **contrasting word** *nevertheless* to establish a limitation on what AI-generated programs can currently catch. While it's often not necessary to find every single structural word in a passage, each one you do find is an opportunity to access the information you need from the passage more efficiently. More specifically, these words can be a great help on Conclusions questions, which require you to keep track of the structure of the passage in order to choose a supported conclusion.

The concept of virtual water is the idea that water is embedded in non-liquid commodities that are traded, such as wheat. If a country imports a certain amount of wheat, it is also saving itself the water required to grow the equivalent amount of wheat. If a country exports wheat, it is also exporting the virtual water associated with growing the wheat. Because virtual water by definition is not a tangible resource, it can be relatively easy for a country to fail to account for the impact of its imports and exports on its water supply. Therefore, this suggests that _____

8 ☐ Mark for Review

Which choice most logically completes the text?

(A) countries should export commodities only if they have a surplus of real water available for use.

(B) countries may accidentally exacerbate a water scarcity if they do not account for virtual water in their trades with other countries.

(C) virtual water can be traded the same way as all other goods and services.

(D) countries with a water shortage should partner with countries with a water surplus in order to augment their supplies.

Why This Question is Hard

A student encountering this passage needs to keep track of both the concept of virtual water and the relevance of the example of wheat to virtual water. Conclusions questions all share an inherent difficulty as well: the incomplete nature of the passage makes it appear as if it could be completed with any answer as long as the answer can be justified logically.

Here's How to Ace It

The **example indicator** *such as* lets you know that wheat is only being used to illustrate the concept of virtual water and is not the main focus of the passage. The repetition of the **continuation** word *also* makes it clear that the second and third sentences relate to explaining the concept of virtual water more clearly. The **conclusion word** *Therefore* indicates that while all of the evidence in the passage matters, special attention should be paid to the evidence immediately before the word, which states that *it can be relatively easy for a country to fail to account for the impact of its imports and exports on its water supply*. The correct answer should be consistent with this sentence and potentially the other explanations given of virtual water.

Choice (A) is wrong because *real water* is not discussed in the passage and the word *only* is an example of **Extreme Language**. Keep (B) because it's a good paraphrase of the final complete sentence and references the middle sentences' use of import and export. Choice (C) is wrong because it's the **Opposite** of what's implied by the passage—virtual water cannot be traded as other goods can. Instead, it is gained or lost as a consequence of trading goods. Choice (D) is wrong because it goes **Beyond the Text**—it's a logical solution to a water shortage but not something actually recommended by the passage itself. The correct answer is (B).

> Conclusions passages often feature more than one type of structural word that can help you understand the connections between ideas in the passage.

Structural Words Drill

Just as you saw in this chapter, this drill contains one question of each type. Practice identifying structural words as you attempt this set and see if it helps your accuracy. Answers and explanations can be found in Chapter 12.

Time: 10 minutes

1 ☐ Mark for Review

The cecal appendix—an anatomical structure present in a wide range of species—was long considered an evolutionary remnant with no meaningful biological function in humans. Research has shown a correlation between appendix presence and longevity in mammals, leading researchers to hypothesize that the organ is not, in fact, _____ but actually serves a useful purpose.

Which choice completes the text with the most logical and precise word or phrase?

(A) vestigial

(B) adaptive

(C) salient

(D) beneficial

2 ☐ Mark for Review

Research has shown that focusing attention on a task impairs one's ability to notice objects that unexpectedly enter the field of vision. Our understanding of this "inattentional blindness" may require some modification, however. Consider a 2023 study by Pascal Wallisch et al. in which participants were asked to count how many times a basketball was passed back and forth. Consistent with earlier studies, the participants failed to notice other objects that slowly entered their field of vision while they were counting. The new study revealed, however, that individuals are surprisingly good at noticing fast-moving objects, even when concentrating on a task.

Which choice best states the main purpose of the text?

(A) It includes the study by Wallisch et al. to challenge the generalizability of the psychological phenomenon known as inattentional blindness.

(B) It discusses the findings of Wallisch et al. to disprove earlier claims that the ability to see unexpected objects is impaired when attention is directed elsewhere.

(C) It supports the conclusion of Wallisch et al. that inattentional blindness depends more on the nature of the task than on the speed of the moving object.

(D) It elaborates upon a flaw in the methodology of inattentional blindness studies such as the one conducted by Wallisch et al. in 2023.

3 🔖 Mark for Review

Text 1

Malaria is transmitted to humans by mosquitoes carrying plasmodium parasites. When the parasites reach the merozoite stage in humans, they can cause debilitating, and often fatal, illness. Researchers seeking to develop a malaria vaccine introduced a genetically altered form of the parasite to humans, and the results are very encouraging. When transmitted to human subjects, the genetically engineered parasite is safe and appears to elicit antibodies that can help guard against malarial infection.

Text 2

After Sean Murphy and his colleagues genetically altered the parasite that causes malaria, the results were heralded as promising for the development of a malaria vaccine. As the researchers acknowledge, though, there is still work to be done. For example, the transmission of the parasite in the study via large numbers of mosquito bites means that the proper dose for an injectable vaccine is still unknown.

Based on the texts, what would the author of Text 2 most likely say about Text 1's characterization of the prospects for a malaria vaccine?

(A) It is overly cautious given that Murphy and his team have succeeded in genetically altering the parasite.

(B) It is appropriate given that Murphy and his colleagues have discovered the mechanism by which malaria is transmitted to humans.

(C) It is prematurely hopeful given the questions that remain regarding delivery of the vaccine.

(D) It is surprising given that most people heralded Murphy and his team's early successes as promising.

4 🔖 Mark for Review

In an article on chemical looping combustion (CLC)—a method of burning fossil fuels while minimizing the release of carbon dioxide—Michael High et al. discuss a strategy for improving the metal oxides traditionally used in the process. One limitation to CLC has been the structural deterioration of the metal oxides over multiple redox cycles, as the metal oxides gain and lose electrons. This shortcoming may be eliminated by a new design strategy for improved copper-based metal oxides that, according to one researcher, "hold great potential for use in the energy processes that are helping us reach net zero."

What does the text most strongly suggest about the metal oxides traditionally used in CLC?

(A) They are structurally flawed and thus render CLC considerably less effective than other methods of reducing carbon emissions.

(B) They are less capable of withstanding multiple redox cycles than the newer copper-based alternatives might prove to be.

(C) They are less effective at minimizing the release of carbon dioxide than are the metal oxides used in other methods of burning fossil fuels.

(D) They typically gain more electrons than they lose over the course of multiple redox cycles.

5 ☐ Mark for Review

In an analysis that grew out of his earlier research into inhibitory control (the brain's ability to override reflexive responses), Dr. Michael Anderson explored whether suppressing negative thoughts might have mental health benefits in times of adversity. Study participants underwent three days of training to learn to suppress distressing thoughts about future events. Contrary to the conventional view that suppression harms mental health, Anderson found that participants, both immediately after the study and when tested again three months later, reported lower levels of depression and anxiety.

Which choice best states the main idea of the text?

 A) While suppressing negative thoughts has been the subject of previous studies, Anderson's was the first to consider its effects on mental health in times of adversity.

B) Research indicates that suppressing negative thoughts will have a rebound effect, causing such thoughts to become more vivid and intrusive.

C) Although the brain is able to override reflexive responses, training is required before a person can suppress negative thoughts about future events.

D) Despite reservations about the benefits of suppressing negative thoughts, research indicates that such suppression might actually improve mental health for some people.

6 ☐ Mark for Review

Utopian societies (such as Brook Farm, Massachusetts, or New Harmony, Indiana) were experiments in communal living that proliferated in mid-nineteenth-century America. In a time of rapid economic change and rising social tensions, the founders of such communities hoped to counter the negative effects of industrial capitalism. Most utopian societies were based on the premise that all residents would live and work in conditions of complete equality. According to one historian, the failure of nearly all utopian societies was due to the tension between individual freedom and the demands of communal societies.

Which quotation from a student research paper best illustrates the historian's claim?

A) "The goal of such utopian societies was to ensure that each individual member would have the opportunity for self-improvement. If all shared equally in the labor, it was hoped, then there would be ample opportunity for leisure and intellectual pursuits."

B) "Reformers quickly came to realize that their attempts to blend individualism with collectivism were inherently untenable. Disillusioned by the demands of collectivist cooperation, many residents soon abandoned these experiments in communal living."

C) "The communities' lofty goals of attempting to reform society while simultaneously emphasizing individual perfectibility led them to undertake many projects that, in the end, were not financially viable."

D) "The leaders of most utopian societies were intellectuals with little to no background in agriculture. All the careful planning in the world could not have prepared them for the physical demands of establishing self-sufficient farming communities."

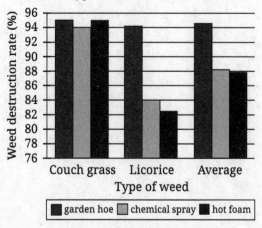

Percentage of Weeds Destroyed Based on Weed Type and Weed Control Method

Most agronomists agree that mechanical weed control methods, such as hoeing, are preferable to chemical herbicides in terms of promoting sustainable agriculture. While particularly effective against annual weeds, mechanical methods can be labor intensive and, over time, can aid in the dispersal of perennial weeds and contribute to soil degradation. Given these limitations, as well as the environmental harms of chemical sprays, Ferhat Kup and Ramazan Saglam conducted a study to test a sustainable alternative for controlling the two most common weeds in cotton fields: couch grass and licorice. They concluded that, while hoeing had the highest success rate at destroying the weeds, hot foam was a viable alternative to spraying chemical herbicides.

Which choice best describes data from the graph that support Kup and Saglam's conclusion?

(A) The application of hot foam was more effective at destroying couch grass than were chemical sprays, while the use of chemical sprays was more effective at destroying licorice than was hot foam.

(B) The use of both hot foam and chemical sprays resulted in weed destruction rates below 85% when applied to infestations of licorice.

(C) The hot foam method was more effective than the spraying method at destroying couch grass and nearly as effective as the spraying method overall.

(D) The effectiveness of all three methods was comparable with respect to couch grass specifically, but hoeing was by far the most effective weed-control method overall with an average weed destruction rate above 94%.

8 ⌖ Mark for Review

Constructive feedback—comments aimed at improving performance—can be invaluable in helping others achieve positive outcomes. Recognizing the benefits, people overwhelmingly report wanting to receive this type of feedback. However, those same people often avoid providing such feedback to others even when it would be helpful. For example, in one pilot study, only 2.6% of participants provided constructive feedback when they observed a situation that their feedback could easily rectify. These findings suggest that _____

Which choice most logically completes the text?

(A) people tend to overestimate the desire of others to receive constructive feedback.

(B) most people provide constructive feedback only when doing so will benefit them.

(C) many people fail to notice opportunities to provide constructive feedback.

(D) the desire for constructive feedback may be greater than the willingness to offer it.

Chapter 8
Understanding
Sentence Function

During the Reading portion of the Reading and Writing modules, you're asked to work through the longest passages you'll see on the Digital SAT in a relatively short amount of time. To access a passage quickly, understanding the roles of sentences can be more important than understanding the details present within those sentences. In this chapter, we'll use the structural words we previously identified and connect them to understand the roles of entire sentences.

THE IMPORTANCE OF FUNCTION

A passive reader absorbs all the words within a passage evenly, and we've mentioned already how this can create breaks in momentum and second guesses that affect accuracy. If structural words were one way to become an active reader, understanding sentence function is the critical next step. Instead of only understanding the role taken on by a single word, using those words to quickly identify what role the entire sentence serves can help you know almost instantaneously which sentence to focus on. With time, you'll notice patterns in how College Board writes its passages and be able to anticipate where you should look in a passage based on its opening sentence. If you know exactly how each sentence contributes to the passage, you're going to avoid losing precious seconds to irrelevant sentences and details and instead can focus on highlighting only what you need.

The Four Main Sentence Functions

Occasionally, especially on literature-based passages, you'll find a sentence that does not neatly fit into one of these roles. Keep your eyes moving forward—either that sentence won't be critical to the passage or you'll be able to understand its relevance by reading the other sentences.

Name	Function Performed
Background	Provides context or information regarding a topic that the author feels is necessary for the reader to understand before any arguments are made. Background sentences are usually factual in nature and often occur at the start of a passage.
Claim	States the author's, an individual's, or a group's main argument, theory, or opinion. A critical feature of a claim is that it is something that can be disagreed with and needs to be supported by evidence.
Objection	Argues against a claim, theory, or opinion made by someone else in the passage. This makes it a claim unto itself, but objections are so frequent on the Reading passages that you want to catch them specifically.
Evidence	Offers details and is used to support Claims or Objections. While most evidence occurs after a claim or objection, it can also come before if the author has chosen to build up to the claim.

Read the following passage and see how you do in determining the role of each sentence by reading our explanation afterwards. We've numbered each sentence for your convenience.

[1] With the initial growth of suburban communities in the mid-twentieth century, residential pools went from the domain of only the wealthiest individuals to attainable amenities for those with more modest incomes. [2] However, this boon came with predictably negative consequences for local wildlife near these communities. [3] Improper drainage of water in pools and spas used for personal recreation has led to widespread contamination of the surrounding landscape that can cause immense environmental damage and even kill plant and animal life. [4] A group of researchers has posited that proper drainage of pool water can help to reverse the damage done to suburban environments. [5] In a survey conducted on soil surrounding residential pools in various American suburbs, the researchers found the toxicity of soil surrounding pools in which the owner had followed the manufacturer's drainage instructions to be 46% lower than the toxicity levels of soil surrounding pools for which the instructions had been followed improperly.

See How You Did

Sentence 1 is **background** explaining the growth of the pool industry.

Sentence 2 is an **objection** explaining that this growth had negative effects.

Sentence 3 is **evidence** further explaining how the proliferation of residential pools was negative.

Sentence 4 is a **claim** by a group of researchers who are proposing a solution to the negative issues.

Sentence 5 is **evidence** that supports the researchers' claim by citing results from their study.

We'll discuss ways to identify these functions throughout the rest of this chapter.

BACKGROUND

Background sentences usually offer context that the author feels is relevant to the passage. In historical passages, some previous event may be discussed. In social and natural science passages, a term may be introduced or explained. In cultural passages, a practice or form of art may be described. While the background information does not always play a critical role in the correct answer choice, recognizing background information can help improve your efficiency by learning to focus your attention elsewhere, especially if any of the passage needs to be reread to determine which answer is a trap. See if you can identify the background information on this Retrieval question and use its role in the passage to find the correct answer.

Reggae is a music genre that evolved from Caribbean calypso, American jazz, and rhythm and blues. Its musical origins can be traced back to the genres ska and rocksteady, both of which began in 1960s Jamaica. The roots of reggae, however, run deeper than its musical influences. Reggae music also has a strong connection to the Rastafari religion, which developed in Jamaica in the 1930s. Proponents of the religion sought an appropriate vehicle for disseminating Rastafari messages, and this desire influenced the lyrical content of what would become reggae music. Due to its memorable rhythms and relatable themes, reggae music quickly gained popularity around the world.

You need to at least read the information contained in background sentences, but what a background sentence really tells you is to keep driving forward until you find an argument—the first argument here is in Sentence 3.

---

1 ☐ Mark for Review

What does the text most strongly suggest about the reggae genre?

(A) It became a way for island nations to deliver news to one another and eventually to the world.

(B) It has not seen the popularity it deserves despite the importance of its messages.

(C) It grew from being a blend of musical styles into music that accompanied religious proceedings.

(D) It evolved from a variety of musical styles but is closely tied to the message of the Rastafari movement.

Why This Question is Hard

The passage spends considerable time discussing music before abruptly switching topics to religion. Also, the answers contain several logical but unsupported assumptions that will be increasingly tempting the more someone knows about reggae music.

Here's How to Ace It

Sentences 1 and 2 here are **background** information. Notice how they only discuss the musical genres connected to reggae without offering any main point or argument. The pivotal word *however* indicates that the next sentence is a shift that should draw your attention, as the passage goes on to say that reggae *has a strong connection to the Rastafari religion*. So, the correct answer is likely to address either the musical or religious influences on reggae, or perhaps both.

Choice (A) is wrong because it goes **Beyond the Text**—while reggae may have been used to *deliver news,* the passage does not offer this as a function of reggae. Choice (B) is wrong because it's the **Opposite** of what's stated in the passage—reggae did in fact gain *popularity*. Choice (C) is wrong because it's **Recycled Language**—while reggae did become a *vehicle* for the *Rastafari religion,* it's not stated that it actually accompanied *religious proceedings,* or formal religious gathering of some sort. Keep (D) because it references both the background information and the connection to the Rastafari movement that comes after the pivot. The correct answer is (D).

CLAIMS

In many ways, claims are at the heart of Reading on the Digital SAT. While the authors of most passages won't frequently make arguments themselves, almost every question references someone's argument or belief. Claims are primarily indicated by **concluding words**, which we covered in the previous chapter. They can also be identified if the question references a hypothesis, theory, or argument, all of which mean a claim was made somewhere in the passage. Lastly, if you catch an **emphasizer** in a sentence, chances are that the author considers that sentence important and it could easily be part of the argument. It seems appropriate to look at claims on a Claims question, so try the one included below and attempt to track both the background information and the claim presented.

Many mental health professionals assert that assessing a person's mental wellbeing requires the trained expertise of a human clinician. A recent study, however, used specially-designed robots to ask questions of children and found that robot-administered questionnaires were more successful in identifying cases of wellbeing-related anomalies than standard clinical methods of testing. Some mental health professionals have expressed concern that such a significant aspect of their profession could be replaced by robots, but the researchers who conducted the study clarified that the robots demonstrated certain technological limitations in their interactions with human patients, and the study's aim was more to investigate the capabilities of the robots rather than create an alternative to human physicians.

If you're running short on time in a given Reading and Writing module but want to maximize your score, try finding the claim in the passage as quickly as possible. What exactly do the *researchers* claim here? The correct answer must address this, even if the other sentences are addressed also.

---

2   🔖 Mark for Review

Which finding, if true, would most directly support the researchers' clarification?

(A) A survey of clinicians showed that very few of them utilize questionnaires in their assessments of a patient's mental wellbeing.

(B) The researchers found that children were more reluctant to answer questions truthfully when asked by human clinicians than they were when asked by robots.

(C) In the researchers' study, no deviations were found in the responses given by the children regardless of whether the questions were administered by a human clinician or a robot.

(D) A review of the study determined that the robots considered only questionnaire responses and were unable to detect fluctuations in the voice that could also speak to mental wellbeing.

Why This Question is Hard

There are multiple opinions to keep track of in this passage, and you need to make sure your answer reflects both the researchers' claim and the interactions between that claim and the other arguments expressed in the passage.

Here's How to Ace It

Virtually every sentence here is some type of **claim**, but the one you're interested in is in the final sentence: *the researchers who conducted the study clarified that the robots demonstrated certain technological limitations in their interactions with human patients*. Therefore, the correct answer should address some limitation to the robots that administered the questionnaires in the researchers' study.

Choice (A) is wrong because it's not relevant to the claim—it doesn't matter what human clinicians do, as the focus of the claim is on the robots. Choices (B) and (C) are wrong because they would do the **Opposite** of the question task—both of these answers would show that the robots performed better than, or at least equal to, human clinicians, and this would weaken, not support, the researchers' claim that the robots have limitations. Keep (D) because if it were true, being *unable to detect fluctuations in the voice* would be a limitation to the robots. The correct answer is (D).

OBJECTIONS

An Objection, as we said before, is a special type of Claim. Authors or people within passages can object to anything: another claim, evidence, or even background information, as you saw with the introductory example. It's even possible for a passage to introduce an objection and then introduce another perspective that objects to the objection. Have no fear, though: objections are easy to spot because they are almost always accompanied by either **pivotal words** or **contrasting words**. After all, any author hoping to write a coherent passage must let the reader know when the argument has changed. You'll frequently see objections on Dual Texts questions, so let's try one of those next.

> Never allow yourself to get distracted by the science on science-based dual texts. You are not being asked to understand or resolve a scientific debate. Here, the only thing you need to know is what the conventional belief is and what Patti and his colleagues from Text 2 say about that belief.

Text 1

Scientists have long been puzzled as to why cancer cells release glucose as waste material, given that the cells need the energy from glucose consumption to fuel their growth. According to the conventional belief, cancer cells should metabolize glucose more readily when interacting with large quantities of glucose. So, why are these cells wasting their fuel? Despite numerous studies, an explanation for this phenomenon has yet to be found.

Text 2

Dr. Gary Patti and colleagues discovered that when cancer cells become fully saturated with glucose, their ability to metabolize glucose diminishes sharply. When the researchers limited the amount of glucose available to cancer cells, the cells efficiently moved almost all provided glucose into their mitochondria. However, as the concentration of glucose surrounding the cells was increased, the cells couldn't keep up with the required speed to move the additional glucose into their mitochondria as well. In his report, Patti stated that cancer cells actually prefer to use glucose efficiently rather than wastefully.

3 🔖 Mark for Review

Based on the texts, how would Patti and colleagues (Text 2) most likely respond to the "conventional belief" discussed in Text 1?

- Ⓐ By suggesting that their research has uncovered a new metabolic mechanism used by cells

- Ⓑ By clarifying that the cells do metabolize glucose efficiently but that previous research may not have considered the possibility of a threshold on this efficiency

- Ⓒ By recommending that more studies be done to detect other forms of waste produced by the cells

- Ⓓ By asserting that it fails to consider other metabolic processes that benefit by using the wasted glucose

Why This Question is Hard

While the first passage poses a question that the second passage eventually provides an answer to, there is still a solid amount of science-heavy background information to read through, and focusing on understanding the science can distract from finding the actual arguments.

Here's How to Ace It

In Text 1, Sentence 1 is **background** to read through before you reach the **claim** in Sentence 2: the conventional belief is that *cancer cells should metabolize glucose more readily when interacting with large quantities of glucose*. Read the rest of Text 1, but your focus now is moving on to Text 2 and finding Patti and colleagues' thoughts on the same topic. After some additional background, we get to the key **objection**, introduced by a **pivotal word**: *However, as the concentration of glucose surrounding the cells was increased, the cells couldn't keep up with the required speed to move the additional glucose into their mitochondria as well*. Therefore, it's not that the cells aren't willing to accept more fuel, it's that they physically cannot keep up their processing efficiency when offered too much fuel.

Choice (A) is wrong because no *new* metabolic mechanism is announced in Text 2. Keep (B) because it's consistent with Patti and colleagues' findings and correctly accounts for the objection using the word *but*. Choice (C) is wrong because it goes **Beyond the Text**—it's not suggested that any *other forms of waste* should be studied. Choice (D) is wrong similarly because no *other metabolic processes* are considered by either passage. The correct answer is (B).

EVIDENCE, PART 1

Claims and objections by themselves don't make sustainable arguments. Without solid evidence, arguments become unsupported opinions and stand little chance of convincing many people of their possible validity. On the SAT, authors and the people they cite will use many different types of evidence to add strength to their arguments and stand a much better chance of gaining supporters. The first types of evidence worth considering are examples, lists, comparisons, and contrasts, which are usually given to you quite directly by **example indicators**, **list indicators**, **comparing words**, and **contrasting words**, respectively, that are being used as part of the argument. Remember: for most questions, it's more important to discover what idea the evidence is supporting than to focus on the nature of the evidence itself. Let's examine a Main Idea question to explore this point more thoroughly.

In 1896, Harvard Observatory director Edward C. Pickering hired a team of women to assist him in mapping and defining every visible star in the sky, including some only visible through photographs taken by telescopes. One such hire was American astronomer Annie Jump Cannon, whose talent for classifying stars quickly and accurately is what drew Pickering to offer her a position on the team. Throughout her career, Cannon manually classified 350,000 stars, and her work at the Observatory formed the foundation of what would become the modern stellar classification system, which organizes stars by temperature and chemical composition, just as Cannon had.

---

4 ☐ Mark for Review

Which choice best states the main idea of the text?

(A) The team of women hired by Pickering was led by Annie Jump Cannon, whose talent for classifying stars quickly was noteworthy.

(B) Pickering and Cannon collaborated on several important astronomical catalogs throughout their time together at the Harvard Observatory.

(C) Though she was involved in a project with great importance to astronomers, Cannon required the use of telescopic photographs to observe some of the stars that she classified.

(D) While part of a team of women hired by Pickering, Cannon made significant contributions to a systematic process for cataloging celestial bodies.

Why This Question is Hard

The mention of two different scientists can create confusion as to which one the author wanted to focus on for a main idea. Additionally, some of the answers contain logical assumptions that would be easy to make based on the mentions of Cannon's talent and the working relationship between Pickering and Cannon.

Here's How to Ace It

Sentence 1 is **background** as it gives the historical context for the passage but makes no actual argument. Sentence 2 is **evidence** as the phrase *One such hire* means that the author wants to give an **example** of someone on Pickering's team. This evidence leads to a **claim** in Sentence 3, that *her work at the Observatory formed the foundation of what would become the modern stellar classification system*. Note that the claim in Sentence 3 has a stronger foundation because of the details given in Sentence 2 regarding Cannon's abilities. On a Main Idea question, if you can identify the claim or statement that the evidence supports, the evidence has done its job and you should instead highlight the claim/statement. In this case, highlight Sentence 3 and compare each answer back to it.

> Don't assume the first name or idea you see in a passage will give you the main idea. You must keep reading until the end of the passage if you want to avoid cleverly constructed traps.

Choice (A) is wrong because it's **Half-Right**—while Cannon's talent is most certainly noteworthy, at least for Pickering, the passage does not state that she *led* the team at any point. Choice (B) is wrong because it goes **Beyond the Text**—it's easy to assume that Pickering and Cannon worked on many catalogs together, but only one such project is discussed in the passage. Choice (C) is wrong because it's **Right Answer, Wrong Question**—it's true according to the first sentence but is not the main idea of the entire passage. Keep (D) as it's a paraphrase of Sentence 3, which we know to be the main idea. The correct answer is (D).

EVIDENCE, PART 2

Not every piece of evidence is accompanied by a clear indicator like the word *such* in the previous passage. Studies, statistics, descriptions, definitions, and even the presence of proper nouns all indicate details, which serve as **evidence** in support of some argument. Remember that you should always be looking for links from one sentence to the next to determine whether the details you find are indeed evidence for a claim or are just background to set up the topic. Purpose questions, specifically sentence function questions, are a great way to practice looking for those links!

A study suggests a link between the rise in mortality rates among working adults in the US and the lack of paid sick leave. Using data from the US Centers for Disease Control and Prevention, the study compared mortality rates among US workers and paid sick leave requirements, including state laws that preempt local governments from enacting paid sick leave mandates. The study determined that four counties that attempted to mandate paid sick leave requirements but were preempted by state laws had a 7.5% higher mortality rate in their working-age population than did counties in states where mandatory paid sick leave was already established.

5 Mark for Review

Which choice best states the function of the underlined sentence in the overall structure of the text?

(A) To contradict the initial claim of the study

(B) To introduce the central conclusion reached by the study

(C) To provide data used to support the study's findings

(D) To describe part of the process used in the study

Why This Question is Hard

Extremely short answers can sometimes provide as much of a challenge as extremely long ones. When the four answers are short and use similar language, it can be difficult to determine what exactly separates them when under time pressure. Also, on sentence function questions, at least one of the wrong answers will accurately describe the function of a sentence in the passage—just not the underlined one you were asked about.

Here's How to Ace It

The first sentence is a **claim** regarding a link between *mortality rates* and *the lack of paid sick leave*. The second sentence is **evidence**, giving a description of the methodology of the study. The third sentence is also **evidence**, giving a description of the results of the study. Even though you should consider the logical flow from claim to methodology to results here, keep the function of the second sentence prominent in your mind as you review the answers.

Choice (A) is wrong because none of the sentences *contradict* each other—the second and third sentences are evidence for the suggestion made in the first sentence. Choice (B) is wrong because it's **Right Answer, Wrong Question**—it perfectly describes the function of the first sentence, not the second. Choice (C) is also wrong because it's **Right Answer, Wrong Question**—it perfectly describes the function of the third sentence rather than the second one. Keep (D) because it correctly identifies the function performed by the evidence in Sentence 2. The correct answer is (D).

PUTTING IT ALL TOGETHER

As mentioned in the previous chapter, Conclusions questions often use multiple types of structural words. It follows, therefore, that they often include a similarly diverse blend of sentence functions as well. By identifying the role of each sentence in a Conclusion, you can quickly find the sentence you need that will be most helpful in completing the passage. Usually, the topic of the passage will be introduced by a **background** sentence, and the information you need about that topic will be contained in a mix of 1–2 **claims**, **objections**, or pieces of **evidence**. Try out the following Conclusions question to see how well you've assimilated the information in this chapter.

It has long been known that both REM and non-REM sleep are key factors in facilitating effective learning, as experiences occurring while awake are encoded into memory. Recently, a team of researchers created a brain model that illustrates how the brain encodes recent data during slow-wave, non-REM sleep and solidifies previous data during REM sleep. However, it is important to acknowledge that these findings are still theoretical and based on observations of individuals with healthy sleeping habits. These researchers therefore imply that _____

> If the incomplete sentence on a Conclusions question mentions a specific group, make sure to prioritize finding exactly what that group says. Even if no specific group is mentioned, the final complete sentence that immediately precedes the incomplete sentence should be heavily considered when choosing an answer.

6 ☐ Mark for Review

Which choice most logically completes the text?

(A) scientists are still baffled as to how the brain encodes memories during both REM and non-REM sleep.

(B) additional models need to be created to predict how proper diet and exercise may affect memory.

(C) more studies need to be conducted to better understand the effects of REM and non-REM sleep.

(D) healthy sleeping habits promote a more thorough encoding of memories than do poor sleeping habits.

Why This Question is Hard

As you examine the answers, each one seems to have a grain of truth to it. None of the answers is obviously outlandish at first glance, and this is a problem particularly on Conclusions questions—the blank at the end of the passage makes it appear that anything that can be linked to the passage logically is correct. This is especially problematic with science, as outside science knowledge is often used to create this logical link in the wrong answers instead of textual support, which is what you must have.

Here's How to Ace It

The first sentence is **background**, explaining a known fact in science. The second sentence is also **background**, offering a description of a study related to the previous fact. The third sentence is an **objection** (using the **pivotal** word *However*) to that background info—the researchers themselves are cautioning people to take their model with a grain of salt. The final sentence should make a **claim** thanks to the concluding word *therefore*, and since the incomplete sentence references the researchers, the correct answer should be as consistent as possible with the researchers' work and comments.

Choice (A) is **Extreme Language**—just because the researchers want more data to validate their model, it does not mean they are totally confused. Choice (B) is wrong because it goes **Beyond the Text**—the passage does not address the link between memory and *proper diet and exercise*. Keep (C) because it urges caution regarding the exact same issue (more data needed) as the team did in its **objection**. Choice (D) is wrong because it also goes **Beyond the Text**—this conclusion is only supported by outside knowledge as *healthy sleeping habits* and *poor sleeping habits* are not compared in the passage. The correct answer is (C).

A NOTE ABOUT CONTINUATIONS

You may have noticed that we've discussed every structural word from the last chapter except for continuations. Continuations don't determine the function of a sentence itself, but rather, tell you that the function of the previous sentence also serves as the function of the sentence containing the continuation. A continuation word means that there's additional background the author wants to share, a second point central to a claim or objection, or an additional piece of evidence that serves a similar supporting role to the first one. Essentially, continuations don't give you new information. They tell you that you can speed up your reading pace a bit if reading more background or evidence, or that you should slow down your pace a bit if reading more aspects to a claim or objection. One of the questions in this chapter's drill features several continuations that may help you cut through a lot of description efficiently—we discuss this in the explanations for the drill.

Sentence Function Drill

Practice determining sentence function as you attempt this chapter's drill and see if it helps your accuracy. Answers and explanations can be found in Chapter 12.

Time: 8 minutes

1 ☐ Mark for Review

The following text is adapted from Franz Kafka's 1912 short story "The Judgment." In the text, Georg, a resident in Germany, is writing to a friend who has left their town and moved to Russia.

So Georg always confined himself to relating the trivial matters that randomly arise from a disorganized memory on a reflective Sunday. His sole desire was to leave intact the picture of the hometown the friend must have constructed over the years and had come to accept. Thus it happened that Georg had informed his friend in three fairly widely spaced letters about the engagement of an inconsequential person to an equally inconsequential girl until, quite contrary to his intentions, the friend became interested in this noteworthy event.

Which choice best describes the function of the underlined sentence in the text as a whole?

(A) It shows that Georg is only writing to assure his friend that nothing significant has changed since he left.

(B) It reveals that Georg misses his friend and is writing to insist he return to their hometown.

(C) It foreshadows a relationship with a young woman that Georg anticipates and is excited to disclose to his friend.

(D) It expresses how increased distance between friends can often strengthen the bonds that they share.

2 ☐ Mark for Review

The following text is from William Beckford's 1887 short story "The History of the Caliph Vathek."

The palace named "The Delight of the Eyes, or the Support of Memory," was one entire enchantment. Rarities collected from every corner of the earth were there found in such profusion as to dazzle and confound, but for the order in which they were arranged. One gallery exhibited the pictures of the celebrated Mani, and statues that seemed to be alive. Here a well-managed perspective attracted the sight; there the magic of optics agreeably deceived it; whilst the naturalist on his part exhibited, in their several classes, the various gifts that Heaven had bestowed on our globe. In a word, Vathek omitted nothing in this palace that might gratify the curiosity of those who resorted to it, although he was not able to satisfy his own, for he was of all men the most curious.

Based on the text, how does Vathek most likely regard the palace?

(A) He is confident that it boasts the greatest collection of its kind on the planet.

(B) He has added to its collection extensively but wishes it were more encompassing.

(C) He wishes its collections were more organized and less confusingly arranged.

(D) He is embarrassed that it does not include the works of great artists.

3 ☐ Mark for Review

Text 1

Overflowing with lush descriptions and weaving myriad story threads across three books, Salman Rushdie's 1981 novel *Midnight's Children* is an allegory that transmutes historical fiction and magical realism. But, at over 600 pages due to its insistence on transposing a nation's story of independence on to the life story of one young boy while referencing literary classics such as *Tristam Shandy*, it may have benefited from its author heeding the call of his editor to rein in some of its cacophonous contradictions and digressions.

Text 2

Salman Rushdie's 1981 novel *Midnight's Children*, a political satire about a boy born in India in a time when the country is shifting from colonial rule to independence, is unashamed in its tendency to mix historical fact and magical realism. Yet the seemingly overwhelming breadth itself tells a story, an epic so sprawling that to exclude even one of the legends or myths would do it a disservice.

Which choice best describes a difference in how the authors of Text 1 and Text 2 view Salman Rushdie's *Midnight's Children*?

(A) The author of Text 1 asserts that novels referencing literary classics such as *Tristam Shandy* should not mix literary genres, while the author of Text 2 suggests that political satire can be combined with magical realism.

(B) The author of Text 1 maintains that Rushdie clearly refused to listen to his editor's recommendations, while the author of Text 2 implies that any editing would have detracted from the political impact of the novel.

(C) The author of Text 1 displays admiration for Rushdie's prose but believes the novel would have been better if it were shorter, while the author of Text 2 agrees that while the novel may be long there is nothing that deserved to be cut from it.

(D) The author of Text 1 expresses frustration with Rushdie's splitting the novel into three books, while the author of Text 2 maintains that a work of political satire must be culturally honest.

4 ☐ Mark for Review

With his novel *The Great Gatsby*, author F. Scott Fitzgerald established himself as a distinctive voice of the Jazz Age. Central to his personal and artistic narrative was his wife and muse Zelda, whom he acknowledged as an inspiration for many female characters in his early short stories and his first successful novel *This Side of Paradise*. Some Fitzgerald biographers contend that Zelda, an artist and writer herself, was more than just an inspiration, pointing to her claims that Fitzgerald extensively borrowed from her own diaries in some of his first acclaimed works.

Which choice best states the main idea of the text?

(A) *The Great Gatsby* and *This Side of Paradise* are largely based on the life of Zelda Fitzgerald.

(B) Zelda Fitzgerald's artistic contributions to the Jazz Age easily rivaled those of her husband, F. Scott Fitzgerald.

(C) Biographers of F. Scott Fitzgerald have greatly underestimated the overwhelming artistic influence of his wife on his writing.

(D) Zelda Fitzgerald may have been more of a vital source for Fitzgerald's early success than he ultimately acknowledged.

As a young producer intent on bringing theater to a wider audience in New York City in the 1950s, Joe Papp staged free Shakespeare productions in non-traditional locations. Although New York's Broadway district was the heart of American theater, Papp believed the district's emphasis on entertainment influenced producers to neglect supporting projects that address contemporary, societal issues. To provide a forum for these projects, Papp founded The Public Theater in 1967. By 1985, according to a designer who worked with Papp, his commitment was unwavering, evidenced by his preference for topical, sometimes controversial, content over even his inventive Shakespeare productions.

Which finding, if true, would most directly support the designer's claim?

(A) Papp joined with notable theater critics such as Brooks Atkinson to fund the Save the Theater District project, which helped the district to survive and thrive today.

(B) Despite several offers to host revivals of various famous musicals, Papp produced *The Normal Heart*, a play that openly protested the government's slow response to the AIDS crisis.

(C) Papp's first Shakespeare productions were staged in neighborhoods outside the Broadway Theater District, featuring diverse casts in non-traditional roles.

(D) By retaining the rights to the musical *A Chorus Line*, a successful production that moved from The Public Theater to Broadway, Papp was able to fund free Shakespeare in the Park for many decades.

A small group of historians have introduced a new theory to explain the hysteria of the Salem witch trials in 1692, in which 200 people were accused of witchcraft. The theory presumes that the erratic behavior exhibited by both the accusers and the accused was due to the presence of ergot, a fungus that grows in wet rye, in their bodies. When ingested, ergot can induce hallucinations and cause gangrene in the limbs. The theory maintains that because Salem residents ate bread mixed from cornmeal and rye flour, many of them could have been exposed to ergot poisoning. According to medical records of the time, however, there were surprisingly few cases of either gangrene or ergot poisoning diagnosed by physicians, suggesting that _____

Which choice most logically completes the text?

(A) the hallucinations caused by ergot were likely experienced by far more than the 200 people accused of witchcraft.

(B) rye fields in Salem must not have been sufficiently damp to encourage and sustain the growth of the fungus.

(C) the people in Salem generally avoided bread made from cornmeal and rye flour, as wheat was more popular in the region.

(D) the theory may be overestimating the influence of ergot poisoning on the hysteria of the Salem witch trials.

Chapter 9
Mastering Process of Elimination

Throughout the Digital SAT, the Process of Elimination is a critical skill, as wrong answers are often easier to eliminate than correct answers are to find evidence for or calculate properly. On Reading especially, you are often confronted with very long answers that are only wrong because of a single word, and that word will be easier to catch if you are looking for flaws in the first place. This chapter will revisit the six most common Digital SAT Reading trap answers and offer examples meant to develop a deeper understanding of each individual trap type.

THE IMPORTANCE OF POE

Just as passive readers consider all of the words in a passage to be equally important, they also consider all of the answer choices to be equally valid until justified as wrong. This creates a fundamental issue: if the focus is on "Which answer is correct?", you'll wind up keeping multiple answers because they sound logically appealing or make sense in the real world. Consider if you've ever attempted to clean out your closet. If you've asked, "What am I keeping?", you probably wind up keeping a lot of stuff, with only a small pile of things that obviously need to go. Similarly on Reading, you may find yourself eliminating the answers that are hopelessly extreme or introduce completely outside ideas but find yourself consistently left with 2–3 answers that all "seem good."

Active readers instead ask, "What answers can be eliminated?" Their focus is on eliminating three of the four answers, every single time. Instead of wondering what *can be* justified, they think about what *can't be* supported. If, in the closet example, you ask, "What ten things am I getting rid of?", you've transformed the task into a quantifiable project rather than an open-ended activity. Similarly on Reading, the question really becomes, "What three answers can be eliminated?" Should you have more than one answer remaining after that question, ask yourself which remaining answers are traps. Before we dive into the types of trap answers again, we must cover a critical reminder:

> **The best reason to eliminate an answer on the SAT is because it's not supported by the passage or not consistent with what you highlighted.**

COMMON TRAP ANSWERS

If all four answers remain after comparing them to your highlighting, **Mark and Move** on from this question for now—come back to it later, after you've answered all of the questions you can answer quickly and easily.

Okay, so you found something to highlight, annotated when needed, and did indeed eliminate 1–2 answer choices. However, 2–3 answers yet remain. At this point, the question shifts to, "What about the wrong answers had me keep them in play initially?" It's extremely likely that the correct answer remains among your options, but the other answers contain cleverly worded traps. The more familiar you are with the traps, the more likely you'll be to catch them on test day. The six most common trap answers on the SAT Reading are as follows.

- Opposite
- Extreme Language
- Recycled Language
- Right Answer, Wrong Question
- Beyond the Text
- Half-Right

AVOIDING ATTRACTORS

We've already covered these traps briefly in the Reading Introduction chapter and have referred to them extensively in the explanations, so hopefully, you already have a decent understanding of how each trap operates. To deepen that understanding, you want to know that each trap type is made up of one or more **attractors**. An attractor is a specific version of the trap that makes a wrong answer appealing at first glance. Not every Opposite answer is contradictory to the passage for the exact same reason, nor does Recycled Language misuse the words from the passage the same way every time. Throughout the rest of this chapter, we'll describe each trap as well as its most common attractors. Feel free to explore them all or jump to the ones you know have given you trouble in the past.

WHY OPPOSITE TRAPS CAN BE DIFFICULT

Opposite trap answers use a single word or phrase that makes the answer convey a tone, viewpoint, or meaning contradictory to what was intended by the author. Since many opposite traps come down to a single opposite word or phrase, they are easy to miss. Furthermore, since many SAT passages are complex and often discuss both sides of an argument, it can be easy to choose an answer related to one side of the argument, just not the one you were supposed to focus on. So, make sure you highlight the argument as well as any words that speak to a positive or negative tone—this way, you stand less of a chance of going in the opposite direction by accident.

Below is a list of the common Opposite attractors:

Attractor Name	Description
Opposite Tone	This attractor specifically applies to Vocabulary questions. In this attractor, one or more answers will be a negative word when the blank calls for a positive word, or vice versa.
Opposite Attitude	This is like Opposite Tone but applies to longer answer choices and reverses which side of an argument someone falls on.
Contradictory Statement	This attractor deals with details rather than arguments; it gets the facts of the passage incorrect.
Opposite Question Task	This attractor weakens a claim when the task was to support it, or vice versa.
Word of Negation	This attractor takes an otherwise perfect answer but adds something like the word "not" or the prefix in- or un- to flip the answer to the opposite meaning.

Opposite Attractors in Action Exercise

For the next five examples, focus entirely on the Process of Elimination. Use the descriptions above and the clues given in each prompt to eliminate the two flawed answers. Check your work using the table in Chapter 12.

> Leonardo da Vinci, renowned as a master artistic innovator, should also be _____ for his scientific forays. For example, he calculated a remarkably close approximation of the gravitational constant centuries before Sir Isaac Newton's groundbreaking work in the field.

i. Should the word to go in the blank be positive, negative, or neutral? Eliminate the two answers that are the opposite **tone** of what should go in the blank:

   a. commended

   b. rebuked

   c. disregarded

ii. Fill in the blank with the leftover word from the first question. Then, eliminate the two answers that represent the opposite **attitude** from the one that the author takes towards da Vinci's approximation:

   a. Da Vinci's work, though admirable, pales in comparison to the work of Sir Isaac Newton.

   b. Da Vinci's calculation was not precise enough to prove useful in the field of astronomy.

   c. Da Vinci's estimation was fairly accurate for its time and predated similar work by another individual.

iii. Eliminate the two answers that **contradict** a statement made in the passage:

   a. Da Vinci was viewed as an amateur artist but a highly regarded scientist.

   b. The work of Sir Isaac Newton predated the work of Leonardo da Vinci.

   c. Leonardo da Vinci may deserve to be celebrated for accomplishments in more than one field.

iv. Eliminate the two answers that, if true, would **weaken** the author's claims regarding da Vinci instead of **strengthening** it:

   a. A biography of Leonardo da Vinci is published that reveals that his work on the gravitational constant was the only notable contribution he made to the sciences.

   b. The memoir of Sir Isaac Newton explains numerous scientific conclusions drawn by da Vinci that Newton's own work confirmed.

   c. An analysis published by an art historian states that da Vinci was most certainly a master artisan, but each of his techniques can be traced back to an artistic predecessor.

   v.   Eliminate the two answers that contain a **word of negation** that disqualifies an otherwise perfectly acceptable conclusion based on the passage:

      a.   Leonardo da Vinci may not deserve to be celebrated for accomplishments in more than one field.

      b.   An individual predominantly known for his work in one area may be worthy of praise in another.

      c.   Da Vinci's approximation was fairly inaccurate, though it did predate similar work by another individual.

WHY EXTREME LANGUAGE TRAPS CAN BE DIFFICULT

Extreme Language trap answers include a word or phrase that takes a stated opinion or viewpoint in the passage too far in a certain direction. Unlike something going Beyond the Text, which means the answer has introduced some completely new idea, most Extreme Language traps are exaggerations in some way of a point the passage or author actually made. The author may approve of an environmental initiative but not be *obsessed* with it. A scientist in a passage may express optimism toward an experiment but not claim that it *proves* anything. Because most Extreme Language answers would become true if the language in them were softened somehow, they can be extremely attractive to someone looking for firm, bold, concrete statements during the part of the SAT that probably feels the most inexact when compared to the inflexible rules of Writing and Math. So, remember that the correct answers to most SAT Reading questions are softer and avoid making definitive statements that could potentially be contradicted by future research.

Below is a list of the common Extreme Language attractors:

Attractor Name	Description
Exaggeration	This attractor is usually seen on Vocabulary questions and brings a positive or negative word to a higher degree than the passage can support.
Judgment / Recommendation	This attractor takes an opinion someone has toward an idea and turns it into either a judgment the individual person has made or a recommended course of action endorsed by the individual. For example, if someone criticizes a city's plan to develop new luxury condos, this does not mean that individual despises the city council or encourages violent protests against the development plan.
Excessive	This attractor takes a piece of evidence and attempts to make a bold claim based on it, such as stating that a single successful experiment *proves* a theory.
Absolute	This attractor uses words such as *always, never, all,* or *only* which allow no room for debate.
Superlative	This attractor uses words ending in *-st* such as *most, best,* or *worst* when no such definitive ranking of an idea was made in the passage.

Extreme Language Attractors in Action Exercise

For the next five examples, focus entirely on the Process of Elimination. Use the descriptions above and the clues given in each prompt to eliminate the two flawed answers. Check your work using the table in Chapter 12.

> Born in 1877 in New York City, Rosalia Edge was an environmentalist who sought to _____ what she considered to be minimal conservation efforts towards many species, especially avians. Notably, she helped established the Hawk Mountain Sanctuary, the land of which had been a hawk target shooting and hunting range for decades before Edge's intervention. In an interview with scientist Rachel Carson regarding her 1962 book *Silent Spring*, Carson claimed that Edge's work was instrumental in facilitating her own ornithological research, particularly concerning hawks and other birds of prey.

  i. Eliminate the two answers that represent an **exaggeration** of the word that should go in the blank:
  - *a.* perfect
  - *b.* improve
  - *c.* idealize

  ii. Fill in the blank with the leftover word from the first question. Then, eliminate the two answers that take an attitude expressed by Edge and turn it into a **judgment** or **recommendation**:
  - *a.* Edge would claim that avian conversation efforts could be further expanded.
  - *b.* Edge would condemn those who enjoy target shooting and hunting for pleasure.
  - *c.* Edge believes that more target shooting and ranges should be turned into avian sanctuaries.

  iii. Eliminate the two answers that are too **excessive** to be supported by a claim or statement from the passage:
  - *a.* Carson's research would have been impossible without the prior work done by Edge.
  - *b.* The fact that people target shoot and hunt hawks proves the necessity for sanctuaries like Hawk Mountain.
  - *c.* Edge's work benefited both the animals themselves and people conducting research on those animals.

  iv. Eliminate the two answers that contain an **absolute** word that invalidates them:
  - *a.* The work performed by Rosalia Edge seems to have produced several positive results.
  - *b.* Many hawk species will eventually be protected by sanctuaries such as Hawk Mountain.
  - *c.* For ornithologists, the study of birds of prey is the only practical career choice.

v. Eliminate the two answers that contain a **superlative** word that invalidates them:

a. Target shooting and hunting are the greatest threat to hawk populations.
b. The establishment of more sanctuaries like Hawk Mountain could aid efforts to protect wild hawk populations.
Carson believed Edge to be the most important influence in Carson's professional career.

WHY RECYCLED LANGUAGE TRAPS CAN BE DIFFICULT

Recycled Language trap answers repeat exact words and phrases from the passage but use those words and phrases incorrectly. Since pacing on Reading is often a struggle, students are looking for any way they can to answer questions efficiently. When you see a string of words such as *advocates of the Chronological Protection Conjecture* used in the passage and then repeated in an answer, it's easy to be drawn to that answer immediately and actively look to knock out the other three answers, or even fail to consider them at all. Additionally, it's not just the repeated words themselves—College Board will often make logical connections between the repeated words that have no flaw except that they are entirely unsupported by the passage, which is, well, the most important thing. So, if you do see repeated words and phrases, double-check them against the passage before ruling on them one way or the other.

> Unsupported connections between ideas are a feature of another trap answer you've seen a bunch, Beyond the Text. Remember that on test day, it doesn't matter if you've identified the trap with its precise name or not—as long as you have a solid reason to eliminate something, do so and move on.

Below is a list of the common Recycled Language attractors:

Attractor Name	Description
Striking Words or Phrases	This attractor recycles at least one extremely memorable word or phrase from the passage.
Words Out of Context	This attractor usually takes two or more words, concepts, or ideas from entirely different parts of the passage and mashes them into a single answer choice.
Unsupported Relationships	This attractor focuses on two or more words, concepts, or ideas from the exact same part of the passage rather than different parts but then compares or contrasts them in a way the passage does not. This attractor could also be considered Beyond the Text, but usually, a relationship in a Beyond the Text trap will involve a concept the passage did not discuss at all.

Recycled Language Attractors in Action Exercise

For the next three examples, focus entirely on the Process of Elimination. Use the descriptions above and the clues given in each prompt to eliminate the two flawed answers. Check your work using the table in Chapter 12.

> The development of theme park attractions has a storied history, and one such attraction, *The Great Movie Ride*, is responsible for the creation of an entire theme park. Historians who study the Walt Disney World resort note that *The Great Movie Ride*, an attraction planned for the existing Epcot theme park, was deemed to represent such a unique and powerful connection to Hollywood and American show business that then-CEO Michael Eisner and President Marty Sklar decided to construct an entire theme park around the ride. Several years later, *The Great Movie Ride* was the centerpiece attraction of the park that would eventually come to be known as Disney's Hollywood Studios.

i. Eliminate the two answers that contain a **striking word or phrase** that only makes the choice appealing because of its memorability from the passage:

   a. American show business has had a major impact on the development of many theme parks.

   b. Disney is often lauded for its ability to create unique and powerful connections between characters.

   c. The design of a theme park ride had implications beyond the ride's original intent.

ii. Eliminate the two answers that contain **words out of context** that have been taken from completely different parts of the passage:

   a. The creation of an entire theme park is often the responsibility of the CEO and the president of the company building the park.

   b. Two individuals saw an opportunity to expand the scope of an upcoming project.

   c. It can take several years to learn how to develop theme park attractions responsibly.

iii. Eliminate the two answers that take two things that are discussed together in the passage and create an **unsupported relationship** between those things:

   a. The development of each theme park attraction has a storied history as interesting as that of *The Great Movie Ride*.

   b. The planning for one theme park had a substantial impact on the eventual existence of another.

   c. Disney CEO Michael Eisner and President Marty Sklar debated whether the more specific Hollywood or the more general American show business should be the main theme of the park.

> Once you check the explanations for this exercise on page 176 and correct any errors, you'll notice that the remaining answer for all three examples uses broader, more general language. It's tempting to want to eliminate bland or generic sounding answers because of how indirectly these answers seem to mirror the passage, but know that many correct SAT answers do indeed paraphrase the passage with this more general language rather than repeat exact words and phrases.

WHY RIGHT ANSWER, WRONG QUESTION TRAPS CAN BE DIFFICULT

Right Answer, Wrong Question trap answers are actually true based on the passage, but they don't answer the question asked. In some ways, this is a more extreme version of Recycled Language—if a student is looking for matching words or phrases to save time, a Right Answer, Wrong Question trap will seem perfect. Furthermore, while many traps are based on misreading or misunderstanding the passage, Right Answer, Wrong Question traps are based on forgetting the question task. These are extremely easy traps to fall into—without the question task, it's going to be nearly impossible to dissuade yourself from an answer that is perfectly consistent with the passage. So, the key to catching these traps is to constantly remind yourself of the question task—all of the reading, highlighting, annotating and Process of Elimination you do should be singularly focused on completing the very specific job given to you by the question.

Below is a list of the common Right Answer, Wrong Question attractors:

Attractor Name	Description
Wrong Sentence Function	This attractor accurately describes a sentence within the passage, just not the sentence asked about by the Purpose question.
Details on a Main Idea Question	This attractor correctly paraphrases an event or idea discussed in the passage but fails to account for at least one additional event or idea. Often, this attractor tries to pass off a single piece of evidence as the main idea.
Details on a Purpose Question	This attractor focuses only on what the author said and ignores why the author may have said it. Like the previous attractor, it usually focuses on a single portion of the passage rather than the passage as a whole.

Right Answer, Wrong Question Attractors in Action Exercise

For the next three examples, focus entirely on the Process of Elimination. Use the descriptions above and the clues given in each prompt to eliminate the two flawed answers. Check your work using the table in Chapter 12.

> The following text is from Robert Louis Stevenson's 1878 short story "A Lodging for the Night."
>
> It was late in November, 1456. The snow fell over Paris with rigorous, relentless persistence; sometimes the wind made a sally and scattered it in flying vortices; sometimes there was a lull, and flake after flake descended out of the black night air, silent, circuitous, interminable. To poor people, looking up under moist eyebrows, it seemed a wonder where it all came from. Master Francis Villon had propounded an alternative that afternoon, at a tavern window: was it only pagan Jupiter plucking geese upon Olympus? or were the holy angels moulting? He was only a poor Master of Arts, he went on; and as the question somewhat touched upon divinity, he durst not venture to conclude.

i.   Eliminate the two answers that describe the function of the **wrong sentence** from the passage rather than the underlined one:
   a.   To describe the unfavorable weather conditions in the city of Paris as seemingly unending
   b.   To characterize a particular group as being astonished regarding the source of precipitation
   c.   To explain a character's hesitancy at pondering subject matter which he does not feel qualified to examine

ii.   Eliminate the two answers that reference only a **detail** from the passage rather than the **main idea** of the passage:
   a.   The snowfall in Paris at the time of the story is mostly unceasing, stopping only occasionally and then starting back up again.
   b.   A character is introduced through the description of a weather phenomenon and an examination into what the source of that phenomenon may be.
   c.   Master Francis Villon offers some alternative explanations for the relentless snowfall that currently dominates the skies of Paris.

iii.   Eliminate the two answers that only reference a **detail** from the passage rather than the **purpose** of the passage as a whole:
   a.   It characterizes Master Francis Villon through his internal reaction to an ongoing snowfall.
   b.   It elaborates upon the sense of awe that a lower class feels when confronted with snowfall.
   c.   It establishes the time and place of the story so the reader can contextualize the events that occur later.

WHY BEYOND THE TEXT TRAPS CAN BE DIFFICULT

Beyond the Text trap answers depend on logical assumptions or outside reasoning but lack actual support in the passage. For some students, these are the most difficult trap answers to catch on the exam. If you think back to the Reading Introduction chapter, the biggest reason that SAT Reading is difficult is that the questions make it sound like, as in English class, an answer can be correct if you can justify it. Well, Beyond the Text traps play into this justification—they rely on you, the student, saying an answer "makes sense" or "could very well be true." Even worse, once you get inside of your head trying to justify one of these answers, you will probably spend valuable time on that justification. Even if you avoid that pitfall, it may be extremely difficult to talk yourself out of an answer once you've logically reasoned it as correct. So, that's why you absolutely must remember that Reading is an open-book test—an answer is correct only because the author said so, meaning that you found actual evidence for the answer and highlighted it.

Below is a list of the common Beyond the Text attractors:

Attractor Name	Description
Too Broad	This attractor generalizes the passage beyond what the evidence can support—it takes a description of one specific event and attempts to make a claim regarding all events of that type.
Too Specific	This attractor is probably the most common type of Beyond the Text trap—it introduces a specific concept or idea that is present only in the answer choice but looks appealing because of its possible relation to the content of the passage.
Outside Knowledge	This attractor introduces a true statement related to the topic or a situation that occurs in the real world. Even statements that are true or situations that exist in reality must have been addressed by the passage in some way to be part of a correct answer.
Predictions of the Future	This attractor makes some statement about what will, might, or should happen in the future when no such forecasting occurred in the passage.

Beyond the Text Attractors in Action Exercise

For the next four examples, focus entirely on the Process of Elimination. Use the descriptions above and the clues given in each prompt to eliminate the two flawed answers. Check your work using the table in Chapter 12.

> The following text is from Thomas Babington Macaulay's 1842 poem "Virginia." The speaker is reciting a song about a military conquest at the request of his audience.
>
> Ye good men of the Commons, with loving hearts and true,
> Who stand by the bold Tribunes that still have stood by you,
> Come, make a circle round me, and mark my tale with care,
> A tale of what Rome once hath borne, of what Rome yet may bear.
> This is no Grecian fable, of fountains running wine,
> Of maids with snaky tresses, or sailors turned to swine.
> Here, in this very Forum, under the noonday sun,
> In sight of all the people, the bloody deed was done.
> Old men still creep among us who saw that fearful day,
> Just seventy years and seven ago, when the wicked Ten bare sway.

i. Eliminate the two answers that are **too broad** to be supported by the passage:

   a. The Romans often commemorated past tragedies through poem and song.

   b. Audiences listening to Roman poets would form a circle around the speakers to better hear them.

   c. Some individuals who witnessed the tragedy referenced in the song were still alive to hear the song.

ii. Eliminate the two answers that are **too specific** to be supported by the passage:

   a. The men of the Commons were honest and genuine individuals who would defend the land if it were attacked again.

   b. The speaker wished to clarify the differences between his tale and those of Grecian fables.

   c. The noonday sun provided optimal lighting for the enemy forces to attack the area.

iii. Eliminate the two answers that make use of **outside knowledge** to make themselves more appealing:

   a. Greek and Roman mythologies share many commonalities, so the speaker provided clarity to avoid any potential confusion.

   b. The good men of the Commons are praised by the speaker before being cautioned to take the speaker's story to heart.

   c. The speaker notes that survivors of wartime tragedies can commemorate those tragedies decades later thanks to a longer human lifespan than in ages past.

iv. Eliminate the two answers that make **predictions of the future** that are not supported by the passage:

 The area is likely to be attacked again as it has already proven a vulnerable target.

The song is meant to serve as a warning of a fate that could befall Rome again.

The bold Tribunes will continue to stand by the good men of the Commons for many years to come.

WHY HALF-RIGHT TRAPS CAN BE DIFFICULT

Half-Right trap answers address only part of a question task or are longer answers divided into one supported half and one unsupported half. As with some of the other traps we've discussed, the presence of something that does match the passage correctly can lead one to assume the entire answer is good to go. To exacerbate this, College Board often places the correct piece of the answer early in the answer choice so that students will seize onto it and decline to investigate the rest of the answer thoroughly. Other times, a claim in a passage has multiple components to it, and when you see an answer that supports one of these components, you may not catch that another answer supports all of them and is therefore the one that would most directly support the claim. So, be sure to read the entire answer choice, and don't stop reading the other answer choices once you've found an answer that you think will work.

Below is a list of the most common Half-Right attractors:

Attractor Name	Description
Only One Half Supported	This attractor is usually a longer answer composed of two distinct halves, often separated by punctuation and/or a transition. While the lengths of each half may vary, one half will be perfectly supported by the passage and the other will not be.
Only Part of a Claim	This attractor appears mostly on Claims questions in which the claim or argument has several different components to it. The trap answer will address one or more aspects of the claim correctly but will leave out at least one aspect of the claim that the correct answer will support.
Consistent with the Chart, Irrelevant to the Claim	This attractor appears on Charts questions and involves data that is consistent with the chart but irrelevant to the argument in the passage. If you've done the Reading chapters in order, you've seen that we call out this trap as "irrelevant to the claim" instead of "Half-Right" because the former is slightly more helpful for explanation's sake. Either way, be ready for these traps, as they are incredibly common.

The "wrong" half of these answers will typically contain an Opposite, Extreme Language, Recycled Language, or Beyond the text trap.

Half-Right Attractors in Action Exercise

For the next four examples, focus entirely on the Process of Elimination. Use the descriptions above and the clues given in each prompt to eliminate the two flawed answers. Check your work using the table in Chapter 12.

> "The Banshee" is a traditional Irish short story attributed to an unknown author. In the story, the author describes a farmer who is one of the central characters in the story.
>
> He was rather dark and reserved in his manner, and oftentimes sullen and gloomy in his temper; and this, joined with his well-known disregard of religion, served to render him somewhat unpopular amongst his neighbours and acquaintances. However, he was in general respected, and was never insulted or annoyed. He was considered as an honest, inoffensive man, and as he was well supplied with firearms and ammunition—in the use of which he was well practised, having, in his early days, served several years in a yeomanry corps—few liked to disturb him, even had they been so disposed.

i. Eliminate the two answers that have **only one half** supported by the passage:

    a. The farmer is described as having a grave and moody disposition, which has led to a lack of respect for him among his neighbors.

    b. The farmer is a firm believer in the virtues of religion, and he conducts himself in an honest and inoffensive manner.

    c. The farmer is not sought out by those around him but does not conduct himself in an inappropriate or belligerent manner.

> "The Banshee" is a traditional Irish short story attributed to an unknown author. In the short story, the author describes the mythical banshee as being a herald of death whose disturbed emotional state reflects the manner of death that will be experienced by the individual she has chosen to haunt: _____

ii. Eliminate the two answers that address **only part of the claim** referenced in the passage above:

    a. "When the death of the person whom she mourns is contingent, or to occur by unforeseen accident, she is particularly agitated and troubled in her appearance, and unusually loud and mournful in her lamentations."

    b. "Some would fain have it that this strange being is actuated by a feeling quite inimical to the interests of the family which she haunts, and that she comes with joy and triumph to announce their misfortunes."

    c. "She always comes at night, a short time previous to the death of the fated one, and takes her stand outside, convenient to the house, and there utters the most plaintive cries and lamentations, generally in some unknown language, and in a tone of voice resembling a human female."

Process of Elimination Drill

Practice looking for and eliminating trap answers when you get down to two or three answer choices. Answers and explanations can be found in Chapter 12.

Time: 10 minutes

1 🔖 Mark for Review

In addition to becoming the first African American to be president of the American Psychological Association, Kenneth Clark was an _____ ending the racial segregation of US schools and spent his career calling for further changes that would even out the academic playing field for Black children.

Which choice completes the text with the most logical and precise word or phrase?

(A) expert on

(B) advocate for

(C) opponent of

(D) adversary to

2 🔖 Mark for Review

The following text is from Emily Brontë's 1847 novel *Wuthering Heights*. Nelly, the narrator, works as a housekeeper at Wuthering Heights, caring for the family's children and an orphan taken in by the family.

> The difference between him and the others forced me to be less partial. Cathy and her brother harassed me terribly: *he* was as uncomplaining as a lamb; though hardness, not gentleness, made him give little trouble.

Which choice best states the main purpose of the text?

(A) To divulge that Nelly finds her position terrifying and potentially harmful

(B) To describe Nelly's resolve to remain at her position in Wuthering Heights

(C) To explain Nelly's devotion to the family that has brought her to Wuthering Heights

(D) To contrast the behaviors of the family's children with those of the orphan

3 ☐ Mark for Review

Text 1

The Loy Krathong festival in Thailand is a centuries-old celebration that involves launching a krathong, or floating lantern, on local waters. The lanterns are wished upon and set to float in various waterways, with the hope that good fortune will come. The krathong is an important material representation of that hope. For example, if the krathong floats back towards the shore, Thai residents believe this means to prepare for potentially unwelcome events.

Text 2

Every year, people come to launch krathongs in the waterways of Thailand, which leaves festival organizers cleaning up the clogged waterways in the following days. In an effort to cut down on the mess and reduce waste, Thai children have created digital versions of these floating lanterns which were projected onto the waterways.

Based on the texts, how would the author of Text 1 most likely respond to the discussion in Text 2?

(A) By noting that a physical aspect of the festival may be lost with the modern changes mentioned in Text 2

(B) By praising the innovation mentioned in Text 2 as a necessary change that will improve future renditions of the festival

(C) By suggesting that all participants in the festival create digital krathongs instead of only the children mentioned in Text 2

(D) By arguing that a centuries-old celebration has become a source of stress rather than one of optimism among Thai residents

4 ☐ Mark for Review

In an effort to make video games more immersive, companies have begun designing and producing virtual reality (VR) headsets that include stereo sound as well as stereoscopic visual sensors that match the orientation of the wearer and align with the visual display. Some headsets have technology that tracks eye movement and is synced with controllers. The semblance to reality that VR provides has applications beyond the gaming world; simulations are used to train medical students for surgeries and to allow military training in a realistic but safe environment.

What does the text most strongly suggest about the applications of virtual reality headsets?

(A) There are still limitations to the technology that have given many people reservations about such an investment.

(B) Virtual reality headsets not only provide more immersive gaming experiences, but they are also useful for training in high-stakes career fields.

(C) Users of VR headsets should make sure to utilize all aspects of the technology present in the device to get the full, immersive experience.

(D) VR headsets allow surgeons and military personnel an opportunity to learn and train at a more rapid pace than ever before.

5 ☐ Mark for Review

The following text is adapted from Edgar Allan Poe's 1839 story "The Fall of the House of Usher."

During the whole of a dull, dark, and soundless day in the autumn of the year, when the clouds hung oppressively low in the heavens, I had been passing alone, on horseback, through a singularly dreary tract of country; and at length found myself, as the shades of the evening drew on, within view of the melancholy House of Usher. I know not how it was—but, with the first glimpse of the building, a sense of insufferable gloom pervaded my spirit.

Which choice best states the main idea of the text?

Ⓐ The narrator discusses the disadvantages of traversing long distances on horseback.

Ⓑ The narrator ponders how a house had looked in previous years.

Ⓒ The narrator details a journey he is on and describes several aspects of it negatively.

Ⓓ The narrator explains the weather he encountered on the way to his destination.

6 ☐ Mark for Review

"Mr. Lismore and the Widow" is an 1883 short story by Wilkie Collins. In the story, Mr. Lismore and the widow meet for the first time. In describing Mr. Lismore's first impression of the widow, Collins contrasts a decision made by the widow regarding her appearance with those made by others, as when Collins writes of her, _____

Which quotation from "Mr. Lismore and the Widow" most effectively illustrates the claim?

Ⓐ "To Mr. Lismore, conscious of the disastrous influence occasionally exercised over busy men by youth and beauty, this was a recommendation in itself."

Ⓑ "Observing the lady as she approached him with the momentary curiosity of a stranger, he noticed that she still preserved the remains of beauty."

Ⓒ "At the same time she evidently held herself above the common deceptions by which some women seek to conceal their age."

Ⓓ "On entering the room, she made her apologies with some embarrassment."

7 ☐ Mark for Review

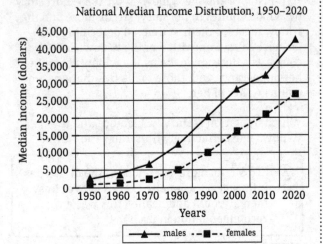

National Median Income Distribution, 1950–2020

males --■-- females

A sociology student is researching the median income of male and female workers in the United States from 1950 to 2020. In the research, the student reads an essay that noted that although women's wages were consistently lower than men's wages, women's wages grew more consistently whereas men's wages stagnated with recessions in the 1960s and 2000s. The student asserts that in the decades directly following these periods of stagnation, men's wages rose more rapidly than women's wages, causing the wage gap to grow even wider.

Which choice most effectively uses data from the graph that support the student's assertion?

Ⓐ The increase in wages from 1970 to 1980 and again from 2010 to 2020 is steeper for males than it is for females.

Ⓑ Women's wages from 1990 to 2000 experienced similar growth to those of men from the same period.

Ⓒ The gap between wages of males and females grows consistently from 1950 to 2020.

Ⓓ The increase in wages for males from 1960 to 1970 and from 2000 to 2010 is not as steep as the increase from 2010 to 2020.

8 ☐ Mark for Review

Found in the icy waters off Greenland, *Liparis gibbus*, a species of snailfish, contains the highest expression of antifreeze proteins ever observed amongst fishes. Researchers from the American Museum of Natural history first discovered this fish by its biofluorescent glow, a rare feature among fish in the Arctic. However, they discovered an even more unusual characteristic when sequencing the DNA of the snailfish—it showed atypically high numbers of genes coded for making antifreeze proteins, which prevent ice crystals from forming inside the fish and thusly prevent the fish from freezing in Arctic waters. This adaptation allows the snailfish to feed and thrive in an environment that is simply too frigid for most fish species. Scientists, however, are concerned with how the snailfish will fare in the face of the increasing temperatures associated with climate change, as _____

Which choice most logically completes the text?

Ⓐ there is a genetic link between the ability of species of fish to produce antifreeze proteins and those species' ability to emit a biofluorescent glow.

Ⓑ species of fish that typically inhabit warmer climates may migrate to the Arctic and compete with the snailfish for resources.

Ⓒ other species of fish may evolve this adaptation and therefore be able to survive in the Arctic environment.

Ⓓ their ability to produce this antifreeze protein may not allow them to survive in warmer waters.

Chapter 10
Working with Poetry

Occasionally, you'll be working through a Reading and Writing module and encounter a question asking about a poem rather than a College Board–authored passage or except from a novel. When this happens, you want to learn to treat the poem as you would any other passage to avoid affecting your momentum. This chapter will help you understand where in the Reading questions you may see poetry and offer you some tools for tackling those questions.

WHY POETRY CAN BE DIFFICULT

On most Digital SAT passages, you're given sentences with relatively clear functions and structural words that help you identify critical components of the passage. Very frequently, the question task directs you to a specific claim, assertion, or statement, and you only need to support that idea or fill in a gap related to that idea. Even in prose passages such as excerpts from novels and short stories, the original author almost certainly wanted the story to have a logical flow and therefore included at least a few phrases that move the content of the story from one idea to the next.

At first glance, poems seem to throw all of this out the window. In an effort to maintain a consistent meter and rhyme scheme, poets appear to disregard traditional sentence structure and include links between ideas that are more about imagery and allegory than pivotal words and evidence. It can be difficult to see where one idea ends and another begins, and even single ideas can stretch the length of the entire poem. Poetry is also the type of writing that you are likely least exposed to, as textbook-style passages are common across almost all disciplines, and people usually have exposure to novels and stories outside of English class.

WHAT CAN MAKE POETRY EASIER

Remember this from earlier: Reading on the Digital SAT is not high school English class, and it's certainly not a college-level creative writing class. It's an open-book test with one correct answer that must be supported by evidence from the passage. You will not be asked to name literary devices or write an essay examining the rhetorical impact of the author's use of symbolism. You will be asked only to identify the part of the poem that provides an answer to the question asked. You need to train yourself to think of a poem as a story with a meter and maybe a rhyme scheme. The following pages will cover four ways to make poems easier in an attempt to direct your eyes to what truly matters on poetry questions and avoid getting caught up in a deep poetic analysis in the middle of the Reading and Writing module. As you go through this chapter, you'll also learn which types of Reading questions may feature poetry texts.

TIP #1: TREAT POEMS AS REGULAR PASSAGES

As authors of literary works, poets still have central arguments or main ideas they wish to stress. For as long as this is true, their work must follow some type of logical structure if it's to be well understood by a future reader. This fact helps you, the test-taker, as well. Regardless of which poem College Board chooses in order to increase the difficulty or complexity of a question, be on the lookout for structural words to help understand sentence function. While poems are organized by line rather than by sentence, most poets still use punctuation to indicate the end of ideas, and so in effect, you still have sentences to refer to. With this in mind, let's look at one of the question types that can feature poetry.

Poetry and Purpose

The first place you may see a poem is on Purpose questions, which, if they appear on your module, will come right after Vocabulary questions. Regardless of whether you're asked for a main purpose, sentence function, or overall structure, all Purpose questions ask you to understand the connection between ideas, and these connections make one of the proposed answers much more likely than the other three. Let's use an Overall Structure question to demonstrate the value of treating the poem like a regular passage.

> Note that it's technically possible for a Vocabulary question to have a poem with the *most nearly mean* question stem, but so far, all released Digital SAT questions with this stem have had prose excerpts rather than poetry ones.

The following text is from Henry Wadsworth Longfellow's 1842 poem "Mezzo Cammin."

> Half of my life is gone, and I have let
>   The years slip from me and have not fulfilled
>   The aspiration of my youth, to build
>   Some tower of song with lofty parapet.
> Not indolence, nor pleasure, nor the fret
>   Of restless passions that would not be stilled,
>   But sorrow, and a care that almost killed,
>   Kept me from what I may accomplish yet;
> Though, half-way up the hill, I see the Past
>   Lying beneath me with its sounds and sights,—
>   A city in the twilight dim and vast,
> With smoking roofs, soft bells, and gleaming lights,—
>   And hear above me on the autumnal blast
>   The cataract of Death far thundering from the heights.

1   🔖 Mark for Review

Which choice best describes the overall structure of the text?

 (A) The speaker reflects on his life with regret, then cautiously considers what awaits him in the future.

(B) The speaker laments his lack of accomplishments, then pledges to attain his goals before he dies.

(C) The speaker defends his shortcomings, then plots to turn back his greatest detractors.

(D) The speaker details how his passions undermined his plans, then admits he cannot stop his further descent into failure.

Why This Question is Hard

The sheer length of the poem combined with what appear to be run-on sentences can make this a slog to work your way through. Additionally, no background information is given besides the author, title, and date, so you are thrust right into this dense bit of text.

Here's How to Ace It

Answers to overall structure questions always have two parts to them, so look for something that separates the rewritten poem above into two halves. The pivotal word *Though* tells you that the first eight lines will make up the first half of the correct answer, while the remaining lines will make up the second half of the correct answer. Look for a claim or main idea in the first half: *I have let the years slip from me and have not fulfilled the aspiration of my youth.* You don't need to read the rest of the information before the pivot over and over—it's just going to be more descriptions of how the author let time go by and didn't accomplish some goals.

Look for a claim or main idea in the second half: *Though, half-way up the hill, I see the past lying beneath me with its sounds and sights…and hear above me on the autumnal blast the cataract of Death far thundering from the heights.* The speaker's past is now beneath him, and he hears Death coming from above. If the past is beneath him, it makes logical sense that the future is above him. Therefore, make an annotation such as "regrets the past, but knows the future is coming."

Keep (A) because it's consistent with the annotation and accounts for the shift between the past and future. Notice that neither half of the poem is particularly optimistic, and this answer accounts for that. Eliminate (B) because it's **Half-Right**—the second half of this answer goes **Beyond the Text**, as the speaker doesn't pledge *to attain his goals before he dies*. Eliminate (C) because not only does the speaker not defend himself, but no mention of his *greatest detractors* (critics) is made. Eliminate (D) because it's the **Opposite** of what's stated in the passage—the author claims that it was *not* the *fret of restless passions* that kept him from his goals. Furthermore, *descent into failure* is **Extreme Language**—the speaker doesn't indicate how successful he will or will not be, only that he may be running out of time to do what he wants to do. The correct answer is (A).

TIP #2: LOOK FOR COMPARISONS

While poems may not have as many structural words as other types of passages, there is one notable exception: comparisons. Because the main argument or idea within a poem may be something abstract that the author wants to communicate in a limited number of lines, the poem may compare the more abstract idea to a far more concrete one. In this way, the readers can grasp the significance of the author's point through their grasp of something far more universal and mundane.

Common Comparisons

On the Digital SAT, you do not need to know and will not be asked to name the different ways poets draw comparisons, but having some familiarity with the types of comparisons may help you approach the texts with more confidence.

Literary Device	Definition	Example
analogy	a comparison between two things, typically for the purpose of explanation or clarification	*Pain, our fire alarm.* *The sharpness of our pain* *Alerts us to an issue* *And rings inside our brain.*
simile	a figure of speech involving the comparison of one thing with another thing of a different kind, used to make a description more emphatic or vivid—typically uses "like" or "as"	*He's got a heart as warm as solid ice,* *A smile as pleasing as spoiled milk,* *An embrace as comforting as a vice,* *And bright eyes that shine like a ruined silk.*
metaphor	a figure of speech in which a word or phrase is directly applied to an object or action to which it is not literally applicable—does not use "like" or "as"	*Our blue car sailed gracefully* *Through the nasty traffic sea,* *We navigated waters rough* *With wisdom of a captain tough.*

While poets use a whole host of other literary devices, we don't recommend studying more than these three. Remember, you won't be asked to identify literary devices, and thinking about them too much means you're spending time trying to understand the passage rather than answering the question.

Poetry and Retrieval

After Purpose questions, the next area you may see a poem is associated with Retrieval and Main Idea questions, which, if you recall, can be mixed together. Retrieval questions are great question types to work on comparisons, as sometimes the question task itself directs you to the comparison you need to focus on. Just as with prose-based literature texts, anything you can conclude about a person or idea from a poem needs to be supported by information you can physically highlight in the text itself.

The following text is from T. S. Eliot's 1922 poem "The Waste Land." The poem describes the scene of a meeting between the narrator and a renowned fortune teller.

> The Chair she sat in, like a burnished throne,
> Glowed on the marble, where the glass
> Held up by standards wrought with fruited vines
> From which a golden Cupidon peeped out
> (Another hid his eyes behind his wing)
> Doubled the flames of seven branched candelabra
> Reflecting light upon the table as
> The glitter of her jewels rose to meet it,
> From satin cases poured in rich profusion.

2 Mark for Review

Based on the text, in what way is the chair that the woman sat in similar to a burnished throne?

- (A) It has a particular shine to it.
- (B) It is made of glass and marble.
- (C) It is engraved with fruit and vines.
- (D) It is reflective and glittery.

Why This Question is Hard

The poem is a single sentence describing a chair with zero pivotal or concluding words that would help quickly find an argument. Additionally, all of the answers are not only short, but use the exact same language as the passage.

Here's How to Ace It

The comparison word *like* indicates a **simile** and helps you immediately focus on the correct comparison. All you are told is that the throne is *burnished*, which means polished by rubbing. If you didn't know that word, you are still told that the chair *Glowed on the marble*, so there is at least something noteworthy about how the chair looks.

Keep (A) because it's consistent either with saying that the Chair is like a highly polished throne or has a glow to it. Eliminate (B), (C), and (D) because they all contain **Recycled Language**—it's not clear from the passage whether *marble, glass, fruited vines,* or *glitter* describe the chair or not. All we know for sure is that the chair *Glowed*. Also, each of these descriptions comes well after the simile that is the focus of the question. The correct answer is (A).

TIP #3: USE THE EXTRA INFORMATION

As you've noticed, all literature-based passages offer an informational blurb before the excerpt that includes the author, date, and title of the work. Sometimes, both prose and poetry blurbs will offer extra information beyond these basic components. When this extra information is present, it's quite telling: College Board would not include it if it wasn't necessary, so if you see a blurb, that must mean the correct answer could not be supported adequately without some additional description.

Poetry and Main Ideas

Mixed in with Retrieval questions will be Main Idea questions, the next type that can have a poem as its passage. Compared to most other texts, poems are less likely to have a single sentence that you can highlight as the main idea. However, when extra information is present in the blurb, you can use this to focus your attention on the phrase most connected to that information—odds are, that phrase or set of lines is your main idea. If no extra information is present on a Main Idea question, use the Annotation box to write a quick summary of the text when needed and remember that the correct answer will address as much of the poem as possible.

> If you see the pronoun "I" in a poem, the speaker is, of course, referring to personal thoughts directly and probably making some type of argument. It's a pretty safe bet that you want to focus your attention on the words around that pronoun.

The following text is adapted from William Shakespeare's 1609 poem "Sonnet 25." In the poem, Shakespeare discusses those with wealth and prestige.

Let those who are in favour with their stars
Of public honour and proud titles boast,
Whilst I, whom fortune of such triumph bars,
Unlook'd for joy in that I honour most.
Great princes' favourites their fair leaves spread
But as the marigold at the sun's eye,
And in themselves their pride lies buried,
For at a frown they in their glory die.

3 Mark for Review

What is the main idea of the text?

(A) The speaker considers the differences between his life and the lives of those considered to be of great fortune.

(B) The speaker desires to have the public stature of great princes.

(C) The speaker is finding inspiration in the stars and the sun.

(D) The speaker believes that fortune comes only to those who have found joy.

Why This Question is Hard

The language chosen by Shakespeare here is, as you might expect, extremely tight. In other words, to meet his chosen style of iambic pentameter, a few of the verbs have been placed at the end of their respective lines, making a few of his points harder to interpret.

Here's How to Ace It

The extra information tells you that Shakespeare *discusses those with wealth and prestige*, so any moment where he addresses those people is an excellent starting point. In addition to highlighting the contrasting word *whilst*, you can highlight *Let those who are in favour with their stars / Of public honour and proud titles boast, / Whilst I, whom fortune of such triumph bars, / Unlook'd for joy in that I honour most*. In other words, people with wealth and prestige may boast about their public recognition or fancy titles, but the speaker finds joy in what he honors, or holds dear.

Keep (A) because it's consistent with the contrast established in the first four lines of the poem. Eliminate (B) because it's **Recycled Language**—*public* stature and *great princes* are both mentioned in the passage, but the speaker does not desire to have or be either of those things. Eliminate (C) because it's also **Recycled Language**—*stars* and the *sun* come from different parts of the passage and neither is associated with the speaker but rather with people who have wealth and prestige. Eliminate (D) because *only* is **Extreme Language**—while the speaker does find *joy* in the things he honors or holds dear, he claims to have done this without great *fortune*. The correct answer is (A).

TIP #4: MATCH IDEA FOR IDEA, NOT WORD FOR WORD

When you think of it, Reading on the Digital SAT is almost a translation exercise, as the correct answer is almost always a paraphrase of the passage rather than a direct quotation. This is doubly true on poetry-based passages, as you may need to translate the language in the poem in addition to the language in the answer choices. However, it really doesn't matter how many synonym hoops College Board makes you jump through—the language in the correct answer will contain the same meaning as that of the poem. As long as you match idea for idea and avoid falling for Recycled Language traps that come from only trying to match word for word, you can navigate the most difficult poetry-based questions.

Poetry and Claims

Unlike the first three question types in this chapter, Claims questions will feature the poetry excerpt in the answer choices rather than in the passage. The passage will usually be short and consist of the typical background sentence and then a claim someone is making about the poem. Highlight the claim in the text and make sure that the poetry excerpt you choose addresses all components of that claim. Remember that the excerpts from the poem in the answer choices will almost certainly use different words from those in the claim, but the meanings of the ideas between the claim and the correct answer will match up.

> You should aim to spend a relatively short amount of time reading the passage and high-lighting the claim on Claims questions with poetry (or prose), as the actual passage is short and the claim always precedes the blank at the end of the passage. Therefore, you have more time to compare each answer back to the claim and look for matches in ideas.

"Lamia" is an 1819 narrative poem by John Keats. The poem describes Lamia, a serpent spirit, who realizes that the man she desires, Lycius, will not accept her serpent form and alters her appearance to attract his affections: _____

---

4 🔖 Mark for Review

Which quotation from the poem most effectively illustrates the claim?

(A) "Whither fled Lamia, now a lady bright, / A full-born beauty new and exquisite? / She fled into that valley they pass o'er / Who go to Corinth from Cenchreas' shore."

(B) "Lamia beheld him coming, near, more near— / Close to her passing, in indifference drear, / His silent sandals swept the mossy green; / So neighbour'd to him, and yet so unseen."

(C) "Thus gentle Lamia judg'd, and judg'd aright, / That Lycius could not love in half a fright, / So threw the goddess off, and won his heart / More pleasantly by playing woman's part."

(D) "The way was short, for Lamia's eagerness / Made, by a spell, the triple league decrease / To a few paces; not at all surmised / By blinded Lycius, so in her comprized."

Why This Question is Hard

Not only is this poem by Keats fairly sophisticated even when read whole, but also on Claims questions about poems, the answers are always broken up into 1- to 4-line excerpts that make it a bit difficult to capture what's going on. Additionally, these four answers are not taken from the exact same portion of the poem, so it's difficult to get a true sense of the story's chronology as you might be able to for normal poetry passages.

Here's How to Ace It

The claim tells you that *Lamia* desires a man named *Lycius* and *alters her appearance to attract his affections*. There are three separate aspects to this claim: the realization that Lycius won't accept how Lamia looks, the altering of Lamia's appearance, and the attraction of Lycius's affections. Remember these two critical points: a tricky wrong answer will address one or two aspects of this claim but not all three, and the correct answer will address all three claims but with different language from that of the question stem.

Choice (A) is wrong because it's **Half-Right**—*now a lady bright, / A full-born beauty new and exquisite* addresses the altering of appearance but neither of the claims regarding Lycius. Choice (B) is wrong because it addresses none of the claim—it would take outside reasoning to connect Lamia watching Lycius approaching in secret to any of the aspects of the claim. Keep (C) because it matches the ideas in the claim: *Lamia judg'd and judg'd aright / That Lycius could not love in half a fright* is the realization that Lycius will not accept Lamia's current form, *So threw the goddess off...by playing a woman's part* covers the altering of Lamia's appearance, and *won his heart / More pleasantly* indicates that Lamia was successful in attracting Lycius's affections. Eliminate (D) because it's also **Half-Right**—while *blinded Lycius, so in her comprized* indicates that Lycius has become smitten with Lamia and thus she has attracted his affection, there is nothing regarding him not accepting her current form, nor is there enough evidence to conclude that the *spell* specifically refers to Lamia's changing of appearance. The correct answer is (C).

POETRY CONVENTIONS 101

Lastly, a word about poetry conventions. In order to keep a consistent meter (the number of syllables per line), poets use their own types of contractions and abbreviations. Below are some of the most common abbreviations you will see on the Digital SAT. Just like literary devices, you won't be explicitly tested on these, but knowing some of the common poetry conventions can help you avoid being unnecessarily tripped up as you read.

Poetic Contraction or Abbreviation	Modern English Word(s)
'tis	it is
'twas	it was
o'er	over
ne'er	never
ere	before
e'en	even
o'	of
an'	and

Poetry Drill

Practice our poetry tips as you attempt this chapter's drill and see if it helps your accuracy. Answers and explanations can be found in Chapter 12.

Time: 10 minutes

1 ☐ Mark for Review

The following text is from Anne Bradstreet's 1678 poem "To My Dear and Loving Husband."

> If ever two were one, then surely we.
> If ever man were loved by wife, then thee.
> If ever wife was happy in a man,
> Compare with me, ye women, if you can.
> <u>I prize thy love more than whole mines of gold</u>
> <u>Or all the riches that the East doth hold.</u>
> My love is such that rivers cannot quench,
> Nor ought but love from thee give recompense.
> Thy love is such I can no way repay;
> The heavens reward thee manifold, I pray.
> Then while we live, in love let's so persever,
> That when we live no more, we may live ever.

Which choice best describes the function of the underlined portion in the text as a whole?

- (A) It measures the depth of the speaker's feelings by comparing them to material wealth.

- (B) It evokes the city where the speaker first met her future husband.

- (C) It emphasizes that the speaker loves her husband more than any other wife could.

- (D) It proposes potential journeys that the speaker wishes to travel on with her husband.

2 ☐ Mark for Review

The following text is from the 1917 poem "Afternoon on a Hill" by Edna St. Vincent Millay, an American poet and playwright.

> I will be the gladdest thing
> Under the sun!
> I will touch a hundred flowers
> And not pick one.
>
> I will look at cliffs and clouds
> With quiet eyes,
> Watch the wind bow down the grass,
> And the grass rise.
>
> And when the lights begin to show
> Up from the town,
> I will mark which must be mine,
> And then start down!

Which choice best describes the overall structure of the text?

- (A) The speaker desires to embark upon a great flurry of activity, then faces the consequences of her actions.

- (B) The speaker expresses an intention to run wild in natural settings, then chooses to seek pleasure in the city instead.

- (C) The speaker declares a desire to enjoy her time at the hillside, then clarifies the circumstances that will cause her departure.

- (D) The speaker depicts her town as precious, then decides she must reexamine her admiration for it.

3 ◫ Mark for Review

The following text is from Lord Byron's 1812 poem "Childe Harold's Pilgrimage." The narrator is describing the beauty of the countryside in Portugal after deciding to leave his home country of England.

> Not in those climes where I have late been straying,
> Though Beauty long hath there been matchless deemed,
> Not in those visions to the heart displaying
> Forms which it sighs but to have only dreamed,
> Hath aught like thee in Truth or Fancy seemed:
> Nor, having seen thee, shall I vainly seek
> To paint those charms which varied as they beamed—
> To such as see thee not my words were weak;
> To those who gaze on thee what language could they speak?

Based on the text, how does the narrator characterize the beauty of the Portuguese countryside?

(A) It is able to be described in only certain languages.

(B) It is comparable to the appearance of other regions the narrator has visited.

(C) It is a valuable subject for an artist's painting.

(D) It is unable to be described with verbal descriptions.

4 ◫ Mark for Review

The following text is adapted from Edward Doyle's 1921 poem "The Stars."

> God loves the stars; else why star-shape the dew
> For the unbreathing, shy, heart-hiding rose?
> And when earth darkens, and the North wind blows,
> Why into stars, flake every cloud's black brew?
> What fitter forms for longings high and true,
> Man's hopes, ideals, than bright orbs like those
> Asbine from Nature's dawn to Nature's close,
> In clusters, prisming every dazzling hue?

Based on the text, what is the primary significance of stars?

(A) Their presence in the nighttime sky acts like a prism used to guide people in the darkness.

(B) Their appearance indicates the dissolution of an ominous weather system that had caused the earth to darken.

(C) Their symmetry represents a balance in life worth striving for even if the stars themselves are not living.

(D) Their shape shows up in a variety of contexts and settings that makes them feel interwoven with nature and life.

5 ☐ Mark for Review

The following text is adapted from Eugene Field's 1897 poem "Beard and Baby."

I say, as one who never feared
The wrath of a subscriber's bullet,
I pity him who has a beard
But has no little girl to pull it!

When wife and I have finished tea,
Our baby woos me with her prattle,
And, perching proudly on my knee,
She gives my petted whiskers battle.

With both her hands she tugs away,
While scolding at me kind o' spiteful;
You'll not believe me when I say
I find the torture quite delightful!

Which choice best states the main idea of the text?

A) The speaker expresses jubilation regarding an interaction with his newborn daughter after years of being unable to conceive a child.

B) Although the speaker expresses sympathy for those who cannot experience a certain interaction, he can experience it and does so joyously.

C) The speaker mourns the lack of understanding he receives from others when he shares his concerns about his child's spiteful nature.

D) As a new phase in the speaker's life takes shape, the speaker expresses his fears concerning the wrath of those he has wronged.

6 ☐ Mark for Review

The following text is adapted from Archibald Lampman's 1888 poem "In October."

Here I will sit upon this naked stone,
Draw my coat closer with my numbed hands,
And hear the ferns sigh, and the wet woods moan,
And send my heart out to the ashen lands;
And I will ask myself what golden madness,
What balmed breaths of dreamland spicery,
What visions of soft laughter and light sadness
Were sweet last month to me.

Which choice best states the main idea of the text?

A) The narrator observes the weather getting colder and reminisces about his experiences in the recent past.

B) The narrator laments not appreciating the beauty and warmth of autumn while it was around and is saddened to notice the change of seasons.

C) The narrator contrasts the naked woods of a looming winter with the yellow and golden leaves of a passing autumn.

D) As the seasons change, the narrator is not sure how to feel about the changing landscape.

7 ☐ Mark for Review

"The Good Part, that shall not be taken away" is an 1842 poem by Henry Wadsworth Longfellow, whose writing style was heavily influenced by the women in his life. The poem describes how the aura of a woman is enhanced by her compassion for others:

_____

Which quotation from "The Good Part, that shall not be taken away" most effectively illustrates the claim?

Ⓐ "And thus she walks among her girls / With praise and mild rebukes; / Subduing e'en rude village churls / By her angelic looks."

Ⓑ "She dwells by Great Kenhawa's side, / In valleys green and cool; / And all her hope and all her pride / Are in the village school."

Ⓒ "Her soul, like the transparent air / That robes the hills above, / Though not of earth, encircles there / All things with arms of love."

Ⓓ "Long since beyond the Southern Sea / Their outbound sails have sped, / While she, in meek humility, / Now earns her daily bread."

8 ☐ Mark for Review

"A Balm for Weary Minds" is a 1906 poem by James E. McGirt. In the poem, which describes the springtime atmosphere, McGirt lauds the season for being refreshing to the mind.

Which quotation from "A Balm for Weary Minds" most effectively illustrates the claim?

Ⓐ "Look at the daisies, see them bend, / Giving their fragrance to each wind."

Ⓑ "What a balm for the mind's the joyous spring, / What fragrant nectar its breezes bring."

Ⓒ "What joy upon the turf to lie / And watch the fleeting butterfly."

Ⓓ "The humming bees as they go and come, / Sipping honey from the bloom."

Chapter 11
Overcoming Challenging Scenarios

On the Digital SAT, you'll encounter a series of Reading questions that College Board deems "hard." While the numbers vary from test to test, it's common for Reading and Writing Module 1 to have somewhere around 3–4 hard Reading questions, while the Harder Module 2 will likely have ten or more hard Reading questions. College Board's definition of "hard" depends on a whole host of difficult-to-quantify factors such as passage and topic complexity. This is further complicated by the fact that each student has very different strengths and weaknesses, and one student's "easy" can be another student's "extremely difficult." This chapter will take you through some scenarios that our students have almost universally found challenging and give you the insight you need to tackle these scenarios when confronted with them on your own exam.

WHAT MAKES A READING QUESTION CHALLENGING?

We could likely write a whole book on this one question, but if you've done all of the Reading chapters up to this point, you probably have a good idea as to what the answer to this question would be.

Acknowledging where you have struggled in the past is the first step toward improving your pacing on any modules or exams that you take in the future.

Here's a list of most (but probably not all) of the features that can make a Reading question "hard":

- a dense, long passage
- a complex or unfamiliar topic
- a sophisticated literature excerpt
- loads of science jargon
- a complicated chart or graph
- a vague question task
- lengthy or similar-looking answer choices
- deceptive traps in the answers

The hardest questions on the Digital SAT will have more than one of these features. Before you dive into exploring how to ace these situations, remember the golden rule for hard questions on the Digital SAT.

Don't attempt a question you *know* will be difficult when you first see it. Skip the question for now, and make sure you've done every question you can answer quickly and easily before spending your valuable time on these questions. If time is about to run out, don't forget to enter a random guess on any question you skipped before the module ends.

From here on out, the description of each scenario will explain why that scenario is difficult, so we won't include "Why This Question is Hard" at the start of each explanation.

SCENARIO 1

Purpose of a Sentence on a Literature-Based Passage

On normal, College-Board authored passages, the goal of the author is to inform or persuade. In both cases, the author must include clear structural words to indicate important shifts in the information and to highlight relevant data, which in turn helps you identify sentence function. However, on literature-based passages, the author's goal is to entertain or perhaps provide some social commentary. These authors had no idea their cherished tales would wind up on the Digital SAT someday, so needless to say, their writing often does not align with how College

Board writes passages. This can make a Purpose question that looks for the function of a sentence more difficult, as you're often reading through multiple descriptions that appear to blend together.

> If the passage doesn't offer you clear connections to focus on, where should you look instead?

The following text is adapted from a translation of Alfred de Musset's 1839 short story "Croisilles." Croisilles is a young man returning home to Paris.

At the beginning of the reign of Louis XV, a young man named Croisilles, son of a goldsmith, was returning from Paris to Havre, his native town. He had been intrusted by his father with the transaction of some business, and his trip to the great city having turned out satisfactorily, the joy of bringing good news caused him to walk the sixty leagues more gaily and briskly than was his wont; for, though he had a rather large sum of money in his pocket, he travelled on foot for pleasure. He was a good-tempered fellow, and not without wit, but so very thoughtless and flighty that people looked upon him as being rather weak-minded.

1 ☐ Mark for Review

Which choice best describes the function of the underlined sentence in the text as a whole?

- (A) It presents a characterization of Croisilles that provides context for the decision Croisilles makes in the previous sentence.

- (B) It explains why Croisilles's father trusted his son with important aspects of his business.

- (C) It illustrates a shortcoming of Croisilles's that may impact his future business dealings.

- (D) It shows why Croisilles does not mind walking even with a large sum of money in his pocket.

Here's How to Ace It

The underlined sentence does not clearly link to any of the previous sentences: it merely continues the description of Croisilles. Highlight it so it stands out that much more to you, and focus on matching idea for idea, not word for word, as you compare each answer to your highlighting.

Keep (A) because the underlined sentence is a description or *characterization* of Croisilles, and if he were *thoughtless* and *flighty* and looked upon as *being rather weak-minded*, this could provide context for why he may have decided to travel *on foot* with a *large sum of money*, something that is not particularly wise. Eliminate (B) because it goes **Beyond the Text**—while Croisilles's *good-tempered* nature may be a logical reason for his father to have *trusted* him with the business, the passage does not offer any reason as to why his father *intrusted* him in the second sentence, just that he did so. Eliminate (C) because it also goes **Beyond the Text**—while *people* look upon Croisilles as *being rather weak-minded*, and it's easy to imagine this perception could affect Croisilles's *future business dealings*, there is no evidence in the passage to conclude anything about the future. The only business discussed in the passage *turned out satisfactorily*, not poorly, for Croisilles. Eliminate (D) because it goes **Beyond the Text**—Croisilles's good-tempered nature could explain why he doesn't mind walking around with *a rather large sum of money in his pocket*, but without any clear structural link between the two sentences, it's unclear. The only reason given in the passage for him choosing to travel by foot this journey is *for pleasure*. The correct answer is (A).

Here's a second example of Scenario 1 to try on your own.

The following text is from Victor Cherbuliez's 1863 novel *Count Kostia*. The protagonist is a widower who has returned to Europe after several years in the Caribbean.

Count Kostia was gifted with a quick and ready intellect, which he had strengthened by study. He had always been passionately fond of historical research, but above everything, knew and wished to know, only that which the English call "the matter of fact." <u>He professed a cold scorn for generalities, and heartily abandoned them to "dreamers"; he laughed at all abstract theories and at the ingenuous minds which take them seriously.</u>

2 ☐ Mark for Review

Which choice best describes the function of the underlined sentence in the text as a whole?

(A) It paints a visual representation of the method by which Count Kostia studies.

(B) It expands upon an idea that is mentioned at the end of the previous sentence.

(C) It exemplifies the types of interactions that Count Kostia has with his acquaintances.

(D) It introduces a viewpoint of Count Kostia's with which the author agrees.

Here's How to Ace It

At first glance, this seems similar to the previous question: the underlined sentence does not clearly link to any of the previous sentences. However, highlight the underlined sentence and proceed to the answers, and let the answers direct you to any sentences that may or may not be relevant.

Eliminate (A) because it's **Recycled Language**—Kostia's *study* is mentioned in the first sentence, but the underlined sentence is not discussing his study habits. Keep (B) because it directs you to the end of the previous sentence, in which Count Kostia only wishes to know the "matter of fact." This is consistent with the underlined sentence, in which Kostia has a cold scorn for those who speak in *generalities*, which are vaguer than facts. So, the underlined sentence does expand on the idea from the sentence before. Eliminate (C) because it's not clear from the passage that the *dreamers* and the *ingenuous minds* who take abstract theories seriously are necessarily *acquaintances* of Kostia's. They could be family, friends, work colleagues, or even people the Count has read about. Eliminate (D) because it's **Half-Right**—the underlined portion does contain Count Kostia's viewpoint, but the author does not express any opinion toward that view. The correct answer is (B).

> When faced with finding the function of a sentence on a Purpose question with a highly descriptive prose passage, go straight to the answers and let them guide both your POE and which sentences you opt to reread.

SCENARIO 2

Dual Texts Questions Looking for Only a Slight Agreement

Many Dual Texts questions want to know how someone from one passage would respond to someone or something from the other. Not only are both arguments often set off by concluding or pivotal words, but the argument of the responder is also frequently contradictory, albeit with some conditions. However, when the question asks for a point on which the authors may agree, suddenly the entire passage could be relevant. After all, you don't know whether or not the agreement will be on the main concept or on some random piece of evidence, and you don't have all day to scour every last word of two different passages, over and over.

> The authors of dual passages rarely agree on their main arguments, which are always claims or objections. So, what types of sentences from the Understanding Sentence Function chapter does that leave to likely contain the points of agreement?

Text 1

Reducing caloric intake through Alternate Day Fasting (ADF) has been theorized to increase longevity. Results from a new study by Leonie Heilbrunn and colleagues compared groups of adult humans and rats in respective ADF programs. Whereas rats compensated for fasting days by overeating on feasting days, people neglected to do so. Researchers did note, however, that people reported increased appetite on feasting days, which suggests that humans may opt to also overeat on feasting days if they commit to ADF for a longer period of time.

Text 2

The potential benefits of ADF extend beyond simply reducing caloric intake by limiting windows of consumption; human participants also experienced better fat oxidation, making more efficient use of the food they did consume. It's important to acknowledge that animals, unsure of sources of food, are driven to consume, but the human brain is more complex, and humans committed to an ADF routine can likely overcome urges to overeat once the benefits of improved health due to weight loss and more efficient processing of food become manifest.

3   Mark for Review

Based on the texts, Heilbrunn's team and the author of Text 2 would most likely agree with which statement about alternate-day fasting?

(A) There is likely to be a difference between how humans and non-humans behave on the feasting days of an ADF program.

(B) A different group of people would have probably exhibited tendencies to compensate by eating more on feasting days.

(C) If people were allowed to choose their own schedules of feast days and fast days, they would probably lose more weight faster.

(D) People are more likely to compensate by overconsuming on feasting days because they have reliable sources of food.

Here's How to Ace It

Just as with our first scenario, the answer choices are the key. Don't hope that you will quickly find the one point of agreement or expect that the point of agreement will be in something easy to find, like the main arguments. Instead, let the answers guide you back to the passages.

Keep (A) because it focuses on a *difference between how humans and non-humans behave*—a quick check of the passages shows that in Text 1, the author discusses how rats overate but humans didn't, and in Text 2, the author explains that the more complex human brain can likely overcome urges to overeat. Eliminate (B) because neither author speculates on what a *different group of people* would do, and Text 2 at least seems to indicate that people might choose to not eat *more* on feasting days. Eliminate (C) because neither author discusses people choosing *their own schedules*—Alternate Day Fasting would mean that everyone (or everything, in the case of the rats) in the study fasts one day and feasts the next day. Eliminate (D) because it goes **Beyond the Text**—neither author states that humans have more *reliable sources of food* than rats do, and whether this is true at all is debatable. The correct answer is (A).

Here's a second example of Scenario 2 to try on your own.

Text 1

In 1944, a team of genetic researchers at Rockefeller Hospital hoped to demonstrate that the polysaccharide hypothesis, which stated that genetic information was carried by sugar molecules, was mistaken. The team concluded that the transmitting particles were instead the nucleic acids DNA and RNA. However, the team's results were initially met with skepticism or outright dismissal by some members of the scientific community, who argued that DNA and RNA were merely inert molecules whose only job was to store phosphorus.

Text 2

After sugar molecules had been discounted as possible carriers of genetic information within the body, some biologists posited that proteins could perhaps serve that role instead. Contrary to this supposition, a 1952 experiment conducted by Alfred Hershey and Martha Chase verified that it was indeed DNA, not proteins, that was responsible for the transfer of genetic material. By studying the process of bacteriophages infecting bacteria, Hershey and Chase discovered that DNA from the bacteriophages enters the host bacterial cell, while most of the protein from the bacteriophage does not.

4 ☐ Mark for Review

Based on the texts, if the Rockefeller Hospital team (Text 1) and Hershey and Chase (Text 2) were aware of the findings of both experiments, they would most likely agree with which statement?

(A) Phosphorus helps feed the nucleic acids responsible for the delivery of genetic material, and those acids in turn help the body more efficiently store phosphorus.

(B) Overall, the impact of bacteriophages infecting bacteria tends to be more harmful to the body than that of polysaccharide consumption.

(C) Genetic material carried by both DNA and RNA tends to enter host bacterial cells with greater frequency than genetic material carried by DNA alone.

(D) The results of the 1944 demonstration were at odds with the beliefs of others in a similar way that the discovery of the 1952 experiment was.

Here's How to Ace It

Don't be intimidated by "aware of the findings of both experiments." This is not some theoretical synthesis task—you only need to see if the statements in the answers appeared in both texts.

Eliminate (A) because *phosphorus* is discussed only at the end of Text 1—additionally, the positive correlation between phosphorus and nucleic acids suggested here goes **Beyond the Text**. Eliminate (B) because it's **Recycled Language**—*polysaccharide* is taken from Text 1 and *bacteriophages infecting bacteria* is taken from Text 2, but they never appear in the same passage and the damage they do to the body is not compared. Eliminate (C) because it also goes **Beyond the Text**—the *frequency* with which RNA and DNA enter host bacterial cells is not discussed, and RNA is not mentioned in Text 2 at all. Keep (D) because both authors reference that the findings they discuss were either *met with skepticism or outright dismissal* or were *Contrary to* a *supposition*. The correct answer is (D).

When faced with finding a point of agreement on a Dual Texts question, go straight to the answers and let them guide you. The point of agreement will likely be in the **Background** information or the **Evidence** rather than in the **Claims** or **Objections**.

SCENARIO 3

Retrieval Questions That Ask You to Summarize a Character Rather Than Identify a Detail

Many Retrieval questions ask you to find a detail from a passage, and that passage usually discussed an innovation, event, or at least a chronological story. All of these things will flow logically as you read them, making it a straightforward (though not necessarily easy) task to locate the required detail. Descriptions of the setting likely occur at the start of a story, and figuring out what challenge someone faced probably comes after some pivotal or contrasting word. However, when College Board uses a literature-based source for its Retrieval questions, you are often plunked down in the middle of some random paragraph without any extra information to guide you. Furthermore, some Retrieval questions are so general in what they ask that they may as well be Main Idea questions, which is why the two often appear together.

The following text is adapted from Park Benjamin's 1881 short story "The End of New York."

Mr. T. A. Edison announced that he had invented everything which, up to that time, anyone else had suggested. He invited all the reporters to Menlo Park, and, after elaborately explaining the merits of a new catarrh remedy, showed some lines on a piece of paper, which, he said, represented huge electro-magnets, which he proposed to set up along the coast, say, near Barnegat. When the enemy's iron ships appeared, he proposed to excite these magnets, and draw the vessels on the rocks. Somebody said that this notion had been anticipated by one Sinbad the Sailor, whereupon Mr. Edison denounced that person as a "patent pirate."

5 🔖 Mark for Review

According to the text, what is true about Edison?

(A) He is a recognized expert of electro-magnets.

(B) He has had many patents stolen from him.

(C) He is confident about his prowess as an inventor.

(D) He is very familiar with the enemy army's position.

If you see a bunch of exact words and terms from the passage in the answers, what trap becomes particularly significant?

Here's How to Ace It

Make sure to read the passage efficiently but carefully. As soon as it becomes obvious that the entire passage is a description of Edison, avoid highlighting what it says about him—you will wind up highlighting everything, which renders the highlighting unhelpful. Instead, know this about the answer choices on these questions—they are likely packed with **Recycled Language** hoping to lure students who were generally confused by the passage and seize upon the hope that such an answer provides. Take the most specific word or phrase in each answer and see if it's used the same way in the passage.

Eliminate (A) because *electro-magnets* is **Recycled Language**—the magnets are only discussed as part of a new invention that Edison has designed, not something he is stated to be a *recognized expert* on. Eliminate (B) because *patents* is also **Recycled Language**—the term *"patent pirate"* is only used to disparage one particular person who is suggested to have invented something before Edison—it's not claimed that *many patents* were stolen from him or that even a single patent was. Keep (C) because the opening line states that *Edison announced that he had invented everything which, up to that time, anyone else had suggested.* He also *invited all the reporters* to explain his new plan elaborately, showing how confident he was in the invention. Eliminate (D) because *enemy* is also **Recycled Language**—the passage discusses the enemy's *iron ships* but not that Edison is *very familiar* with the enemy's *position*. The correct answer is (C).

Here's a second example of Scenario 3 to try on your own.

The following text is adapted from Edward George Bulwer-Lytton's 1834 novel *The Last Days of Pompeii*.

Nature had sown in the heart of this poor girl the seeds of virtue never destined to ripen. The lessons of adversity are not always salutary—sometimes they soften and amend, but as often they indurate and pervert. If we consider ourselves more harshly treated by fate than those around us, and do not acknowledge in our own deeds the justice of the severity, we become too apt to deem the world our enemy, to case ourselves in defiance, to wrestle against our softer self, and to indulge the darker passions which are so easily fermented by the sense of injustice.

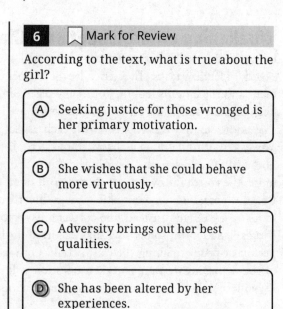

6   ☐ Mark for Review

According to the text, what is true about the girl?

(A) Seeking justice for those wronged is her primary motivation.

(B) She wishes that she could behave more virtuously.

(C) Adversity brings out her best qualities.

(D) She has been altered by her experiences.

Here's How to Ace It

Look for possible instances of **Recycled Language** in each answer by finding the most specific word or phrase and comparing it back to the passage.

Eliminate (A) because *justice* is **Recycled Language**—the word is used only as part of the author's description of how lessons of adversity cause some people to become virtuous and others to become twisted. Eliminate (B) because *virtuously* is **Recycled Language**—the girl has *seeds of virtue never destined to ripen*, meaning that there are certain positive qualities she will not possess. The passage does not claim to what extent the girl *wishes* for anything. Eliminate (C) because *Adversity* is **Recycled Language**—the word is used in the passage to describe the lessons people experience and how the lessons shape them. If anything, this answer is also the **Opposite** of the passage, as the author indicates that the girl has developed bad qualities, not good ones. Keep (D) because by stating that the girl has *seeds of virtue never destined to ripen*, the author indicates that the girl could have been virtuous but is not. For the girl, this would mean that the *lessons of adversity* have indurated and perverted the girl rather than softened and amended her, but either way, they most certainly have changed her. The correct answer is (D).

When faced with a Retrieval question asking for a conclusion about a character from a literature-based passage, find the most specific words and phrases in the answer choices and compare them back to the passage to catch **Recycled Language**.

SCENARIO 4

Weakening an Argument on a Claims Question

In many ways, illustrating an argument and supporting an argument are almost (but not exactly) identical tasks. Theoretically, the former is looking for an exemplification of an argument and the latter is looking for a new piece of evidence to bolster an argument. In practice, both of these variations on Claims questions are handled the exact same way: find the answer that addresses and is consistent with each aspect of the claim. However, when you are asked to weaken or undermine a claim, things get a little trickier. For one, the correct answer does not need to address each aspect of the claim: it only needs to contradict one part of it. Furthermore, the correct answer won't directly call out a flaw in the original claim—after all, College Board is not going to go out of its way to directly contradict the scientists and historians it cites in its own passages. Instead, the correct answer to a weaken question introduces some alternative explanation for something that occurred in the passage or cites new data that the original person or people making the claim could not possibly have accounted for. Lastly, at least one of the wrong answers on a weaken question will strengthen or support the claim instead, and if you lose sight of the question task for even a moment, that answer will be mighty appealing.

To protect itself from predators such as snails, *Trifolium repens* (white clover) produces small amounts of cyanide in its leaves. These cyanide stores, however, are affected by the cold: if the plant's leaves freeze, the internal system keeping *T. repens* safe from its own cyanide can rupture, potentially killing the plant. Therefore, *T. repens* plants in cities with colder climates must adapt accordingly. University of Toronto graduate student Ken Thompson noted that temperatures in city centers are warmer than those in city outskirts due to population density and subsequently questioned why more clover colonies are not found in the center of colder climate cities. He hypothesized that while the centers of colder cities may be warmer than the outskirts, this must in some way pose a significant challenge for *T. repens*, causing the plant to prefer the colder temperatures of a city's outskirts.

As you examine the answer choices, ask yourself: Are any of these answers potentially irrelevant to the claim entirely?

7 ☐ Mark for Review

Which finding, if true, would most directly weaken the student's hypothesis?

(A) The genes that control cyanide production in *T. repens* are also susceptible to changes in moisture and aridity in the plant's habitats.

(B) In cold climate cities with wide temperature fluctuations, snails prey on *T. repens* more frequently in city centers than in city outskirts.

(C) *T. repens* growing in cities with warmer climates are consumed by snails at a similar rate to those growing in cities with colder climates.

(D) *T. repens* grows evenly throughout colder cities, but the population density of city centers leads to more frequent removal of *T. repens* clusters from those areas.

Here's How to Ace It

Highlight the hypothesis in the last sentence as you normally would, but don't neglect the importance of the **evidence** in the previous sentence that caused the student to arrive at his hypothesis in the first place. When College Board wants to weaken an argument, it is much more likely to focus on a feature of the evidence that led to the hypothesis rather than contradict a feature of the hypothesis itself.

Eliminate (A) because it's irrelevant to the claim—the *genes that control cyanide production* are not discussed in the passage, but more importantly, *moisture and aridity* are not part of the student's hypothesis. Eliminate (B) because it's the **Opposite** of the question task—if *T. repens* stopped attempting to grow in city centers due to more frequent predation from snails, this would support, not weaken, the hypothesis that *T. repens* must have some reason for going to the city outskirts instead. Eliminate (C) because it's irrelevant to the claim—the student's hypothesis is only about *colder climates*, so the rate of snail predation on *T. repens* in warmer climates would not affect it. Keep (D) because if the presence of more people in the city center led to a greater likelihood of *T. repens* cluster removal, this would make it appear to the student that *T. repens* prefers to grow in the outskirts. Notice how this answer focused on the population density that was evidence for the student's hypothesis rather than the hypothesis itself. The correct answer is (D).

Here's a second example of Scenario 4 to try on your own.

The mouse universe experiments, a series of trials conducted by behavioral researcher John B. Calhoun, attempted to demystify some aspects of modern human behavior. Sponsored by the National Institute of Mental Health, Calhoun bred a population of mice that was given everything it needed except for one critical component: adequate space. As the population multiplied, the social structure and reproductive norms broke down, with females failing to attract male suitors, who focused on solitary activities. Calhoun found that the stress of competition in such a crowded environment resulted in near societal extinction and stated that this finding could apply to humans as well.

8 ☐ Mark for Review

Which finding, if true, would most directly undermine Calhoun's findings?

(A) In several trials during Calhoun's experiments, erratic behavior unrelated to reproductive activity was observed in several of the male mice.

(B) In several trials during Calhoun's experiments, societal structure was maintained in mouse habitats where relatively few mice capable of breeding were present.

(C) In several trials that were not part of Calhoun's experiments, large, breeding populations of mice eventually experienced near societal extinction.

(D) In several trials that were not part of Calhoun's experiments, mouse reproductive rates correlated positively with increasing population regardless of restrictions on habitat size.

Here's How to Ace It

Highlight the finding in the last sentence as you normally would, but don't neglect the importance of the **evidence** in the previous sentence that caused Calhoun to state his findings. This time around, the evidence is the result of an experiment rather than an observation, but because both are meant to support a claim, they should be treated the exact same way.

Eliminate (A) because it's irrelevant to the claim—*erratic behavior unrelated to reproductive activity* doesn't relate to Calhoun's findings, which were primarily related to examining societal breakdown through reproductive activity. If anything, mice exhibiting weird behaviors during one of Calhoun's trials might strengthen the idea that there was a societal breakdown. Eliminate (B) because it's irrelevant to the claim—if *few mice capable of breeding were present* and this helped maintain societal structure, this would not undermine the idea that too many mice break down societal structure, as the slower population growth of the mice would have prevented them from running out of room as quickly in the first place. As in (A), this may actually support Calhoun's hypothesis, as he could state that societal structure is maintained only when the population remains small. Eliminate (C) because it's the **Opposite** of the question task—such a result would greatly support Calhoun's findings. Keep (D) because part of Calhoun's results indicated that *reproductive norms broke down*—if instead, *reproductive rates correlated positively with increasing population*, this would undermine Calhoun's findings. The correct answer is (D).

> When faced with weakening or undermining a claim, keep the evidence that led to the claim in mind, as that is what College Board will often address in the correct answer. Anticipate a blend of irrelevant and strengthen answers as you apply POE.

SCENARIO 5

Tables with A Large Number of Disparate Variables

Many students prefer tables to bar graphs and line graphs because, generally, they are easier to read—tables are effectively text presented in an organized manner. Most tables feature a handful of rows and columns that all relate to a single idea, such as the percentages of elements located in different dust clouds or the number of highways built in different countries. Sometimes, however, tables will display a series of variables that don't share an obvious relation. These tables can also feature words instead of numbers, making it slightly more difficult to just grab the one piece of information you need. Lastly, the size of the table itself can seem overwhelming and start distracting you with its density before you even get a chance to focus on what you should: the question task.

Fundamental Number of Chromosomes and Hybridization Preferences of Wild and Captive Rainbowfish Species

Name of rainbowfish species	Number of specimens included in study	NF	Wild vs. captive	Willingness to hybridize
Running River	6	48	captive	yes
Red	7	48	captive	yes
Threadfin	4	48	captive	no
Ornate	4	50	captive	no
Cairns	4	56	wild	no

Australia and New Guinea are host to many ecologically diverse species of rainbowfish. Though these rainbowfish species share habitats, few of them appear willing to hybridize, or cross-breed, so researchers rely on cytogenetic analysis to explain how so many varieties of rainbowfish developed. Recently, 25 fish specimens from five rainbowfish species were studied to identify which genetic factors may influence a given rainbowfish species to hybridize. Researchers began their analysis by examining the genetic sequences of the specimens and determined the species' fundamental number of chromosomes (NF). The preliminary findings indicated that a lower NF may influence rainbowfish species to be willing to hybridize. However, a student evaluating the same data argues that a low NF is unlikely to be the sole determinant for a fish's willingness to cross-breed or not.

9 ☐ Mark for Review

Which choice best describes data from the table that support the student's argument?

(A) The same number of Ornate and Threadfin rainbowfish were used in the study and the two species are unwilling to hybridize, but they have different NFs.

(B) The Threadfin rainbowfish in the study had the same NF as the Running River and Red rainbowfish but does not willingly hybridize with other species.

(C) More Running River rainbowfish and Red rainbowfish were used in the study than any other captive fish species, and both of these species were willing to hybridize.

(D) The Cairns Rainbowfish has the highest NF of any species included in the study and was the only wild fish used in the study.

What variables should you actually care about according to the student's argument?

Here's How to Ace It

Double down on the student's argument that follows the pivotal word *However* in the final sentence—the only variables the student argues about are *NF* and *willingness to hybridize*. While you can't highlight these terms in the table, do your best to stay focused on them and even consider writing them down on scratch paper if it will help you maintain your focus.

Eliminate (A), (C), and (D) immediately as each fails to focus only on the relevant variables from the claim—(A) and (C) focus on the *number of specimens included in [the] study*, and (D) focuses on *wild* vs. captive. It's irrelevant that these three answers describe the table accurately—they either discuss *NF* or *willingness to hybridize*, but not both as they must. Keep (B) as this would support the student's argument—Threadfin rainbowfish have the exact same (and the lowest) *NF* as Running River and Red rainbowfish do and yet do not have a *willingness to hybridize*, so a low NF *is unlikely to be the sole determinant for a fish's willingness to cross-breed*. The correct answer is (B).

Here's a second example of Scenario 5 to try on your own.

Origin Languages of the Garifuna Language
and Sample Words with Translations

Source language	Percentage of Garifuna derived from source language	Sample word	English translation
Arawak	45%	wéyu	day
Carib	25%	watu	fire
French	15%	milu	thousand
English	10%	marin	mosquito
Spanish	5%	ayi	yes
African languages	<1%	Garifuna	Garifuna

Garifuna, a member of the Arawakan family of languages, is spoken in the northern area of Central America and is made up of numerous words taken directly from Caribbean and European languages. Many concepts within the language will be expressed differently when spoken by a male speaker or a female speaker. Terms used by males tend to be derived from the Carib language, while terms used by females tend to be derived from Arawak. Words to express numbers, meanwhile, tend to be derived from French. Interestingly, the word Garifuna itself is derived from African languages, which is surprising given that _____

10 Mark for Review

Which choice most effectively uses data from the table to complete the statement?

(A) two languages account for the majority of the words spoken in Garifuna, but the discrepancy between the percentages of words contributed by those languages is quite large.

(B) there is a relative lack of African influence in most of the Garifuna language compared to the influences of the Arawak and Carib languages on gendered terms and the French influence on numerical terms.

(C) the origin of some common Garifuna words such as "yes" and "fire" derive from Spanish and Carib, respectively, rather than the less common "mosquito," which derives from English.

(D) female terms, which are derived from the Arawak language, make up much more of the Garifuna language than male terms, which are derived from the Carib language.

Here's How to Ace It

Notice that the incomplete sentence begins with a statement saying that *the word Garifuna itself is derived from African languages* and then establishes a contrast with the word *surprising*. Therefore, the completion of the statement must address this variable. It's fine if other variables are referenced in the correct answer because this time there is no argument that depends on the connection between two variables specifically, as in the previous question. However, the correct answer must mention something in regard to African languages.

Eliminate (A), (C), and (D) immediately as each fails to focus on the only relevant variable in the statement—the percentage of Garifuna words derived from African languages. All three of these answers introduce a comparison between two or more of the languages discussed in the table, but none of those languages are the African languages referenced in the incomplete statement. Keep (B) as this would successfully complete the statement—African languages only account for less than 1% of all Garifuna words, and yet the word Garifuna itself came from these African languages rather than Arawak, Carib, or French, which all contributed far greater percentages of words. The correct answer is (B).

> When faced with a large table packed with disconnected variables on a Charts question, do whatever is needed to keep your focus on the only variables that matter to the claim or statement. Eliminate answers that neglect to discuss one or more of the relevant variables.

SCENARIO 6

Conclusions Questions That Lack a Clear Focus

Most Conclusions questions introduce their main subject in the first sentence, and your only job is to find the critical 1–2 pieces of evidence related to that subject. While these questions are rarely "easy," because your job is to provide a conclusion or claim, the evidence will support only one of the correct answers. If you find the evidence and highlight it, you'll rarely be led astray. However, some Conclusions questions are so meandering that they seem to shift topics every single sentence, and by the end of them, you may feel as though you're in a very different place from where you started. Harder Conclusions questions can also be science-dense or can contain a multifaceted and difficult-to-follow description of a historical event or a cultural item.

Extreme cold weather endangers a plant's survival as low temperatures freeze cell membranes, which in turn decreases the plant's epidermal thickness. When temperatures reach a low but non-lethal range from 0–15 degrees Celsius, plants respond by increasing the rigidity of their cells, protecting damage to the cell membrane to some extent. But a plant's long-term survival depends on its ability to evolve epigenetic, or environmentally-driven, adaptations, such as the ability to produce anti-freeze proteins that inhibit freezing in plant cells even at below-freezing temperatures. Agricultural scientists experimenting on *Zea mays* (maize) crops have successfully transferred single genes that have encoded anti-freeze proteins into the plants and allowed *Z. mays* to survive up to one degree below freezing, suggesting that _____

---

11 ☐ Mark for Review

Which choice most logically completes the text?

Ⓐ anti-freeze proteins are capable of protecting *Z. mays* crops if their cells are not too rigid.

Ⓑ *Z. mays* is one of the only types of crops that will accept a single gene transfer.

Ⓒ if *Z. mays* plants can evolve this adaptation on their own, the range of low temperatures they can endure may increase.

Ⓓ anti-freeze proteins are incapable of adequately protecting *Z. mays* plants from low temperatures.

> What was the last idea introduced before the blank? How does that help you?

Here's How to Ace It

Don't get too bogged down in the descriptions of cell membranes and epigenetic adaptations. The last idea before the blank states that *scientists experimenting on Zea mays (maize) crops have successfully transferred single genes that have encoded anti-freeze proteins into the plants and allowed Z. mays to survive up to one degree below freezing*. Therefore, *Z. mays* using such a feature to help survive freezing temperatures is at least possible, even if they had a little help. Stay consistent with this idea and don't be tempted to choose answers that go beyond what this limited information can support.

Eliminate (A) because it's **Recycled Language**—increasing the *rigidity* of their cells is part of a plant's response to cold weather, but the development of *anti-freeze proteins* is an adaptation for *long-term survival*. The two features are not discussed together in the passage. Eliminate (B) because it's **Extreme Language**—it's not known from the passage whether *Z. mays* is one of the *only* crops that will accept a single gene transfer. Keep (C) because it's already been demonstrated in the passage that *Z. mays* specimens with anti-freeze proteins can at least survive *up to one degree below freezing*, so this should also be true if they were able to produce the proteins naturally. Eliminate (D) because this is the **Opposite** of what the passage shows—the anti-freeze proteins were actually quite capable of *protecting Z. mays plants*, at least up to a degree below freezing. The correct answer is (C).

Here's a second example of Scenario 6 to try on your own.

Azerbaijani Ashiq is an art form that incorporates storytelling, dance, instrumental and choral music, and poetry into a live performance. It is considered a symbol of Azerbaijan culture, which has Turkic, Caucasian, and Iranian influences. The primary characteristic of an Azerbaijani Ashiq performance is the presence of the kopuz, a stringed instrument, and modern-day Azerbaijani Ashiq comprises over 200 songs and nearly 2,000 poems. Each region of the country, including Kalbajar, Ganya, Touz, Borchali, and Gazakh, performs the art of the Azerbaijani Ashiq a little differently, such as incorporating rustic art, wind instruments, or omniscient narrators. This suggests that _____

12 ☐ Mark for Review

Which choice most effectively completes the text?

(A) the exact composition of any Azerbaijani Ashiq piece may be influenced by the region in which it's performed.

(B) any Azerbaijani Ashiq performance must incorporate art, music, and narration.

(C) the significance of Azerbaijani Ashiq is in its preservation of the Turkic, Caucasian, and Iranian cultures.

(D) the art form is marked by rigid consistency in a wide variety of locations and cultures.

Here's How to Ace It

As fascinating as it is to learn every detail of the Azerbaijani Ashiq, notice the word *This* at the start of the incomplete idea—it's directing you to the last complete idea before the incomplete sentence, which states that *Each region of the country…performs the art of the Azerbaijani Ashiq a little differently, such as incorporating rustic art, wind instruments, or omniscient narrators*. Regardless of any other details concerning the art form, this idea must be present in any acceptable conclusion.

Keep (A) because it's a rather direct paraphrase of the last complete idea. Eliminate (B) because it's **Extreme Language**—it's not stated that an Azerbaijani Ashiq performance *must* incorporate each of these elements. The passage states that it depends on the region as to which of these elements will be included. Eliminate (C) because it goes **Beyond the Text**—the fact that the Azerbaijani Ashiq draws influence from these three cultures does not support that it helps to preserve these cultures, even if that seems logically true. Eliminate (D) because it's the **Opposite** of what's stated by the last complete idea—different elements are incorporated into the Azerbaijani Ashiq based on the region its performed in. The correct answer is (A).

> When faced with a dense, meandering passage on a Conclusions question, keep your focus on the last idea before the blank. Be prepared for a wide variety of trap answers based on different components of the passage that a student could get distracted by.

Challenging Scenarios Drill

Try to use all of your skills as you attempt this chapter's drill and see how much your accuracy has improved. Answers and explanations can be found in Chapter 12.

Time: 8 minutes

1 ☐ Mark for Review

The following text is adapted from Beatrice Harraden's 1894 short story "The Bird On its Journey."

Miss Blake, who never listened to what anyone said, took it for granted that the little girl was the tuner for whom M. le Proprietaire had promised to send.

"Really, it is quite abominable how women thrust themselves into every profession," she remarked, in her masculine voice. "It is so unfeminine, so unseemly."

There was nothing of the feminine about Miss Blake; her horse-cloth dress, her waistcoat and high collar, and her billycock hat were of the masculine genus; even her nerves could not be called feminine.

Which choice best states the function of the underlined sentence in the text as a whole?

(A) It presents the background information that is described in the subsequent sentences.

(B) It states an opinion made by a character who the text later describes in further detail.

(C) It generates a comparison between two characters described in the excerpt.

(D) It expounds on the prior sentence's portrayal of the character.

2 ☐ Mark for Review

Text 1

After being freed from slavery in 1817, John Edmonstone became a taxidermist and professor in Scotland. He taught the craft of taxidermy to Charles Darwin, who attended the University of Edinburgh in 1826. Because Edmonstone had spent time performing taxidermy in warm environments, he learned techniques to speed up the process before bird specimens decomposed. His teaching allowed Darwin to successfully preserve Galapagos finch individuals, and Darwin would likely not have become as famous as he did without the techniques he learned from Edmonstone.

Text 2

While John Edmonstone did contribute greatly to the field of taxidermy, Charles Darwin would still have been the most influential figure of evolution without learning from Edmonstone. Edmonstone only taught Darwin different methods for the preservation of birds, but Darwin also analyzed tortoises, kangaroos, platypuses, bees, ants, and barnacles. Without Edmonstone's influence, Darwin's work may have been forced to exclude bird species, but he almost certainly still would have had enough evidence to formulate his theory of evolution.

Based on the texts, the author of Text 1 and the author of Text 2 would most likely agree with which statement?

(A) Without Edmonstone, Charles Darwin would not have been able to develop his theory of evolution.

(B) Darwin taught Edmonstone how to properly preserve birds after learning the techniques on his travels.

(C) John Edmonstone's expertise in the taxidermy of birds contributed to the development of a theory.

(D) Edmonstone and Darwin equally contributed to the development of the field of evolution.

3 ☐ Mark for Review

The following text is adapted from Ivan Turgenev's 1872 novella "Torrents of Spring."

In one of the outlying streets of Moscow, in a gray house with white columns and a balcony, warped all askew, there was once living a lady, a widow, surrounded by a numerous household of serfs. Her sons were in the government service at Petersburg; her daughters were married; she went out very little, and in solitude lived through the last years of her miserly and dreary old age. Her day, a joyless and gloomy day, had long been over; but the evening of her life was blacker than night.

Based on the text, what is true of the widow?

(A) Some people dislike that her family has left her.

(B) Many people would disregard her were it not for her unique-looking house.

(C) Her family has come to understand her negative tendencies.

(D) Her experiences have become even less positive now that she is older.

4 ☐ Mark for Review

The ability of our machines to perform tasks has improved greatly with the addition of artificial vision systems such as cameras and motion detection. Certain types of automobiles are now self-driving as they can detect obstacles and adjust their speed accordingly. Crop monitoring devices can now "spot" dryness in the soil and adjust irrigation frequency. However, the inability of an artificial system to adapt to a change in terrain (which causes light to refract differently) limits the applicability of these systems to some extent. Researchers at MIT are attempting to develop an artificial eye that converges all of the light rays from numerous sources into one spot on a single image sensor, regardless of the refractive index of the media the light rays travel through.

Which finding, if true, would most directly undermine the researchers' attempt?

(A) Different image sensors are needed to process visual stimuli from land versus visual stimuli underwater.

(B) Previous prototypes of the artificial eye utilized two or more cameras, the weight of which made the model essentially immobile.

(C) The cost to develop technologies such as self-driving cars and crop monitoring systems is an impediment for most investors.

(D) It is determined that amphibians, which often experience changes in terrain from land to water, demonstrate better vision in the water.

5 ☐ Mark for Review

Records of Scraping by Fish Species
of Different Sizes

Species Name	Records of scraping	Percentage of scraping conducted on sharks	Common FL (cm)
Yellowfin tuna	47	96%	150
Southern Bluefin tuna	17	94%	160
Skipjack tuna	4	0%	80
Hawaiian salmon	38	71%	69

Parasites can deplete their hosts of resources and energy and cause damage to the regions of the hosts' bodies on which they live. Ocean-dwelling fishes are hosts to a diverse array of parasites, but their ecosystem provides limited options for parasite removal. A 2022 study showed that, in an attempt to rid their bodies of parasites, offshore fish will scrape their bodies against other fish, including sharks. The researchers surmise that fish prefer to scrape against sharks, whose skin is rougher than that of other fish species, but they suggest that this interaction is limited to fish of a certain size, as smaller fish (those with shorter fork lengths, or FL) may be more at risk of predation. However, using data from this study, a marine biologist asserts that a smaller fish size does not necessarily indicate a preference for scraping.

Which choice best describes data from the table that support the marine biologist's assertion?

Ⓐ Skipjack tuna were recorded to scrape against sharks 0% of the time and have a common FL of 80 cm, while Hawaiian salmon were recorded to scrape against sharks 71% of the time and have a common FL of 69 cm.

Ⓑ Yellowfin tuna and southern Bluefin tuna have common FLs of 150 cm and 160 cm, respectively, and were recorded to scrape against sharks 96% and 94% of the time, respectively.

Ⓒ Skipjack tuna were recorded scraping only 4 times, suggesting a preference for a different parasite removal method other than scraping.

Ⓓ The larger tuna species observed in the study were recorded to scrape against sharks more than 90% of the time.

6 ☐ Mark for Review

In Arabic music, maqam is a system of melodic composition that relies on improvisation to define the patterns and pitches within musical pieces. Maqam pieces do not exhibit regular patterns, although there are scales within the system that use consistent modulation and notes. In addition, most defining principles of the maqam system were passed down by oral tradition rather than written record, leading some to claim that modern maqam is an approximation of traditional maqam. Therefore, some musicologists have commented that

_____

Which choice most logically completes the text?

(A) the lack of a written record for maqam was likely influenced by the extreme difficulty in composing music that lacks a regular pattern.

(B) while some of the general principles of maqam music are known, both its nature and its method of preservation will lead to inconsistency among maqam compositions.

(C) although those who originally composed maqam pieces may have been Arabian musicians, they passed down their knowledge of systems to musicians of many diverse ethnicities.

(D) before the invention of the maqam system, Arabian musicians borrowed heavily from the established melodies of other cultures.

Chapter 12
Reading Drills: Answers and Explanations

CHAPTER 5: READING INTRODUCTION

Diagnostic Drill (Page 48)

Throughout these explanations, we'll first *italicize* the words or phrases that help identify the question type. Any other *italicized* text in the main body of the explanation references either a clue, evidence, or argument from the question or passage that should be highlighted or a direct quote from the answer choices.

1. **A**   This is a Vocabulary question, as it asks for a *logical and precise word or phrase* to fill in the blank. The blank should describe the correlation between hemoglobin's oxygen-binding affinity and levels of acidity and carbon dioxide, so look for and highlight clues in the passage about that correlation. Highlight that *Elevated physical activity* prompts *increased carbon dioxide production*, and highlight the result of this, which is that *hemoglobin exhibits a decreased propensity to bind with additional oxygen molecules*. Since an increase in one element of the correlation results in a decrease in the other, a good word to enter in the annotation box would be "opposite" or "contrasting."

    - (A) is correct because *inverse* matches "opposite."

    - (B) is wrong because it's the **Opposite** of what's presented in the passage—in a direct relationship, the variables should all increase or all decrease.

    - (C) is wrong because *present* doesn't match "opposite."

    - (D) is wrong because an *alternating* correlation would mean that the correlation goes back and forth from direct to inverse, which the passage does not support.

2. **D**   This is a Purpose question, as it asks for the *function of the second sentence* in the passage. Read the passage and highlight clues in the sentence before and after that can help understand the function of the underlined sentence. In the sentence after, highlight that *Li and his colleagues published a paper considering the veracity of this second theory but concluded that it does not account for* certain evidence. Therefore, a good function of the underlined sentence to enter in the annotation box would be "introduce a theory that had a flaw."

    - (A) is wrong because it's **Extreme Language**—the passage does not offer *proof* of the theory from the first sentence. Furthermore, the underlined sentence doesn't offer any *new parameters*, as it presents only a contradictory theory to that of the first sentence.

    - (B) is wrong because it goes **Beyond the Text**—it's not known from the passage that the second theory is newer and therefore an *update* of any accepted theory, nor does the underlined sentence offer any *evidence*.

    - (C) is wrong because the underlined sentence does not cite any *technological advances* that may have corrected an error in the formation of the original theory.

    - (D) is correct because it's consistent with the highlighting and annotation—note that this answer doesn't just focus on the underlined sentence, but rather, the underlined sentence and its connection to the sentence after it.

3. **A** This is a Dual Texts question, as it asks what *the author of Text 2* would say about *the underlined claim in Text 1*. Read Text 1 and highlight the underlined portion, which is that *Moon rocks were so similar in isotopic composition to rocks on Earth that they link the Moon only to Earth and negate any trace of a foreign entity*. Then, read Text 2 and highlight what its author says about the same topic: if the *Moon formed in a mere few hours after Earth's impact with Theia*, this *could explain why the new moon retained material from Earth in its crust and lost vestiges from other parts of the solar system*. Therefore, the author of Text 2 has offered a scenario in which a foreign entity (Theia) could most certainly have been involved in the moon's formation. Enter "Text 2 doesn't discount foreign entity" into the annotation box.

- (A) is correct because it's consistent with the highlighting and annotation—the alternate explanation given by the author of Text 2 could explain why the Moon appears to have been influenced only by the Earth and not any foreign entities.

- (B) is wrong because it's **Recycled Language**—*isotopic similarity* is a phrase constructed from the underlined claim in Text 1 and has nothing to do with Text 2's agreement. Even more importantly, the author of Text 2 wouldn't *agree* with the claim, as the author offers an alternative theory.

- (C) is wrong because it's also **Recycled Language**—*other parts of the solar system* is lifted directly from the end of Text 2, but the author does not comment on whether material from those regions was *present* in the area surrounding the impact. Instead, the author focuses only on a timeline that might explain why the Moon's formation seems to have been influenced only by the Earth.

- (D) is wrong because it's **Extreme Language**—while there's no doubt the author of Text 2 would want anyone involved in the debate to consider the new timeline, nothing in the passage is *criticizing* the claim in Text 1. The author of Text 2 only proposes an alternate theory rather than makes any criticisms of Text 1.

4. **B** This is a Retrieval question, as it asks for a detail based on the text. Look for and highlight information about how *the abbé* reacts *when he sees a bird's nest in the mailbox*. Highlight the abbé's reaction: seeing the birds makes him *smile* and he says *"Rest easy, little one, I know you. Twenty-one days to hatch your eggs and three weeks to raise your family; that is what you want? You shall have it."* The *abbé* is promising to let the birds hatch their eggs despite the location of their nest inside the mailbox. The correct answer should be as consistent as possible with these details.

- (A) is wrong because it's **Half-Right**—the second half of this answer is supported, but the passage doesn't state that the abbé *questions the wisdom of the bird's nesting location*. He accepts it without any negative comment.

- (B) is correct because it's consistent with the highlighting—it's clear from the context of the passage that this is not a normal spot for birds to nest, as the abbé has to *take away the key* in order for them to have peace.

- (C) is wrong because it's the **Opposite** of the abbé's reaction—the passage makes it clear he will leave the birds be.

- (D) is wrong because it's also **Half-Right**—the abbé's smile may indeed be *amusement*, but the passage makes no comment on how *serious* the situation truly is.

5. **B** This is a Main Idea question, as it asks for the *main idea of the text*. Look for and highlight information that can help identify the main idea. While there is certainly a lot of sorrow expressed in the passage, only the line *On my heart is the black badge of exile* explains what the speaker is mournful about: being exiled from somewhere. Highlight the final three lines as the main idea. The correct answer should be as consistent as possible with this portion of the passage.

- (A) is wrong because it goes **Beyond the Text**—as logical as it is to assume that someone who is exiled *has been left alone*, it's entirely possible the speaker was exiled along with others. The passage does not mention this either way.

- (B) is correct because it's consistent with the highlighted portion of the passage—*dismayed* matches *mournful* and *exile* could be *separated from a particular location*.

- (C) is wrong because it's **Recycled Language**—the *thunder moving* and *rain heard beating* are similes to help explain the speaker's feelings, not actual instances of *bad weather*.

- (D) is wrong because it's the **Opposite** of the speaker's feelings toward wherever he has been banished from (it's unknown if this place was even *his home*.) Wherever it was, he feels *shame* and was not *eager to leave*.

6. **C** This is a Claims question, as it asks which finding *would most directly support her (Hirsch's) claim*. Look for and highlight the claim in the passage, which is that *in-person meetings were more dynamic interactions than Zoom meetings*. The premise of this claim, which should also be highlighted, is that *Communicating through a camera and a screen can decrease sensory engagement...as well as other neural signaling cues.* The correct answer should be as consistent as possible with this claim and its premise.

- (A) and (D) are wrong because they're the **Opposite** of the question task—if Zoom meetings had a *greater variety of vocal intonations* than in-person meetings, this would weaken, not support, Hirsch's claim. Similarly, it would also weaken Hirsch's claim if participants *in both Zoom and in-person meetings* received and acknowledged facial expressions on a *relatively equal* level.

- (B) is wrong because it's irrelevant to the claim—Hirsch's claim compares Zoom meetings to in-person meetings but does not focus on the *middle* of one versus the *beginning or end* of the other.

- (C) is correct because it's consistent with the highlighted claim—if *Neural signaling cues... appeared less frequently* during Zoom meetings than face-to-face conversations, that would be directly in line with Hirsch's claim.

7. **D** This is a Charts question, as it asks for *data from the table* that will *complete the example*. Read the title, variables, and units from the table. Then, read the passage and highlight the statement containing the same information, which is that *as the tarragon's concentration increased, the cytotoxic reduction percentage decreased*. The correct answer should offer accurate information from the table that is consistent with this claim and completes the example given regarding the MCF-7 cancer cell.

- (A) and (B) are wrong because they're each consistent with the table but irrelevant to the claim—the example begins with an MCF-7 cancer cell and must conclude with one in order to properly track the effect of an increase in tarragon concentration.

- (C) is wrong because it's irrelevant to the claim—the passage started with the highest tarragon concentration, so the correct answer should show a decrease in tarragon concentration along with an increase in reduction percentage, but this answer references the cisplatin-treated cell instead.

- (D) is correct because it's consistent with the table and the highlighted claim—if you consider the completed example in reverse, an increase in tarragon concentration from 100mg to 1,000 mg led to a decrease in cytotoxic reduction percentage from 94% to 53%, which is in line with the claim.

8. **C** This is a Conclusions question, as it asks what *most logically completes the text*. Look for the main focus of the passage, which is *the sweet potato crop*. Then, highlight the main points made regarding this focus: first, the passage states that there are *those who believe the crop was brought to the island by Polynesian explorers who were active at the time*. Then, an alternate theory states that the *sweet potato arrived at the island* by *seed dispersal from migratory seabirds*. The final sentence offers a hypothetical statement considering the implication if *sweet potato seeds arrived both through twelfth-century human visitors and seed dispersal via seabirds that had lived thousands of years ago*. If this were true, then both theories regarding the sweet potato crop's arrival could be correct. The correct answer should be as consistent as possible with this conclusion.

- (A) is wrong because it goes **Beyond the Text**—while the nature of archaeological surveys involves digging up the land at times, it's not claimed on the passage that this *accidentally disrupted* any evidence.

- (B) and (D) are wrong because they also go **Beyond the Text**—it's not stated which seeds are *easier to study* in the passage or that there is now a debate as to when the *Easter Island settlement was founded*.

- (C) is correct because it's consistent with both the highlighted theories and the implications of the hypothetical in the last sentence.

CHAPTER 6: EXPLORING ADVANCED VOCABULARY

Advanced Vocabulary Drill (Page 64)

1. **A**

Who/What	what observers and educators feel about the difficulty of engaging younger generations with historical content
Clue	*defies that thinking*
Transition	*while*
Annotation	"believe" or "think"

- (A) is correct because *suppose* matches "believe."

- (B) and (C) are wrong because they go **Beyond the Text**—just because the observers or educators believe something does not mean they can *empathize* with it or even *understand* it well.

- (D) is wrong because *deny* is the **Opposite** of "believe."

2. **C**

Who/What	support for the concept of virtual water
Clue	*has gained traction*
Transition	*however*
Annotation	"unanimous" or "undisputed"—note the word *not* before the blank.

- (A) and (B) are wrong because *determined* and *isolated* don't match "unanimous."

- (C) is correct because *universal* matches "unanimous."

- (D) is wrong because *waning* (decreasing) is the **Opposite** of unanimous.

3. **B**

Who/What	Hogan's interaction with the diverse arrangement of projects
Clue	*wrote novels and poetry, penned a script for a PBS documentary about Native American freedom of religion, and collaborated with other authors for National Geographic nonfiction books*
Annotation	"worked on" or "produced"

- (A) and (D) are wrong because *settled for* and *agonized over* both go **Beyond the Text**—it's not known whether these projects were something that Hogan grudgingly agreed to or stressed herself thinking about.

- (B) is correct because *contributed to* matches "worked on."

- (C) is wrong because *recommended against* is the **Opposite** of "worked on."

4. **B**

Who/What	Fe del Mundo's interaction with the first modern pediatric healthcare system in the Philippines
Clue	*recognized for several innovations*
Annotation	"founding" or "creating"

- (A) is wrong because *revitalizing* (bringing back to life) would mean the system existed previously.

- (B) is correct because *pioneering* matches "founding" the first of something.

- (C) is wrong because *repudiating* (rejecting) is the **Opposite** of "founding."

- (D) is wrong because *monetizing* (making profitable) goes **Beyond the Text**—it's unknown whether the system made money or not nor is it stated if that was a goal of del Mundo's.

5. **D**

Who/What	the second way al-Jazari contributed to the field of mathematics
Clue	*he invented the elephant clock, a clock that uses water to maintain time*
Annotation	"inventive" or "creative"

- (A) is wrong because *whimsical* goes **Beyond the Text**—an elephant clock may sound quirky in name to some, but the author gives no such opinion toward the device itself.

- (B) and (C) are wrong because *debatable* and *incendiary* (provoking a reaction) are both negative opinions, but if anything, the author is positive towards al-Jazari's contributions.

- (D) is correct because *innovative* matches "inventive."

6. **D**

Who/What	a description of Brandur
Clue	*The neighbours thought he must have money hidden away somewhere* and knew he *had accumulated large stores of various kinds*
Annotation	"wealthy" or "rich"

- (A) and (B) are wrong because *sumptuous* and *opulent* (both meaning luxurious) go **Beyond the Text**—one could have a considerable amount of money without living luxuriously or decorating himself.

- (C) is wrong because *thunderous* (booming) doesn't match "wealthy."

- (D) is correct because *affluent* matches "wealthy."

CHAPTER 7: IDENTIFYING STRUCTURAL WORDS

Structural Words Drill (Page 86)

1.   **A**   In this Vocabulary question, *but* is a **pivotal word** that establishes a shift in the belief of how useful the cecal appendix is.

Who/What	the cecal appendix
Clue	*no meaningful biological function*
Transition	*but actually serves a purpose*
Annotation	"meaningless" or "useless"—note the word *not* in front of the blank

- (A) is correct because *vestigial* (now functionless) matches "meaningless."

- (B) is wrong because *adaptive* doesn't match "meaningless."

- (C) and (D) are wrong because *salient* (significant) and *beneficial* are the **Opposite** of "meaningless."

2.   **A**   In this Purpose question, *however* is a **pivotal word** that is used twice to impose a limitation of how well we understand inattentional blindness, stating that our understanding *may require some modification*. The correct answer should account for this idea that inattentional blindness does not always manifest the same way.

- (A) is correct because it accounts for the presence of the pivotal word and notes some inconsistencies in observations of inattentional blindness.

- (B) is wrong because *disprove* is **Extreme Language**—just because some individuals still notice fast-moving objects in their field of vision, an individual could still fail to notice other objects when focused on a task.

- (C) is wrong because it goes **Beyond the Text**—it's not stated in the passage which aspect affects inattentional blindness more.

- (D) is wrong because the *flaw* present in the passage is with any attempt to generalize inattentional blindness, not with Wallisch et al.'s experiment.

3.   **C**   In this Dual Texts question, *though* is a **pivotal word** in Text 2 that is used to caution that more work needs to be done, and the **example indicator** *For example* introduces one specific idea that needs to be looked into further. Therefore, the author of Text 2 is likely to going to remind others that more work needs to be done before passing judgment on the efficacy of a malaria vaccine.

- (A) is wrong because *overly cautious* is the **Opposite** attitude of that expressed in Text 1, which calls the results *very encouraging*.

- (B) is wrong because while Murphy and his colleagues *genetically altered the parasite that causes malaria*, the team is not described as having *discovered* the mechanism itself.

- (C) is correct because it accounts for the pivotal word, and the *questions that remain* are consistent with the *unknown* given in the example.

- (D) is wrong because while it's true that the results from Murphy and his team were *heralded*, *very encouraging* results from a different study wouldn't be surprising, as the results in both studies were positive. Also, it's not known that *most* people heralded the results, so this answer is also **Extreme Language**.

4. **B** In this Retrieval question, *This shortcoming may be eliminated* is a **contrasting phrase** in the last sentence that links the two sentences and indicates that the *new design strategy* may address a flaw in CLC.

   - (A) is wrong because it goes **Beyond the Text**—no other existing *methods of reducing carbon emissions* are mentioned in the text. Only one with *great potential* is discussed, which means this newer method does not yet exist.

   - (B) is correct because it accounts for the contrast stated within the last two sentences regarding how the newer method may address a known flaw of CLC.

   - (C) is wrong because it's **Recycled Language**—CLC uses metal oxides, but this answer compares them as if they were entirely different processes.

   - (D) is wrong because it goes **Beyond the Text**—while the passage does mention that the metal oxides used in CLC *gain and lose electrons*, it's not stated whether they *gain more electrons than they lose*.

5. **D** In this Main Idea question, *Contrary to* is a **contrasting phrase** in the final sentence that indicates that Anderson's results contradict the idea that *suppression harms mental health*. His patients, who had undergone suppression training, *reported lower levels of depression and anxiety*.

   - (A) is wrong because it's **Extreme Language**—it's not known from the passage that Anderson was the *first* to consider the effects of suppression on mental health in times of adversity.

   - (B) is wrong because it goes **Beyond the Text**, which doesn't discuss a *rebound effect* that makes thoughts *more vivid and intrusive*.

   - (C) is wrong because it's **Extreme Language**—while it's possible to assume that suppression training helped Anderson's patients, it's not supported to say it is *required* in order to override reflexive responses.

   - (D) is correct because it captures both the traditional view and the contradictory results found by Anderson in his study.

6. **B** In this Claims question, *According to one historian* is a concluding phrase that helps you identify the historian's claim quickly. While the rest of the passage is certainly helpful background, the correct answer must first and foremost be consistent with the final sentence, which contains this claim.

   - (A) is wrong because it's **Right Answer, Wrong Question**—this answer perfectly supports the premise of utopian societies from the second to last sentence, but does not address the historian's claim in the last sentence.

- (B) is correct because this quotation would address *the tension between individual freedom and the demands of communal societies* by calling the situation *inherently untenable* (unsustainable) and stating that the experiments were *soon abandoned*.

- (C) and (D) are wrong because they each go **Beyond the Text**. While both offer examples of potential issues with utopian societies (finance and agriculture), neither of them addresses *the tension between individual freedom and the demands of communal societies*, which is the crux of the historian's claim.

7. **C**   In this Charts question, *concluded* is a concluding phrase that directs you fairly quickly to the most relevant part of the passage. The goal is to choose an answer that directly addresses this conclusion while also presenting accurate data from the graph.

- (A) is wrong because it's the **Opposite** of the claim—the claim is that *hot foam was a viable alternative to spraying chemical herbicides*, but the second half of this answer calls out an instance (licorice) in which chemical herbicides outperformed hot foam.

- (B) is wrong because it's consistent with the graph but irrelevant to the claim—the answer should focus on how *hot foam was a viable alternative to spraying chemical herbicides*, but this answer focuses on both of them performing below a certain level.

- (C) is correct because it's consistent with the graph and relevant to the claim—while it begins nearly identically to (A), the second half of the answer continues to reference how *hot foam was a viable alternative to spraying chemical herbicides*.

- (D) is wrong because it's consistent with the graph but irrelevant to the claim—the claim made by Kup and Saglam references hot foam and spraying. While the two acknowledge that hoeing is the most effective weed control method, the **pivotal word** *while* indicates that the last part of the sentence is their actual conclusion.

8. **D**   In this Conclusions question, *though* is a pivotal word that shifts the focus of the passage from the idea that people want to receive constructive feedback to the idea that they avoid giving such feedback. Later, the example indicator *For example* makes it clear that the author wants to explain the second idea more completely. Therefore, this disparity between wanting to receive and wanting to provide should be accounted for in any conclusion to the passage.

- (A) is wrong because it goes **Beyond the Text**—the passage doesn't discuss the level to which one group estimates the desires of others to receive feedback.

- (B) is wrong because it's **Recycled Language**—this answer misuses the word *benefits* from the second sentence to make an unsupported claim about those who provide feedback, whereas the word is used in the second sentence to discuss those who want to receive feedback.

- (C) is wrong because it goes **Beyond the Text**—the passage doesn't discuss to what extent people *fail to notice opportunities* to provide feedback.

- (D) is correct because it captures the relationship of the two statements on either side of the pivotal word.

CHAPTER 8: UNDERSTANDING SENTENCE FUNCTION

Sentence Function Drill (Page 104)

1.   **A**   In this Purpose question, the underlined sentence is **evidence** that describes Georg's motivation. The following sentence is a **claim** based on the evidence that explains that Georg chooses letters as a way to accomplish his goal. The correct answer should be consistent with this evidence and reference the claim it supports.

   - (A) is correct because it's consistent with the evidence and claim—though *only* may seem extreme, the passage states his *sole desire* was to ensure his friend kept a certain image of their hometown intact.

   - (B) is wrong because it goes **Beyond the Text**—the passage offers no support for the idea that Georg *misses* this particular friend.

   - (C) is wrong because it's **Recycled Language**—the *young woman* referenced is marrying someone else, not Georg.

   - (D) is wrong because it goes **Beyond the Text**—even if this may be true in the real world, there needs to be explicit mention of this goal in the passage somewhere.

2.   **B**   In this Retrieval question, look for the sentence with a structural word or phrase to separate **claims** from **evidence**. The passage opens with a description of a palace, and the words *there*, *One gallery*, and *Here* help you understand that the second, third, and fourth sentences are just continuing to offer more descriptions of the palace and its contents. Read these as efficiently as possible: what you really want is a claim regarding Vathek. The concluding phrase *In a word* that begins the last sentence lets you know that you've found the claim that all of the evidence was building up to. Highlight this sentence and compare it to the answers.

   - (A) is wrong because it goes **Beyond the Text**—though Vathek has added a lot to the collection, he does not compare its grandeur to any other collections of its kind.

   - (B) is correct because it's consistent with the claim made about Vathek and the palace in the final sentence.

   - (C) is wrong because it's **Recycled Language**—it misuses the words *confound* and *arranged* from the second sentence to make an unsupported statement about Vathek himself.

   - (D) is wrong because it's the **Opposite** of the passage—the evidence in the third sentence implies that at least some *works of great artists* are present in one of the galleries.

3.   **C**   In this Dual Texts question, be on the lookout for each author's **claim** or **objection** regarding *Midnight's Children*. After the pivotal word *But* in Text 1, the author reveals a criticism of the novel, that *it may have benefited from its author heeding the call of his editor to rein in some of its cacophonous contradictions and digressions*. After a similar pivotal word, *Yet*, in Text 2, the author praises the novel, stating that *the seemingly overwhelming breadth itself tells a story, an epic so sprawling that to exclude even one of the legends or myths would do it a disservice*. Notice how the author of Text 1 discusses

some positives but wants to primarily focus on a negative, while the author of Text 2 discusses a potential negative before primarily focusing on a positive. The correct answer, and any annotation you make, should account for this difference.

- (A) is wrong because the author of Text 2 does not state that one should not *mix literary genres,* only that the author of *Midnight's Children* should have listened to his editor more. Additionally, the author of Text 2 does not offer personal feelings as to whether *political satire can be combined with magical realism.* If anything, calling the novel *unashamed* for combining these genres would be a criticism rather than a suggestion.

- (B) is wrong because while the author of Text 2 states that removing anything from the novel would be a disservice, this author does not specifically say that doing so would have affected the *political impact* of the novel. Also, it's not known from Text 1 that Rushdie *refused* to listen to his editor at all, just that he didn't reduce the length of the book.

- (C) is correct because it's consistent with both claims and accounts for the pivotal words included in each of them.

- (D) is wrong because the author of Text 1 does not specifically express *frustration* with the decision to make the novel three books, only with the overall length of the novel. Additionally, the author of Text 2 does not mention being *culturally honest* in the praise for the book.

4. **D** In this Main Idea question, look for the sentence with a structural word or phrase to separate **claims** from **evidence**. After two **background** sentences describing Fitzgerald and the influence of his wife Zelda on his career, the last sentence offers the concluding word *contend* to indicate a claim. This claim is more of an objection due to the contrasting phrase *more than just an inspiration.* The correct answer should be as consistent as possible with this final sentence, which serves as the main idea of the passage because of its use of structural language.

- (A) is wrong because it goes **Beyond the Text**—Zelda may have served an inspiration for the female characters in *This Side of Paradise*, but that doesn't mean the book is *based on* her life. Furthermore, she is not given any connection to *The Great Gatsby* from the first sentence.

- (B) is wrong because it's **Extreme Language**—while the claim indicates that Zelda's influence may be underestimated, there's not enough support to say that she *easily rivaled* her husband's contributions.

- (C) is wrong because it's the **Opposite** of what's stated by the passage—it's the *Fitzgerald biographers* themselves who are arguing Zelda was more than just an inspiration, and they don't call out any other group of biographers for having *greatly underestimated* Zelda's influence.

- (D) is correct because it's not only consistent with the claim but also consistent with the background evidence from the second sentence—Fitzgerald did acknowledge his wife's contributions, but not as much as he probably should have, according to the claim made in the last sentence.

5. **B** In this Claims question, you first need to read a **background** sentence, an **objection** that introduces a conflict, and another piece of **background** explaining the founding of Papp's theater. Do read these, but don't forget that the question stem itself tells you to look for the designer's **claim**, which is that Papp's *commitment was unwavering, evidenced by his preference for topical, sometimes controversial, content over even his inventive Shakespeare productions.* In other words, once Papp founded his theater, he went out of his way to present works that addressed the *contemporary, societal issues* that he felt most of Broadway neglected. The correct answer should offer **evidence** that would most support this claim.

- (A) is wrong because it's irrelevant to the claim—a project to save the theater district doesn't address Papp's preference for showcasing topical, controversial works over traditional Broadway entertainment.

- (B) is correct because it's consistent with the designer's claim—Papp is showing preference for something addressing a controversial topic over something offering entertainment.

- (C) and (D) are wrong because they're irrelevant to the claim—these answers discuss Papp's work outside of the theater, while the claim focuses on Papp's work in the theater itself.

6. **D** In this Conclusions question, the first sentence is **background** that tells you there is a theory, but not what the theory is. The second sentence is a **claim** which tells you the theory that the passage will focus on. The third sentence is **evidence** explaining the connection between ergot and hallucinations. The fourth sentence is an additional **claim** related to the original theory and explaining how residents may have become exposed to ergot. Most importantly, the last sentence is an **objection** stating that *there were surprisingly few cases of either gangrene or ergot poisoning diagnosed by physicians.* The correct answer should offer a conclusion based on this objection and reference the claims and evidence from earlier as needed.

- (A) is wrong because, if anything, it's the **Opposite** of what's implied by the passage—while the actual number of those affected is not given, the objection in the passage implies that the impact of ergot is overstated, not understated.

- (B) and (C) are wrong because each goes **Beyond the Text**—while either of these being true would certainly reduce the prevalence of ergot, note that the objection is focused on *medical records*, not agricultural or dietary ones.

- (D) is correct because it's consistent with the objection and its connection to the theory from earlier in the passage—if there were *surprisingly few cases of either gangrene or ergot poisoning*, then it's at least possible that the *influence of ergot poisoning* may have been overestimated.

CHAPTER 9: MASTERING PROCESS OF ELIMINATION

Opposite Attractors in Action Exercise (Page 110)

Which Answers to Eliminate and Why

i.	b, c – both negative words when a positive word should go in the blank
ii.	a – pales in comparison b – not precise enough
iii.	a – amateur b – predated
iv.	a – only notable contribution c – can be traced back to an artistic predecessor
v.	a – not c – inaccurate

Extreme Language Attractors in Action Exercise (Page 112)

Which Answers to Eliminate and Why

i.	a, c – both exaggerated forms of improve
ii.	b – condemn those who enjoy shooting and hunting c – more…should be turned into…sanctuaries
iii.	a – impossible b – proves
iv.	b – will c – only
v.	a – greatest c – most

Recycled Language Attractors in Action Exercise (Page 114)

Which Answers to Eliminate and Why

i.	a – American show business b – unique and powerful connection
ii.	a – entire theme park and CEO and president c – responsible/responsibly, several years, and theme park attractions
iii.	a – each… has a storied history as interesting as that of The Great Movie Ride c – more specific Hollywood or the more general American show business

Right Answer, Wrong Question Attractors in Action Exercise (Page 116)

Which Answers to Eliminate and Why

i.	*a* – gives the function of the second sentence *c* – gives the function of the last sentence
ii.	*a* – accurately describes the second sentence only *c* – accurately describes the fourth sentence only
iii.	*b* – accurately describes the third sentence only *c* – accurately describes the first sentence only

Beyond the Text Attractors in Action Exercise (Page 118)

Which Answers to Eliminate and Why

i.	*a* – often commemorated *b* – Audiences listening to Roman poets would form a circle around the speakers
ii.	*a* – would defend the land if it were attacked again *c* – optimal lighting
iii.	*a* – Greek and Roman mythologies share many commonalities *c* – longer human lifespan than in ages past
iv.	*a* – likely to be attacked again *c* – will continue to stand by…for many years to come

Half-Right Attractors in Action Exercise (Page 120)

Which Answers to Eliminate and Why

i.	*a* – *lack of respect* is **Opposite**—the text says *he was in general respected* *b* – *believer in the virtues of religion* is **Opposite**—he has a *well-known disregard for religion*
ii.	*b* – *joy and triumph* would not address a *disturbed emotional state* without some further explanation by the author *c* – this answer does not address that the Banshee's mood *reflects the manner of death that will be experienced by the individual she has chosen to haunt*

Process of Elimination Drill (Page 121)

1. **B** In this Vocabulary question, you must catch the clue that comes after the blank to know for certain whether Clark was for or against ending racial segregation.

Who/What	Clark's interaction with ending racial segregation
Clue	*calling for further changes that would even out the academic playing field for Black children*
Annotation	"supporter of" or "champion of"

- (A) is wrong because it's **Extreme Language**—it would be excessive to claim that Clark is an *expert* on something just because he wanted it to happen.

- (B) is correct because *advocate for* matches "supporter of."

- (C) and (D) are wrong because *opponent* and *adversary* are the **Opposite** tone of "supporter."

2. **D** In this Purpose question, the first sentence indicates that the passage focuses on a difference, while the second sentence is evidence explaining that difference.

- (A) is wrong because it's **Recycled Language**—two of the children may harass Nelly *terribly*, which is a striking word, but this doesn't mean she *finds her position terrifying*, and *potentially harmful* would be going even further **Beyond the Text**.

- (B) and (C) are wrong because each goes **Beyond the Text**—it's too specific of a conclusion to say either that Nelly expresses *resolve* to stay at her job despite some difficult children to manage or that she feels a *devotion* to the family employing her.

- (D) is correct because the main difference explained in the evidence is that of behavior.

3. **A** In this Dual Texts question, make sure to start with Text 2, as the answers focus on the author of Text 1's reply. Wrong answers will likely focus on the wrong author's view.

- (A) is correct because it's consistent with the relationship between the passages—if *children have created digital versions of these floating lanterns*, something like the krathong floating back to shore would be impossible, and the author of Text 1 states that *The krathong is an important material representation*.

- (B) and (C) are wrong because they're **Right Answer, Wrong Question**—if anything, these opinions are what the author of Text 2 may feel or agree with regarding the children's digital lanterns, not the author of Text 1.

- (D) is wrong because it goes **Beyond the Text**—it's too general of a claim to say that the entire celebration *has become a source of stress rather than one of optimism* just because Thai residents believe a krathong floating back to shore means to prepare for *potentially unwelcome* events.

4. **B** In this Retrieval question, the last sentence explicitly discusses applications of VR headsets. The correct answer must be consistent with this sentence but also not go beyond what this sentence can support.

- (A) is wrong because it goes **Beyond the Text**—any *limitations* to VR technology would be drawn from a student's real-world knowledge, as no such limitations are discussed in the passage.

- (B) is correct because it's consistent with the highlighting—it's a paraphrase of the last sentence that captures both of its points.

- (C) is wrong because it's **Recycled Language**—it takes *immersive*, VR *headsets*, and *technology* out of context to create an unsupported recommendation.

- (D) is wrong because it goes **Beyond the Text**—it's too specific of a claim to state that the learning will now occur at *a more rapid pace than ever before*.

5.   **C**   In this Main Idea question, all you receive is a series of descriptions. Look for an answer that summarizes all of them rather than focuses too sharply on one single description.

- (A) is wrong because it's **Recycled Language**—the narrator may mention *length* and *horseback* in the same sentence but does not discuss any *disadvantages* of traveling long distances on horseback.

- (B) is wrong because it goes **Beyond the Text**—using outside logic, it's easy to imagine someone pondering how an older house used to look, but no such thoughts are described in the passage.

- (C) is correct because it's consistent with each detail given by the narrator and summarizes all of the sentences without focusing too much on just one of them.

- (D) is wrong because it's **Right Answer, Wrong Question**—this answer captures only the descriptions in part of the first sentence and neglects to mention the description of his destination as well.

6.   **C**   In this Claims question, the claim in the second sentence of the passage has two aspects: *a decision made by the widow regarding her appearance* and a contrast with the decisions *made by others*. The correct answer must address both aspects of the claim.

- (A) and (B) are wrong because they're **Half-Right**—each makes some reference to *beauty*, which is connected to appearance, but neither makes a contrast and (A) does not seem to even relate to the widow directly.

- (C) is correct because it references both aspects of the claim—a decision the widow made to not conceal her *age*, and the fact that *some women* choose to do so.

- (D) is wrong because it's irrelevant to the claim, addressing neither aspect of it.

7.   **A**   In this Charts question, make sure to highlight the student's assertion. Remember that an answer being accurate based on the line graph is not enough—it must also address the student's assertion, which is specifically about the *decades directly following these periods of stagnation*.

- (A) is correct because it's consistent with the graph and the claim—both 1970–1980 and 2010–2020 follow the periods of stagnation in the 1960s and 2000s, and in both cases, men's wages grew at a sharper rate than did women's in those years.

- (B) is wrong because it's consistent with the graph but irrelevant to the claim—the student's claim is that *men's wages rose more rapidly*, not that that the rise was similar, and 1990–2000 is not a decade that directly follows a period of stagnation.

- (C) is wrong because it's not consistent with the graph nor is it relevant to the claim—the gap grows larger at some decade markers than others, and the correct answer should focus only on *the decades directly following these periods of stagnation.*

- (D) is wrong because it's consistent with the graph but irrelevant to the claim—while 1960 to 1970 and 2000 to 2010 may not have the steepest increases for men's wages, the focus should be on *the decades directly following these periods of stagnation*, not the periods of stagnation themselves.

8. **B** In this Conclusions question, don't lose focus on the incomplete sentence—it makes it clear that the correct answer must reference something to do with the *increasing temperatures associated with climate change*. Also don't forget that the last complete sentence before the incomplete sentence always plays a role in the correct answer.

- (A) is wrong because it's **Recycled Language**—while both *antifreeze proteins* and a *biofluorescent glow* are discussed in the passage, this answer creates an unsupported relationship between them.

- (B) is correct because it's consistent with both the incomplete sentence and the last complete sentence—if temperatures increase due to climate change, the Arctic environment may no longer be *too frigid for most fish species.* If other fish species migrated to these now warmer waters, this may make it harder for the snailfish to *feed and thrive* there.

- (C) and (D) are wrong because both go **Beyond the Text**—there is no evidence in the passage to support a specific claim like *other species of fish may evolve this adaptation* or that the snailfishes' *antifreeze protein may not allow them to survive in warmer waters.*

CHAPTER 10: WORKING WITH POETRY

Poetry Drill (Page 136)

1. **A** In this Purpose question, focus on the "I" pronoun and subsequent comparison within the underlined portion, which is *I prize thy love more than whole mines of gold.* The lines after this continue to expand upon the comparison, so a good annotation would be "show that she values her love more than gold."

- (A) is correct because it's consistent with the underlined portion and the annotation.

- (B) is wrong because no named *city* is referenced in the underlined portion.

- (C) is wrong because *more than any other wife could* is **Extreme Language**—it's clear that the speaker loves her husband a lot, but there's no support for the idea that another woman couldn't love her own husband more.

- (D) is wrong because it's **Recycled Language**—the reference to the *East* is part of the mention of wealth, not a *travel* destination.

2. **C**   In this Purpose question, use the passage of time *And when* in the third stanza to mark the transition from one set of activities to another. Initially, the speaker will *touch a hundred flowers* and *look at cliffs and clouds*. However, once *the lights begin to show / Up from the town*, she will *then start* her way down. Based on this, a good annotation would be "she will explore nature and head down to town once lights come on."

- (A) is wrong because it's **Half-Right**—no *consequences* are discussed in the third stanza of the poem.

- (B) is wrong because it goes **Beyond the Text**—it's not stated that the speaker will necessarily *run wild* while on the hillside nor that she will head down to the city specifically for *pleasure*.

- (C) is correct because it's consistent with the highlighting and annotation and also accounts for the transition in the poem.

- (D) is wrong because the speaker never describes the town as *precious* nor does she claim to have *admiration for it*.

3. **D**   In this Retrieval question, use the extra information to contextualize the story—the narrator is describing the *beauty of the countryside in Portugal*. Use the "I" pronoun to locate the narrator's main claim: *Nor…shall I vainly seek / To paint those charms which varied as they beamed—To such as see thee not my words were weak*. The narrator is claiming that his words are not strong enough to properly describe the charms of the countryside. Even if this translation is not obvious, going straight to the answers and comparing them back to the passage will help identify inconsistencies.

- (A) and (C) are wrong because each is **Recycled Language**—the words *language* and *paint* appear in the passage, but the narrator neither claims that *only certain languages* can describe the beauty nor that the countryside could inspire *an artist's painting*.

- (B) is wrong because it's the **Opposite** of what's stated in the first few lines of the poem—if the *climes* where the author has been visiting and the *visions* the narrator sees *Hath aught like thee* (have nothing like you do), he is stating that the Portuguese countryside contains beauty he has not seen before.

- (D) is correct because it's consistent with the highlighting and the narrator's claim that he doesn't have words strong enough to describe the Portuguese countryside.

4. **D**   In this Retrieval question, the passage does not provide a clear moment in which the significance of stars is given explicitly. Therefore, go straight to the answers and match them to the passage idea for idea rather than word for word.

- (A) and (B) are wrong because each has **Recycled Language**—stars *prisming every dazzling hue* does not mean stars *act like a prism used to guide people*, and the *earth darkens* and the *North wind blows* does not indicate an *ominous weather system that had caused the earth to darken*.

- (C) is wrong because it goes **Beyond the Text**—while the star is apparently a great form for man's hopes and ideals, nothing is discussed about the *symmetry* representing a *balance in life*. Furthermore, *not living* is a **Recycled Language** trap taken from *unbreathing* in the second line.

- (D) is correct because it's consistent with the description of stars in the poem—in three separate instances (each ending with a question mark), the speaker describes ways that we find stars occurring naturally or relevant to the lives of people.

5. **B** In this Main Idea question, note the pivotal word *But* in the first stanza stating that the speaker pities someone who *has a beard / But has no little girl to pull it*. Later, when discussing his own baby pulling his beard, note the "I" pronoun indicating a claim or opinion: *You'll not believe me when I say / I find the torture quite delightful!* The two main ideas then are that the speaker enjoys this interaction with his daughter and that he feels bad for those who cannot have such an interaction.

    - (A) is wrong because it's **Half-Right**—nothing in the passage supports that the speaker and his wife were *unable to conceive a child*.

    - (B) is correct because it's consistent with the two highlighted main ideas.

    - (C) is wrong because it's **Recycled Language**—it misuses *You'll not believe me* and *spiteful* from the poem to create a concern that the speaker does not express.

    - (D) is wrong because it's also **Recycled Language**—it misuses *feared* and *wrath* from the poem to create another concern that the speaker does not express.

6. **A** In this Main Idea question, the term *last month* at the end of the poem indicates a passage of time that sets up a contrast between two moments in the narrator's life. In the first four lines, the tone is more negative and the narrator seems to be dealing with cold and wet weather. In the last four lines, the tone is more positive and the narrator is thinking about the balmier (warmer) weather and laughter of the previous month. The correct answer should address the contrast between these two ideas.

    - (A) is correct because it's consistent with the contrast between and descriptions of the two moments in the narrator's life.

    - (B) is wrong because it's the **Opposite** of what is implied by the poem—the narrator seems to recall fondly *the beauty and warmth* of the past month rather than being upset for *not appreciating* it.

    - (C) is wrong because it's **Recycled Language**—it misuses *naked, woods,* and *golden* to make an unsupported claim.

    - (D) is wrong because it's the **Opposite** of what is implied by the poem—the narrator has a clear feeling toward the changing landscape (he doesn't like it compared to the previous month.)

7. **C** In this Claims question, immediately highlight the claim in the shorter passage, which is that *The poem describes how the aura of a woman is enhanced by her compassion for others.* Go straight to the answers and remember to match them to the passage idea for idea rather than word for word.

    - (A) is wrong because it's **Half-Right**—while this answer may describe the woman's aura in terms of her looks, there is nothing about *her compassion for others*.

    - (B) is wrong because it's also **Half-Right**—while this answer may discuss the woman having *compassion for others* (it does not directly describe her as compassionate, but her *hope* and *pride* in the school expresses at least some positive emotions), there is nothing that could mean her *aura is enhanced*.

- (C) is correct because it's consistent with the highlighted claim—*Her soul, like the transparent air / That robes the hills above . . . encircles . . . All things* could be the same as the woman's aura being enhanced, and *her compassion for others* could be *all things with arms of love*.

- (D) is wrong because it addresses neither aspect of the claim, only that the woman now works for a living and probably did not before.

8. **B** In this Claims question, immediately highlight the claim in the shorter passage, which is that *the poem… describes the springtime atmosphere*, and *McGirt lauds the season for being refreshing to the mind*. Go straight to the answers and remember to match them to the passage idea for idea rather than word for word.

- (A), (C), and (D) are wrong because they're **Half-Right**—each answer describes only an aspect of the *springtime atmosphere*. While (C) does include praise for the season, calling it a *joy*, none of these answers claims that the season is *refreshing to the mind*.

- (B) is correct because it's consistent with the highlighted claim—*a balm for the mind's the joyous spring* could mean that spring is refreshing to the mind, and the *fragrant nectar* and the *breezes* could be part of the *springtime atmosphere*.

CHAPTER 11: OVERCOMING CHALLENGING SCENARIOS

Challenging Scenarios Drill (Page 158)

1. **B** In this Purpose question, the pronoun *It* following the underlined portion indicates that the lines after will refer back to the underlined portion. The underlined portion includes an opinion of Miss Blake, and the lines after go on to describe her. Therefore, a good annotation would be "include an opinion stated by one of the characters."

- (A) is wrong because the information presented in the underlined portion, Miss Blake's opinion about women thrusting themselves into every profession, is not referenced in any of the *subsequent sentences*.

- (B) is correct because it's consistent with the annotation and the passage does go on to describe Miss Blake in *further detail*.

- (C) is wrong because there is not a second character described in the excerpt.

- (D) is wrong because it's **Right Answer, Wrong Question**—while the later sentences do expand on the description of Miss Blake as *masculine*, the first time this description is given is in the underlined sentence, not the *prior sentence*.

2. **C** In this Dual Texts question, go straight to the answers after reading both passages. Remember that the point of agreement is unlikely to be on the main arguments but rather on a detail such as background information or evidence.

- (A) is wrong because it's **Extreme Language**—neither author claims that Darwin *would not have been able to develop his theory* at all, just that he may *not have become as famous as he did* or may have been forced to exclude bird species.

- (B) is wrong because it's the **Opposite** of Text 1—Edmonstone taught Darwin the preservation techniques, not the other way around.

- (C) is correct because both authors acknowledge Edmonstone's taxidermic contributions to Darwin's theory. The point of disagreement is only on the impact of the contribution, but both authors agree that a contribution was there.

- (D) is wrong because neither author claims that the two men *equally contributed*—both acknowledge Darwin as the author of the theory but debate Edmonstone's level of impact.

3. **D** In this Retrieval question, go straight to the answers rather than highlighting every last idea about the widow, as it will be difficult to know which true detail the answers will focus on.

- (A) is wrong because it goes **Beyond the Text**—the widow's husband (through death) and children (through work and marriage) have left her, but the opinion of *Some people* toward those departures is not included in the passage.

- (B) is wrong because it's **Extreme Language**—though the widow's house is described, it's not described as *unique-looking* nor is it known whether *Many people would disregard* the widow if she lived in a home with less warping to it.

- (C) is wrong because it goes **Beyond the Text**—while families often do learn to live with a more negative family member, no comment is made in the passage about the widow's own family doing so.

- (D) is correct because it's consistent with the final sentence, while *Her day* had been *joyless and gloomy...the evening of her life was blacker than night*. The metaphor of day and night for the earlier part and later part of her life explains that her experiences *have become even less positive now that she is older*.

4. **A** In this Claims question, make sure to highlight the claim (or in this case, attempt), which is in the last sentence. Also note the information that occurs after the pivotal word *However*, as this relates to why the researchers are attempting to develop an artificial eye in the first place.

- (A) is correct because if *Different image sensors* are needed to process visual stimuli on the land versus in water, which are two different types of terrain, then the *single image sensor* that the researchers are attempting to build would not be sufficient.

- (B) is wrong because it's irrelevant to the claim—*Previous prototypes* being too heavy because of multiple cameras does not mean this issue will extend to the researchers' artificial eye.

- (C) is wrong because it's **Recycled Language**—*self-driving cars* and *crop monitoring systems* are taken from earlier in the passage and are not stated to be in the same cost category as the researchers' artificial eye. Additionally, there is not any evidence to suggest that *cost* is a hurdle the researchers are facing.

- (D) is wrong because it goes **Beyond the Text**—the ability of living beings to see better in one terrain type than another is irrelevant to what an artificial eye may experience.

5.   **A**   In this Charts question, highlight the assertion in the final sentence and notice that it focuses only on two of the variables from the table: size, represented by *Common FL*, and *Percentage of scraping conducted on sharks*. Also note the pivotal word *However* at the start of the assertion, which makes the sentence before important: *smaller fish* may choose not to scrape up against sharks because of the *risk of predation*. The correct answer should focus primarily on the connection, or rather the lack of connection, between FL and the percentage of scraping conducted on sharks.

- (A) is correct because it demonstrates that a smaller fish, the *Hawaiian salmon*, opted to scrape against sharks 71% of the time, while a larger fish, the *Skipjack tuna*, never opts to scrape against sharks. This is consistent with the marine biologist's assertion, which is that *size does not play a role* in whether a fish decides to scrape against a shark.

- (B) and (D) are wrong because they're the **Opposite** of the question task—if anything, these would support the researchers' claim, not the biologist's, that only larger fish risk scraping up against sharks.

- (C) is wrong because it's irrelevant to the claim—the total number of recorded scraping incidents is not part of the marine biologist's assertion.

6.   **B**   In this Conclusions question, work backwards from the incomplete idea. The pivotal word *Therefore* tells you to focus on the evidence immediately before the incomplete idea, which is that *most defining principles of the maqam system were passed down by oral tradition…leading some to claim that modern maqam is an approximation of traditional maqam*. The continuation phrase *In addition* at the start of this sentence means that the sentence before is also connected to the conclusion—the sentence before states that *Maqam pieces do not exhibit regular patterns*. Therefore, there are multiple reasons why a maqam piece one hears today could be different from another maqam piece. The correct answer should be as consistent as possible with this conclusion.

- (A) is wrong because it's **Recycled Language**—*written record* and *regular patterns* are taken from different parts of the passage, and no link is established between them relating to the *extreme difficulty* of maqam pieces.

- (B) is correct because it's consistent with both pieces of evidence concerning maqam.

- (C) is wrong because it's **Half-Right**—the second half of the answer goes **Beyond the Text**, as it is unknown whether maqam music was passed down to *musicians of many diverse ethnicities*.

- (D is wrong because it also goes **Beyond the Text**—it's not known from the passage that it was necessary for Arabian musicians to have *borrowed heavily* from other cultures.

Part III
SAT Advanced Writing Strategies

Chapter 13
Writing
Introduction

You already know from the Reading and Writing Introduction that the Writing portion of the module consists of Rules questions and Rhetoric questions (and if that isn't familiar, go back and read the Reading and Writing intro because it contains a lot of helpful information about the structure of the RW module!). In this chapter, we're going to take a closer look at exactly what topics make up each of these sections and their frequency. We'll also preview what Writing topics are covered in this book.

RULES

One of the most important things to know about the Rules portion of the RW module is that the number of topics is limited. There are plenty of writing rules in the real world, but only a very small number of them are tested on the Digital SAT. Knowing exactly what topics are tested will allow you to quickly identify how to approach each question, which will improve your time and accuracy. The chart below breaks down the Rules topics and their frequency.

Rules Topic	Description	Frequency
Question vs. statement	Tests whether the sentence should end with a question mark or a period (exclamation marks may show up as well) and the correct phrasing of the question or statement	Uncommon
Connecting clauses	Separating the text into two sentences by ending the first with a period or putting a semicolon, a colon, a comma, and/or a coordinating conjunction between clauses	Very common
Verb form	Choosing the correct form of a verb in order to produce a complete sentence	Very common
Describing phrases	Tests whether matching punctuation (two commas, two dashes, or possibly two parentheses) should surround a phrase	Common
No punctuation	Gives the option to use punctuation where there isn't a reason to use any	Common
Lists	Forming a simple list with commas or a complex list with semicolons	Uncommon
Subject-verb agreement	Choosing a singular verb to match with a singular subject or a plural verb to match with a plural subject	Common
Pronouns	Choosing the correct pronoun to match with a singular or plural antecedent, and possibly choosing between pronouns with and without apostrophes	Common
Verb tense	Choosing a verb in the correct tense to match the clues in the text	Common
Noun apostrophes	Determining the correct plural and/or possessive form of a noun	Uncommon
Modifiers	Identifying a modifier and making it modify something logical	Uncommon

These are the only topics that are tested on Rules, which means that you won't be tested on spelling, being concise, frequently confused words (like *affect* and *effect*), formal and informal language, capitalization, constructing a paragraph, or any of the numerous other skills that are needed in order to be a good writer. As we'll discuss in more detail in the next chapter, knowing and being able to recognize this limited set of topics will greatly help your score.

The frequencies that we included in this chart are based on the Digital SATs that have been released so far, which is a limited sample. It's impossible to say for sure exactly which topics will show up on your individual test. Furthermore, you're going to have only about 5–9 Rules questions per module, so it's not likely that you'll see more than a few from each topic. That being said, as a high-scorer, you'll want to master all of these topics if you want to get to 100% on Rules. You never know if College Board might decide to put 3 questions from an uncommon topic area in a given module.

In this book, we are not going to go over every Rules topic. Instead, we're going to focus on the ones that College Board is most likely to rate as Hard, as well as some trickier questions on various topics. If you're not familiar with any of the Rules topics from the chart, you may want to read through the Writing chapters of *Digital SAT Premium Prep* first to get a handle on the basics and to ensure you know how to approach the topics that aren't included in this book.

It's also worth noting that Rules questions go from easy to hard within that Rules portion of the module. The questions aren't grouped by these topics in any way. Whenever you decide to do Rules questions, feel free to skip around within that section and do whatever's easiest for you first. The types of questions we go over in this book will be more likely to show up toward the end of the Rules questions and in the harder second module.

RHETORIC

Rhetoric questions include only two types: transitions and Rhetorical Synthesis, in that order, so we won't bother putting them in a chart. Both of these are virtually guaranteed to show up in at least one module on your test. You'll likely see 1–4 transition questions and 0–6 Rhetorical Synthesis questions per module.

If you're not sure where to even start with these questions, first check out the Rhetoric chapter of *Digital SAT Premium Prep*, which explains how the questions work and provides a basic approach for each of the two Rhetoric question types. Then, the chapters in the book you're reading right now will give you more examples of harder questions on these topics as well as some strategies for approaching them.

CONCLUSION

If you need to work on Rules questions, move on to the next chapter because it provides some more in-depth information on the topics mentioned in this lesson. On the other hand, if you'd like to work on either transitions or Rhetorical Synthesis, feel free to skip directly ahead to those chapters.

Chapter 14
Rules Topics and
How to Spot Them

If you want to work through the RW module efficiently, it's not enough to know the Writing rules. You also need to be able to recognize when each is being tested, which will be a key focus throughout the Rules chapters, beginning with this one.

In the Writing Introduction, you saw a list of all of the Rules topics that can appear on the Digital SAT. In this chapter, we're going to take a closer look at these topics to show you how to spot them. First, let's talk about why and how to determine when a punctuation or grammar topic is being tested.

As you may have seen in *SAT Premium Prep* or one of our other books, our basic approach for Rules questions tells you to begin by looking at the answer choices. That's different from the way you should approach other questions, particularly for reading comprehension and transitions, but there's a good reason for this difference. If you start by reading the passage on a Rules question, it's not going to get you very far. That's because the passage contains a blank, and you'll truly have no idea what should go in the blank because it involves one or more words. So, to speed things up, look at the answer choices first so that you can see what those words are *and* determine what topic is being tested. There's no point in even thinking about whether you have a complete sentence if, say, apostrophes on nouns are changing in the answer choices. The way you read the sentence, and whether you even need to read any more of the text besides that one sentence, is determined by the topic of the question, which is determined by what's changing in the answer choices.

Let's revisit the Rules topics we went over in the Writing Introduction, but this time we'll see what the answer choices might look like for each one so that you can start to spot these topics right away.

Rules topic	Example of answer choices	Description of answer choices	Additional notes
Question vs. statement	A. was the study funded. B. was the study funded? C. the study was funded. D. the study was funded?	Typically, two answers end in a question mark and two end in a period (there could also be a wrong answer ending with an exclamation mark). There will usually be two different wording options as well—one that's appropriate for a question and one that's appropriate for a statement.	You'll need to determine whether the answer should be a question or a statement and how it should be phrased. Typically, two answers have inconsistent phrasing. For example, (A) and (D) are almost certainly wrong because in a statement the subject (*the study*) usually comes before the verb (*was*), while in a question, the verb usually comes before the subject.

Rules topic	Example of answer choices	Description of answer choices	Additional notes
Connecting clauses	A. documents, they B. documents. They C. documents and they D. documents they	Punctuation will vary in the answer choices, with a combination of these options: period, semicolon, comma by itself, comma + FANBOYS (for, and, nor, but, or, yet, so), FANBOYS by itself, no punctuation, colon.	If the sentence contains two independent clauses, (B) is the answer because the other three can't connect independent clauses. When the sentence contains two independent clauses, (A), (C), and (D) represent what you will almost certainly see in the wrong answers. The right answer can vary as there are several ways of connecting independent clauses.
Verb form	A. share B. sharing C. having shared D. to share	Verbs will change in the answer choices, but specifically, you'll see a "to" form and/or one or more -ing forms.	The answer is going to be either the "regular" or main verb form (like (A) here), the -ing form, or the "to" form. If you see more than one answer in the same form, like (B) and (C) here, they're almost certainly both wrong. We don't expect College Board to ask you to choose between two answers in the same form.

Rules topic	Example of answer choices	Description of answer choices	Additional notes
Describing phrases	A. author Aparna B. author, Aparna C. author, Aparna, D. author—Aparna	You may not always be able to spot when this topic is being tested, but if you see dashes, it's almost certainly this topic. Furthermore, if you see commas before and after a word or phrase, as in (C), that's a good clue it could be testing this topic. These questions usually don't include semicolons or periods in the answers.	If the answer contains a longer phrase and gives you the option to put punctuation before and after, just before, just after, or not at all, you can likely eliminate the options that put punctuation only before or only after the phrase. For this rule, the phrase either gets punctuation before and after the phrase or doesn't get punctuation at all.
No punctuation	A. of B. of: C. of, D. of—	You won't be able to spot these just from looking at the answers, but you'll know you're dealing with punctuation and can consider the various punctuation rules to decide whether any punctuation is needed.	If, as in our example, the punctuation follows a preposition (like *of*), there's a good chance that punctuation shouldn't be used, as prepositions usually aren't followed by punctuation. However, there are rare cases where punctuation can be used in such a place.

Rules topic	Example of answer choices	Description of answer choices	Additional notes
Lists	A. Baltimore; *Titanic*, B. Baltimore, *Titanic*, C. Baltimore; *Titanic*; D. Baltimore, *Titanic*;	Basic lists separated by commas won't be easy to spot by looking at the answer choices, as they'll look like other punctuation questions. Complex lists separated by semicolons are usually easier to spot, though. As in this example, you'll see semicolons and commas in at least two spots, and you probably won't see periods or FANBOYS words. For connecting clauses, the other topic that involves semicolons, you typically won't see the semicolon appear in multiple places in the answers.	The format of these answers suggests that the list involves semicolons, so the correct answer probably isn't (B) since that has only commas. Choice (C) also isn't the best guess because it puts *Titanic* by itself as a list item. A list item could be as short as a single word, but it's not all that likely in these sentences.
Subject-verb agreement	A. drives B. drive C. were driving D. have driven	The answers will contain verbs, and three of them will be plural and one will be singular, or three will be singular and one will be plural.	The answer is virtually guaranteed to be (A) here because it's the "odd one out"—all of the other options are plural. We don't think College Board will test tense or verb form in the same question as subject-verb agreement based on what we have seen so far.

Rules topic	Example of answer choices	Description of answer choices	Additional notes
Pronouns	A. some B. it C. they D. one	You'll see pronouns in the answer choices, typically a form of *it*, a form of *they*, and two oddball answers. Occasionally, apostrophes are also tested, in which case the answers will be *it's*, *its*, *they're*, and *their*.	The answer is almost certainly (B) or (C) here. College Board is testing you on whether the word the pronoun refers to is singular or plural, so whether this word is an "it" or a "they." The other two answers, whatever they are, are almost guaranteed to be wrong.
Verb tense	A. wrote B. will write C. was writing D. writes	Verbs will be changing in the answer choices, but you won't see the hallmarks of verb form or subject-verb agreement (both of which can also contain different tenses). In other words, all of the answers will produce a complete sentence and will agree with the subject.	Students often assume all verb questions test tense because the other verb topics can involve tense changes. Save yourself time and effort by learning to recognize verb form and subject-verb agreement. Consider tense only after you've ruled out those topics.
Noun apostrophes	A. dog's paws B. dogs paws C. dogs paw's D. dog's paw's	The answers will usually contain at least two nouns with apostrophes on them in some answers but not others.	It's very unlikely to have two plural, non-possessive nouns in a row like (B), so this is almost certainly wrong. Likewise, (C) puts two nouns next to each other but the first one is plural and not possessive, another unlikely scenario.

Rules topic	Example of answer choices	Description of answer choices	Additional notes
Modifiers	A. Oluo wrote a book B. Oluo's book was written C. it was Oluo who wrote a book D. the book of Oluo was written	The answers will say something similar but with the words in a different order. You could also say that the subjects of the answers vary.	It's common that two answers will refer to the same thing, such as (B) and (D) here, which both refer to the book. In that case, neither one can be right. Furthermore, answers that begin with *it, there was,* or anything else that doesn't refer to something specific are almost certainly wrong, which eliminates (C). The answer is almost certainly (A). Note that you might see some answers that don't "sound good" (like *the book of Oluo* in (D)), but don't waste time thinking about that, since these questions are just testing you on matching the modifier with what it describes.

As you can see from the chart, some of these topics (such as apostrophes with nouns) will be very easy to spot. Others, such as some of the punctuation topics, can be a bit more ambiguous. When it comes to punctuation topics, if you're unable to tell which topic is being tested (or at least likely being tested) from looking at the answer choices, go ahead and read the text to see if you can determine whether there is a need for punctuation based on any of the various rules. Just knowing that the question is dealing with punctuation at least directs you to think about the structure of the sentence rather than other features.

You may also find it helpful to know that you don't always need to read the full text of the passage for a Rules question. Rules passages do tend to be shorter, so you won't save yourself tons of time, but if you know the question is dealing with punctuation within a single sentence, there's no point in reading any other sentences in the passage. It's always fine to read more if you need to, but that's likely going to be helpful only on question vs. statement, the connecting clauses questions that involve transitions (we'll go over them in the next chapter), verb tense, and possibly pronouns.

In the next two chapters, we'll take a closer look at a few of the trickier topics and harder questions within punctuation and grammar, in that order. Then we'll revisit identifying the topic, and you'll practice with the tips you learned in this chapter.

Chapter 15
Tricky Punctuation

You may find that you tend to get punctuation questions right but miss one or two on occasion. This chapter may help you fill in the few remaining gaps by examining some harder ways College Board can test punctuation.

As we've been doing throughout this book, we'll give you fair warning that this chapter does *not* cover all of the punctuation topics. Some, such as Question versus Statement, tend to be ranked Easy or Medium and don't seem to give high-scorers much trouble. Others, such as Lists, are straightforward even when they're ranked Hard, and we've covered all of the basics for these topics in *Digital SAT Premium Prep*. Instead, for this lesson, we're specifically looking at the types of punctuation questions College Board tends to rank Hard as well as the nuances of these questions that high-scorers tend to get hung up on.

Let's start with questions that ask you to connect independent clauses. As you should already know, two independent clauses can be connected in the following ways:

> FANBOYS is an acronym for the coordinating conjunctions, which are **F**or, **A**nd, **N**or, **B**ut, **O**r, **Y**et, **S**o.

- Period (make each independent clause its own sentence)
- Semicolon
- Comma + FANBOYS
- Colon

Even after you've mastered those rules, there's a version of this question that we think may still trick you. Here's an example.

---

1   ⚑ Mark for Review

In 2022, evolutionary biologist Elizabeth Sinclair, ecologist Martin Breed, and colleagues published a study regarding a giant seagrass meadow in Shark Bay, off the coast of Western _____ genetic testing, the team determined that the meadow is actually a single clone of Poseidon's ribbon weed, *Posidonia australis*, that has grown to a size of 70 square miles over the course of its 4,500-year lifetime, making it the world's largest organism.

Which choice completes the text so that it conforms to the conventions of Standard English?

- (A) Australia. Using
- (B) Australia, using
- (C) Australia using
- (D) Australia and using

Why This Question is Hard

When you read the first part of the sentence and look at the answer choices, here's what you might think it's saying: *In 2022, evolutionary biologist Elizabeth Sinclair…published a study regarding a giant seagrass meadow in Shark Bay, off the coast of Western Australia, using genetic testing.* In that case, you're going to pick (B)—and get the question wrong. This sentence as we just wrote it makes perfect sense and is correctly punctuated on its own. However, if we read the rest of the sentence, it says *the team determined that the meadow is actually a single clone… that has grown to a size of 70 square miles….* This also sounds fine on its own, but we need to identify that it's an independent clause. Since the first part is also an independent clause, now we have two independent clauses separated by only a comma, which is never allowed.

So, if you don't finish reading the sentence, you can easily make a mistake by assuming that *using genetic testing* belongs with the first part of the sentence. To avoid making a mistake, you need to recognize that the parts of the text before and after *using genetic testing* are both independent clauses. There's a comma after *using genetic testing*, but a comma alone can't connect two independent clauses. Therefore, the answer choice needs to provide a punctuation option that will properly connect the independent clauses. That eliminates (B), (C), and (D), as those represent the three standard ways you *can't* punctuate two independent clauses. Thus, (A) has to be the answer, and it makes each of the independent clauses its own sentence, with *Using genetic testing* belonging to the second one.

Here's How to Ace It

It's common that for Hard questions on connecting independent clauses the second independent clause will begin with some type of describing phrase that may seem like it's part of the first independent clause, which can make it tempting to stop reading there. Instead, make it a habit to always read the entire sentence and consider whether it has two independent clauses. Better yet, if you see a period or a semicolon in the answer choices, determine whether you have independent clauses both before and after where the period or the semicolon would go, in which case that's your answer.

Let's try another one.

<table>
<tr><td>2</td><td>☐ Mark for Review</td></tr>
</table>

Previously, it was believed that the Amazon rainforest had been wilderness, untouched by human intervention. The updated perspective is that humans arrived in the Amazon at least 10,000 years ago and began cultivating certain plants there at least 8,000 years _____ making the jungle into a network of gardens, Indigenous people domesticated the cocoa tree, the Brazil nut, and the rubber tree.

Which choice completes the text so that it conforms to the conventions of Standard English?

(A) ago,

(B) ago

(C) ago;

(D) ago and

Why This Question is Hard

As with #1, when you start from the beginning of the sentence, you'll probably assume that *making the jungle into a network of gardens* goes with the first part. Including this phrase, it's an independent clause, and it makes perfect sense! However, that then leaves a comma and an independent clause in the rest of the sentence, and we know that two independent clauses can't have only a comma in between.

Here's How to Ace It

Start by looking at the answers instead of reading the passage. Choice (C) has a semicolon, which is used to connect two independent clauses, so instead of just reading the sentence on its own, try reading it in two parts—one part before the semicolon and one part after. Are they both independent clauses? Yes! So, (A), (B), and (D) have to be eliminated, and (C) is the answer because it's the only one that can connect two independent clauses.

Let's look at another type of connecting independent clauses question that College Board tends to rate Hard.

---

3 ☐ Mark for Review

The first interpretation of the Endangered Species Act by the US Supreme Court was the 1978 case *Tennessee Valley Authority v. Hill*, which halted the construction of the Tellico Dam in Tennessee because it would endanger the snail darter fish in the Little Tennessee River. The dam was completed in _____ the passage of a public works appropriations bill earlier that year made the project exempt from the Endangered Species Act.

Which choice completes the text so that it conforms to the conventions of Standard English?

(A) 1979 however,

(B) 1979, however;

(C) 1979, however,

(D) 1979; however,

Why This Question is Hard

Most Digital SAT Writing questions test only one skill, but this type of question tests two: connecting independent clauses *and* transition placement. Even if you do well with the transition questions that come after Rules, this is a different type of skill because instead of choosing the transition word, you're deciding which part of the sentence it belongs with. This is also less rule-based than the other Rules topics since you need to actually understand the content of the passage and not just the structure of the sentence.

Here's How to Ace It

Hopefully, you don't find it difficult to eliminate (A) and (C) here. When you look at the two parts of the sentence, you'll discover that both are independent clauses, so they can't be connected with just commas. Next is the harder part: you need to determine which side of the sentence the transition goes with. Start with the first part of the sentence. If *however* goes with the first part, that means *The dam was completed in 1979* would disagree with what came before. This could work because the previous sentence says that the dam's construction was *halted*. It's not a bad idea to try it the other way, though. If *however* goes with the second part of the sentence, then the completion of the dam would need to contrast with the bill exempting the dam from the Endangered Species Act. These ideas don't contrast—they agree because the second part of the sentence helps explain why the dam was completed. Thus, the correct answer must be (B) because the contrast word needs to go in the first part of this sentence to go against what was stated in the sentence before.

We'll also note that it's possible to see a question like this that doesn't contain two independent clauses but is instead a single independent clause where the transition falls in the middle and is just separated by commas. So, while questions that look like this usually contain two independent clauses, be sure to verify that before eliminating the answers with just commas.

Let's try another one, this time with a same-direction transition.

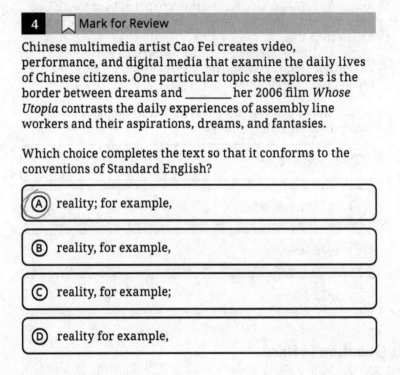

4 ☐ Mark for Review

Chinese multimedia artist Cao Fei creates video, performance, and digital media that examine the daily lives of Chinese citizens. One particular topic she explores is the border between dreams and _____ her 2006 film *Whose Utopia* contrasts the daily experiences of assembly line workers and their aspirations, dreams, and fantasies.

Which choice completes the text so that it conforms to the conventions of Standard English?

(A) reality; for example,

(B) reality, for example,

(C) reality, for example;

(D) reality for example,

Why This Question is Hard
By its nature, this type of question tends to be rated Hard, for the reasons we mentioned on question 3.

Here's How to Ace It
Like before, start by determining whether the sentence contains two independent clauses. It does, so that means (B) and (D) are out. Next, decide which half of the sentence *for example* belongs with. If it goes in the first part of the sentence, then *One particular topic she explores is the border between dreams and reality* would need to be an example of what's stated in the first sentence, which is that Fei's work examines *the daily lives of Chinese citizens*. It sounds more like the first part of this sentence is elaborating on Fei's focus, rather than providing an example, as *the border between dreams and reality* doesn't have a clear connection to *daily lives of Chinese citizens*. Try putting the transition with the second part of the sentence. In that case, the description of *Whose Utopia* needs to be an example of what's in the first half, the topic of *the border between dreams and reality*. Is the film an example of that? Yes! The second part of the sentence mentions *daily experiences* versus *aspirations, dreams, and fantasies*, and it's providing the name of a specific work in order to give an example of how Fei explores this topic. Thus, *for example* needs to go in the second part of the sentence, so eliminate (C) and choose (A).

Let's take a look at another topic that College Board tends to rank Hard and that students tend to struggle with: colons. As we noted earlier, a colon can be used to connect two independent clauses. Even if you don't often do this in your own writing, it's important to know that this is possible. It's also a reminder of why POE is so helpful: you may not *want* to use a colon within a sentence, but if the other three answers break the punctuation rules, then you have to pick the colon even if it's not your preferred way of writing the sentence. You also need to know that, in order to use a colon, the first part of the sentence—the part before the colon—must be an independent clause. However, the second part of the sentence doesn't have to be. It can be an independent clause, or it can be a list or even a single item. But it needs to elaborate on the first part in some way. It's not *describing* the first part; it's essentially saying what the first part is or explaining what the first part means.

Although you're probably fairly comfortable picking a colon when the second part involves a list, College Board still ranks almost all questions where colons are correct as Hard. It's also worth noting that lists aren't always easy to spot, so even if you feel more comfortable with this usage, you may struggle to notice the list. Let's try a couple examples of questions involving colons.

---

5   🔖 Mark for Review

The reason the majority of the poetic works of the aqyns—speakers of extemporaneous, song-like soliloquies—have been lost is at least partially due to the nomadic lifestyle of the Kyrgyz and Kazakh _____ their lack of permanent settlements has resulted in significant limitations on written records. Thus, oral tradition has been the aqyns' primary means of recording and transferring knowledge.

Which choice completes the text so that it conforms to the conventions of Standard English?

(A) peoples, though

(B) peoples:

(C) peoples,

(D) peoples though

Why This Question is Hard

If you read this text, you will probably think to yourself that you'd like to put a period or maybe a semicolon between the two independent clauses. Of course, those options don't show up in the answers! That's why it's best not to come up with a way of writing the sentence on your own. Use POE instead, and it will save you time and help you avoid making a mistake. Many students, when they see that the period and semicolon aren't in the answers, are likely to overlook the colon because they don't see a list or they simply don't like colons. (If that's you, get used to it! Colons are okay!) Instead, they might look at an answer like (A) because it appears technically correct. This does produce a complete sentence that's punctuated correctly. But given that two options have *though* and two don't, it's important to consider whether this transition is appropriate.

The first part of the sentence states that the *nomadic lifestyle* of these people has caused their *poetic works* to have been *lost*, and the second part says *their lack of permanent settlements has resulted in significant limitations on written records*. They're basically saying the same thing! So, we definitely can't use *though* here, and (A) and (D) are out. You should already know that a comma by itself can't work in between two independent clauses, so (C) can't work, and thus the answer has to be (B).

Here's How to Ace It

Again, make sure you are looking at the answers and using POE instead of trying to fill in the blank yourself. Consider all of the options fairly, and eliminate ones that violate the rules. When a sentence has two independent clauses, a period, a semicolon, and a colon can all work, at least the way they're tested on the SAT. This means that you're not going to see more than one of those in the answers for a sentence with two independent clauses, unless the answer choice makes some other type of error. If you ever see a question with transition words in only some of the answers, make sure to consider the meaning of the text and whether the transition word matches with those ideas or not.

---

6 🔖 Mark for Review

The surface of the Moon primarily features two distinct geological _____ Lunar Maria, flat areas dark in color and composed of basaltic lava that were formed by ancient volcanic activity, and Lunar Highlands, rugged mountains made up of anorthositic rock that cover most of both the far and near sides of the moon.

Which choice completes the text so that it conforms to the conventions of Standard English?

(A) regions:

(B) regions.

(C) regions,

(D) regions;

Why This Question is Hard

If you start from the beginning of the sentence and see the option with the period, you may be tempted to go ahead and pick it, since the first part could be a sentence on its own. Hopefully by now you've realized that this isn't a good strategy! If you think about it a little more, you may notice that there's also a semicolon, which also works with two independent clauses, and likewise with a colon. That should give you a real hint. Only one answer can be right, so maybe this text doesn't contain two independent clauses. Keep reading. The part after the blank mentions *Lunar Maria* and then gives a description of it that's surrounded by commas; then there's the word *and* and the name and description for *Lunar Highlands*. If it helps, ignore the describing phrases separated by commas. In that case, it just says "Lunar Maria and Lunar Highlands." Of course, that isn't an independent clause. It's a list of two things. This means (B) and (D) are definitely out because the second part isn't independent.

Next, compare (A) and (C). You should be thinking at this point that the colon works because the second part explains the first by stating what the *two distinct geological regions* are, so keep (A). As for (C), this option doesn't make it clear that Lunar Maria and Lunar Highlands are the two regions; the comma could make this look like a list of three separate things, which isn't what the sentence is trying to say. Thus, the answer must be (A). Remember, with a colon, the first part must be an independent clause, but the second part doesn't have to be.

Here's How to Ace It

As before, looking at the answers first and carefully using POE are your best friends. Suppose you see answers like (B) and (D), one with a semicolon and one with a period. Unless the sentence includes a list (the other use for semicolons—but periods normally don't show up on those questions), then neither option could be correct since a period and a semicolon are interchangeable on the SAT. Remember, on the SAT, a period, a semicolon, and a colon all work equally well to connect two independent clauses. If you see more than one of those show up in the answers (without any other changes), chances are the sentence doesn't contain two independent clauses.

Now, let's move on to one final topic that is frequently rated Hard by College Board: describing phrases. These are phrases that add additional detail to the main meaning of a sentence and, using our terminology, can be either Specifying or Extra. Specifying phrases are essential to a sentence's meaning—the sentence changes its meaning or doesn't make sense without the phrase. Thus, Specifying Information shouldn't be separated from the rest of the sentence in any way. By contrast, Extra Information isn't essential to the sentence's meaning. Removing Extra phrases results in a sentence that still means the same thing and is just a little less detailed. Since these phrases aren't essential, they're separated from the rest of the sentence with commas, dashes, or parentheses (if the Extra phrase comes in the middle of the sentence, it needs matching punctuation both before and after it).

One reason this topic is often rated Hard is that in the real world it comes with a lot of gray areas. This is one punctuation rule that can have some flexibility, in that there are places where one person might use a comma and another person might not, and either could be fine. Of course, those gray areas aren't tested on the Digital SAT. The only way College Board tests this topic is in a way in which the answer is very clear according to the rules. Another "gray area" with this question type is that sometimes a sentence can legitimately be written with or without punctuation, depending on the meaning you wish to convey. Here's an example:

My sister who's older than I am is going to summer camp.

My sister, who's older than I am, is going to summer camp. My sister—who's older than I am—is going to summer camp. My sister (who's older than I am) is going to summer camp.

Both of these sentence variations can be correct, but they suggest different things. In the first example, the describing phrase *who's older than I am* isn't separated with punctuation, so it's Specifying. That means that it's being used to specify which sister we're talking about, so this sentence implies that the speaker has more than one sister. It's the one who's older who is going to summer camp. Presumably, there's also a younger sister, so the speaker is specifying which sister is going to camp.

On the other hand, the second sentence separates the phrase with punctuation (any of the three can work here), suggesting that the phrase is Extra and we don't need to specify which sister we're talking about. This implies that the speaker only has one sister (or the audience is already aware of which sister is being discussed), and the Extra information is just giving an additional detail that isn't needed in order to know who we're referring to.

Again, don't worry about sentences like this on the SAT. The Writing passages are short, and it's not at all likely that you'll have to infer something like whether a person has one or more sisters in order to answer these questions. Here's basically how these questions can appear:

1. Sentences in which it's 100% clear whether the phrase is Specifying or Extra
2. Sentences in which the original sentence already has punctuation or lacks punctuation before or after the phrase, so you only need to match that and not decide whether the phrase is Specifying or Extra
3. Sentences in which it may not be clear whether the phrase is Specifying or Extra, but only one answer is possible. The wrong answers make other punctuation errors, so you can get the answer through POE without deciding whether the phrase is Specifying or Extra.

As you can see from the list above, you'll only need to determine whether a phrase is Specifying or Extra in cases that don't have ambiguity. Of course, that's coming from the perspective of grammar experts, though, and *you* might have trouble understanding the difference, so try the following exercise to practice distinguishing Specifying Information from Extra Information. Then, try some example SAT questions.

Describing Phrases Exercise

Directions: If the sentence needs punctuation before and/or after the bolded phrase(s), add it. If the sentence is correct as written, put a check mark next to it. Answers can be found in Chapter 20.

_____ ✓ 1. This morning I couldn't find the shirt **that always gives me luck on test days.**

_____ ✓ 2. The flowers **in the garden** still need to be watered.

_____ 3. Split weight training—**a workout style that involves exercising different parts of the body on different days**—is popular with both beginners and advanced lifters.

_____ ✓ 4. Before his Hollywood success with science fiction action films such as *Robocop* and *Starship Troopers*, Dutch filmmaker **Paul Verhoeven** was highly acclaimed for his romantic drama *Turkish Delight*.

_____ ✓ 5. I can tell that the cat **with the orange hair** has been napping on my clean clothes.

_____ 6. **Made from overlapping horizontal slats,** Venetian blinds (and the shadows they formed) were a visual trope of the film noir genre.

_____ 7. **As demonstrated by Albert Einstein,** the speed of light **in a vacuum** is the same for any observer regardless of how fast that observer is traveling.

_____ ✓ 8. German Baroque composer **Georg Philipp Telemann** wrote the first known concerto for viola.

_____ ✓ 9. The new store at the intersection of Main Street and Second Avenue is hiring anyone **who is able to lift more than fifty pounds**.

_____ 10. Though the term *houndstooth* for the textile pattern was not used until the 1930s, evidence **of the pattern** dates back to the Bronze Age and has been found in the Hallstatt Celtic Salt Mine, **the world's oldest salt mine.**

7 ☐ Mark for Review

Dominican American poet and translator Rhina Espaillat is known for rhyming poems that follow traditional forms and focus on everyday experiences. These include _____ that describe episodes from her own family life.

Which choice completes the text so that it conforms to the conventions of Standard English?

(A) sonnets, referred to by the poet as "snapshots"

(B) sonnets referred to by the poet as "snapshots"—

(C) sonnets referred to by the poet as "snapshots,"

(D) sonnets, referred to by the poet as "snapshots,"

Why This Question is Hard

College Board ranks most questions in the describing phrases topic as Medium or Hard, as it's a topic students tend to struggle with. Many students don't know the rule being tested and tend to rely on sound or how the sentence feels, which often results in a wrong answer.

Here's How to Ace It

Don't do the hard work yourself. First, identify that describing phrases is the topic being tested. The punctuation in the answers includes only commas and dashes, and they appear around a specific phrase. That's a solid clue that describing phrases are being tested. Use Process of Elimination instead of trying to decide for yourself how the sentence should be punctuated.

Choice (A) puts a comma before the phrase but not after, which means that the main meaning of the sentence is *These include sonnets* and the whole rest of the sentence, *referred to by the poet as "snapshots" that describe episodes from her own family life*, is a describing phrase. This could potentially work, so keep (A). Choice (B) puts a dash after *"snapshots,"* which would suggest that the phrase beginning with *that* is Extra. However, phrases beginning with *that* are always Specifying and shouldn't be separated with punctuation, so (B) can't be right. Choice (C) makes the same mistake by putting a comma before the phrase beginning with *that*. Choice (D) puts commas around the phrase, suggesting that the main meaning of the sentence is *These include sonnets…that describe episodes from her own family life*. Compare this meaning to (A). In (A), the *poet* refers to the sonnets as "snapshots" that describe something, whereas in (D), the poet refers to the sonnets as "snapshots," and these sonnets describe something. Choice (D) makes a lot more sense because the commas separate the poet's name for the sonnets and the rest of the sentence explains what the sonnets do. Thus, (D) is the answer.

8 ☐ Mark for Review

According to a recent study by a team of researchers including biologist Jessica Carson of the Liverpool School of Tropical Medicine and chemist Bart Kahr of New York University, heating samples of the commonly used _____ in a household microwave oven rearranges the compound's crystal structure, making it significantly more effective against malaria-carrying mosquitoes resistant to other methods of chemical control.

Which choice completes the text so that it conforms to the conventions of Standard English?

(A) insecticide, deltamethrin

(B) insecticide deltamethrin

(C) insecticide deltamethrin,

(D) insecticide, deltamethrin,

Why This Question is Hard

As before, this topic tends to be considered harder. Furthermore, if you look at the answers, you'll notice that you have the option to use two commas and the option to use no commas, which means you have to figure out for yourself whether the phrase is Extra or Specifying.

Here's How to Ace It

Notice that you have the four combinations in the answers: comma before, comma after, two commas, no commas. In that case, if you can't find any other reason to use a comma (besides possibly for Extra Information), you can go ahead and eliminate (A) and (C). Remember, the rule is either two commas or no commas, so just the comma before or just the comma after can't work (unless it's there for another reason, but there isn't another reason here). Next, try it with the commas. If there are commas around *deltamethrin*, that suggests that the name is Extra and that the sentence still works without the word, so read the sentence without it: … *heating samples of the commonly used insecticide in a household microwave oven rearranges the compound's crystal structure*. This meaning suggests that there is only one *commonly used insecticide*, but logically, surely there are multiple commonly used insecticides. Thus, the name of the insecticide is Specifying, not Extra. It specifies which commonly used insecticide the sentence is discussing. In that case, it shouldn't have any punctuation around it, and the answer must be (B).

9 ☐ Mark for Review

The ubiquitous _____ may soon have a new application. Titanium dioxide is a crucial component of dye-sensitized solar cells, an emerging technology promising lower production costs compared to conventional solar panels made of crystalline silicon.

existing or being everywhere at once; widespread

Which choice completes the text so that it conforms to the conventions of Standard English?

- (A) pigment used to give many household products their brilliant white color
- (B) pigment, used to give many household products their brilliant white color
- (C) pigment, used to give many household products their brilliant white color,
- (D) pigment used to give many household products their brilliant white color,

Why This Question is Hard

It's on the tricky describing phrases topic. Furthermore, it gives the option to use two commas or no commas, which means you have to decide whether the phrase is Specifying or Extra.

Here's How to Ace It

Notice the same four comma options as last time. As with question 8, there is no other reason to use a comma in this sentence, so (B) and (D) can be eliminated because each has only a single comma. Another way to eliminate them is to use the rule that a single punctuation mark can't come in between a subject (*pigment*) and its verb (*may...have*). Next, try out the Extra option, (C), by removing the phrase surrounded in commas from the sentence. In that case, it reads *The ubiquitous pigment may soon have a new application*. That probably sounds a bit weird, as we don't know what *ubiquitous pigment* is being discussed. The phrase *used to give many household products their brilliant white color* is Specifying. (Note that this phrase could start with "that is" and function the same way, and phrases beginning with "that" are always Specifying.) Since the phrase is Specifying, it shouldn't have any commas around it, so the answer is (A).

As you can see from the example questions in this chapter, following our basic approach helps avoid many errors. If you start with what's changing in the answers, identify what topic is being tested, and use Process of Elimination, you'll be much less likely to miss a question. Of course, knowing the rules is key as well, so if you still struggle to remember any, keep studying them until you know them cold.

Try the following drill for more hard questions on the topics from this lesson.

Tricky Punctuation Drill

Time: 10 minutes

Answers and explanations can be found in Chapter 20.

1 ☐ Mark for Review

A behavior of domesticated cats that has inspired multiple theories as to its motivation is that of kneading, or making _____ rhythmic pushing and pulling of the paws against soft surfaces such as pieces of furniture or carpets.

Which choice completes the text so that it conforms to the conventions of Standard English?

(A) biscuits; a

(B) biscuits: a

(C) biscuits a

(D) biscuits. A

2 ☐ Mark for Review

After working as an educator in his native Trinidad, Henry Sylvester Williams immigrated to Canada, where he studied law and co-founded a hockey league for people of color. In 1900 Williams organized the First Pan-African Conference in _____ in 1903 he moved to what is now South Africa to practice law.

Which choice completes the text so that it conforms to the conventions of Standard English?

(A) England, and

(B) England,

(C) England and

(D) England

3 ☐ Mark for Review

In traditional Korean woodworking, master carpenters called Daemokjang supervised the ornamental painters, roof tile makers, porters, masons, and plasterers. During the Korean eras of the Unified Silla, the Goreyeo, and the Joseon Periods, carpentry was a highly prestigious _____ builders often holding vaunted governmental positions.

Which choice completes the text so that it conforms to the conventions of Standard English?

(A) craft, the

(B) craft, and the

(C) craft; the

(D) craft. The

4 ☐ Mark for Review

In 1974, American singers Cher and Sonny Bono's pop music duo known as *Sonny and Cher*—as well as their marriage—came to an end. The dissolution of their act was not the end of Cher's singing _____ she would go on to record several disco and pop hits throughout the following decades.

Which choice completes the text so that it conforms to the conventions of Standard English?

(A) career; however,

(B) career however

(C) career, however,

(D) career, however;

5 ☐ Mark for Review

There are eleven distinct styles for reciting the Vedic mantras, ancient Indian religious _____ the Ghanapatha is the most complex, as it involves repeating the words backward and forward.

Which choice completes the text so that it conforms to the conventions of Standard English?

(A) texts

(B) texts:

(C) texts,

(D) texts while

6 ☐ Mark for Review

Burmese amber, fossilized tree resin from the Hukawng Valley in northern Myanmar, dates to the Cretaceous period and contains over two thousand species of flora and fauna, the vast majority of which are terrestrial arthropods. The amber has preserved some marine _____ this finding indicates that the amber is from a tropical forest near the ocean.

Which choice completes the text so that it conforms to the conventions of Standard English?

(A) organisms. Though,

(B) organisms, though,

(C) organisms, though;

(D) organisms, though

7 ☐ Mark for Review

According to the El-Sayed rule, electrons are more likely to switch to different electronic states when the electrons' vibrations are sustained during the change, as any change in vibration will be compensated by an adjustment in orbital motion. Proposed by Egyptian-American physical _____ in the 1960s, this rule is helpful for explaining phosphorescence and certain processes of atomic decay.

Which choice completes the text so that it conforms to the conventions of Standard English?

(A) chemist, Mostafa A. El-Sayed

(B) chemist Mostafa A. El-Sayed,

(C) chemist Mostafa A. El-Sayed

(D) chemist, Mostafa A. El-Sayed,

8 ☐ Mark for Review

In their study of domestic feline facial expressions, researchers Lauren Scott and Brittany Florkiewicz cataloged 276 differentiated intraspecific facial signals. Because wild cats and the ancestors of domesticated cats are solitary creatures, the majority of these cats' interactions with one another are considered competitive and aggressive. Domesticated cats have spent a large quantity of time together in non-adversarial _____ developing around 120 distinctly friendly facial expressions, according to Scott and Florkiewicz's observations.

Which choice completes the text so that it conforms to the conventions of Standard English?

(A) settings, however

(B) settings, however,

(C) settings, however;

(D) settings; however,

9 ☐ Mark for Review

Invented in 1991 by Dr. David Huang and colleagues, optical coherence tomography (OCT) is analogous to ultrasound imaging, though OCT uses light instead of _____ measuring light waves, OCT generates a detailed cross-sectional representation of the retina.

Which choice completes the text so that it conforms to the conventions of Standard English?

(A) sound and by

(B) sound by

(C) sound, by

(D) sound. By

10 ☐ Mark for Review

The lowland peat swamp forests on the island of Sumatra in Indonesia are lacking in nutrients but contain significant amounts of carbon. Because of agriculture, logging, and the production of palm oil, only 11% of these poorly studied swamp forests still _____ growing in a protected and predominantly undisturbed swamp forest, the recently discovered tree *Lophopetalum tanahgambut* is the only known species of its genus that has certain leaves in a pseudoverticillate arrangement.

Which choice completes the text so that it conforms to the conventions of Standard English?

(A) exist,

(B) exist and

(C) exist;

(D) exist

Chapter 16
Tricky Grammar

Only a few grammar topics are tested on the Digital SAT, but College Board can still find ways to trick students who are comfortable with those grammar rules. By familiarizing yourself with the approaches in this chapter, you'll better equip yourself to avoid any grammatical difficulties on test day.

In this chapter, we'll take a look at a few other Rules topics, ones that don't involve punctuation. Again, this won't cover every single non-punctuation Rules topic. We've chosen question types that tend to be ranked Hard and that high-scorers tend to struggle with.

Our first two topics look different but test something similar: subject-verb agreement and pronoun-antecedent agreement. Both question types require you to find another word and determine whether it's singular or plural. We'll start with subject-verb agreement.

---

1 ☐ Mark for Review

Gustav Holst's *The Planets*, an orchestral suite composed in the 1910s and consisting of seven movements, _____ not only to the planets themselves but also to their corresponding astrological personas, such as Saturn, the Bringer of Old Age, and Neptune, the Mystic.

Which choice completes the text so that it conforms to the conventions of Standard English?

(A) refer

(B) refers

(C) were referring

(D) have referred

Why This Question is Hard

The word right before the blank is *movements*, which is plural. That could make you want to pick (A)...or (C) or (D). (The fact that all three of those are plural actually suggests that none of them could be right.) The subject comes way earlier in the sentence: *The Planets*. This is another way the question tries to trick you, because *Planets* is also plural. However, the passage says that *The Planets* is *an orchestral suite*, so that phrasing means that the subject is actually singular, so (B) has to be the answer, as it's the only singular verb in the answer choices.

> Say "it" or "they" before each verb to test whether the verb is singular ("it") or plural ("they").

Here's How to Ace It

The biggest key to solving a subject-verb agreement question is to realize that agreement is the topic being tested. It'll save you a lot of time because you won't bother to consider tense or anything else related to verbs. Since (B) is singular and the other three options are plural, the question must be testing subject-verb agreement. Not only that, but you already know that (B) is almost certainly the answer because it's the odd one out. You should still find the subject to confirm, but recognizing this pattern can help immensely in avoiding a mistake.

Try the following exercise for more practice with subject-verb agreement. Then, try the Subject-Verb Agreement Drill for SAT-style questions on this topic.

Subject-Verb Agreement Exercise

Directions: Highlight the subject for the verb in brackets and circle the correct verb in the brackets. Answers can be found in Chapter 20.

1. Outselling books by authors who are far more famous now, Marie Corelli's occult romance novels, most of which fantasize about the potential spiritualized powers of electricity or radium, {was | were} attempts to give her theories of spiritual evolution a rational basis by assimilating ideas derived from contemporary science and technology.

2. Engraver and satirist William Hogarth's *Gin Lane*, a visual retrospective about the devastating effects of this newfangled spirit on the lives of London's poor, visually {portray | portrays} a frightful panorama of poverty, addiction, insanity, and violence.

3. Solitary confinement, which is today widely reviled as a severe punishment that calls to mind banging, buzzers, and unruly inmates, {was | were} originally inspired by Quaker ideas about the redemptive powers of silence and solitude.

4. The renowned French writer Charles Perrault, inspired by ancient folklore, myths, and fairy tales, {were | was} well known for having transcribed enchanting tales of "Cinderella," "Sleeping Beauty," and "Little Red Riding Hood," immortalizing them in his iconic book "Tales of Mother Goose."

5. Young tendrils of a pea plant, an annual with a life cycle of one year, often {grows | grow} in a pattern that resembles that of a child exploring the world and seeking things to climb.

6. Each of the dogs, all of whom were trained for at least two months, {have mastered | has mastered} the numerous skills necessary to be an effective guide dog for a visually impaired person.

7. Even the most dedicated teachers of literature, brimming with passion for artistic education, {are | is} often disillusioned when students do not share the same love of reading.

8. Many biographies written about Michael Jackson, a famous performer who began his long professional musical career at age 5 and who is widely revered as "King of Pop," {begin | begins} with descriptions of Jackson's unhappy childhood.

Subject-Verb Agreement Drill

Answers and explanations can be found in Chapter 20.

---

1 ☐ Mark for Review

Scientists in the field of quantum mechanics, in which particles behave in perplexing ways that defy classical intuition, _____ that the act of observing an object can fundamentally alter its properties, leading to the phenomenon known as the observer effect.

Which choice completes the text so that it conforms to the conventions of Standard English?

Ⓐ have discovered

Ⓑ has discovered

Ⓒ is discovering

Ⓓ discovers

---

2 ☐ Mark for Review

The thought-provoking portrayals of artist Amrita Sher-Gil, best known for her captivating and emotionally charged paintings that bridge the gap between traditional Indian aesthetics and Western modernization, _____ a lasting impact on the art world through her depiction of the complexities of human existence.

Which choice completes the text so that it conforms to the conventions of Standard English?

Ⓐ has left

Ⓑ is leaving

Ⓒ have left

Ⓓ leaves

---

3 ☐ Mark for Review

The work of prolific writer and diarist Anaïs Nin delves deep into the complexities of human emotions. The author's sensual and introspective prose, which often blurs the boundaries between reality and fiction, _____ both societal and artistic norms, paving the way for a more liberated and authentic self-expression.

Which choice completes the text so that it conforms to the conventions of Standard English?

Ⓐ challenge

Ⓑ challenges

Ⓒ have challenged

Ⓓ are challenging

---

4 ☐ Mark for Review

Lulu Washington, a visionary choreographer and dance educator, has carved an indelible ← *not able to be forgotten or removed* mark on the world of dance with her innovative and intricate movement compositions. Her choreographic style of seamlessly blended elements of contemporary, African, and jazz dance _____ a captivating tapestry of rhythm and expression.

Which choice completes the text so that it conforms to the conventions of Standard English?

Ⓐ is

Ⓑ were

Ⓒ are

Ⓓ have been

---

5 ☐ Mark for Review

In 1943, James Wright, a researcher at General Electric, was tirelessly striving to develop a substitute for rubber. His exhaustive experimentation on a myriad of substances, including many mixtures of solids and liquids, _____ finally and unexpectedly fruitful when he inadvertently combined boric acid with silicone oil, creating a peculiar substance that possessed astonishingly unique properties. This fortuitous fusion birthed Silly Putty, a malleable and viscous material that defied conventional classification.

Which choice completes the text so that it conforms to the conventions of Standard English?

(A) were

(B) have been

(C) are

(D) was

6 ☐ Mark for Review

The failure of the consumer-level video cassette recorder known as Betamax can be attributed to tough competition from VHS, which secured movie studio licensing and gained widespread consumer adoption. Additionally, the fateful decision of Sony's executives to keep Betamax exclusive to their own products _____ detrimental to its wide acceptance, allowing VHS to become the dominant video cassette format.

Which choice completes the text so that it conforms to the conventions of Standard English?

(A) were

(B) was

(C) are

(D) have been

Next, let's see how pronoun agreement is tested.

---

2 🔖 Mark for Review

An ancient stringed Chinese instrument known as the guqin is often associated with high class and refinement. The guqin is a very quiet instrument and ranges about four octaves; _____ can also produce a wide range of plucking and harmonic sounds.

Which choice completes the text so that it conforms to the conventions of Standard English?

(A) one

(B) this

(C) they

(D) it

Why This Question is Hard

The topic of the passage is *the guqin*. It's tricky because the text is describing guqins in general, but grammatically, the subject is singular because it says *the guqin*. That's what the blank is referring back to, so because it's singular, the answer is (D), not (C) as some students might want to pick. Choice (C) is also appealing because the part of the sentence after the semicolon sounds perfectly fine with "they," but the problem is that there isn't a plural noun for "they" to refer back to. Remember, a pronoun refers back to something that was specifically stated. Since the text specifically said *The guqin* (singular), the blank must be singular in order to agree. This is another example of why it's so important to follow the rules. Note that (A) and (B) aren't specific enough to refer back to *The guqin*.

Here's How to Ace It

Use the rules and the strategy, not your ear! You might think (C) sounds better than (D), but that doesn't matter. You're never being tested on sound. It's a good idea to highlight the word or phrase that the pronoun refers back to and annotate whether it's singular or plural. This will help you to avoid making a mistake.

Try the following exercise for more practice choosing between singular and plural pronouns.

Pronoun Agreement Exercise

Directions: Highlight the word or phrase that the pronoun refers back to (the antecedent) and circle the correct pronoun to agree with it. Answers can be found in Chapter 20.

1. The debate team assessed {their | its} performance after a recent competition in which another school surprised the competitors with a sweep of the categories.

2. Each of the schools' logos contained an image of the school district's mascot within {it | them}.

3. The pistol shrimp developed a frustrating trait: {their | its} claws can be shut hard enough to create a shock wave that interferes with sonar communication used by scientists to search for shipwrecks.

5. The researcher focused on removing the observer-expectancy effect and the sampling bias to ensure that {they | it} didn't affect the results of the survey.

5. Drawing asteroids and comets to {themselves | itself}, Jupiter protected Earth for millions of years by reducing the number of impacts Earth experienced and ultimately making it habitable.

Next, let's look at another grammar topic that students often struggle with: verb tense. Chances are, you don't have too much difficulty choosing whether a verb should be past, present, or future in most cases, but you may find it a bit more challenging to decide what specific form of each of those tenses is needed.

Here's an example.

---

3 ☐ Mark for Review

Since the beginning of the 19th century, puppeteers in Sicily _____ theatrical performances known as the Opera dei Pupi. The repertoire performed by the puppets ranges from short, humorous stories to medieval romances and Shakespearean plays.

Which choice completes the text so that it conforms to the conventions of Standard English?

(A) will stage

(B) staged

(C) have staged

(D) had staged

Why This Question is Hard

It's not at all hard to tell that the blank shouldn't be present or future tense, but unfortunately that only eliminates (A). There are three answers that seem related to past tense, and students often struggle to differentiate among these three—the simple past, present perfect, and past perfect, respectively.

Here's How to Ace It

Learn to recognize when each tense should be used and look for clues in the sentence or the rest of the passage. In this case, the answer is (C), because present perfect is used to describe something that started in the past and continues to the present. That's exactly the situation in this passage because the performance type started in the *beginning of the 19th century*, and the second sentence uses present tense to suggest that it still happens today. So, the present perfect tense with the helping verb *have* is correct.

Take a look at the following chart for some suggestions on differentiating tenses.

Tense	What it looks like	When it's used	Common clues
Simple past	Most simple past tense verbs end in *-ed*, but some (like *brought*, *went*, and *did*) are irregular.	For something that happened in the past, usually once or at a specific time	• References to specific dates or times • If it's not any of the other tenses in this chart
Present perfect	Present perfect verbs always start with the helping verb *has* (singular) or *have* (plural).	For something that started in the past and continues to today or happened an unspecified number of times in the past and could happen again	• The word *since* suggesting something happening over a period of time • A reference to something that has happened multiple times going up to the present (such as *this month* or *in the past ten years*)

Tense	What it looks like	When it's used	Common clues
Past perfect	Past perfect verbs always start with the helping verb *had*.	For something that happened prior to another event that already occurred in the past	• Another verb in the sentence that is already in simple past tense, and this event happened before the event the other verb refers to • Hypothetical statements with the word *if* • The sentence indicating something having happened "by" a certain time • The word *until* suggesting that a past action or event has ended
Past progressive	It will be in the form "was _____ing" or "were _____ing."	To refer to someone being in the process of doing something when some other past-tense event happened	• The word *when* appearing later in the sentence (someone was doing something *when* something else happened)

> You don't need to know the names of these tenses for the SAT, but make sure you know how to use them.

Next, try the following exercise and drill for more practice with verb tense.

Verb Tense Exercise

Directions: Highlight the clue(s) in the sentence and circle the correct verb to match. Answers can be found in Chapter 20.

1. I {watched | had watched | was watching} a video on my phone when a call startled me.

2. They {wanted | had wanted | have wanted} to go to the amusement park until they found out how much it was going to cost.

3. By the time the late bell rang, I {had completed | completed | have completed} the warm-up.

4. We {went | have gone | had gone} to the supermarket earlier today.

5. My friend Sam {goes | went | has gone} to the supermarket five times already this week.

Verb Tense Drill

Answers and explanations can be found in Chapter 20.

---

1 ☐ Mark for Review

American inventor Buckminster Fuller strove to pioneer technology that focused on obtaining the greatest gain from the smallest energy contribution. After co-inventing a map that accurately represented Earth's features when printed on a two-dimensional surface in 1943, Fuller _____ an educational simulation called the World Peace Game, which allowed players to use the map to attempt to solve real-world problems, such as overpopulation.

Which choice completes the text so that it conforms to the conventions of Standard English?

(A) was developing

(B) developed

(C) develops

(D) had developed

---

2 ☐ Mark for Review

Researchers at the University of Melbourne _____ the idea of using renewable energy to split water into its components to generate a renewable way to harvest hydrogen when they identified a challenge: freshwater sources are limited in some areas, so an alternative source, such as hydrogen in the air, needs to be explored.

Which choice completes the text so that it conforms to the conventions of Standard English?

(A) were exploring

(B) explore

(C) have been exploring

(D) will explore

3 Mark for Review

After starting her profession by helping families in Chicago navigate adoptions, American social worker Delia Villegas Vorhauer transitioned to a role directing a program that strove to provide vocational instruction and English lessons to non-native speakers. While Vorhauer's heritage was Mexican, she _____ deeply involved in supporting the Puerto Rican community, coordinating a conference focused on Puerto Rican affairs and earning a presidential award for her work.

Which choice completes the text so that it conforms to the conventions of Standard English?

(A) became

(B) will become

(C) has become

(D) is becoming

4 Mark for Review

By the time UNESCO incorporated Al Sadu, a form of Bedouin embroidery utilizing geometrical shapes to create a pattern, into the UNESCO List of Intangible Cultural Heritage in Need of Urgent Safeguarding in Kuwait in 2020, the practice _____ popularity in two main settings: urban towns, where it was primarily practiced by men, and desert communities, where it was primarily practiced by women.

Which choice completes the text so that it conforms to the conventions of Standard English?

(A) gained

(B) will gain

(C) has gained

(D) had gained

5 Mark for Review

Christiaan Barnard, a cardiac surgeon from South Africa, _____ a remedy for intestinal atresia, a condition that primarily affects infants, in 1953 and completed research on tubercular meningitis when he performed the world's first human-to-human heart transplant operation in 1967.

Which choice completes the text so that it conforms to the conventions of Standard English?

(A) already developed

(B) had already developed

(C) already develops

(D) was already developing

6 Mark for Review

Inspired by a similar play by French-Canadian playwright Michel Tremblay, Tomson Highway, an Indigenous Canadian author, published *The Rez Sisters* in 1986. The two-act play represents the experiences, hopes, and dreams of seven female characters in a genuine way. The play was intended to launch a cycle of seven plays, but the cycle _____ completed.

Which choice completes the text so that it conforms to the conventions of Standard English?

(A) is never

(B) was never

(C) had never been

(D) will never be

7 ☐ Mark for Review

In Turkish, Georgian, and Armenian societies, a poetic, singing bard—known as an ashik—traditionally accompanied his or her refrain with a long-necked lute. In modern settings, an ashik is typically a professional musician who _____ multiple instruments and a wide variety of musical pieces.

Which choice completes the text so that it conforms to the conventions of Standard English?

(A) would master

(B) had mastered

(C) has mastered

(D) will master

8 ☐ Mark for Review

Roberts's triangle theorem, named after British mathematician Samuel Roberts, who developed it in 1889, is utilized in discrete geometry to verify that the minimum number of triangular faces for any simple arrangement of lines is two fewer than the number of lines. Roberts _____ the theorem in 1889, but some mathematicians didn't accept it until 1979 when it was elaborated on by other mathematicians.

Which choice completes the text so that it conforms to the conventions of Standard English?

(A) had proposed

(B) is proposing

(C) was proposing

(D) proposes

There's one final grammar topic to go over: modifiers. These questions are generally ranked Medium or Hard because the topic is one that many students aren't familiar with. Let's begin with an example.

---

4 ▢ Mark for Review

In the 1780s, English philosopher and social theorist Jeremy Bentham proposed a design for a prison that would enable a single guard to observe the totality of the population of prisoners, though the guard would not be able to observe everyone all at once. Derived from the Greek word for "all seeing," _____ to act as though they were being watched at all times, since they could never be sure whether or not the guard was observing them at a given moment.

Which choice completes the text so that it conforms to the conventions of Standard English?

Ⓐ the term "panopticon" was selected for the prison, which was designed to compel the prisoners

Ⓑ the panopticon was designed to compel the prisoners

Ⓒ there was the panopticon, which was said to theoretically compel all prisoners

Ⓓ the single guard would have a view of all prisoners, who would be compelled

---

Why This Question is Hard

One reason these questions are often ranked Hard is that many students don't even realize what's being tested. They think the question is testing what order the words should go in, perhaps for the sake of being concise or to avoid awkward language. But, that's not what these questions are testing at all. Modifier questions don't have to be hard for *you*, as long as you recognize them and know the rule. If you do that, you'll find that these questions can actually be relatively quick and easy.

Here's How to Ace It

If you're familiar with the list of Rules topics we went over earlier, then you'll be able to use what's changing in the answers to recognize that question 4 must be a modifier question, and you'll know to immediately look for a modifier. Since the modifier says *Derived from the Greek word for "all seeing,"* the answer needs to begin with something that could be derived from a Greek word. The only answer that works for that is (A) because a *term* can be derived from another word. None of the other answers begin with something that can be derived from a word.

Try the following exercise and drill for more practice with this topic.

Modifier Exercise

Directions: Highlight the misplaced modifier. Draw an arrow to what it's currently modifying. Circle the noun that the modifier *should* be modifying. Answers can be found in Chapter 20.

1. Ringing loudly, Katelyn was awakened by the alarm clock going off at 6:00 AM.

2. On top of the whiteboard, my teacher had placed colorful decorations.

3. My sister had to go to the nurse with a headache.

4. Buried under a pile of clothes, I finally found my headphones.

5. While taking a quiz, Jason's patience was tested by the many confusing questions.

> So far, we've only seen College Board test modifiers at the beginning of a sentence.

Modifier Drill

Answers and explanations can be found in Chapter 20.

One of the most important inventions in the history of chemistry, the periodic table had several important precursors, such as the Law of Octaves first published by British chemist John Newlands in 1865. Named in analogy to the notes of a musical scale, _____

Which choice completes the text so that it conforms to the conventions of Standard English?

(A) Newlands organized the chemical elements by atomic weight and found a repeating pattern in their properties.

(B) the properties of chemical elements followed a repeating pattern when Newlands arranged these elements in order of atomic weight.

(C) chemical elements' properties showed a repeating pattern when the elements were ordered according to atomic weight.

(D) the Law of Octaves stated that the properties of chemical elements arranged according to atomic weight show a repeating pattern.

The National Film Registry, which is operated by the staff of the Library of Congress, seeks to preserve culturally and historically significant American movies that are nominated through a public ballot. By the time of its 20th anniversary in 2008, _____ These included popular full-length features as well as documentaries, short films, and other visual media.

Which choice completes the text so that it conforms to the conventions of Standard English?

(A) the Registry had added 500 movies to its collection.

(B) 500 movies were added to the Registry's archive.

(C) the members of the staff had selected 500 movies for addition to the Registry.

(D) there were 500 movies in the Registry's collection.

3 ▢ Mark for Review

The Earth is an oblate spheroid rather than a perfect sphere, meaning that its circumference is largest along the Equator and smallest from pole to pole. Located only one degree of latitude south of the Equator, _____ making it the farthest point on the planet's surface from the center despite the volcano's significantly lower elevation above sea level compared to that of Mt. Everest.

Which choice completes the text so that it conforms to the conventions of Standard English?

(A) the distance from the summit of the Ecuadorian volcano Chimborazo to the Earth's center is 3,967 miles,

(B) 3,967 miles of distance separate the summit of the Ecuadorian volcano Chimborazo from the Earth's center,

(C) there are 3,967 miles between the Earth's center and the summit of the Ecuadorian volcano Chimborazo,

(D) the summit of the Ecuadorian volcano Chimborazo is at a distance of 3,967 miles from the Earth's center,

4 ▢ Mark for Review

Cornelia Walker Bailey was a renowned storyteller and historian of the Geechee-Gullah people, a distinctive African American population of the southeastern US coast. Traveling to West Africa in 1989, _____

Which choice completes the text so that it conforms to the conventions of Standard English?

(A) there were many cultural similarities between the farming communities in Sierra Leone and Bailey's Geechee family and neighbors.

(B) Bailey noted many similarities between the culture of farming communities in Sierra Leone and the Geechee culture of her family and neighbors.

(C) the similarities between the culture of farming communities in Sierra Leone and the Geechee culture of Bailey's family and neighbors were noted in her account.

(D) Bailey's works noted many similarities between the culture of farming communities in Sierra Leone and the Geechee culture of her family and neighbors.

5 ☐ Mark for Review

A team of researchers led by biologist Marc Badger of the University of California, Berkeley, used a high-speed camera to study how Anna's hummingbirds (*Calypte anna*) are able to fly through an opening smaller than their wingspans. Flying more slowly and turning sideways, _____ close to their bodies as they carefully navigate the opening. The researchers hope to use the results to help engineers develop more maneuverable small aerial vehicles.

Which choice completes the text so that it conforms to the conventions of Standard English?

(A) the researchers found that the hummingbirds flutter their wings

(B) the hummingbirds' wings flutter

(C) the hummingbirds flutter their wings

(D) their study showed that hummingbirds keep their wings fluttering

And that wraps up some grammar topics that you might have had a bit of trouble with previously—and hopefully will be able to get right every time from now on. In the next chapter, we'll revisit the Rules question types and how to identify them so that you can get even faster and better at identifying when each topic is being tested.

Chapter 17
Rules Conclusion: Identifying Question Types, Saving Time, and Smart Guessing

Before we move on to the Rhetoric questions, we'll wrap up Rules by revisiting how to identify the topics (now that you are more familiar with them) and providing some miscellaneous tips that will help you get every last point.

If you have worked through the three preceding Rules chapters, you should now have a pretty solid idea of how to identify the question types we went over in this book. You may want to revisit the chart on page 194, now that you're more familiar with some of the topics, to see what to look for in the answers to identify each question type.

IDENTIFYING PUNCTUATION TOPICS

When it comes to punctuation topics, it takes a lot of practice to be able to identify what's likely being tested based on what you see in the answer choices. (Notice we say *likely* being tested, because you really can't tell for sure without reading the sentence.) You may find it helpful to look back at drills and practice tests you've completed to see for yourself what the answer choices tend to look like for the various types of punctuation questions. In some cases—for example, if the answers contain only a single word with different punctuation marks after it—you probably won't be able to tell what specific topic is tested at all. That being said, it still saves some time to look at the answers and merely identify that punctuation is changing, as that removes some topics from consideration. When in doubt, go to POE and eliminate any answer that violates any of the punctuation rules.

SMART GUESSING ON PUNCTUATION QUESTIONS

If you learn the rules, you shouldn't ever have to guess on a punctuation question, especially because most people find the Rules questions better to do early on, so you shouldn't be running out of time on these. Nevertheless, savvy test-takers may be able to have a good guess of what the answer is even before they read the text. Then, they can read the text to confirm.

Here are some ways to do that:

POE situation	Example	How it can help	Be careful of...
Period and semicolon	A. series, the B. series. The C. series; the D. series the	Choices (B) and (C) are essentially the same here, since a semicolon functions the same way as a period, so neither one can be correct.	Semicolons can also be used in lists. Questions on complex lists with semi-colons usually don't give you the option to use a period, but it's something to keep in mind.

POE situation	Example	How it can help	Be careful of...
Odd one out	A. computer. B. computer, and C. computer; D. computer	Choices (A), (B), and (C) are all possible ways to connect two independent clauses, so they're more or less interchangeable on the SAT. Choice (D) is the only one that can't connect two independent clauses, so it's likely that the sentence doesn't contain two independent clauses and (D) is the answer.	A semicolon or a comma followed by *and* could potentially be used for a list instead, so confirm that there isn't a list in the sentence.
Describing phrases without matching punctuation	A. author, who gave the speech B. author, who gave the speech, C. author who gave the speech D. author who gave the speech,	With describing phrases, if the phrase is Extra, it needs commas before *and* after it, and if it's Specifying, then it doesn't get any punctuation. This eliminates (A) and (D) right away.	There are other reasons to use commas, so (A) or (D) could be correct if the phrase is Specifying but there is another reason to use a single comma, or if it's Extra but the second comma comes later on in the original sentence. This rule works if there aren't any other commas or reasons to use commas in the sentence.
Standard format for connecting independent clauses	A. painting, the B. painting the C. painting. The D. painting and the	Two independent clauses can be separated into two sentences with a period or can be in the same sentence with a semicolon or a comma + FANBOYS. The three wrong answers are almost always the following: a comma by itself, no punctuation, and a FANBOYS word by itself. If you see this pattern, chances are there are two independent clauses and the answer that's not one of these three is correct.	If the sentence doesn't contain two independent clauses, there could be another reason to use a comma, use the word *and* by itself, or not use punctuation at all.

IDENTIFYING GRAMMAR TOPICS

Grammar topics are much easier to spot. You'll be able to tell from the part of speech in the answer choices whether the question is testing pronouns, nouns with apostrophes, or verbs. The two areas that are a little trickier to identify are the specific verb topics (verb form, subject-verb agreement, and tense) and modifiers. We'll take a closer look at identifying verb topics later in this chapter. Modifier questions are easy to spot *as long as you know how to recognize them*. Remember, modifier questions are the only ones that have a whole phrase changing in the answer choices. So, the answer choices don't show you that the question is testing modifiers, since the modifier normally comes before the blank, but if you're a savvy test-taker, then you'll know that that's the only topic that could be tested if entire phrases are changing in the answer choices.

SMART GUESSING ON GRAMMAR QUESTIONS

As we noted with punctuation questions, you shouldn't have to guess on grammar questions since they are so rule-based. However, as with punctuation questions, there are a few ways you may be able to get an idea of what is likely or not likely to be correct just by comparing the four answers. Here are some details:

POE situation	Example	How it can help	Be careful of...
Subject-verb agreement	A. was B. is C. were D. has been	Three answers are singular, and only one—(C)—is plural. In that case, chances are the question is testing subject-verb agreement and (C) has to be the answer because it's the odd one out.	Although we haven't seen College Board do this so far, it's possible that a question could test both tense and subject-verb agreement in the same question. In that case, one of the other options could be correct because it's the right tense and number.
Weird answers on pronoun questions	A. they B. this C. one D. it	Generally, on pronoun questions, you are really just choosing between a form of *it* and a form of *they*, so (B) and (C) aren't at all likely to be correct.	Although we haven't seen College Board do this so far, there's a remote possibility that one of the "weird" answers could be correct.
Repeat answers on modifier questions	A. Liu's research won several awards B. Liu won several awards for her research C. several awards were given to Liu for her research D. the research conducted by Liu won several awards	Choices (A) and (D) both begin with *research* (be careful with the possessive in (A)), so neither can be correct because modifier questions generally test you only on what the subject or beginning of each answer choice is.	Although we haven't seen this so far, it's possible to have a modifier elsewhere in the sentence. If the modifier comes after the blank, look at what's at the end of each answer choice instead.

THE THREE VERB TOPICS

In this book, we covered two of the three verb topics: subject-verb agreement and verb tense. You should already have an idea of what those questions look like from the Tricky Grammar lesson. Verb form questions also contain verbs in the answer choices, but they are testing you on something different: the construction of the sentence. If a sentence uses an incorrect form of a verb (for example, *My brother wanting a toy* or *My brother to want a toy* instead of *My brother wants a toy*), it won't be a complete sentence. Try the following exercise to practice identifying the three verb topics. Being able to identify which of the three topics is tested will save you a lot of time and help you avoid making mistakes!

Verb Topic Identification Exercise

Directions: Identify whether each set of answer choices is likely testing verb form, subject-verb agreement, or verb tense. Answers can be found in Chapter 20.

1. A) walk
    B) walks
    C) has walked
    D) was walking

Topic: _____Subject verb agreement_____

2. A) had written
    B) wrote
    C) will write
    D) writes

Topic: _____verb tense_____

3. A) to go
    B) going
    C) having gone
    D) go

Topic: _____verb form_____

4. A) began
    B) to begin
    C) begin
    D) have begun

Topic: _____verb form_____

5. A) approach
   B) have approached
   C) are approaching
   D) has approached

Topic: _____ Subject verb agreement _____

6. A) would share
   B) are sharing
   C) share
   D) have shared

Topic: _____ verb tense _____

Now you have learned all of the extra tips and tricks we can come up with for Rules questions. If you need to work on Rhetoric questions, continue to the next two chapters.

Chapter 18
Tricky Transitions

If you're reading this book, there's a good chance you find some transition questions easy. Some of these questions are quite straightforward, and if you read a lot, you may find yourself filling in a logical transition yourself as you read the sentences. On the other hand, if you've chosen to work through this chapter, you're probably struggling with some of the more challenging transition questions. Transition questions can be hard in two different ways. In this chapter, we'll examine both.

CONFUSING RELATIONSHIPS

Our basic strategy for transition questions tells you to determine whether the ideas agree, disagree, or involve a time change. It's a good idea to highlight the words that demonstrate this relationship and then use the annotation box to write down what the relationship is. Then, eliminate answers that don't match the relationship you wrote down, and use POE on anything that is remaining.

If you're not already using that strategy, try it out first. We think it will go a long way toward improving your performance on transition questions. One of the most common mistakes students make on transition questions is to look at the answers too early. Once they see a transition they like, they read the passage with that transition in mind, looking for a way to make the meaning of the text work with their desired answer. Of course, the answer that you choose before reading is, statistically, going to be wrong 75% of the time, so this is a really bad strategy. It's easy to interpret the text through the lens of an incorrect transition and convince yourself that it makes sense. Instead, as with Reading questions, make sure you understand the passage and the relationship between the ideas *before* even glancing at the answer choices. It'll make a big difference!

On the other hand, perhaps you're already using this strategy, and it's working on a lot of the questions, but occasionally you struggle to identify the relationship between the ideas. It may be that the passage is on a difficult topic and you have a hard time understanding what each sentence is saying. Or, the sentences may seem like they neither agree nor disagree. There are also some transitions that are very specific and can be difficult to predict if you're not familiar with them. Let's take a look at some examples and see how to work through them.

---

1 ☐ Mark for Review

While neutron stars and white dwarfs are both remnants of stellar evolution, their origins differ in some key ways. For example, white dwarfs are the final evolutionary state of stars with low or medium mass; neutron stars, _____ are formed from the collapsed cores of massive supergiants.

Which choice completes the text with the most logical transition?

(A) nevertheless,

(B) however,

(C) likewise,

(D) therefore,

Why This Question is Hard

Sometimes, when the blank appears in the middle of the sentence, you're being asked to determine how the two halves of the sentence relate. In this case, that could be challenging because unless you're an astronomy whiz, it's tough to understand from the sentence whether white dwarfs and neutron stars are formed in a similar way or in different ways. Instead, the clue for the answer comes in the sentence before: it says *their origins differ*, so that's how you know to annotate "disagree." This eliminates (C) and (D), but another way this question is tricky is that it contains two opposite-direction answers. *Nevertheless* is used to dismiss a previous statement, as you might do with the word "anyway." Is that the relationship here? No, because there's no information suggesting that neutron stars' formation is affected by or related to that of white dwarfs. *However* is a contradicting transition, which is more appropriate for the relationship here, given that the sentence before said their origins *differ*, so (B) is the correct answer.

Here's How to Ace It

When the blank comes in the middle of the sentence, sometimes it's about the relationship between the two parts of the sentence, but other times the clue comes elsewhere or the blank is related to the sentence before. Make sure to read the whole text before trying to understand the meaning of difficult portions of text.

2 Mark for Review

Jessie Redmon Fauset is best known for her role as the literary editor of the NAACP's official magazine, *The Crisis*. Starting in 1919, she used her position to introduce the works of young Black writers to a wider audience, and, _____ to launch the careers of many of the best-known authors of the Harlem Renaissance, including Langston Hughes, Anne Spencer, and Claude McKay. Fauset was also an author in her own right: among many other works, her novels *There is Confusion* and *Plum Bun* were groundbreaking portrayals of middle-class African American life partially based on her own experiences.

Which choice completes the text with the most logical transition?

(A) in other words,

(B) by contrast,

(C) thus,

(D) for example,

Why This Question is Hard

It may not look like this sentence needs a transition at all, as it could appear that Fauset *used her position* simply to do two things. But, of course, there's going to be a transition, so try to determine the relationship between the ideas by considering their meaning. In the first part of the sentence, she introduced writers' works, and in the second part of the sentence she launched well-known authors' careers. These ideas agree, so (B) is out, but three answers remain. Hence, this question is hard in part because identifying the general direction (agree or disagree) doesn't get you that far. You'll have to make that relationship more specific.

It may seem at first like the blank should be something like "additionally" if the ideas in this sentence represent two things Fauset did. However, *introduce* and *launch...careers* seem like very similar things. It doesn't make that much sense to say that she separately introduced the works of young Black writers and launched authors' careers. Recognizing this, you may then draw the conclusion that introducing the writers' works is what helped launch their careers, so the second part is a result of the first. In that case, you have your answer as (C), as *thus* is the only option that functions in this way. (If you found (A) appealing, note that *in other words* is used for a restatement, but introducing people's works doesn't necessarily mean that those people will launch careers, so the two ideas aren't just saying the same thing.)

Here's How to Ace It

If more than one answer agrees or disagrees—or even before you look at the answers—make your annotation more specific if you're able to. Writing "agree," "disagree," or "time change" is the bare minimum. We encourage you to be more specific about the relationship anytime you can. That being said, in some cases you might have to consider each answer choice individually. This isn't typically the best strategy because, as stated earlier, it can be easy to read the sentences with an incorrect transition and convince yourself that it makes sense. But as a last resort, cross off any answers that definitely don't represent the relationship between the ideas.

3 ☐ Mark for Review

Seafloor spreading occurs when volcanic activity forms new oceanic crust. Seafloor spreading as the cause of continental drift was proposed by American geologists Harold Hess and Robert Dietz in the 1960s. _____ the movement of the continents had been proposed by Alfred Wegner in 1912, but he did not specify the mechanics responsible for the movement.

Which choice completes the text with the most logical transition?

(A) Previously,

(B) Meanwhile,

(C) Still,

(D) In other words,

Why This Question is Hard

It's a bit difficult to tell what kind of word is needed in the blank here. It could seem like the ideas agree, as Wegner proposed the same theory, but it could also seem like the ideas disagree because of the change in time periods and the fact that Wegner's theory lacked specifics. In fact, it's a time-change question. Although time-change transitions are often easier to understand than other types of transitions, the time-change relationship can be difficult to identify if the passage doesn't already have a word like "earlier" or "second" to give you a strong clue about what the blank should be.

Here's How to Ace It

If you truly have no idea what to write down in the annotation box, you can start with POE, but take your time and be cautious. In this case, (A) clearly works because, of course, 1912 was before the 1960s. Choice (B), therefore, doesn't work since this wasn't at the same time. Choice (C) is a contrast transition that doesn't work in this context because the author isn't dismissing or countering anything. Choice (D), *In other words,* is used for a restatement, but this sentence is providing new information, not merely restating what was said in the last sentence. Thus, (A) has to be the answer. Remember, annotating the relationship, as specifically as you can, before using POE is the best strategy. However, if the blank seems as if it could go different ways, it's okay to go to POE as long as you have a good understanding of how each transition should be used, which is our next topic.

Unfamiliar Transitions

Sometimes you understand the relationship between the ideas well, but you're not familiar with one or more of the transitions in the answer choices. You are probably comfortable with transitions such as *however*, *for example*, and *in addition* and use them in your everyday writing. Let's take a look at some other transitions that have shown up or could show up on the Digital SAT. If you're aiming for a top Writing score, you'll want to understand how each of these is used.

Transition	Direction	What it means/How it's used
Accordingly	Agree	"going along with this"—a statement that naturally follows the one before
As such	Agree	"because of this"—used for the consequence of a specific feature of the last thing mentioned
Be that as it may	Disagree	Used to state something that is true in spite of the last statement
Consequently	Agree	"as a result"
Granted/To be sure	Disagree	Used for a statement that the author is giving in to or conceding that disagrees with the author's argument
Hence	Agree	The same as "thus" and "therefore"
In fact	Usually agree	Used to reinforce the previous statement by adding evidence to support it (occasionally it can correct a false statement as well)
In other words	Agree	Used to say essentially the same thing as the previous sentence but, literally, in other words
Likewise/similarly	Agree	Used for a second example or an additional, separate thing that shares a similarity with the last thing mentioned
Subsequently	Time change	Same as "next," "then," or "after that"
That is	Agree	Used to clarify the last thing stated by saying it another way or being more specific
That said	Disagree	Acknowledges the previous point but goes against it (similar to "nevertheless")
To that end/to this end/ to these ends/to those ends	Agree	"End" in this context refers to a goal, so it means "with that goal in mind" and is used when the previous sentence stated what someone wanted to do and this sentence states what the person did or will do in pursuit of that goal

In the following chart, we've grouped Digital SAT transitions into categories. Keep in mind that two transitions in the same category may not always be interchangeable, but they perform similar roles. Also, this list isn't comprehensive, but we think the vast majority of the transitions that will appear on your test are in this list. The starred ones are the most common transitions on the Digital SAT.

Same-Direction Transitions

Transition	What it means/How it's used
Consequence	A result of previously given evidence—accordingly, as a result*, as such, consequently*, fittingly, for this reason, for that reason, hence, in turn, therefore*, thus, to that end
Reinforcement	A statement that provides evidence for a previous claim or otherwise reinforces it—indeed, in fact
Additional point	Further support for a claim—additionally, besides, furthermore, in addition, moreover*
Restatement	The same as the previous claim but using different words— in other words, that is
Comparison	The subject of this statement has a similarity to the subject of the previous statement—likewise*, similarly
Specification	A more specific detail regarding the previous claim—in particular, specifically*
Example	An example that illustrates the previous claim—for example*, for instance*
Generalization	A broader claim related to previous statements— in many cases, ultimately

Opposite-Direction Transitions

Transition	What it means/How it's used
Dismissal	An acknowledgment of what was stated but then a contradicting viewpoint—after all, be that as it may, despite this, in any case, nevertheless*, nonetheless, regardless*, still, that said
Concession	Concedes (gives in to) a statement that goes against the author's main point—admittedly, granted, to be sure
Contradiction	An opposing statement to what was previously stated—by comparison, by contrast*, conversely, however*, in comparison, in contrast, instead, on the contrary, rather, though
Alternative	Not a contradiction of the previous statement but another option or differing view— alternately, alternatively, on the other hand
Correction	Goes against the previous statement by correcting it—actually, in fact

Time-Change Transitions

Now that you know the types of relationships and the common transitions words, try the following drill to test your abilities.

Transition	What it means/How it's used
Before	A statement referring to something that happened prior to something else in the text—earlier, first, firstly, first of all, in the first place, previously
After	A statement referring to something that happened after something else in the text or at the very end—afterward, finally, in conclusion, in sum, in summary, in the end, lastly, later, next, second, secondly, soon, subsequently, then, to conclude, to sum up
Now	A statement describing current conditions or events happening simultaneously in different places—currently, elsewhere, increasingly, in the meantime, meanwhile, nowadays, there, today

Tricky Transitions Drill

Time: 10 minutes

Answers and explanations can be found in Chapter 20.

---

1 | Mark for Review

Evidence-based research can be conducted using a quantitative method, a qualitative method, or a mixture of both. A quantitative approach is associated with the traditional scientific method, utilizing an experimental setting to acquire and analyze data that can be extrapolated to other populations. _____ a qualitative approach gathers data from different sources to explore the complexity of a situation based on observation and perception. While both research approaches are valid, the nature of the research question often determines which approach is better suited to provide substantial evidential support.

Which choice completes the text with the most logical transition?

- (A) Therefore,
- (B) Additionally,
- (C) In contrast,
- (D) Specifically,

---

2 | Mark for Review

Global grouping theory examines how the selection of individuals to compose a group influences the learning and performance of those group members. A like-skilled tiered system places individuals with similar backgrounds and skills together, such as separating students by level of proficiency to promote a personalized learning environment in which all students within each group improve their learning at a pace suited to their ability. _____ a cross-sectional system places individuals with a variety of backgrounds and skills together as a group, such as combining students of different proficiencies into a group and thereby encouraging group members to learn from each other.

Which choice completes the text with the most logical transition?

- (A) Consequently,
- (B) Alternatively,
- (C) For instance,
- (D) In particular,

3 | Mark for Review

Russian-American author and philosopher Ayn Rand is best known for her novels, such as *The Fountainhead*, a major literary success that led to her fame as a novelist. Following this career achievement, she went on to publish *Atlas Shrugged*, a best-selling novel in which she debuted her philosophy known as Objectivism. After the book received negative reviews from intellectuals, _____ Rand was discouraged from publishing fiction and subsequently promoted her political philosophy through non-fiction writing.

Which choice completes the text with the most logical transition?

(A) additionally,

(B) indeed,

(C) though,

(D) thus,

4 | Mark for Review

Between 2009 and 2018, researchers surveyed various groups of Americans four separate times and tracked their accuracy on five multiple-choice questions about objective financial knowledge as well as their self-rated confidence in financial knowledge on a scale of 1–7. The results of these surveys showed a decline in accurate understanding of financial concepts over the years with a slight increase in the number of "don't know" responses. _____ the concerning trend of decreased financial knowledge occurred simultaneously with an increase in self-confidence scores, indicating that more people felt confident in their financial skills in spite of lower knowledge scores.

Which choice completes the text with the most logical transition?

(A) In other words,

(B) Nevertheless,

(C) Therefore,

(D) Similarly,

5 ☐ Mark for Review

In 1905, physicist Albert Einstein suggested that comparing the movements of a spring-clock located at the equator to one located at either pole under similar conditions would support his theory of relativity. Many experiments were subsequently conducted to test the theory of relativity using subatomic particles instead; _____ it was not until 1971 that astronomer Richard Keating and physicist Joseph Hafele tested the effects of kinetic and gravitational time dilation by taking four atomic clocks aboard commercial airlines that flew in opposite directions around the world twice. The movement of the atomic clocks was then compared to the movement of clocks that had remained at the US Naval Observatory.

Which choice completes the text with the most logical transition?

(A) as a result,

(B) indeed,

(C) regardless,

(D) moreover,

6 ☐ Mark for Review

Fossil evidence shows that many dinosaurs had feathers far earlier than originally thought, with feathers possibly appearing around 250 million years ago and contributing to dinosaurs' survival in the harsh volcanic winters that occurred during the mass extinction at the end of the Triassic period. _____ the presence of feathers is just one of many possible reasons accounting for the spread and diversification of dinosaurs into the subsequent Jurassic period.

Which choice completes the text with the most logical transition?

(A) Consequently, .

(B) Specifically,

(C) Moreover,

(D) Granted,

7 ☐ Mark for Review

LED technology offers potential benefits to public lighting (street lights and outdoor home lights, for example) by significantly reducing energy costs and carbon emissions through improved energy efficiency. _____ increased usage of LEDs for public lighting has led to shifts in the composition of spectral emissions, such as higher concentrations of blue emissions, that have dire consequences for certain fauna and flora sensitive to these emissions.

Which choice completes the text with the most logical transition?

(A) That said,

(B) As a result,

(C) Additionally,

(D) In fact,

8 ☐ Mark for Review

When biologist James Watson and physicist Francis Crick introduced their model describing the structure of DNA in 1953, they also hypothesized that DNA was replicated in a semiconservative manner. _____ each DNA strand serves as a template on which a new strand is synthesized, resulting in two new strands of DNA that each contain a strand of parent DNA and a strand of a new DNA. It was not for another five years that an experiment conducted by geneticists Matthew Meselson and Franklin Stahl was able to prove that Watson and Crick's hypothesis was correct.

Which choice completes the text with the most logical transition?

(A) That is,

(B) Moreover,

(C) Nevertheless,

(D) Likewise,

9 ☐ Mark for Review

Famous for his self-portraits, still-life paintings of sunflowers, and notable works such as *The Starry Night* and *The Potato Eaters*, Vincent van Gogh was a Dutch Post-Impressionist artist regarded as both talented and troubled. Over a span of 10 years, van Gogh completed over 900 paintings and over 1,000 paper sketches, with many of his famous paintings completed during his hospitalization in a psychiatric facility in Paris. During his lifetime, van Gogh did not achieve a successful career as an artist, having only ever sold one painting; _____ though, it was his death that led to public awareness of his paintings and letters, many of which were later dedicated to the Van Gogh Foundation and are currently viewed by over two million people each year at the Van Gogh Museum.

Which choice completes the text with the most logical transition?

(A) as a result,

(B) specifically,

(C) ultimately,

(D) in other words,

10 ☐ Mark for Review

Traditionally, large flood basalt eruptions have been believed to occur in regions where deep mantle material can reach the Earth's surface in low-pressure environments in which tectonic plates are very thin. A recent study developed an alternative hypothesis that the rare trace elements found in many flood basalt eruptions in regions of thin tectonic plates suggested a high-pressure environment. Using computer simulations, the team of researchers found that high-pressure magmas can resemble low-pressure magmas on a chemical level at high temperatures regardless of the depth of the mantle source; _____ the compositions of trace elements found in flood basalts are unreliable at predicting the depths from which the magma was generated.

Which choice completes the text with the most logical transition?

(A) be that as it may,

(B) nevertheless,

(C) moreover,

(D) in other words,

Chapter 19
Tricky Rhetorical Synthesis

Although Rhetorical Synthesis questions appear last in the RW module, they can actually be a relatively easy way to pick up points early on, since they can often be done quickly. If you're still missing a handful of Rhetorical Synthesis questions, the examples and strategies in this lesson should help you get to 100% on these.

Although Rhetorical Synthesis questions might have seemed tough when you first saw them, hopefully you've realized by now how quick, simple, and easy the vast majority of them are. Our strategy is to highlight the purpose stated in the question and then go straight to the answers, since the answers generally don't make factual errors in combining the bullet points. All you need to do is check whether each answer fulfills what the question is asking for.

Following that strategy, you should be able to get at least 90% of the Rhetorical Synthesis questions right. However, there are a few ways College Board can make these questions a bit trickier. Let's take a look.

While researching a topic, a student has taken the following notes:

- Batik is an Indonesian art of creating patterns on cloth by applying wax that resists dye.
- A canting is a type of tool with a spout to add wax to the cloth.
- It allows the artist to hand-draw patterns of dots and lines.
- A cap is a copper stamp that adds a pattern of wax to the cloth.
- It allows the artist to easily replicate a pattern over a large section of cloth.

1   ☐ Mark for Review

The student wants to emphasize an advantage of the cap for batik. Which choice most effectively uses relevant information from the notes to accomplish this goal?

(A) Batik artists can use a canting or a cap to create a pattern on cloth.

(B) Different tools are used in batik, an Indonesian art of creating patterns on cloth by applying wax.

(C) A cap allows a batik artist to stamp a pattern over a large section of cloth instead of drawing each pattern by hand.

(D) A batik artist uses a canting to hand-draw a pattern of dots and lines on a cloth.

Why This Question is Hard

The task is asking about an *advantage* of the cap, but the word *advantage* doesn't appear in the bullet points, so the answer requires you to draw a conclusion about what might be advantageous even if it might not explicitly be stated as such.

Here's How to Ace It

If you're following our strategy, you shouldn't be reading the bullet points first anyway. You can start by eliminating anything that doesn't clearly seem like an advantage or doesn't relate to the topic. Choices (B) and (D) don't mention *the cap* at all, for instance, so they can't be right. Between (A) and (C), (C) much more clearly seems like an advantage because it says *instead of drawing each pattern by hand*, which implies that this method is faster and/or easier than an alternative. Choice (A) states that the cap can be used, but there's no mention of anything that might be advantageous. However, it's always okay to check the bullets to make sure. In doing so, you'll see the same advantage stated in the last bullet point that is in (C).

While researching a topic, a student has taken the following notes:

- Neptunism was a geologic theory that held that all rocks are formed by minerals precipitating from the ocean.

- German geologist Abraham Werner was a supporter of neptunism.

- It is now known that the rock limestone is formed by minerals precipitating from the ocean.

- Plutonism was a geologic theory that held that all rocks are formed underground from magma.

- Scottish geologist James Hutton was a supporter of plutonism.

- It is now known that the rock granite is formed underground from magma.

2 ☐ Mark for Review

The student wants to make a generalization about how rocks are formed. Which choice most effectively uses relevant information from the notes to accomplish this goal?

(A) Rocks can be formed in multiple ways, such as from minerals in the ocean and from magma.

(B) Neptunism and plutonism were two geologic theories supported by different geologists.

(C) German geologist Abraham Werner suggested that rocks are formed by minerals precipitating from the ocean, which is true about limestone.

(D) Limestone is formed by minerals precipitating from the ocean, while granite is formed underground from magma.

Why This Question is Hard

Questions that ask for a generalization are usually going to be ranked Hard. That's because the answer is less explicitly stated than it is for other Rhetorical Synthesis questions. In fact, we've seen some examples of these questions where the topic of the text wasn't even stated in the correct answer. The answer for a generalization question will usually be a broader claim that the bullets can support, rather than a specific detail from the bullets. You may need to actually read the bullets for this type of question. Likewise, if the question asks for a summary of the text, you will probably need to read in order to get the main idea.

Here's How to Ace It

If we start by looking at the answers, we can definitely eliminate (B) because it doesn't mention rocks or their formation. Choice (A) probably seems like a good match because it makes a broad statement about *how rocks are formed*, whereas (C) and (D) mention specific types of rock (limestone and granite), which would be less in line with a *generalization*. Read the bullets to confirm if needed. Since (C) and (D) focus on specific types of rocks and (A) is about rocks in general, (A) is the correct answer. Again, starting with the answers can help a lot. If you read the bullets first, you may be tempted to pick an answer that seems closer to what the bullets are focusing on, but Rhetorical Synthesis questions are all about the stated task, and (A) is the only answer that fulfills that task.

While researching a topic, a student has taken the following notes:

- The sakman is a sailing boat traditionally built by the Chamorro people of the Mariana Islands.
- Accounts describe it as being capable of averaging a speed of more than 20 miles per hour.
- The sakman consists of two hulls, one smaller than the other, and a triangular sail.
- The art of building the sakman was lost during the 19th century due to pressure from colonial powers.
- Modern Chamorro artisans have revived the tradition.

3 ☐ Mark for Review

The student wants to introduce the sakman and emphasize its speed. Which choice most effectively uses relevant information from the notes to accomplish these goals?

(A) Modern Chamorro artisans have revived the tradition of building the sakman, a sailing boat with two hulls.

(B) The art of building the sakman was lost during the 19th century, but Chamorro artisans have revived the tradition in the modern day.

(C) The sakman is a sailing boat traditionally built by the Chamorro people; it consists of two hulls, one smaller than the other, and a triangular sail.

(D) The sakman, a sailing boat from the Mariana Islands, has been described as being capable of averaging over 20 miles per hour.

Why This Question is Hard

There are two goals stated in the question. Some students might pick an answer that fulfills only one of the two goals.

Here's How to Ace It

Always highlight the goal or goals and eliminate any answer that doesn't completely fulfill them. In this case, (A), (B), and (C) don't mention the speed of the sakman, so they have to be eliminated, and (D) is the answer. Choice (D) also fulfills the first goal of introducing the sakman by stating what it is.

While researching a topic, a student has taken the following notes:

- Jhumpa Lahiri is an author and professor born in London, England, to Bengali Indian parents.

- She published her novel *The Namesake* in 2003.

- The central character in the novel is a young Indian-American man born and raised in the United States.

- Another central character is the main character's mother, who is adjusting to life in the United States.

- A film adaptation of *The Namesake* was released in 2007.

---

4 ☐ Mark for Review

The student wants to introduce the novel *The Namesake* to an audience already familiar with Jhumpa Lahiri. Which choice most effectively uses relevant information from the notes to accomplish this goal?

(A) Author and professor Jhumpa Lahiri's novel *The Namesake* was adapted into a film in 2007.

(B) Jhumpa Lahiri's 2003 novel *The Namesake* features a central character who was born in the US and his mother, who is adjusting to life in the US.

(C) *The Namesake*, a 2003 novel by London-born author and professor Jhumpa Lahiri, includes central characters who have different connections to the US.

(D) Jhumpa Lahiri's characters include those born in the US and those adjusting to life in the US.

Why This Question is Hard

Once again, there are two parts to the goal. Not only does the answer need to introduce the novel, but it also needs to keep in mind that the audience is *already familiar with Jhumpa Lahiri*. In that case, the answer must not give any description to Lahiri, since the audience is already familiar with her.

Here's How to Ace It

Consider both parts of the goal when using POE. Choice (D) doesn't mention the novel at all, so it can't be right. Then, while (C) in particular may be appealing, both (A) and (C) give a description of Lahiri. Since the audience is familiar with her, these answers can't be correct. Choice (B) is the only one that introduces the novel and doesn't give any background to Lahiri.

Now that you have seen some examples of harder Rhetorical Synthesis questions, which hopefully don't seem too hard after all, try the following exercise and drill to further hone your skills.

Rhetorical Synthesis Exercise

Directions: Cross off answer choices that don't fulfill the stated goal(s), without any reference to the bullet points, as they're not provided. Answers can be found in Chapter 20.

1. **Goal:** The student wants to emphasize the scale of the crop loss and state why it occurred.

    A.   Out of the 15 million acres of crops in Nebraska, 100,000 acres were lost.

    B.   At the time of the wildfires, Nebraska had 15 million acres of crops.

    C.   Over 100,000 acres of crops were lost in Nebraska due to the wildfires.

2. **Goal:** The student wants to make a generalization about the type of study the researchers conducted.

    A.   Ethnographic research can be used to draw conclusions about populations of people.

    B.   The researchers' study showed that the residents of Greenville were concerned about economic conditions.

    C.   Researchers conducted a study to determine how residents viewed local economic conditions.

3. **Goal:** The student wants to describe fexofenadine to an audience already familiar with antihistamines.

    A.   Antihistamines such as fexofenadine block histamine receptors in the body.

    B.   Fexofenadine, an antihistamine, blocks histamine receptors in the body and is used to treat physical allergy symptoms.

    C.   The second-generation antihistamine medication fexofenadine is used to treat physical allergy symptoms such as rhinitis and urticaria.

4. **Goal:** The student wants to emphasize a potential criticism of the Slow Streets Act.

    A.   By reducing the speed limit in places with high foot traffic, the act could prevent injuries to pedestrians.

    B.   The act could inadvertently put pedestrians at risk by increasing their exposure to pollutants from car exhaust.

    C.   Currently, an average of ten pedestrians is hit by cars every year.

5. **Goal:** The student wants to present the study results to an audience unfamiliar with PFAS.

    A. The study showed that the water contained a higher amount of PFAS (harmful chemicals that build up in people's bodies) than was legally permitted.

    B. The levels of PFAS in the water supply were concerning to researchers because they exceeded maximum permitted levels.

    C. PFAS, harmful chemicals that build up in people's bodies, are subject to a legal maximum level in certain regions.

Tricky Rhetorical Synthesis Drill

Time: 10 minutes

Answers and explanations can be found in Chapter 20.

---

1 ⚑ Mark for Review

While researching a topic, a student has taken the following notes:

- Although other programming languages existed in the 1960s, BASIC was designed specifically to be easy to use.
- Hungarian-born mathematician John Kemeny, one of the creators of BASIC, was a professor at and later president of Dartmouth College.
- American mathematician Thomas Kurtz, the other creator of BASIC, joined Dartmouth College as a professor.
- Kemeny wrote the first version of BASIC after experimenting with other programming languages used to teach students computer programming.
- Kurtz worked on later versions and gave the programming language the name BASIC from one of his papers.

The student wants to compare the two men's work on the BASIC programming language. Which choice most effectively uses relevant information from the notes to accomplish this goal?

(A) Many programming languages existed in the 1960s, but BASIC, created by Kemeny and Kurtz, was designed to be easy to use.

(B) Although Kurtz gave the programming language its name, Kemeny wrote the first version of BASIC.

(C) While both Kemeny and Kurtz worked in mathematics at Dartmouth College, Kemeny eventually became the president of the institution.

(D) Kemeny and Kurtz didn't write the first version of BASIC together; Kemeny wrote the first version on his own.

---

2 ⚑ Mark for Review

While researching a topic, a student has taken the following notes:

- The Patagonian Desert is located in South America.
- The desert has an area of 259,847 square miles.
- The Patagonian Desert covers 3.8% of the South American continent.
- The Gobi Desert is located in Asia.
- The desert has an area of 500,002 square miles.
- The Gobi Desert covers 2.9% of the Asian continent.

Which choice most effectively uses information from the given sentences to emphasize the relative sizes of the two deserts' areas?

(A) Comparing South America and Asia, 259,847 square miles is 3.8% of South America's area, and 500,002 square miles is 2.9% of Asia's area.

(B) Even though the Gobi Desert (500,002 square miles) is larger than the Patagonian Desert (259,847 square miles), the Patagonian Desert covers a greater percentage of its continent.

(C) The areas of the Patagonian Desert and the Gobi Desert, respectively, are 259,847 and 500,002 square miles.

(D) In South America is the Patagonian Desert, which is 259,847 square miles, and in Asia is the Gobi Desert, which is 500,002 square miles.

---

3 ☐ Mark for Review

While researching a topic, a student has taken the following notes:

- In the Chesapeake Bay, the overall population of seagrass, which includes widgeon grass and eelgrass, has plummeted in recent years.
- A team at the Virginia Institute of Marine Sciences (VIMS) wanted to know how widgeon grass has affected the overall seagrass population.
- The team used decades of watershed modeling and water quality data to track the changes in the populations of seagrass.
- The seagrass population's proportion of widgeon grass increased because widgeon grass can tolerate the warmer waters resulting from climate change.
- However, widgeon grass is more sensitive to water quality changes, leading to some years with greater die-offs of the overall seagrass population.

The student wants to emphasize the aim of the research study. Which choice most effectively uses relevant information from the notes to accomplish this goal?

(A) A team at VIMS used decades of watershed modeling and water quality data for a study on the seagrass population in the Chesapeake Bay.

(B) A Virginia Institute of Marine Sciences team found that widgeon grass, a type of seagrass, is sensitive to changes in water quality.

(C) Due to the work of a team at VIMS, it's now known that widgeon grass can tolerate heat but not water quality changes.

(D) A research team at the Virginia Institute of Marine Sciences investigated the effect of widgeon grass on the seagrass population.

4 ☐ Mark for Review

While researching a topic, a student has taken the following notes:

- Animals have different ways to escape predators, including losing an appendage.
- Many species of lizards use this defense strategy.
- Shedding an appendage as a defense is called autotomy.
- The act of shedding a tail is known as caudal autotomy.
- Some lizards can regrow their tails after caudal autotomy.

The student wants to explain what caudal autotomy is. Which choice most effectively uses relevant information from the notes to accomplish this goal?

(A) Autotomy is one of many defense strategies used by animals.

(B) Having encountered a predator, a lizard can shed its tail, a strategy known as caudal autotomy.

(C) When it's trying to escape, a lizard may use a defense strategy.

(D) After caudal autotomy, some lizards can regrow their tails.

5 ☐ Mark for Review

While researching a topic, a student has taken the following notes:

- Potable water is water that is safe and suitable for drinking as well as cooking and hygiene.
- Stanford professor William Mitch studied the potability of treated and recycled wastewater.
- Wastewater that is treated at potable reuse treatment plants goes through reverse osmosis treatment.
- Wastewater that is treated at conventional wastewater treatment plants goes through less extensive treatments.
- Potable reuse treatment plants can help supplement cities' drinking water supplies, especially ones located in drier or drought-ridden areas.

The student wants to provide an overview of potable reuse water. Which choice most effectively uses relevant information from the notes to accomplish this goal?

(A) Wastewater can go through different levels of treatment at different types of treatment plants.

(B) Potable reuse treatment plants treat wastewater with reverse osmosis to produce clean water that can be used to supplement cities' drinking water supplies.

(C) Potable water can be produced at conventional or potable reuse treatment plants.

(D) Cities may need to supplement their drinking water supplies with water that comes from wastewater treatment plants.

6 ☐ Mark for Review

While researching a topic, a student has taken the following notes:

- Since public goods belong to the whole society, economists must evaluate the value of public goods without the market.
- One method is to use a contingent valuation, sometimes referred to as a willingness-to-pay, approach.
- People are asked how much they would be willing to pay for a public good.
- Since the public good is usually part of a larger system, it is difficult for people to identify the value of that specific good.
- The difficulty in identifying the value of a particular public good in a collection is called the embedding effect.

The student wants to summarize the embedding effect. Which choice most effectively uses relevant information from the notes to accomplish this goal?

(A) Economists attempting to find a value for a public good may use a contingent valuation or willingness-to-pay approach.

(B) When asked how much they would pay for a public good, people have difficulty identifying the value of a public good that is part of a larger system.

(C) One issue that economists have when trying to find a value for a public good is the embedding effect.

(D) The value of public goods is not determined by the market since these goods belong to the whole society.

7 ☐ Mark for Review

While researching a topic, a student has taken the following notes:

- Sterlin Harjo (born 1979) is a filmmaker and a member of the Seminole Nation of Oklahoma.
- He created the comedy TV show *Reservation Dogs* with Taika Waititi.
- *Reservation Dogs* premiered in 2021 on the streaming service Hulu.
- The show was the first one to feature all Indigenous writers and directors as well as an almost entirely Indigenous cast.
- *Reservation Dogs* won an Independent Spirit Award for Best New Scripted Series.

The student wants to begin a narrative about Harjo's award-winning TV show. Which choice most effectively uses relevant information from the notes to accomplish this goal?

(A) In 2021, *Reservation Dogs* premiered on Hulu; it would later win an award.

(B) Harjo, who created a show with Taika Waititi, would see that show win an Independent Spirit Award.

(C) *Reservation Dogs* was the first TV show to feature all Indigenous writers and directors, and it won an Independent Spirit Award for Best New Scripted Series.

(D) In 2021, filmmaker and member of the Seminole Nation Sterlin Harjo created a comedy TV show called *Reservation Dogs*.

8 ☐ Mark for Review

While researching a topic, a student has taken the following notes:

- The Dodo bird verdict is a claim about the effectiveness of different types of psychotherapy.
- According to the verdict, all empirically validated psychotherapies are equally effective.
- It also states that the common factors of all psychotherapies, such as a warm and respectful therapist, produce results.
- However, studies have shown that specific psychotherapies are more effective for specific disorders.
- Other studies have shown that some psychotherapies are unhelpful or even harmful.

The student wants to explain a disadvantage of following the Dodo bird verdict when delivering psychotherapy. Which choice most effectively uses relevant information from the notes to accomplish this goal?

(A) The Dodo bird verdict claims that empirically validated psychotherapies are equally effective.

(B) Psychotherapies can have common factors, such as a warm and respectful therapist, which produce effective results according to the Dodo bird verdict.

(C) Psychotherapists who believe that their particular psychotherapy is effective based on the Dodo bird verdict may deliver psychotherapy that is not effective for a specific disorder or may even be harmful.

(D) The results of psychotherapy can be effective, unhelpful, or even harmful.

9 ☐ Mark for Review

While researching a topic, a student has taken the following notes:

- Exoplanets are planets that are located outside of the Solar System.

- One method astronomers use to find exoplanets is called transit, or looking for the light of stars blocked by exoplanets.

- 4,132 exoplanets have been discovered using transit.

- Another method is radial velocity or looking for changes in colors of light due to exoplanets' orbits.

- 1,068 exoplanets have been discovered using radial velocity.

The student wants to make and support a generalization about methods used to find exoplanets. Which choice most effectively uses relevant information from the notes to accomplish this goal?

(A) The different methods that astronomers use to find exoplanets have had varying levels of success, as the examples of transit and radial velocity demonstrate.

(B) Using radial velocity, astronomers have discovered 1,068 exoplanets.

(C) Exoplanets have been discovered using transit and radial velocity.

(D) When using transit, astronomers look for exoplanets blocking the lights of stars.

10 ☐ Mark for Review

While researching a topic, a student has taken the following notes:

- Medical student Lauren Scott and evolutionary psychologist Brittany Florkiewicz wanted to learn more about how cats communicate with each other.

- They reviewed hours of videos of cats at a cat café.

- They identified 276 distinct facial expressions that cats used when interacting with other cats.

- The majority of the facial expressions were either distinctly aggressive (37%) or distinctly friendly (45%).

- The other 18% of the facial expressions were too ambiguous to categorize.

The student wants to summarize the study's findings. Which choice most effectively uses relevant information from the notes to accomplish this goal?

(A) According to Scott and Florkiewicz, cats use over 250 facial expressions when communicating with other cats, with the majority either being friendly or aggressive.

(B) Reviewing hours of videos of cats, Scott and Florkiewicz identified 276 facial expressions in cats.

(C) Scott and Florkiewicz found that almost 20% of cat's facial expressions were too ambiguous to categorize as aggressive or friendly.

(D) To find the results of their study, which focused on the facial expressions cats use with other cats, Scott and Florkiewicz used hours of videos of cats.

Chapter 20
Writing Drills:
Answers and
Explanations

CHAPTER 15: TRICKY PUNCTUATION

Describing Phrases Exercise (Page 211)

1. No punctuation is needed, as this phrase is specifying which shirt was lost.

2. No punctuation is needed, as this prepositional phrase is specifying which flowers need to be watered.

3. The phrase should have matching punctuation before and after, as it's a noun phrase and thus Extra Information.

4. No punctuation is needed, as the person's name specifies which Dutch filmmaker the sentence is discussing. If you remove his name, the sentence no longer makes sense, so it's Specifying.

5. No punctuation is needed, as this prepositional phrase is specifying which cat was napping on the clothes.

6. The phrase needs a comma after it, as it's Extra Information.

7. The first phrase needs a comma after it, as it's Extra Information. The second phrase shouldn't have punctuation around it, as it's specifying the location of light that is being discussed.

8. No punctuation is needed, as the person's name specifies which composer the sentence is discussing. If you remove his name, the sentence no longer makes sense, so it's Specifying.

9. No punctuation is needed, as the phrase is specifying which people are being hired. If the phrase is removed, the sentence says that the store is hiring anyone, which changes the meaning of the sentence.

10. The first phrase shouldn't have punctuation around it because it's specifying what type of evidence the sentence is discussing. The second phrase should have a comma before it, a dash before it, or parentheses around it since it's a noun phrase and thus Extra Information.

Tricky Punctuation Drill (Page 216)

1. **B**   In this Rules question, punctuation is changing in the answer choices. Look for independent clauses. The first part of the sentence says *A behavior of domesticated cats that has inspired multiple theories…is that of kneading, or making biscuits,* which is an independent clause. The second part of the sentence is not an independent clause but provides a definition for the cat behavior. Eliminate any option that doesn't correctly connect the independent clause to the definition.

    *   (A) is wrong because a semicolon can't be used when the second part isn't an independent clause.

    *   (B) is correct because a colon is used when the second part of the sentence elaborates on the first.

- (C) is wrong because some type of punctuation is needed in between the independent clause and the definition.

- (D) is wrong because the period makes the definition its own sentence, which doesn't work because it's not an independent clause.

2. **A** In this Rules question, punctuation is changing in the answer choices. Look for independent clauses. The first part of the sentence says *In 1900 Williams organized the First Pan-African Conference in England*, which is an independent clause. The second part says *in 1903 he moved to what is now South Africa to practice law*, which is also an independent clause. Eliminate any answer that can't correctly connect two independent clauses.

- (A) is correct because it connects the independent clauses with a comma + a coordinating conjunction *(and)*, which is acceptable.

- (B) is wrong because a comma without a coordinating conjunction (FANBOYS) can't connect two independent clauses.

- (C) is wrong because a coordinating conjunction *(and)* without a comma can't connect two independent clauses.

- (D) is wrong because some type of punctuation is needed in order to connect two independent clauses.

3. **A** In this Rules question, punctuation is changing in the answer choices. Look for independent clauses. The first part of the sentence says *During the Korean eras…carpentry was a highly prestigious craft*, which is an independent clause. The second part of the sentence says *the builders often holding vaunted governmental positions*, which is a describing phrase and not an independent clause. Eliminate any option that doesn't correctly connect the independent clause to the describing phrase.

- (A) is correct because the phrase is Extra Information and therefore should be separated with a comma.

- (B), (C), and (D) are wrong because these are all ways to connect two independent clauses, but the second part isn't independent.

4. **D** In this Rules question, punctuation with a transition is changing in the answer choices. Look for independent clauses. The first part of the sentence says *The dissolution of their act was not the end of Cher's singing career.* There is an option to add *however* to this independent clause. This statement does contrast with the previous sentence, which states that the *pop music duo…came to an end*, so *however* belongs in the first part of the sentence. Eliminate options with *however* in the second part.

- (A) is wrong because it puts *however* with the second independent clause.

- (B) is wrong because some type of punctuation is needed in order to connect two independent clauses.

- (C) is wrong because the sentence contains two independent clauses, which cannot be connected with commas alone.

- (D) is correct because it puts *however* with the first independent clause and puts a semicolon between the two independent clauses.

5. **B**   In this Rules question, punctuation is changing in the answer choices. Look for independent clauses. The first part of the sentence says *There are eleven distinct styles for reciting the Vedic mantras...*, which is an independent clause. The second part explains that *the Ghanapatha is the most complex...*, which is also an independent clause. Eliminate any answer that can't correctly connect two independent clauses.

- (A) is wrong because some type of punctuation is needed in order to connect two independent clauses.

- (B) is correct because a colon is an acceptable way to connect two independent clauses if the second part elaborates on the first, which it does here.

- (C) is wrong because a comma without a coordinating conjunction (FANBOYS) can't connect two independent clauses.

- (D) is wrong because the two ideas don't contrast with each other, so *while* isn't appropriate.

6. **C**   In this Rules question, punctuation with a transition is changing in the answer choices. Look for independent clauses. The first part of the sentence says *The amber has preserved some marine organisms.* There is an option to add *though* to this independent clause. This statement does contrast with the previous sentence, which states that the majority of species found in the amber *are terrestrial arthropods*, so *though* belongs in the first part of the sentence. Eliminate options with *though* in the second part.

- (A) is wrong because it puts *though* with the second independent clause.

- (B) and (D) are wrong because the sentence contains two independent clauses, which cannot be connected with commas alone.

- (C) is correct because it puts *though* with the first independent clause and puts a semicolon between the two independent clauses.

7. **C**   In this Rules question, commas are changing in the answer choices. The commas are moving around the name of the person, so determine whether there is a reason to use any commas. The phrase *physical chemist* is a title for El-Sayed, so no punctuation should be used. Eliminate answers that use punctuation.

- (A) and (D) are wrong because a comma isn't used after a title.

- (B) is wrong because *in the 1960s* shouldn't be surrounded by commas as it's part of the introductory phrase.

- (C) is correct because titles before names have no punctuation.

8. **B**   In this Rules question, punctuation is changing in the answer choices. The main meaning of the sentence is *Domesticated cats have spent a large quantity of time together in non-adversarial settings... developing around 120 distinctly friendly facial expressions....* The word *however* is Extra Information as it's not essential to the sentence's meaning. It should therefore be set off with matching punctuation before and after. Eliminate answers that do not have matching punctuation before and after *however*.

- (A) is wrong because it uses a comma before *however* but not after.

- (B) is correct because it uses a comma before and after the Extra Information.

- (C) is wrong because a semicolon links two independent clauses, but the part after *however* isn't an independent clause.

- (D) is wrong because a semicolon links two independent clauses, but the part after *settings* isn't an independent clause.

9. **D** In this Rules question, punctuation is changing in the answer choices. Look for independent clauses. The first part of the sentence says …*optical coherence tomography…is analogous to ultrasound imaging, though OCT uses light instead of sound*, which is an independent clause. The second part says *by measuring light waves, OCT generates a detailed cross-sectional representation of the retina*, which is also an independent clause. Eliminate any answer that can't correctly connect two independent clauses.

- (A) is wrong because a coordinating conjunction *(and)* without a comma can't connect two independent clauses.

- (B) is wrong because some type of punctuation is needed in order to connect two independent clauses.

- (C) is wrong because a comma without a coordinating conjunction (FANBOYS) can't connect two independent clauses.

- (D) is correct because the period makes each independent clause its own sentence, which is fine.

10. **C** In this Rules question, punctuation is changing in the answer choices. Look for independent clauses. The first part of the sentence says *Because of agriculture…only 11% of these poorly studied swamp forests still exist*, which is an independent clause. The second part says *growing in a protected and predominantly undisturbed swamp forest, the recently discovered tree…is the only known species of its genus…*, which is also an independent clause. Eliminate any answer that can't correctly connect two independent clauses.

- (A) is wrong because a comma without a coordinating conjunction (FANBOYS) can't connect two independent clauses.

- (B) is wrong because a coordinating conjunction *(and)* without a comma can't connect two independent clauses.

- (C) is correct because a semicolon can connect two independent clauses.

- (D) is wrong because some type of punctuation is needed in order to connect two independent clauses.

CHAPTER 16: TRICKY GRAMMAR

Subject-Verb Agreement Exercise (Page 221)

1. Subject: *novels*. Verb: *were*.
2. Subject: *Gin Lane*. Verb: *portrays*.
3. Subject: *Solitary confinement*. Verb: *was*.
4. Subject: *Charles Perrault*. Verb: *was*.
5. Subject: *tendrils*. Verb: *grow*.
6. Subject: *Each*. Verb: *has mastered*. (The pronoun *each* is singular.)
7. Subject: *teachers*. Verb: *are*.
8. Subject: *biographies*. Verb: *begin*.

Subject-Verb Agreement Drill (Page 223)

1. **A** In this Rules question, verbs are changing in the answer choices, so it's testing consistency with verbs. Find and highlight the subject, *Scientists*, which is plural, so a plural verb is needed. Write an annotation saying "plural." Eliminate any answer that is not plural.

   - (A) is correct because it's plural.

   - (B), (C), and (D) are wrong because they are singular.

2. **C** In this Rules question, verbs are changing in the answer choices, so it's testing consistency with verbs. Find and highlight the subject, *portrayals*, which is plural, so a plural verb is needed. Write an annotation saying "plural." Eliminate any answer that is not plural.

   - (A), (B), and (D) are wrong because they are singular.

   - (C) is correct because it's plural.

3. **B** In this Rules question, verbs are changing in the answer choices, so it's testing consistency with verbs. Find and highlight the subject, *prose*, which is singular, so a singular verb is needed. Write an annotation saying "singular." Eliminate any answer that is not singular.

   - (A), (C), and (D) are wrong because they are plural.

   - (B) is correct because it's singular.

4. **A** In this Rules question, verbs are changing in the answer choices, so it's testing consistency with verbs. Find and highlight the subject, *style*, which is singular, so a singular verb is needed. Write an annotation saying "singular." Eliminate any answer that is not singular.

   - (A) is correct because it's singular.

   - (B), (C), and (D) are wrong because they are plural.

5. **D**   In this Rules question, verbs are changing in the answer choices, so it's testing consistency with verbs. Find and highlight the subject, *experimentation*, which is singular, so a singular verb is needed. Write an annotation saying "singular." Eliminate any answer that is not singular.

   - (A), (B), and (C) are wrong because they are plural.

   - (D) is correct because it's singular.

6. **B**   In this Rules question, verbs are changing in the answer choices, so it's testing consistency with verbs. Find and highlight the subject, *decision*, which is singular, so a singular verb is needed. Write an annotation saying "singular." Eliminate any answer that is not singular.

   - (A), (C), and (D) are wrong because they are plural.

   - (B) is correct because it's singular.

Pronoun Agreement Exercise (Page 226)

1. Antecedent: *debate team*. Pronoun: *its*. (Even though a team has multiple people on it, the word is still singular.)
2. Antecedent: *Each*. Pronoun: *it*. (The pronoun *each* is singular.)
3. Antecedent: *The pistol shrimp*. Pronoun: *its*.
4. Antecedent: *the observer-expectancy effect and the sampling bias*. Pronoun: *they*.
5. Antecedent: *Jupiter*. Pronoun: *itself*. (Pronoun questions can have either a form of "they" or a form of "it" as the correct answer, but forms of "it" are more common on the harder questions since we tend to think of things as plural when they're not.)

Verb Tense Exercise (Page 228)

1. was watching (past progressive)
2. had wanted (past perfect)
3. had completed (past perfect)
4. went (simple past)
5. has gone (present perfect)

Verb Tense Drill (Page 229)

1. **B**   In this Rules question, verbs are changing in the answer choices, so it's testing consistency with verbs. Find and highlight the subject, *Fuller*, which is singular, so a singular verb is needed. All of the answers work with a singular subject, so look for a clue regarding tense. The first part of the sentence states that the blank happened *After* something in *1943*, and the description of Fuller's simulation is also in past tense with the use of the word *allowed*. Highlight this verb as well as the other clues and write an annotation that says "past." Eliminate any answer not in past tense.

   - (A) is wrong because the sentence implies that Fuller completed the simulation and isn't discussing a time when he was in the process of developing it.

- (B) is correct because it's in simple past tense, which is appropriate for something that was created at a specific time.

- (C) is wrong because it's in present tense.

- (D) is wrong because the sentence doesn't suggest that this development occurred before another past development.

2. **A**   In this Rules question, verbs are changing in the answer choices, so it's testing consistency with verbs. Find and highlight the subject, *Researchers*, which is plural, so a plural verb is needed. All of the answers work with a plural subject, so look for a clue regarding tense. This sentence later says *when they identified a challenge*, so the verb should be in past tense and should suggest that the researchers were in the process of doing something at the same time that they identified the challenge. Highlight this clue and write an annotation that says "past." Eliminate any answer not in past tense.

- (A) is correct because it's in past progressive tense, suggesting that the researchers were in the process of exploring something *when they identified a challenge.*

- (B) is wrong because it's in present tense.

- (C) is wrong because it doesn't agree with the highlighted phrase later in the sentence, as *have been exploring* goes up to the present but the highlighted phrase uses a past tense verb.

- (D) is wrong because it's in future tense.

3. **A**   In this Rules question, verbs are changing in the answer choices, so it's testing consistency with verbs. Find and highlight the subject, *she*, which is singular, so a singular verb is needed. All of the answers work with a singular subject, so look for a clue regarding tense. The previous sentence and this sentence use past tense verbs: *transitioned* and *was*. Highlight those verbs and write an annotation that says "past." Eliminate any answer not in past tense.

- (A) is correct because it's in past tense.

- (B) is wrong because it's in future tense.

- (C) is wrong because *has become* goes up to the present, but everything in the passage is in past tense.

- (D) is wrong because it's in present tense.

4. **D**   In this Rules question, verbs are changing in the answer choices, so it's testing consistency with verbs. Find and highlight the subject, *practice*, which is singular, so a singular verb is needed. All of the answers work with a singular subject, so look for a clue regarding tense. The beginning of the sentence says *By the time UNESCO incorporated Al Sadu...into the UNESCTO List...in 2020*, so the blank happened before 2020, which is already in the past. Highlight these clues and write an annotation that says "past." Eliminate any answer not in past tense.

- (A) is wrong because the past perfect is needed in order to indicate what happened prior to the 2020 incorporation.

- (B) is wrong because it's in future tense.

- (C) is wrong because *has gained* goes up to the present, but the time period in the text stops in 2020.

- (D) is correct because the past perfect tense is appropriate here to show what had happened prior to 2020.

5. **B** In this Rules question, verbs are changing in the answer choices, so it's testing consistency with verbs. Find and highlight the subject, *Barnard*, which is singular, so a singular verb is needed. All of the answers work with a singular subject, so look for a clue regarding tense. The blank is describing something Barnard had already done (*in 1953*) by the time he did something *in 1967*. Highlight these clues and write an annotation that says "past." Eliminate any answer not in past tense.

- (A) is wrong because the past perfect is needed in order to indicate what happened prior to the 1967.

- (B) is correct because the past perfect tense is appropriate here to show what had happened prior to the 1967 transplant.

- (C) is wrong because it's in present tense.

- (D) is wrong because this tense would suggest that the 1953 work happened at the same time as the 1967 transplant, which isn't correct.

6. **B** In this Rules question, verbs are changing in the answer choices, so it's testing consistency with verbs. Find and highlight the subject, *cycle*, which is singular, so a singular verb is needed. All of the answers work with a singular subject, so look for a clue regarding tense. This sentence uses a past tense verb: *was intended*. Highlight this verb and write an annotation that says "past." Eliminate any answer not in past tense.

- (A) is wrong because it's in present tense.

- (B) is correct because it's in past tense.

- (C) is wrong because past perfect isn't appropriate here, as the cycle's completion isn't being compared in time to any other past event.

- (D) is wrong because it's in future tense.

7. **C** In this Rules question, verbs are changing in the answer choices, so it's testing consistency with verbs. Find and highlight the subject, *musician*, which is singular, so a singular verb is needed. All of the answers work with a singular subject, so look for a clue regarding tense. This sentence uses the present tense verb *is* and begins with *In modern settings*. Highlight these clues and write an annotation that says "present." Eliminate any answer not in present tense.

- (A) is wrong because the word *would* isn't appropriate here since the sentence isn't hypothetical.

- (B) is wrong because it's in past perfect tense.

- (C) is correct because the present perfect tense is appropriate for something that happened over time and continues to today.

- (D) is wrong because it's in future tense.

8. **A** In this Rules question, verbs are changing in the answer choices, so it's testing consistency with verbs. Find and highlight the subject, *Roberts*, which is singular, so a singular verb is needed. All of the answers work with a singular subject, so look for a clue regarding tense. This sentence says *some mathematicians didn't accept it until 1979*, which is already in the past, and Roberts's proposal occurred before that *in 1889*. Highlight these phrases and write an annotation that says "past." Eliminate any answer not in past tense.

- (A) is correct because it's in past perfect tense, indicating that this action was completed before another action.

- (B) and (D) are wrong because they're in present tense.

- (C) is wrong because the sentence isn't discussing something that happened while Roberts was in the process of proposing his theorem.

Modifier Exercise (Page 233)

1. Misplaced modifier: Ringing loudly. Currently modifying: Katelyn. Should be modifying: alarm clock.
2. Misplaced modifier: On top of the whiteboard. Currently modifying: my teacher. Should be modifying: colorful decorations.
3. Misplaced modifier: with a headache. Currently modifying: the nurse. Should be modifying: My sister.
4. Misplaced modifier: Buried under a pile of clothes. Currently modifying: I. Should be modifying: my headphones.
5. Misplaced modifier: While taking a quiz. Currently modifying: Jason's patience. Should be modifying: Jason.

Modifier Drill (Page 234)

1. **D** In this Rules question, the subjects of the answers are changing, which suggests it may be testing modifiers. Look for and highlight a modifying phrase: *Named in analogy to the notes of a musical scale*. Whatever is *Named in analogy to the notes* needs to come immediately after the comma. Eliminate any answer that doesn't start with something that can be named in a certain pattern.

- (A) is wrong because *Newlands* is an individual who wasn't named in a pattern.

- (B) and (C) are wrong because *properties* wouldn't be named in relation to *notes of a musical scale*.

- (D) is correct because *the Law of Octaves* could have been named in relation to *notes of a musical scale*.

2. **A** In this Rules question, the subjects of the answers are changing, which suggests it may be testing modifiers. Look for and highlight a modifying phrase: *By the time of its 20th anniversary in 2008.* Whatever had its *20th anniversary in 2008* needs to come immediately after the comma. Eliminate any answer that doesn't start with something that could have had its *20th anniversary.*

- (A) is correct because *the Registry* could have had its *20th anniversary.*

- (B) is wrong because *500 movies* is plural and can't have *its 20th anniversary.*

- (C) is wrong because *the members of the staff* is plural and can't have *its 20th anniversary.*

- (D) is wrong because *there were* doesn't provide something that could have had an anniversary.

3. **D** In this Rules question, the subjects of the answers are changing, which suggests it may be testing modifiers. Look for and highlight a modifying phrase: *Located only one degree of latitude south of the Equator.* Whatever is *Located only one degree of latitude south of the Equator* needs to come immediately after the comma. Eliminate any answer that doesn't start with something that can be located in this spot.

- (A) and (B) are wrong because a *distance* or *miles* can't be *Located* in a specific spot.

- (C) is wrong because *there are* doesn't provide something that could be located somewhere.

- (D) is correct because *the summit* could be *Located only one degree of latitude south of the Equator.*

4. **B** In this Rules question, the subjects of the answers are changing, which suggests it may be testing modifiers. Look for and highlight a modifying phrase: *Traveling to West Africa in 1989.* Whoever traveled *to West Africa in 1989* needs to come immediately after the comma. Eliminate any answer that doesn't start with someone or something that could travel *to West Africa.*

- (A) is wrong because *there were* doesn't provide someone who could have traveled.

- (B) is correct because *Bailey* could have traveled *to West Africa*

- (C) is wrong because *similarities* can't travel *to West Africa.*

- (D) is wrong because *Bailey's works* can't travel *to West Africa.*

5. **C** In this Rules question, the subjects of the answers are changing, which suggests it may be testing modifiers. Look for and highlight a modifying phrase: *Flying more slowly and turning sideways.* Whatever is *flying* and *turning sideways* needs to come immediately after the comma. Eliminate any answer that can't fly or turn sideways.

- (A) is wrong because *researchers* can't fly and turn sideways.

- (B) is wrong because the *wings* themselves don't fly or turn sideways.

- (C) is correct because *hummingbirds* can fly and turn sideways.

- (D) is wrong because a *study* can't fly and turn sideways.

CHAPTER 17: RULES CONCLUSION: IDENTIFYING QUESTION TYPES, SAVING TIME, AND SMART GUESSING

Verb Topic Identification Exercise (Page 241)

1. Subject-verb agreement—three options are singular and one is plural.
2. Verb tense—all of the answers are in "main verb" form, and all could work with a singular subject.
3. Verb form—there's a "to" verb and two *-ing* verbs.
4. Verb form—there's a "to" verb.
5. Subject-verb agreement—three options are plural and one is singular.
6. Verb tense—all of the options are in "main verb" form, and all could work with a plural subject.

CHAPTER 18: TRICKY TRANSITIONS

Tricky Transitions Drill (Page 251)

1. **C** This is a transition question, so follow the basic approach. Highlight ideas that relate to each other. The preceding sentence states that *A quantitative approach is associated with the traditional scientific method*, and this sentence states that *a qualitative approach gathers data from different sources*. These ideas disagree, so an opposite-direction transition is needed. Make an annotation that says "disagree." Eliminate any answer that doesn't match.

   - (A), (B), and (D) are wrong because *Therefore, Additionally,* and *Specifically* are same-direction transitions.

   - (C) is correct because *In contrast* is an opposite-direction transition.

2. **B** This is a transition question, so follow the basic approach. Highlight ideas that relate to each other. The preceding sentence states that *A like-skilled tiered system places individuals with similar backgrounds and skills together*, and this sentence describes a how a *cross-sectional system places individuals with a variety of backgrounds and skills together*. These ideas disagree, since they describe two different systems, so an opposite-direction transition is needed. Make an annotation that says "disagree." Eliminate any answer that doesn't match.

   - (A), (C), and (D) are wrong because *Consequently, For instance,* and *In particular* are same-direction transitions.

   - (B) is correct because *Alternatively* is an opposite-direction transition.

3. **C** This is a transition question, so follow the basic approach. Highlight ideas that relate to each other. The preceding sentence describes Rand's success with *Atlas Shrugged*, and this sentence reveals the *negative reviews* that *discouraged* her from writing fiction. These ideas disagree, so an opposite-direction transition is needed. Make an annotation that says "disagree." Eliminate any answer that doesn't match.

    • (A), (B), and (D) are wrong because *additionally, indeed,* and *thus* are same-direction transitions.

    • (C) is correct because *though* is an opposite-direction transition.

4. **B** This is a transition question, so follow the basic approach. Highlight ideas that relate to each other. The preceding sentence states that *The results of these surveys showed a decline in accurate understanding of financial concepts*, and this sentence states that *the concerning trend…occurred simultaneously with an increase in self-confidence scores*. These ideas disagree, as there's a contrast between *decline* and *increase* as well as between people's accuracy and confidence, so an opposite-direction transition is needed. Make an annotation that says "disagree." Eliminate any answer that doesn't match.

    • (A), (C), and (D) are wrong because *In other words, Therefore,* and *Similarly* are same-direction transitions.

    • (B) is correct because *Nevertheless* is an opposite-direction transition.

5. **B** This is a transition question, so follow the basic approach. Highlight ideas that relate to each other. The first part of the sentence says *Many experiments were subsequently conducted to test the theory of relativity using subatomic particles instead*, and the second part of the sentence says *it was not until 1971* that scientists did an actual test with the poles of the Earth. These ideas agree because the second part emphasizes that earlier tests did not follow Einstein's suggestion, so a same-direction transition is needed. Make an annotation that says "agree." Eliminate any answer that doesn't match.

    • (A) is wrong because the second part of the sentence is not a *result* of the first part of the sentence.

    • (B) is correct because *indeed* supports and reinforces the previous idea.

    • (C) is wrong because *regardless* is an opposite-direction transition.

    • (D) is wrong because the second part of the sentence is not an additional point beyond the ideas in the first part of the sentence.

6. **D** This is a transition question, so follow the basic approach. Highlight ideas that relate to each other. The preceding sentence states that *many dinosaurs had feathers far earlier than originally thought* and that the features contributed to their *survival* during a *mass extinction*, and this sentence states that this is *just one of many possible reasons* dinosaurs survived and spread into the next period. These ideas disagree, as the second sentence is lessening the previous statement by noting that it's only one of many reasons, so an opposite-direction transition is needed. Make an annotation that says "disagree." Eliminate any answer that doesn't match.

    • (A), (B), and (C) are wrong because *Consequently, Specifically,* and *Moreover* are same-direction transitions.

    • (D) is correct because *Granted* is used to concede a point, so it is an opposite-direction transition.

7. **A** This is a transition question, so follow the basic approach. Highlight ideas that relate to each other. The first sentence mentions *potential benefits* of LED technology, and this sentence mentions the *dire consequences* of the compositional changes. These ideas disagree, since the passage shifts from benefits to negative consequences, so an opposite-direction transition is needed. Make an annotation that says "disagree." Eliminate any answer that doesn't match.

    -   (A) is correct because *That said* is used to acknowledge a point and then go against it, so it is an opposite-direction transition.

    -   (B), (C), and (D) are wrong because *As a result, Additionally,* and *In fact* are same-direction transitions.

8. **A** This is a transition question, so follow the basic approach. Highlight ideas that relate to each other. The preceding sentence states that Watson and Crick *hypothesized that DNA was replicated in a semiconservative manner*, and this sentence states that *each DNA strand serves as a template on which a new strand is synthesized*. These ideas agree, so a same-direction transition is needed. Make an annotation that says "agree." Eliminate any answer that doesn't match.

    -   (A) is correct because this sentence is a clarification of the previous sentence.

    -   (B) and (D) are wrong because the second sentence is not an additional point beyond the ideas in the first sentence.

    -   (C) is wrong because *Nevertheless* is an opposite-direction transition.

9. **C** This is a transition question, so follow the basic approach. Highlight ideas that relate to each other. The first part of the sentence says *van Gogh did not achieve a successful career as an artist, having only ever sold one painting,* and the second part of the sentence says *it was his death that led to public awareness of his paintings and letters*. These ideas agree, so a same-direction transition is needed. Make an annotation that says "agree." Eliminate any answer that doesn't match.

    -   (A) is wrong because the second part of the sentence is not a *result* of the first part of the sentence.

    -   (B) is wrong because the second part of the sentence is not a more specific detail related to the first part of the sentence.

    -   (C) is correct because *ultimately* suggests something that eventually occurred, which is described in the second part of the sentence.

    -   (D) is wrong because the second part of the sentence is not a restatement of the information in the first part of the sentence.

10. **D** This is a transition question, so follow the basic approach. Highlight ideas that relate to each other. The first part of the sentence says *researchers found that high-pressure magmas can resemble low-pressure magmas…regardless of the depth,* and the second part of the sentence says *the compositions of trace elements found in flood basalts are unreliable at predicting the depths from which the magma was generated.* These ideas agree, as the second part of the sentence explains the significance of the findings in the first part, so a same-direction transition is needed. Make an annotation that says "agree." Eliminate any answer that doesn't match.

   - (A) and (B) are wrong because *be that as it may* and *nevertheless* are opposite-direction transitions.

   - (C) is wrong because the second part of the sentence is restating the previous idea rather than providing an additional point.

   - (D) is correct because *in other words* is a same-direction transition that restates the previous information, which is the relationship between the two parts of the sentence.

CHAPTER 19: TRICKY RHETORICAL SYNTHESIS

Rhetorical Synthesis Exercise (Page 260)

1. Eliminate (A) because it doesn't state why the crop loss occurred. Eliminate (B) because it doesn't mention the scale of the crop loss or why it occurred.
2. Eliminate (B) and (C) because they don't mention any *type* of study.
3. Eliminate (A) and (B) because they say what antihistamines are, but the audience is already familiar with them.
4. Eliminate (A) because preventing injuries would be a potential benefit, not a potential criticism. Eliminate (C) because it doesn't mention the act.
5. Eliminate (B) because it doesn't define PFAS; this term should be defined since the audience is unfamiliar with it. Eliminate (C) because it doesn't mention the study or its results.

Tricky Rhetorical Synthesis Drill (Page 262)

1. **B** This is a Rhetorical Synthesis question, so follow the basic approach. Highlight the goal(s) stated in the question: *compare the two men's work on the BASIC programming language.* Eliminate any answer that doesn't fulfill this purpose.

   - (A) is wrong because it doesn't specify what exactly each person contributed to *BASIC*.

   - (B) is correct because it shows each person's contribution to *BASIC*.

   - (C) is wrong because it doesn't mention *BASIC*.

   - (D) is wrong because it doesn't specify Kurtz's contribution to *BASIC*.

2. **B** This is a Rhetorical Synthesis question, so follow the basic approach. Highlight the goal(s) stated in the question: *emphasize the relative sizes of the two deserts' areas*. Eliminate any answer that doesn't fulfill this purpose.

 - (A) is wrong because it doesn't mention the *two deserts*.

 - (B) is correct because it compares the sizes of both deserts in relation to each other and the size of their respective continents.

 - (C) and (D) are wrong because they don't explain the sizes of the deserts in relation to each other or their respective continents.

3. **D** This is a Rhetorical Synthesis question, so follow the basic approach. Highlight the goal(s) stated in the question: *emphasize the aim of the research study*. Eliminate any answer that doesn't fulfill this purpose.

 - (A), (B), and (C) are wrong because they don't state what the study was aiming to do.

 - (D) is correct because it states the effect the scientists were studying.

4. **B** This is a Rhetorical Synthesis question, so follow the basic approach. Highlight the goal(s) stated in the question: *explain what caudal autotomy is*. Eliminate any answer that doesn't fulfill this purpose.

 - (A) is wrong because it only describes *autotomy* in general and doesn't specifically focus on *caudal autotomy*.

 - (B) is correct because it states a specific example of *caudal autotomy*.

 - (C) is wrong because it doesn't mention *caudal autonomy*.

 - (D) is wrong because it only describes something that happened after *caudal autotomy* and not what it is.

5. **B** This is a Rhetorical Synthesis question, so follow the basic approach. Highlight the goal(s) stated in the question: *provide an overview of potable reuse water*. Eliminate any answer that doesn't fulfill this purpose.

 - (A) and (D) are wrong because they don't specifically mention *potable reuse water*.

 - (B) is correct because it describes how *potable reuse water* is created from *wastewater* and summarizes the process described in the notes.

 - (C) is wrong because it says where *potable water* is created but not what it is.

6. **B** This is a Rhetorical Synthesis question, so follow the basic approach. Highlight the goal(s) stated in the question: *summarize the embedding effect*. Eliminate any answer that doesn't fulfill this purpose.

 - (A) and (D) are wrong because they express aspects of the notes other than the *embedding effect*.

 - (B) is correct because it describes the definition of the *embedding effect* as stated in the notes.

 - (C) is wrong because it doesn't *summarize* the embedding effect, as it only mentions the effect rather than providing its definition from the notes.

7. **D**   This is a Rhetorical Synthesis question, so follow the basic approach. Highlight the goal(s) stated in the question: *begin a narrative about Harjo's award-winning TV show.* Eliminate any answer that doesn't fulfill this purpose.

    •   (A) is wrong because a sentence that's beginning a narrative shouldn't skip ahead to what happened *later*.

    •   (B) is wrong because it doesn't introduce the show, which it would need to do in order to *begin a narrative* about the show.

    •   (C) is wrong because a sentence that's beginning a narrative should introduce the show by providing background information.

    •   (D) is correct because it includes background information about the TV show that can be elaborated upon.

8. **C**   This is a Rhetorical Synthesis question, so follow the basic approach. Highlight the goal(s) stated in the question: *explain a disadvantage of following the Dodo bird verdict when delivering psychotherapy.* Eliminate any answer that doesn't fulfill this purpose.

    •   (A) and (B) are wrong because they describe the verdict in general without specifying *a disadvantage*.

    •   (C) is correct because it describes how the therapy may not be effective or may be harmful.

    •   (D) is wrong because it focuses on all results of psychotherapy in general rather than *a disadvantage of following the Dodo bird verdict*.

9. **A**   This is a Rhetorical Synthesis question, so follow the basic approach. Highlight the goal(s) stated in the question: *make and support a generalization about methods used to find exoplanets.* Eliminate any answer that doesn't fulfill this purpose.

    •   (A) is correct because it presents a *generalization* about how astronomers find exoplanets and mentions *examples* that *support* this generalization.

    •   (B), (C), and (D) are wrong because they include specific details instead of a *generalization*.

10. **A**   This is a Rhetorical Synthesis question, so follow the basic approach. Highlight the goal(s) stated in the question: *summarize the study's findings.* Eliminate any answer that doesn't fulfill this purpose.

    •   (A) is correct because it specifies the general *findings* of the study.

    •   (B) and (C) are wrong because each mentions specific details instead of summarizing the findings from the last three bullet points.

    •   (D) is wrong because it focuses on the methods instead of the *findings*.

Part IV
SAT Advanced
Math Strategies

Chapter 21
Math Section
Introduction

INTRODUCTION

If you're aiming for the highest score on the SAT, you probably already have a broad range of math skills. In fact, you probably know the math required to answer almost every question on the Math modules. So why aren't you already scoring an 800?

You may be surprised to learn that what's holding you back is *not* content knowledge. Students who score in the high 600s have roughly the same amount of mathematical knowledge as those who score in the high 700s. Knowing more math is not the key—you have likely already learned almost every concept that's tested. You might feel frustrated that what you *can* do on a timed Math module doesn't match what you think you *should* be able to do.

The test-writers set out to make things difficult in multiple ways. They restrict your time while making you feel like you have to do all sorts of time-consuming algebraic manipulation. They make you feel rushed and then put in trap answers that you might get if you calculate something incorrectly or misread the question because you're in a hurry. The next several chapters will show you how to work around those challenges and even turn some of them to your advantage.

WHAT'S IN THE MATH CHAPTERS

To improve your score, you need to do the following four things. We will address each of them in its own chapter.

Chapter 22: Use Your Pacing Strategies and POOD. Develop a pacing strategy to move through the modules efficiently, and understand your Personal Order of Difficulty (POOD) so you can spend your time where it will help your score the most.

Chapter 23: Use Your TPR Math Tactics. Learn how to approach SAT Math questions in ways that aren't what the test-writers or your teachers at school would tell you to do. These are tried and true methods that improve both speed and accuracy, courtesy of your friends at the Princeton Review (TPR).

Chapter 24: Use the Built-In Calculator. The testing app has a calculator built into it, and this is a powerful tool that can make a major difference in your pacing, which in turn increases your score.

Chapter 25: Use Your Math Knowledge. Review some of the basics and learn new math content that will help on harder questions.

After you've become an expert in those four areas, **Chapter 26** will give you an opportunity to put everything together in a comprehensive drill, and **Chapter 27** has detailed explanations for all of the drill questions in the preceding chapters.

Finally, the book includes access to a full Math module online via your Student Tools. This is a harder second module to let you put your skills to the test. This full module is **not** the time to fall back on old habits. Apply your pacing strategy, think about your Personal Order of Difficulty, and use all of the tactics and tools from this book.

A NOTE ABOUT MATH CONTENT

This book will not cover every possible math topic that you could see on the SAT. It won't show you how to isolate a variable, set up a proportion, or turn a sentence into an equation, although you'll do all of those things while working the example questions. Those basics, and many more, can be found in the *Digital SAT Premium Prep* book. If you need to review some math content or some of the core techniques you encounter in this book, please consider picking up a copy of *Digital SAT Premium Prep* and using the two books together to fully prepare for the SAT. If you are reading this book after taking a Princeton Review class or working with one of our tutors, you can brush up on math with those course materials instead.

TAKE CHARGE

To do your best on the SAT Math section, you want to be an *active* test-taker. Passively doing what the test-writers expect will probably get you an OK score, but to get a great score you need to approach the test in new ways. This may include skipping around in the module instead of doing the questions in order, starting with the answers instead of writing out an algebraic equation, or using the built-in calculator instead of solving a graphing question by hand.

WORK SMARTER

The techniques and strategies in this part of the book are not that hard to learn, but they will not be second nature to you. Make sure that you focus on actively putting them into practice, not just passively reading them. Your goal is to internalize everything in the following chapters. When you have internalized a concept, you no longer consciously think about what to do—you simply do it.

Successfully incorporating these techniques requires three things: an open mind, practice, and review. Some of the techniques may feel awkward at first. You may even ask yourself why you should try something new if you can already get the question right another way. This is a valid question. The answer is that the way to get a high math score consistently is through transferable skills. If you have a consistent approach, you can apply that to many questions, not just to the one question where you happened to know the math content well.

Internalizing new skills takes practice. Think about your musical or athletic activities: the first time you try to play a new chord or learn a new serve, it probably doesn't go perfectly. You know how to do it, but the coordination and muscle memory aren't there yet. While taking a standardized test isn't a physical activity (you don't even have to pencil in bubbles anymore!), the same principle applies. Much of what you read in this section may seem basic. Only practice, however, will make the way you approach questions feel natural and automatic.

The second reason to practice what you see in the next few chapters is more pragmatic: if you were happy with your SAT Math score, you wouldn't be reading this. Do not merely skip to the drills and practice module and work them the old way. Even if you ultimately decide that your way is better on some questions, practice the new approaches. You may find yourself using them more often than you expected, and, even if you use your old approach sometimes, you're now making an *active* choice to do so.

It is often said that the definition of insanity is doing the same thing over and over again while expecting different results. Don't drive yourself crazy with meaningless practice; there is a better way. It involves keeping an open mind and being willing to adjust. Apply what you learn in these pages to every single question you work on. You will be pleased with the results.

Finally, review your work. Don't just count up your right and wrong answers and feel happy or disappointed. Ask yourself what happened. Reinforce things that you did well and had success with. Identify times when you were missing some content knowledge or overlooked a chance to use a new technique. Read the detailed explanations that come after the example questions or in Chapter 27. These will help you understand why you missed a question, identify a faster way to get it right, or confirm that you did it exactly right the first time.

Over time, you will begin to see patterns emerging. For example, you might notice that you tend to rush through algebra problems and make careless errors. On the other hand, you might find yourself getting more questions right and feeling less stressed about time because you're improving at recognizing the best approach.

LET'S GET STARTED!

That's a lot of theory and concept, and it might not feel solid to you until you apply it to the SAT Math section. It's time to turn your attention to pacing and POOD before moving on to new tactics and tools.

Chapter 22
Use Your Pacing
Strategies and
POOD

The SAT Math section is less about hard math and more about time. If you've taken a full test, you probably noticed this on the second module when you were trying to get hard questions right with very little time remaining. Read on to start thinking about ways to move through the Math section more efficiently.

MATH PACING

It's very easy to lose time trying to finish a question that you know you *should* be able to get right. As you know, however, the test-writers intentionally limit your time. They want to make it extremely difficult for even diligent students who are great at math to get an 800. Your goal, then, is to make active, almost aggressive, decisions about where to spend your time. Keep moving, and don't get stuck in the *should*.

Here's some advice to consider while you develop your individual pacing strategy.

Work in Bite-Sized Pieces—Sometimes, a complicated algebra question or long word problem can feel overwhelming. Take it one step at a time, keep your pencil moving, use the built-in calculator, and stay focused. Completing one step often makes the next step much clearer.

Use Process of Elimination. We will talk more about using POE on math questions in the next chapter, but remember that eliminating three answers is just as good as picking one. After every bite-sized piece, check to see whether you can cross out any answers.

Mark for Review—If you start working on a question but can't figure out the next bite-sized piece, flag it to come back to later. It might make more sense when you return to it, and then you can finish it. If not, it's time to guess.

Guessing is Good—Even test-takers who score in the upper 700s miss a question or two. You're not letting anyone down if you guess on some questions. You might guess right, and you're saving time for the questions you understand and know you can get right.

Find the Fill-ins—If you're down to a handful of questions, attempt as many of the remaining fill-in questions as you can. If you guess on a multiple-choice question, you have a 25% chance of guessing right, and your odds get even better if you use POE, Ballparking (another word for estimating), and your knowledge of trap answers to eliminate one or two answers. Your odds of randomly guessing the correct answer on a fill-in question are much lower. If you have no idea how to approach a specific fill-in question, however, go ahead and guess something that seems reasonable.

MATH POOD

You already know the idea behind Personal Order of Difficulty (POOD) from the introductory chapters in this book. If you worked through the Reading and Writing chapters first, you know how to apply the concept to the Reading and Writing section of the test. One of the major differences between the Reading and Writing section and the Math section is that the Math section is not organized by topic or question type. Instead, the questions increase in difficulty throughout the module. Or at least the test-writers think they do. In fact, a "hard" math question just means that a lot of test-takers miss it. They could miss those questions because they don't understand the math, but they also could have made a mistake or fallen for a trap answer. You will apply the techniques in this book to avoid mistakes and trap answers, so some of those "hard" questions might not be hard for you. Take each module in your *Personal* Order of Difficulty instead of using the order College Board has presented to you.

There are several approaches you can take with your POOD. Perhaps you want to do all the word problems at once while your brain is in that mode. Or word problems might be tiring so you want to space them out. Geometry might be your favorite thing in the world, so you want to seek out the geometry questions and make sure you get them right. You might even end up doing the questions in order, but don't let that be your default habit. Make an active, informed decision about every question.

A Note About Question Numbering

While there are some hard questions on the first Math module, the questions in the following drill and throughout the Math portion of this book are numbered 1–22 based on where they are likely to appear in a harder second Math module on the real SAT. This will give you a sense of how hard the question is supposed to be and whether you agree with the test-writers about the difficulty level.

POOD Drill

The following drill will give you a sense of your current POOD, and you will revisit the drill later to see whether your opinions have changed after working through the next few chapters.

It is important that you **NOT** try to answer these questions. Each question in the drill will be used later in the book as an example of a specific approach. If you do them now using your old habits, you will not get the full benefit of this book.

All you should do now is put the questions in order based on your Personal Order of Difficulty. Read the nine questions, and then use the worksheet at the end to mark them 1–9 in order from easiest to hardest based on your current strengths and weaknesses.

7 ☐ Mark for Review

$$\frac{3a-1}{7b+2} = c$$

The given equation relates the distinct positive numbers a, b, and c. Which equation correctly expresses $7b + 2$ in terms of a and c?

(A) $7b + 2 = 3a - 1 - c$

(B) $7b + 2 = \frac{c}{3a-1}$

(C) $7b + 2 = \frac{3a-1}{c}$

(D) $7b + 2 = 3ac - c$

9 ☐ Mark for Review

The circumference of a circle is equal to twice its area. What is the area of the circle?

(A) π

(B) 2π

(C) 4π

(D) 16π

10 ☐ Mark for Review

The function v models the value of a truck and is defined by $v(m) = 35{,}000(0.99)^m$, where m is the number of months after purchase. Which of the following best models the value of the truck y years after purchase?

(A) $v(y) = 35{,}000(0.99)^{\frac{y}{12}}$

(B) $v(y) = 35{,}000(0.99)^{12y}$

(C) $v(y) = 35{,}000(12 \times 0.99)^{12y}$

(D) $v(y) = (35{,}000 \times 12)(0.99)^{\frac{y}{12}}$

11 ☐ Mark for Review

$$8|x - 3| - 11|x - 3| = -48$$

What is the negative solution to the given equation?

12 ◻ Mark for Review

$$y = 4x^2 - 4x + 3$$
$$y = 3x + 2$$

At how many points do the graphs of the given equations intersect in the xy-plane?

(A) 0

(B) 1

(C) 2

(D) 3

14 ◻ Mark for Review

A certain amusement park sells two types of passes: half-day passes and all-day passes. The amusement park charges $40 for a half-day pass and $80 for an all-day pass. The amusement park sold a total of 70 passes one day for a total of $4,600. How many all-day passes did the amusement park sell?

☐

19 ◻ Mark for Review

x	$g(x)$
-6	172
-4	86
-2	0

The table shows three values of x and their corresponding values of $g(x)$. If function g is defined by $g(x) = cx + d$, where c and d are constants, what is the value of $c + d$?

(A) -129

(B) -86

(C) -45

(D) 43

20 ◻ Mark for Review

$$(x + 3)^2 + y^2 = 9$$

The equation shown represents a circle in the xy-plane. A new circle is created by shifting the given circle up 4 units. Which of the following equations represents the new circle?

(A) $(x - 1)^2 + y^2 = 9$

(B) $(x + 3)^2 + (y - 4)^2 = 9$

(C) $(x + 3)^2 + (y + 4)^2 = 9$

(D) $(x + 7)^2 + y^2 = 9$

21 🔖 Mark for Review

In triangles PQR and STU, side PQ has the same length as side ST, and side QR has the same length as side TU. Which additional piece of information is needed to determine whether triangle PQR is congruent to triangle STU?

(A) The length of side PR

(B) The measure of angle P

(C) The measures of angles Q and T

(D) No additional information is necessary.

POOD RANKING

Question	My POOD Ranking
7	✍
9	✍
10	✍
11	✍
12	✍
14	✍
19	✍
20	✍
21	✍

Chapter 23
Use Your TPR Math Tactics

Now that you're taking an active approach to the SAT Math modules and thinking about strategies to help with pacing, it's time focus on some tactics to help you achieve your pacing goals.

REVIEW BEFORE READING

This chapter will be much more productive if you're already familiar with the tactics. If you have the *Digital SAT Premium Prep* book or your student manual from a TPR course or tutorial, these strategies are covered in detail there. We will review them here, but go back to your other materials first if you're not sure what PITA, Plugging In, or the Word Problem Basic Approach refers to.

IT'S THE SAT

One way to ensure that you have enough time to spend on the questions that are hard for you is to find the most efficient way to correctly answer the questions you feel are easy or medium in difficulty. Test-takers often run out of time because they do too much "real math" on the easy and medium questions instead of getting them right a faster way and moving on. This does *not* mean that you should rush on easier questions; rushing leads to mistakes. Instead, treat the SAT as, well, the SAT.

Remind yourself throughout the test that this isn't a math test at school: you don't have to show your work, you don't get partial credit, and there isn't a "right way" to solve the problem. You just need to click the correct answer on the screen, and no one in a single university admissions department will know (or care) how you got there.

Sometimes, yes, you have to sit there and just do the math. Many other times, however, what looks like an algebra or geometry question doesn't need a lot of algebra or geometry. These are questions that you are probably getting right already but might be spending more time on than you need to. Let's pick up the pace and talk about things that start with P.

RTFQ

OK, this one doesn't start with P, but it's still important! One of the best ways to save time *and* avoid trap answers on SAT Math questions is to **R**ead **T**he **F**inal **Q**uestion.

Consider the following question:

> **7**   Mark for Review
>
> When graphed in the *xy*-plane, at what point (x, y) does the graph of $2y - x = 6$ intersect the *x*-axis?
>
> Ⓐ $(-6, 0)$
>
> Ⓑ $(0, 3)$
>
> Ⓒ $(0, 6)$
>
> Ⓓ $(3, 0)$

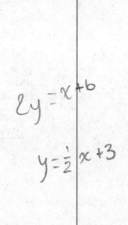

Recall that the question numbers in this book indicate approximately where the question would appear on the 22-question harder second module. Question 7 is not going to be the hardest question on the test, and the majority of high-scorers can expect to get it right. However, did you catch the trap? RTFQ one more time: which intercept are you looking for? Your math classes in school have probably conditioned you to put this equation into the format $y = mx + b$, where *b* represents the *y*-intercept. Remember, though: this isn't math class. It's the SAT. If you fell into your school habits and solved for the *y*-intercept, you would get (B). This question, on the other hand, is asking where the graph intersects the *x*-axis, which means $y = 0$. Slow down, read carefully, and avoid the kind of mistake that you'll regret when you get your score report back. Always RTFQ and jot down some key words on your scratch paper to make sure you know exactly what you are looking for. (The correct answer is (A), but we'll get to that in a minute.)

POE

Ah, now this one starts with P! Using the Process of Elimination (POE) on a standardized test is almost certainly something you did before you ever cracked open an SAT book. If you read the verbal part of this book first, you already know that POE is always the final step on Reading and Writing questions. Here's how to use POE to improve your pacing and maximize your score on the Math section.

First, focus on the word *process*. This implies an action on your part, and it helps you take control of the SAT. Because you have an on-screen answer eliminator and scratch paper, none of this needs to happen in your head. Use all of the tools available to you to work actively and keep track of where you are.

Second, anticipate the kinds of trap answers the test-writers are going to use, and turn that against them by eliminating those answers. Look back at the previous question. Once you RTFQ and catch that it's about the *x*-intercept, use POE to cross off any answer choice that represents a *y*-intercept:

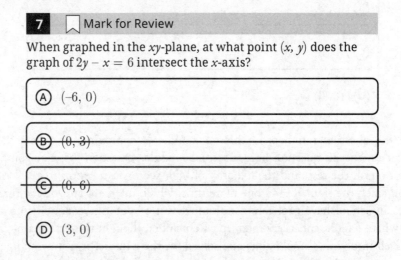

Notice how this simple technique avoids the obvious traps and cuts your answer choices in half simply by reading, with no math required. There are often more subtle trap answers, too. Choice (D) has the correct *y*-coordinate, but the point is not even on the line. Does 2(0) − 3 = 6? No, it does not, but 2(3) − 0 = 6. Choice (D) is what you would get if you mixed up the *x*- and *y*-coordinates. Get rid of this trap, as well, and you're left with only one answer, (A), which is correct.

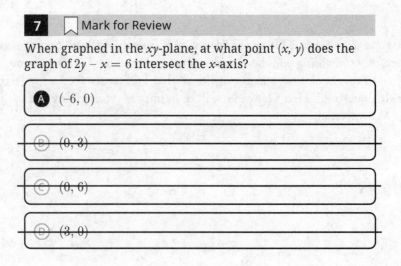

The message here is that the wrong answers on SAT Math questions are not random. The test-writers think about ways that test-takers could misread a question or make a math error, and then they put the results of those mistakes in the answer choices. When you RTFQ and use POE, you completely sidestep many of those traps.

Try the next two questions on your own, and then check the explanations. To get the most out of these examples, don't just do the questions; instead, see whether you can spot the traps in the questions and answers.

---

8 ☐ Mark for Review

The population of a certain town increased by 20% in one year. The following year, the town's population decreased by 20%. What was the net change in the town's population over the two-year period?

(A) It decreased by 10%.

(B) It decreased by 4%.

(C) It stayed the same.

(D) It increased by 4%.

---

9 ☐ Mark for Review

$$x^2 + y^2 = 360$$
$$y = -3x$$

The given system of equations has a solution at (x, y). What is the value of y^2?

(A) −18

(B) 6

(C) 36

(D) 324

$x^2 + 9x^2 = 360$

$10x^2 = 360$

$x^2 = 36$

$x = 6$

$36 + y^2 = 360$

$y^2 =$

Here's How to Ace #8

The question asks for a net change over time. The main trap answer is (C). Many students will be tempted to think that the 20% increase is canceled out by the 20% decrease, making the net change 0. It's a good rule of thumb that, if you arrive at an answer by simply thinking for a few seconds, that answer is probably wrong. To see why percentages don't work that way, use some real numbers. Make the original population 100. One year later, it will increase by 20% to 120.

The population then decreases by 20%, so take 20% of 120 and subtract it from 120: $120 - \left(\frac{20}{100}\right)(120) = 120 - 24 = 96$. The population decreased by $100 - 96 = 4$ out of the original 100, which is a 4% decrease. The correct answer is (B).

Here's How to Ace #9

The question asks for a value based on a solution to a system of equations. You can eliminate (A) before doing any work because a squared term cannot be negative—the SAT does not test imaginary numbers. To solve algebraically, substitute $-3x$ for y in the first equation to get $x^2 + (-3x)^2 = 360$, which becomes $x^2 + 9x^2 = 360$, and then $10x^2 = 360$. Divide both sides of the equation by 10 to get $x^2 = 36$. That's answer choice (C), but are you done? No! The final question asks for the value of y^2, not x^2. Choice (C) is a trap answer. Cross it out and do a little more math: plug 36 into the first equation for x^2 to get $36 + y^2 = 360$. Subtract 36 from both sides of the equation to get $y^2 = 324$. Does that answer the final question? Yes! Pick (D) and move on.

Call on the Calculator
Questions about solutions to a system of equations are a great chance to use the built-in calculator. We'll show you more about that later in this book.

There is another solid, algebra-free way to solve #9. If you've practiced using the built-in calculator—and by the end of this book you will have!—you know that it's quite easy to enter both equations and then scroll and zoom to see the point(s) of intersection. There are two points, at $(-6, 18)$ and $(6, -18)$. Since the question asks for the value of y^2, it doesn't matter which y-value you use: $18^2 = 324$ and $(-18)^2 = 324$. How are the test-writers trying to trick you this time? Let's look at those answer choices again:

Choice (A) is the y-coordinate of one of the points of intersection. That leaves out a math step.

Choice (B) is the x-coordinate of one of the points of intersection. That leaves out a math step *and* has the wrong coordinate.

Choice (C) is the x-coordinate of one of the points of intersection squared. That's the right math with the wrong coordinate.

Choice (D), of course, is correct.

Remember to always, *always* RTFQ. Whether you use algebra or the built-in calculator, the correct answer is (D).

PLUGGING IN THE ANSWERS (PITA)

The steps for using PITA are below. If you need a refresher on the basics, review that part of your *Digital SAT Premium Prep* book, class Manual, or other Princeton Review resource.

> To solve a problem by plugging in the answers:
>
> 1. Rewrite the answer choices on your scratch paper and label them.
> 2. Starting with one of the middle answer choices, work the steps of the problem.
> 3. Look for something in the question that tells you what must happen for the answer to be correct.
> 4. When you find the correct answer, STOP.

Here's an example to refresh your memory.

8 🔖 Mark for Review

A store reduces the price of a certain item by 20% and then reduces that price by 15%. If the final price of the item is $170, what was its original price?

Ⓐ $140

Ⓑ $185

Ⓒ $200

Ⓓ $250

Here's How to Ace It

The question asks for the original price of an item. Back in algebra class, your teacher would have wanted your work to look something like this:

$$x - 0.2x - 0.15(x - 0.2x) = 170$$
$$x - 0.2x - 0.15x + 0.03x = 170$$
$$0.68x = 170$$
$$x = 250$$

Depending on how you feel about algebra, this might seem OK, and algebra skills will be necessary on *some* SAT questions. This is the SAT, however, not algebra class, and you need to save time for the harder questions, so look for a way to get this question right that's faster and less complicated to set up. That way is PITA.

The question asks for the original price of an item, and it's a multiple-choice question. That means that the original price *must* be $140, $185, $200, or $250. Because the correct answer is right in front of you, you do not need to use algebra. Instead, plug in the answers. Follow the PITA steps above and start by rewriting the answers on your scratch paper. They represent possible values for the original price, so label them that way.

Original Price

A) $140
B) $185
C) $200
D) $250

Starting with a middle number might help you determine which direction to go if the first number doesn't work, so try (B) or (C). The math will be easier with a round number, so (C) is a good place to start. Plug in $200 for the original price, and work the steps of the question one at a time. Take 20% of 200 to get $\left(\frac{20}{100}\right)$ $200 = $40. The store *reduces* the price by 20%, so subtract $40 from $200 to get $160. Next, take 15% of this new price to get $\left(\frac{15}{100}\right)$ $160 = $24. This is another reduction, so subtract: $160 − $24 = $136. The question states that the final price is $170, not $136, so (C) is wrong. The final price is too low, so the original price was also too low; eliminate (A) and (B), as well.

Your scratch paper should look something like this:

Original Price	20%	New Price	15%	Final Price = 170?
A) $140				too small
B) $185				too small
C) $200	40	200 − 40 = 160	$\left(\frac{15}{100}\right)$ 160 = 24	160 − 24 = 136
D) $250				

Only (D) is left, so it must be correct. Don't spend any more time on this question; click (D) and move on.

Depending on how things go with POE and ballparking, you might need to plug in more than one answer. If you needed to try (D) on the previous question, for example, you would follow the exact same arithmetic steps with the value in (D) as the starting point:

Original Price	20%	New Price	15%	Final Price = 170?
A) $140				too small
B) $185				too small
C) $200	40	200 − 40 = 160	$\left(\dfrac{15}{100}\right)$ 160 = 24	160 − 24 = 136
D) $250	50	250 − 50 = 200	$\left(\dfrac{15}{100}\right)$ 200 = 30	200 − 30 = 170 ✔

It's important not only to know how to use PITA but also to recognize *when* you can use it.

> Three ways to know that it's time for PITA:
>
> 1. There are numbers in the answer choices.
> 2. The question asks for a specific amount. Look for phrases like "the number of," "what was," or "how many."
> 3. You have the urge to write an algebraic equation to solve the problem.

When you see some or all of these features in a question, recognize that it's a potential PITA question. Sometimes it won't work or there will be a more efficient way to answer the question, but PITA should be the first thing you consider. This also applies to questions that are about something other than algebra, such as geometry.

Try applying the same PITA steps on the following geometry question; then read the explanation to see how you did.

9 ☐ Mark for Review

The circumference of a circle is equal to twice its area. What is the area of the circle?

Ⓐ π

Ⓑ 2π

Ⓒ 4π

Ⓓ 16π

Here's How to Ace It

The question asks for the area of a geometric figure. That means the question is asking for a specific value. Check the answers: there are numbers in order. Are you tempted to start writing an equation to relate the circumference and area of a circle? You probably are, but don't do it. This question ticks all three boxes for PITA, so use it.

Strike Won!

When you plug in, start with the easier of the two middle choices. The first one you do is likely to be the slowest, as you're still working your way through the problem, so don't complicate it. Subsequent tries should be faster and are likely to be more straightforward than writing out equations.

First, rewrite the answer choices on your scratch paper and label them "area." Next, start with one of the middle numbers. Since 4 should work well with both circumference and area, start with (C). Write down the formula for the area of a circle. You can always click open the reference sheet in the testing app if you forget it. The formula is $A = \pi r^2$. Plug in 4π for the area, and the formula becomes $4\pi = \pi r^2$. Divide both sides of the equation by π to get $4 = r^2$, and then take the positive square root of both sides of the equation to get $2 = r$. If the radius is 2, what is the circumference? Write down that formula, which is $C = 2\pi r$. Plug in 2 for r to get $C = 2\pi(2)$, which becomes $C = 4\pi$. That's the same as the area you plugged in, but the question states that *the circumference of a circle is equal to twice its area*, so eliminate (C).

The circumference needs to be greater than the area, so try a smaller value for the area. You might notice that an area of 2π will make the radius a square root, so leave (B) for now and try (A). Plug in π for the area, and the area formula becomes $\pi = \pi r^2$. Divide both sides of the equation by π to get $1 = r^2$, and then take the positive square root of both sides of the equation to get $1 = r$. If the radius is 1, the circumference formula becomes $C = 2\pi(1)$, and then $C = 2\pi$. If the circumference is 2π and the area is π, the circumference is twice the area. This matches the information in the question, so stop here. The correct answer is (A).

That's Plugging In the Answers! It turns algebra into arithmetic, requires less thinking about how to set things up, makes it more likely that you will catch any calculation errors, and avoids trap answers. Seek opportunities to use PITA, and apply this method as often as possible on the Math modules.

PLUGGING IN (YOUR OWN NUMBERS)

Sometimes, instead of plugging in the answer choices, you will plug in numbers that you come up with yourself. The purpose is to replace variables with numbers to turn an algebra question into an arithmetic question. Like PITA, this approach will help you get questions right more quickly than you might with algebra. It will also help you avoid setting something up incorrectly or making an algebra mistake—exactly the kind of thing the test-writers *want* you to do.

> Plugging In is easy. It has three steps:
>
> 1. Pick numbers for the variables in the question.
> 2. Use your numbers to find an answer to the question. Circle your answer.
> 3. Plug your number(s) for the variable(s) into the answer choices and eliminate choices that don't equal the answer you found in Step 2.

Unlike PITA questions, which are about specific values and numbers, Plugging In questions are about relationships among values and variables. That's why questions about equivalent expressions are a great chance to plug in.

Here's an example.

---

14 🔖 Mark for Review

$$\frac{6x(6x+10)+4(6x+10)}{3x+5}$$

For all positive values of x, which of the following is equivalent to the given expression?

- (A) $\dfrac{3x+2}{3x+5}$
- (B) $\dfrac{36x^2+24x+20}{3x+5}$
- (C) $\dfrac{36x^2+24x+100}{3x+5}$
- (D) $12x+8$

$2(6x+4) = 12x+8$

Here's How to Ace It

The question asks for an equivalent expression. First, remind yourself that this is not algebra class; it's the SAT. Don't just automatically start doing algebra. Second, notice that the question asks about equivalent expressions and has variables in the answer choices. The correct answer will have the same value as the first expression for any value of x, so plug in your own number for x. Follow the Plugging In steps shown above. First, pick a number to plug in. Unless there's a good reason not to use it, 2 is usually a good choice. It's small, so the math should be easier, and it avoids some potential pitfalls that can happen with 0 and 1.

Next, plug in 2 for x, and the expression in the question becomes $\dfrac{6(2)[6(2) + 10] + 4[6(2) + 10]}{3(2) + 5}$.

Simplify to get $\dfrac{12(12 + 10) + 4(12 + 10)}{6 + 5}$, and then $\dfrac{12(22) + 4(22)}{11}$. There are several ways to finish the arithmetic from here. One is to divide both 22s by 11 to get $12(2) + 4(2)$, which becomes $24 + 8$, and then 32. This is the target value; write it down and circle it.

Finally, plug $x = 2$ into all four answer choices, and eliminate any that do not match the target value. Choice (A) becomes $\dfrac{3(2) + 2}{3(2) + 5}$, then $\dfrac{6 + 2}{6 + 5}$, and finally $\dfrac{8}{11}$. This does not match the target value of 32, so eliminate (A). Choice (D) becomes $12(2) + 8$, then $24 + 8$, and finally 32. This matches the target value, so keep (D). Because you avoided 0 and 1, it is unlikely that any other answer choice will work, but check (B) and (C) just in case. Notice that they have the same denominator as the original expression, which you already know is 11 when $x = 2$, so only work with the numerators. The numerator in (B) becomes $36(2)^2 + 24(2) + 20$. Simplify to get $36(4) + 48 + 20$, then $144 + 68$, and finally 212. Since $\dfrac{212}{11} \approx 19.3$, not 32, eliminate (B). The only difference between (B) and (C) is + 20 or + 100 in the numerator, so the numerator of (C) is $144 + 48 + 100 = 292$. Since $\dfrac{292}{11} \approx 26.5$, not 32, eliminate (C). The correct answer is (D).

The previous question had both of the big clues that you can plug in your own numbers. Here they are so you can be on the lookout.

> Two ways to know to use Plugging In:
>
> 1. The question asks about a relationship between variables or numbers. Look for phrases such as "equivalent expression" or "in terms of."
> 2. There are variables in the answer choices.

Sometimes it's not quite as obvious, but identifying that you can plug in will help you get the question right faster and avoid mistakes.

Take a look at this one.

---

12 ☐ Mark for Review

The value of p is 85% less than the value of r, and the value of r is 125% greater than the value of s. What percent of s is p? (Disregard the percent sign when entering your answer.)

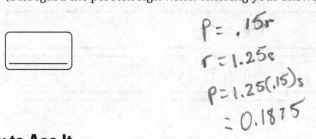

$$p = .15r$$
$$r = 1.25s$$
$$p = 1.25(.15)s$$
$$= 0.1875$$

Here's How to Ace It

The question asks for a value based on percentages. You saw a similar question earlier and discovered the sneaky trap answers you can expect to see on percent questions. However, this one doesn't have answer choices at all; it's a fill-in question! How can plugging in work without answer choices? It still works because all of the values in the question are related to each other by percentages, not by real numbers. That opens the door to plugging in your own number. Because *percent* means "out of 100," the perfect number to plug in is—you guessed it—100.

Since p is related to r and r is related to s, start with s. Make $s = 100$. The question states that *the value of r is 125% greater than the value of s*. You are probably used to automatically converting percentages to decimals, and that works well when the percent is between 0 and 100. It can get more complicated when the percent is a decimal or greater than 100, so using fractions is safer on the SAT. In this case, write 125% as $\dfrac{125}{100}$. Because you plugged in 100, the math is easy, and 125% of 100 is $\frac{125}{100}(100) = 125$. Read carefully! Does $r = 125$? No, r is 125% *greater than* s, so $r = 100 + 125$, or $r = 225$.

The question also states that *the value of p is 85% less than the value of r*. Take 85% of 225 to get $\frac{85}{100}(225) = 191.25$. Subtract that from the value of r to get $p = 225 - 191.25$, or $p = 33.75$. Once again, plugging in 100 pays off: what percent of 100 is 33.75? It's 33.75%, of course. The fill-in box does not accept the percent sign, but it does give you room for five characters when the answer is positive, so do not round up or down. The correct answer is 33.75.

Let's look at another question that provides an example of how Plugging In can help.

---

10 ☐ Mark for Review

The function v models the value of a truck and is defined by $v(m) = 35,000(0.99)^m$, where m is the number of months after purchase. Which of the following best models the value of the truck y years after purchase?

Ⓐ $v(y) = 35,000(0.99)^{\frac{y}{12}}$

Ⓑ $v(y) = 35,000(0.99)^{12y}$

Ⓒ $v(y) = 35,000(12 \times 0.99)^{12y}$

Ⓓ $v(y) = (35,000 \times 12)(0.99)^{\frac{y}{12}}$

Here's How to Ace It

The question asks for a function that models a specific situation. You should recognize that the function is in the form of the exponential growth and decay formula, which is *final amount =* *(original amount)*$(1 \pm rate)^{number\ of\ changes}$. Nothing in the question gives a reason to change the original amount or the rate, so eliminate (C) because it changes the rate and (D) because it changes the original amount. You just used one of your SAT skills, POE, to cut the answers in half very quickly. Now use another SAT skill, Plugging In, to find the correct answer.

The only change indicated in the question is in the units of the number of changes. You know that there are 12 months in a year, and you probably think you know whether (A) or (B) is correct. Keep in mind, however, that picking an answer after thinking for a few seconds often leads to a trap answer, so plug in to double check. Plug in $m = 24$ for the number of months. This is equivalent to 2 years, so $y = 2$. Plug $y = 2$ into the exponent in (A) to get $\frac{2}{12} = \frac{1}{6}$ months. That's not 24 months, so eliminate (A). Plug $y = 2$ into the exponent in (B) to get $12(2) = 24$ months. That's 24 months, so the correct answer is (B).

Was your instinct correct, or would you have rushed your way into the wrong answer? Either way, it's not worth the risk. When a growth and decay question changes units, always plug in to check.

WORD PROBLEM BASIC APPROACH

You are now well aware that PITA and Plugging In work on word problems, and you are also learning that identifying the most efficient approach quickly is a great way to increase your pacing. That's one reason it's important to have a consistent approach for SAT word problems and follow it every time.

Here's that approach:

Word Problem Basic Approach

1. **Read the Final Question (RTFQ)**—Understand the actual question being asked. Write down key words.
2. **Let the answers point the way**—Use the answer type to help determine how to start working on the question.
3. **Work in bite-sized pieces**—Find one piece to start with; then work piece-by-piece until the final question has been answered.
4. **Use POE**—Check to see whether any answers can be eliminated after each bite-sized piece.

You hopefully already know this approach from other work you've done with the Princeton Review or from reading the *Digital SAT Premium Prep* book. You have also applied it several times already in this chapter, even if you weren't aware of it.

Treat the first step literally: read the end of the question first and then go back and read more of the question as you work each Bite-Sized Piece. This way, you aren't wasting time doing unnecessary work.

Let's imagine two different approaches to the next question.

15 ⚑ Mark for Review

A cargo ship currently holds two-thirds of its maximum capacity by weight. If seven tons of cargo were added to the ship, it would hold 75% of its maximum capacity. What is the maximum capacity, in tons, of the ship?

(A) 48

(B) 60

(C) 84

(D) 96

Here's How to Ace It

Here's how your friend who is stuck on a 650 Math score and can't figure out why would approach this question.

OK, my algebra teacher told me to use a variable for an unknown value, so I'll call the max capacity x. The ship has two-thirds of that.

$$\frac{2}{3}x$$

Now we need to add 7 tons to that.

$$\frac{2}{3}x + 7$$

Then it would hold 75% of its max capacity, so...I think that means equals? And 75% is 0.75, I'm sure of that.

$$\frac{2}{3}x + 7 = 0.75x$$

Cool, now I just need to solve for x. Ugh, there's a fraction and a decimal. OK, calculator time.

[entering in a calculator] zero point seven five minus two *oops, I pressed equals too soon*

[entering in a calculator, again] zero point seven five minus two divided by three equals

0.08333 and so on

OK, so 7 = 0.083x. Now divide to solve for x and I get 84.337 blah blah blah. That's close to 84, so I think it's (C). Those numbers were pretty messy though; maybe I should check them again...

Back to reality: your friend got the question right, but it took a while, there were several places to make a mistake, and your friend doesn't sound very confident. Here's how you, the SAT expert, will approach this question:

The final question asks for a specific value, and I see numbers in the answers, so it's a PITA question. Let me write down key words, including the units because I know they like to mess with that. I'll write down the answers and label them while I'm at it.

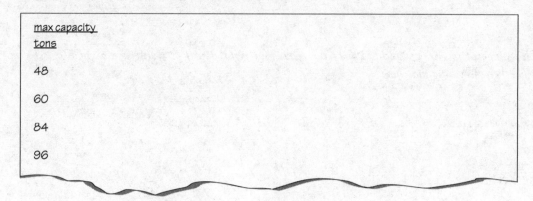

60 is a round number in the middle so I'll start there. Time to read more of the question in bite-sized pieces. Oh look, I can figure out $\frac{2}{3}$ of the max capacity.

Now we add 7 tons.

max capacity tons	$\dfrac{2}{3}$	+7	
48			
60	$\dfrac{2}{3}(60) = 40$	40 + 7 = 47	
84			
96			

It's supposed to end up with 75% of the max, and right now I'm trying a max of 60. Let's see whether everything matches.

max capacity tons	$\dfrac{2}{3}$	+7	75% of max	
48				
60	$\dfrac{2}{3}(60) = 40$	40 + 7 = 47	0.75(60) = 45	*47 is close to 45, but no; bye (B)*
84				
96				

I'm not sure which direction to go, but those numbers were close, so probably not (D). I'll try (C). The arithmetic will go faster this time because it's the same steps I just did.

max capacity tons	$\dfrac{2}{3}$	+7	75% of max	
48				
~~60~~	$\dfrac{2}{3}(60) = 40$	40 + 7 = 47	0.75(60) = 45	*47 is close to 45, but no; bye (B)*
84	$\dfrac{2}{3}(84) = 56$	56 + 7 = 63	0.75(84) = 63	*That worked! I rule. Next question.*
96				

Yes, you do rule! The first two steps of the Word Problem Basic Approach are vital to a solid pacing strategy. By focusing on the final question and the answer type, you can get started on the first Bite-Sized Piece right away. If you don't see a good place to start, skip that question and come back to it later.

Here's a summary of the differences between PITA questions and Plugging In questions. Internalize these clues so you recognize chances to use these approaches right away.

	Plugging In the Answers (PITA)	Plugging In your own number
Question	Asks for a specific value	Relationship among values
Answers	Numbers in order	Include variables or unknowns

Look for these clues in the following question, and then apply the best approach. Hint: it's not algebra.

---

21 🔖 Mark for Review

A player in a certain video game earn 700 points per match for the first 12 matches the player wins, and then 500 points per match for each match won after that. If a veteran player has won m matches, where $m \geq 12$, which function f gives the total number of points the player has earned by winning matches?

Ⓐ $f(m) = 500m - 6,000$

Ⓑ $f(m) = 500m + 2,400$

Ⓒ $f(m) = 500m + 8,400$

Ⓓ $f(m) = 1,200m - 6,000$

Here's How to Ace It

The question asks for a function that represents a certain situation. The question is about the relationship between the number of matches and the number of points, and the answer choices contain variables, so this is a good chance to plug in some numbers. You might think, however, that you already know the answer. Over the first 12 matches, the player earns $(700)(12) = 8,400$ points. After that, it's 500 points for each of m matches, and that's $500m$. Choice (C) is looking really good.

What if you plug in to check? In one possible scenario, the player earns 8,400 points for winning 12 matches, which means that $f(12)$ should equal 8,400. Plug 12 into each answer choice to see what happens. Choice (A) becomes $f(12) = 500(12) - 6,000$, then $f(12) = 6,000 - 6,000$, and finally $f(12) = 0$. This is definitely not 8,400, so eliminate (A). Choice (B) becomes $f(12) = 500(12) + 2,400$, then $f(12) = 6,000 + 2,400$, and finally $f(12) = 8,400$. Huh, that's interesting; keep (B). Choice (C) isn't going to work because 500(12) + 8,400 is greater than 500(12) + 2,400; eliminate (C). Choice (D) becomes $f(12) = 1,200(12) − 6,000$, then $f(12) = 14,400 − 6,000$, and finally $f(12) = 8,400$. This also works, so keep (D). Notice that the tempting but wrong answer (C) is already gone!

Try a second scenario with the two remaining answer choices. Make $m = 14$, so the player earns the initial 8,400 points plus another (2)(500) = 1,000 points for winning two more matches, for a total of 8,400 + 1,000 = 9,400 points. Plug $m = 14$ into (B) and (D) to see whether they equal 9,400. Choice (B) becomes $f(14) = 500(14) + 2,400$, then $f(14) = 7,000 + 2,400$, and finally $f(14) = 9,400$. This matches the target number of points, so keep (B). Choice (D) becomes $f(14) = 1,200(14) − 6,000$, then $f(14) = 16,800 − 6,000$, and finally $f(14) = 10,800$; eliminate (D). The correct answer is (B).

Why didn't (C) work? What's happening here is that the player earned 500 points for every match won, plus an additional 200 points per match for the first 12. That's why you add 2,400 instead of 8,400 to 500m. Even if that makes sense now, don't try to think your way through a question like this on the test. The test-writers have a few varieties of this kind of question, and they *always* include very tempting trap answers. Instead, you got the question right confidently by doing some basic arithmetic. Algebra is always there when you need it, but never lose sight of the test-taking tactics that are both faster and safer.

Sometimes, of course, you *do* need algebra. Always RTFQ, then try to use your new skills—POE, PITA, and Plugging In—before giving in and using algebra if nothing else works.

Here's an example.

---

14 | Mark for Review

A certain amusement park sells two types of passes: half-day passes and all-day passes. The amusement park charges $40 for a half-day pass and $80 for an all-day pass. The amusement park sold a total of 70 passes one day for a total of $4,600. How many all-day passes did the amusement park sell?

45

Call on the Calculator
Believe it or not, the built-in graphing calculator would save some time and effort on this question. You will see how in the next chapter.

Here's How to Ace It

The question asks for a value given a specific situation. RTFQ and write down "how many all-day passes?" That's a specific value, so it sounds like PITA so far! The answers contain…oh no, there are no answers, so PITA is unavailable. So is POE, because there's nothing to eliminate. Plugging In works for relative values, but these are all specific values equal to other specific values. The only option left is to work in Bite-Sized Pieces. In this case, that involves translating English into math and solving simultaneous equations.

Use h to represent the number of half-day passes and a to represent the number of all-day passes. If you use x and y or different variables, write down what they represent to keep things straight. The total amount the amusement park charges for half-day passes becomes $40h$, and the total amount charged for all-day passes becomes $80a$. The question states that the total amount for the day was 4,600, so one equation is $40h + 80a = 4,600$. The question also states that the *amusement park sold a total of 70 passes*, and there are only two types of passes, so the other equation is $h + a = 70$.

Check the key words that you wrote down from the final question: the question asks for the number of all-day passes, so you want to solve for a. Find a way to make the h-terms disappear. Multiply the entire second equation by −40 to get $-40h - 40a = -2,800$. Now the two equations have the same h-value with opposite signs, so stack and add the equations.

$$
\begin{array}{r}
40h + 80a = 4,600 \\
+ \underline{(-40h - 40a = -2,800)} \\
40a = 1,800
\end{array}
$$

Divide both sides of the resulting equation by 40 to get $a = 45$. The correct answer is 45.

Questions like the previous one are pretty rare on the SAT, but you could see one. You might also see questions that deal with quadratics, systems of equations, and graphing that can't be solved by using PITA or Plugging In. The good news is that sometimes your new skills *will* work on those questions, and you have another great tool: the built-in calculator.

We will show you many things about the built-in calculator in the next chapter, but first it's time to practice the skills you just learned.

Use Your TPR Math Tactics Drill

Use PITA, Plugging In, and/or the Word Problem Basic Approach on each of the following six questions. Don't forget to RTFQ and look for chances to POE, too. If you want to try out your pacing and POOD strategies, set a timer for 6 minutes. Keep in mind that the question number represents approximately where it would appear in a harder second module.

Answers and explanations can be found in Chapter 27.

---

7 ☐ Mark for Review

$$y = x^2 + 2$$
$$y + 2x = 5$$

Which of the following ordered pairs (x, y) is a solution to the given system of equations?

Ⓐ $(-3, 11)$

Ⓑ $(-1, 3)$

Ⓒ $(3, -1)$

Ⓓ $(11, -3)$

---

13 ☐ Mark for Review

A rectangle has a perimeter of 52 centimeters. The length of the rectangle is l centimeters, and the width is w centimeters. The value of l is 2 less than 6 times the value of w. What is the value of l?

Ⓐ 4

Ⓑ 9

Ⓒ 18

Ⓓ 22

---

14 ☐ Mark for Review

$$v = \frac{1}{2}at^2$$

The velocity, v, of an object t seconds after beginning to accelerate from rest at a constant acceleration, a, is modeled by the given formula. According to the formula, what is the ratio of the velocity of the object t seconds after the object begins to accelerate to the velocity of the object $2.5t$ seconds after the object begins to accelerate?

Ⓐ $\frac{4}{25}$

Ⓑ $\frac{2}{5}$

Ⓒ $\frac{5}{2}$

Ⓓ $\frac{25}{4}$

---

19 ☐ Mark for Review

A large bag of dry dog food contains 150 cups of kibble. Which equation represents the total number of large bags, L, needed to feed a dog two cups of kibble three times per day for d days?

Ⓐ $L = 25d$

Ⓑ $L = 50d$

Ⓒ $L = \frac{d}{25}$

Ⓓ $L = \frac{d}{50}$

(handwritten work)

$2l + 2w = 52 \qquad l + w = 26$

$l = 6w - 2 \qquad 6w + w - 2 = 26$

$l = 24 - 2 \qquad\qquad 7w = 28$

$= 22 \qquad\qquad\qquad w = 4$

$L = \frac{6d}{150} = \frac{d}{25}$

20 ⬛ Mark for Review

Given the inequality $y < 6x + 7$, which of the following tables gives three possible values of x and their corresponding values of y?

(A)

x	y
-2	-6
1	13
4	31

(B)

x	y
-2	-6
1	10
4	28

(C)

x	y
-2	-5
1	10
4	31

(D)

x	y
-2	-4
1	10
4	28

21 ⬛ Mark for Review

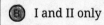

$$(x + c)(x + 5) = x + 5$$

In the given equation, c is a constant and $c < 4$. Which of the following are solutions to the equation?

   I. -5
  II. $1 - c$
 III. $-c$

(A) Neither I, II, nor III

(B) I and II only

(C) I and III only

(D) II and III only

Chapter 24
Use the Built-in Calculator

One of the most useful tools that the test-writers provide for you in the testing app is the built-in calculator. Knowing when and how to use this tool will help you get easy and medium questions right faster, and it will make some harder questions much easier. Read on to learn everything you need to know about taking advantage of this feature.

CALCULATOR CONFIDENCE

The built-in calculator is an amazing tool. In order to take full advantage of the built-in calculator in the Math modules, however, you need to be completely comfortable using it. Like playing your favorite video game, you want to get to the point at which you do things automatically without having to think about them or hunt for the correct button. While the calculator at Desmos.com is quite similar to the one in the testing app, it is best to use the one in the testing app so everything feels natural and normal on test day.

Open the Bluebook app and log in. Click on Test Preview, then Next, then select SAT Suite of Assessments under Test Type, and click Next. Click Close, and then click on the Question 1 of 8 button at the bottom, followed by Go to Review Page. Click Next to move to the Math section; then click Close on the notification. Now you are in a section with several practice math questions. The questions are less important than being able to open the calculator and do some untimed practice.

Before continuing, read the *Digital SAT Calculator Guide* available online. Practice with the basics of opening the calculator, resizing and moving it, entering math calculations, and creating graphs. Here are a few things to keep in mind that will help you use the calculator fluidly.

- The graphing area is larger and easier to see with the calculator expanded.
- Practice clicking and dragging to move the calculator around on the screen. That way, you can enter information from the question without having to write it down or memorize it, and you can use the answer eliminator tool at the same time as the calculator.
- Practice scrolling and zooming in the graphing area. There are buttons on the screen for zooming in and out, and using a mouse scroll wheel or pinching on a trackpad will also work. Click and drag to move the graphing area to find what you need on the graph.
- If you close the calculator after finishing one question and reopen it to work on another question later, it will appear exactly the way you left it before. Make sure you delete anything from the entry field that doesn't apply to the current question. You might want to click the Home button (the one with the icon of a house) to recenter and restore the graphing area to its default size.

You should also practice using the entry fields. It is possible to click the keyboard icon and click buttons in the on-screen keyboard to enter what you need, but almost everything can be typed directly in a field using a computer keyboard. Here are a few hints.

- Press the forward slash (/) for fractions.
- Hold the Shift key and press the backslash (\) to enter the absolute value symbol.
- Holding the Shift key and pressing 6 is a shortcut for entering exponents.
- Use the right arrow on your keyboard frequently when entering things like fractions, exponents, and parentheses. This completes that part of the entry before you start something new.
- **Always** double-check that what you entered matches the information in the question.

Finally, here are some features of the graphing calculator that you might not be aware of. We will use several of these later in the chapter.

- The calculator shows a graph only when the equation has x and/or y. If you need to graph an equation with other letters for the variables, which could happen on a word problem, replace those letters with x and y and write down which is which.

- Most hand-held graphing calculators create a graph only when the equation starts with "$y =$." The built-in calculator, on the other hand, will graph an equation in any form. Save time and avoid mistakes by entering expressions and equations in the form given in the question rather than converting them.

- When you enter a quadratic as an expression (without "= 0"), the graph is a parabola. When you enter a quadratic as an equation (with "= 0"), the solutions are shown as vertical lines. Get used to both graph displays because you want to be able to enter a quadratic in any form and find the solutions or number of solutions. Rearranging the equation takes time and could lead to a mistake.

> **Equations and Inequalities**
> These points about the graphing calculator refer to equations, but don't forget that the calculator can be used for graphing inequalities as well.

- When entering a function, remember that $f(x) = y$. You can enter y instead of $f(x)$ to save yourself a couple of keystrokes. The built-in calculator will recognize and graph $f(x)$, as well.

- If you want to copy an equation or expression, start by entering the equation in the first entry field. Click on the ⚙ icon, then on the 🗐 icon to make a copy. This will come in handy when you want to enter four answer choice equations that only have small differences.

- The 〰 button hides the graph of whatever is in that entry field. This can be useful if you have multiple graphs showing at once and want to isolate two of them to compare. Each graph is a different color, but if you have trouble differentiating colors, you can also use this button to hide and show graphs to determine which graph goes with which equation.

- Once you have entered the equation(s), you can make the graphing area larger by clicking the « button to hide the entry fields. Don't forget to click » when you're done so you can enter something new.

- Most graphs have gray dots that show key points such as an x-intercept or a vertex. These dots disappear when you scroll or zoom. To bring them back, either click on the graph itself (not just in the graphing area) or on the entry field.

- The button contains several graph settings. Most of these will not be useful on the SAT, but clicking to make the text bigger and bolder or selecting Reverse Contrast might make things easier to see. Experiment so you know how you want to set things up on test day.

- You might see a slider tool appear when you enter a letter other than *x* or *y*. This will be quite useful on some questions with constants, as you will see later in this chapter.

Calculator Choices

You might feel more comfortable using your familiar hand-held calculator and/or scratch paper for basic calculations. You might also have a graphing calculator that you like using, but you might be surprised by how much more powerful and easy it is to use the built-in calculator. Use the built-in calculator for every example in this chapter to get used to it and discover what it can do.

GRAPHING WITH THE BUILT-IN CALCULATOR

Questions that ask about the graphs of functions or equations are the most obvious place to use the built-in calculator. Let's take a look at a typical question.

---

5 ☐ Mark for Review

$$-4x + 2y = 10$$
$$8x + 3y = 29$$

When graphed in the *xy*-plane, the graphs of the equations in the given system of equations intersect at the point (x, y). What is the value of *x*?

Ⓐ 0

Ⓑ 1

Ⓒ 4

Ⓓ 7

POOD Point

Questions in this book are numbered based on where they are likely to appear in a harder second module. This is #5, so your goal is to get it right quickly, avoid mistakes, and save time for harder questions.

$$7y = 49$$
$$y = 7$$
$$8x + 21 = 29$$
$$x = 1$$

Here's How to Ace It

The question asks for the value of the *x*-coordinate of the solution to a system of equations. If your brain is in school mode, you're probably thinking about solving simultaneous equations; that is the *least* efficient way to work this question. If your brain is in SAT mode, you should be thinking that a question asking for a specific value with numbers in the answer choices is a great chance to use PITA; that will be a much more efficient approach. However, there's something even better than PITA on questions like this, and that's the built-in calculator.

Open the calculator and enter each equation in an entry field. The built-in calculator will graph these equations the way they are; you don't need to convert them into a "*y* =" form the way you would on a hand-held graphing calculator. The graphing area shows two lines:

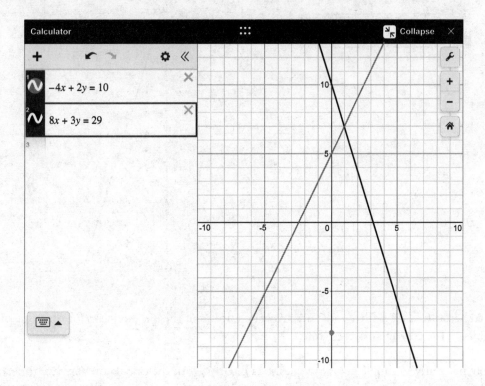

If the calculator is expanded with the default settings, you won't even need to scroll or zoom to see the point of intersection. If you had scrolled or zoomed on an earlier question, click the home button to reset everything. Find the gray dot at the point of intersection: click on one of the lines or one of the equations if it isn't there. Click on the gray dot to show the coordinates of the point.

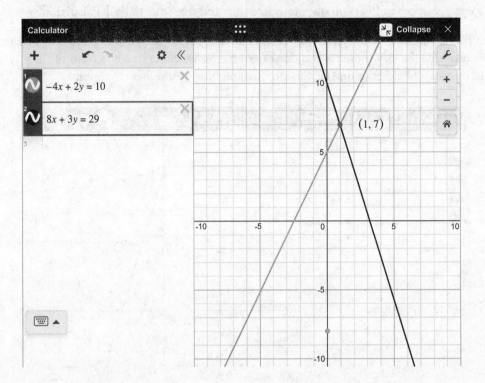

Remember to RTFQ! Both 1 and 7 are answer choices, but the question asks for the value of *x*, which is 1. The correct answer is (B).

By solving relatively simple graphing questions like this with the calculator, you save time and avoid potential mistakes. It's not just for lines, either: questions about parabolas, such as ones that ask about the solutions or vertex, can also be answered quickly with the built-in calculator.

Uncomplicate with the Calculator

There are two common ways for the test-writers to make graphing questions more complicated and make you think that the built-in calculator won't work: asking about the number of solutions and using constants.

Here's one about the number of solutions.

---

12 🔖 Mark for Review

$$y = 4x^2 - 4x + 3$$
$$y = 3x + 2$$

At how many points do the graphs of the given equations intersect in the *xy*-plane?

(A) 0

(B) 1

(C) 2

(D) 3

$4x^2 - 4x + 3 = 3x + 2$

$4x^2 - 7x + 5 = 0$

Here's How to Ace It

The question asks for the number of points of intersection in a system of equations. If you catch it, you can use POE and eliminate (D) right away because a parabola and a line can never intersect three times. Then open the built-in calculator and enter both equations. Scroll and zoom as needed and look at the gray dots.

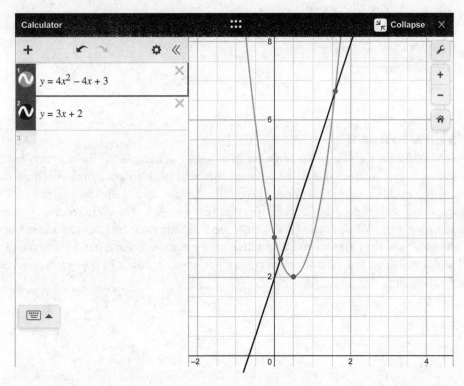

Note that there are four gray dots. The one at the bottom is the vertex of the parabola, and the one on the *y*-axis is the *y*-intercept of the parabola. Focus on where the line intersects the parabola, and see that there are two points of intersection marked by dots. It doesn't matter what the coordinates are because the final question simply asks for the number of points of intersection. Therefore, the correct answer is (C).

If you want to see how much time you saved by using the built-in graphing calculator on the previous question, try solving it algebraically. Better yet, don't: you have better things to do with your time, both now and on the SAT.

Questions about the number of solutions could involve a single linear equation, a system of two linear equations, a single quadratic equation, or a system of one linear and one quadratic equation. In all four cases, the test-writers might include a constant, a letter that represents a fixed value.

The next example adds a constant to the mix and gives you a chance to use the built-in calculator's slider tool.

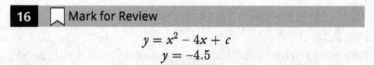

16   🔖 Mark for Review

$$y = x^2 - 4x + c$$
$$y = -4.5$$

When graphed in the *xy*-plane, the graphs of the given system of equations intersect at exactly one point. If *c* is a constant, what is the value of *c*?

$$\boxed{-0.5}$$

Here's How to Ace It

The question asks for the value of a constant in a system of equations. The question mentions graphs, so your first instinct should be to open the built-in calculator. Enter both equations, and you will see additional options under each one. You can ignore the place to put in a range for *y* because the second equation already specifies that $y = -4.5$. The useful tool is the one that says "add slider" for *c*. Click that, and you now see a default value of 1 for *c*, a slider from -10 to 10, and graphs of the parabola and line. Click on the equation of the parabola to see the gray dots. The parabola and line do not intersect, so $c = 1$ does not result in the graphs intersecting at exactly one point.

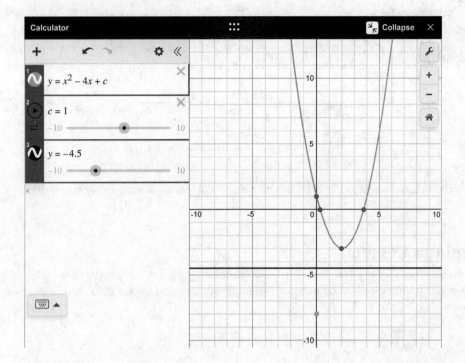

Click and hold the circle under the slider for c (you can still ignore the one for y), and slide it in either direction. When you move the slider to the right, the parabola moves up and gets farther away from the line. Thus, a value of c that is greater than 1 will not make the graphs intersect at exactly one point. Move the slider to the left, and the parabola moves down and gets closer to the line. Keep an eye on those gray dots to see when one appears at the intersection of the line and the parabola. It might help to zoom in to be able to see clearly as you make small adjustments on the slider. If the dots disappear, click on one of the equations again. When $c = -0.5$, there is exactly one point of intersection.

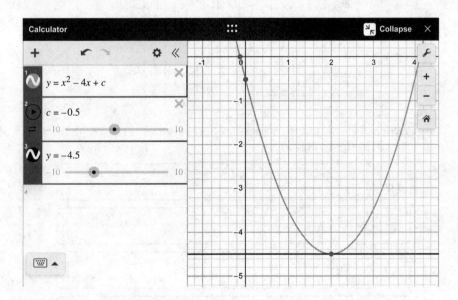

The correct answer is -0.5.

The slider tool also works well combined with PITA, but be aware that you might need to click it open and adjust the range if the numbers in the answer choices are less than −10 or greater than 10. In those cases, it will usually be easier to type in your own numbers for the constant.

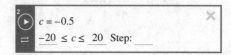

As with the other calculator features, *practice* to get comfortable with using the slider.

Calculator Combos

The built-in calculator is a tool that you can use in combination with the tactics you learned in the previous chapter. See if you can spot a good combined approach for the following example.

4   Mark for Review

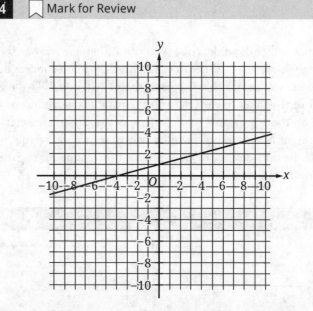

Which of the following equations best represents the graph shown in the *xy*-plane?

(A) $y = \frac{1}{4}x + 1$

(B) $y = -\frac{1}{4}x + 1$

(C) $y = \frac{1}{2}x + 1$

(D) $y = -\frac{1}{2}x + 1$

Here's How to Ace It

This is question #4 in the harder second module, so you want to make sure you get it right but also finish it quickly. Start with some POE: the line goes up from left to right, so it has a positive slope. Eliminate (B) and (D) because they have negative slopes. Both of the remaining answer choices have the same *y*-intercept, so that won't help you to eliminate further.

You might feel like you can estimate based on the steepness of the slope, start counting up and over, or use two points to calculate the slope. If you are absolutely certain that one of those methods will get you the correct answer and is faster than using the built-in calculator, go for it. But at least consider the calculator method. You're down to two answer choices, so enter the equations from (A) and (C). To enter the one in (C), you can copy the first one using the steps from earlier in this chapter and change the 4 to a 2, or you can enter the second equation directly. Zoom in a little to see the *x*-intercepts more clearly. The calculator will show this:

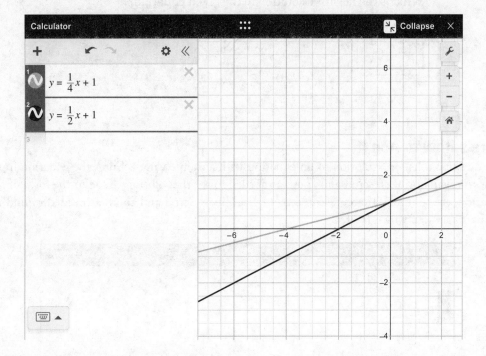

The graph of the first line intersects the *x*-axis at (–4, 0) and intersects the *y*-axis at (0, 1). Both of these match the graph in the question, so $y = \dfrac{1}{4}x + 1$ is the equation of the line. The correct answer is (A).

OTHER WAYS TO USE THE BUILT-IN CALCULATOR

Questions that ask about the graphs of functions or equations are the most obvious place to use the built-in calculator, but it is also useful on other questions.

Basic Algebra

Questions that ask you to solve for *x* without explicitly mentioning graphs or the *xy*-plane can still be graphed and solved. Some fill-in questions will ask you for the positive or negative solution, so be sure to look up the correct value after you graph the equation.

Here's a question involving absolute value that would take multiple steps to solve algebraically but becomes much easier with the help of the built-in calculator.

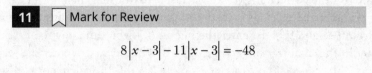

11 🔖 Mark for Review

$$8\left|x-3\right|-11\left|x-3\right|=-48$$

What is the negative solution to the given equation?

$$\boxed{-13}$$

$(-3|x-3| = -48$

$|x-3| = 16$

Here's How to Ace It

The question asks for a solution to an equation with absolute values. Enter the equation in the built-in calculator; then scroll and zoom as needed to see the solutions. Due to the form of this equation, the solutions are represented by vertical lines. Scroll and zoom as needed to find the negative solution, which is −13.

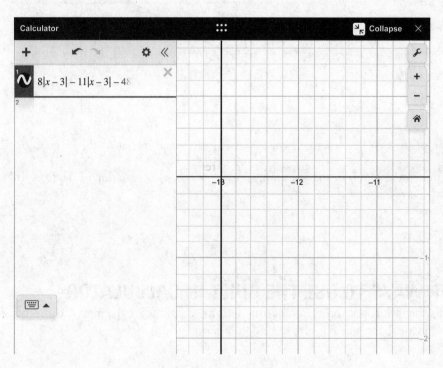

That's all you have to do! No solving; no having to remember how absolute value works; no chance of messing up a sign. Just graph it, answer it, and leave it. The correct answer is –13.

Word Problems

Don't forget about the calculator when you're doing word problems. If a question involves solving for a value in an equation or system of equations, the built-in calculator can be a useful tool.

You already saw the following question in the previous chapter and answered it correctly using simultaneous equations. Take another look and see whether the built-in calculator can speed things up.

---

14   🔖 Mark for Review

A certain amusement park sells two types of passes: half-day passes and all-day passes. The amusement park charges $40 for a half-day pass and $80 for an all-day pass. The amusement park sold a total of 70 passes one day for a total of $4,600. How many all-day passes did the amusement park sell?

___45___

$40h + 80a = 4600$

$h + a = 70$ $40a = 1800$

$40h + 40a = 2800$ $4a = 180$

                      $a = 45$

Here's How to Ace It

The question asks for a value given a specific situation. RTFQ and write down "how many all-day passes?" This is a fill-in question, so it isn't possible to use PITA. Instead, start the same way you would if you were going to solve algebraically, and translate the English into math.

Remember that the built-in calculator shows a graph only when you use x and y, so use x to represent the number of half-day passes and y to represent the number of all-day passes. Write this down so you don't forget which is which. Translate the total amount the amusement park charges for half-day passes as $40x$, and translate the total amount charged for all-day passes as $80y$. The question states that the total amount for the day was 4,600, so one equation is $40x + 80y = 4,600$. The question also states that the *amusement park sold a total of 70 passes*, and there are only two types of passes, so the other equation is $x + y = 70$.

Enter both equations in the built-in calculator; then scroll and zoom as needed to see the point of intersection. Click on the gray dot to see that the coordinates are (25, 45). The question asks for the number of all-day passes, so check your scratch paper: you used y to represent the number of all-day passes, so you're looking for the y-value, which is 45. The correct answer is 45.

Statistical Measures

Finally, be aware of two calculator shortcuts that can save time on statistics questions. If you type *mean* or *median* followed by a list of numbers in parentheses, the calculator will find the mean or median for you. There are buttons for these statistical measures in the *functions* menu on the keypad, but typing it into the entry field is faster. There is also a button for standard deviation, but you will never need to calculate standard deviation on the SAT.

Use the built-in calculator to get the relatively easy question below correct even faster.

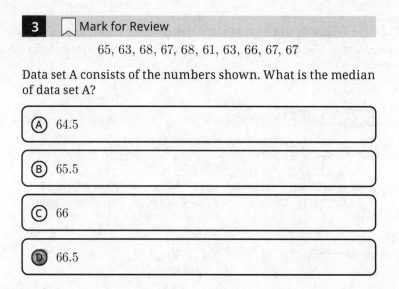

3 ☐ Mark for Review

65, 63, 68, 67, 68, 61, 63, 66, 67, 67

Data set A consists of the numbers shown. What is the median of data set A?

(A) 64.5

(B) 65.5

(C) 66

(D) 66.5

Here's How to Ace It

The question asks for the median of a list of numbers. There are two elements that make this question trickier than it might appear. First, the numbers are out of order, so you would need to take time putting them in order before finding the median. Second, there are 10 numbers in the list. In lists with an even number of numbers, the median is the average of the two middle numbers. If you take the average of the two middle numbers without putting the numbers in order first, you get 64.5, which is trap answer (A). If you put the numbers in order but miscount, you could fall for trap answer (C). If you don't RTFQ and solve for the mean instead of the median, you get 65.5, which is trap answer (B).

That's a lot of work and potential mistakes to get #3 on the harder second module right! Instead, use the built-in calculator. Type median(65,63,68,67,68,61,63,66,67,67) and look in the lower right corner of the entry field.

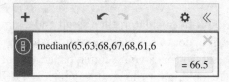

The median is 66.5, and you're done. If the answer choices were fractions instead of decimals, you could click the button with a fraction image to the left of the entry field to change the form of the answer.

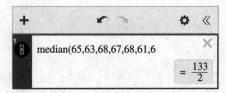

The correct answer is (D).

Use the Built-in Calculator Drill

As you are discovering with some of these examples, there is more than one way to answer many questions on the SAT Math section, and sometimes you will combine multiple skills and tools. In the following drill, however, focus on using the built-in calculator. Try the questions yourself, set a five-minute timer if you want to practice your pacing, and then read the explanations in Chapter 27 to see whether you found the most efficient way to get the correct answer.

14 ☐ Mark for Review

$$\sqrt{4x + 28} = \sqrt{(x + 4)^2}$$

What is the positive solution to the given equation?

2

$4x + 28 = x^2 + 8x + 16$

$x^2 + 4x - 12 = 0$

$x^{-2} \quad 6$

15 ☐ Mark for Review

$$36x^2 + bx + 9 = 0$$

If b is a constant, for which of the following values of b will the given equation have no real solutions?

(A) −36

(B) 16

(C) 36

(D) 324

16 ☐ Mark for Review

$$4x^4 - 88x^3 + 228x^2$$

One of the factors of the given expression is $x - a$, where a is a positive constant. What is the greatest possible value of a?

$88x^2 - 298$

19

17 ☐ Mark for Review

$$y = (x - 5)^2 = x^2 - 10x + 25$$
$$y = 8x - 56$$

The graphs of the equations in the given system of equations intersect at the point (a, b). What is the value of $a + b$?

(A) −11

(B) 12

(C) 15

(D) 25

$x^2 - 10x + 25 = 8x - 56 \qquad y = 16$
$x^2 - 18x + 81 = 0 \qquad x = 9$

19 ☐ Mark for Review

$$2x^2 + 8x + 2 = 0$$

One of the solutions to the given equation can be written as $-2 - \sqrt{c}$, where c is a constant. What is the value of c?

(A) 3

(B) 4

(C) 10

(D) 48

$x = \dfrac{-8 \pm \sqrt{64 - 16}}{4} = \dfrac{-8 \pm \sqrt{48}}{4}$

$= \dfrac{-8 - 4\sqrt{3}}{4} = -2 - \sqrt{3}$

Chapter 25
Use Your Math Knowledge

This chapter covers the advanced algebra, graphing, coordinate geometry, and geometry/trig content that you will need to know to get a top score on the SAT Math section. Use this chapter in combination with everything you've learned so far.

IT'S STILL THE SAT

All the skills and tools you learned about in Chapter 22 and Chapter 23 give you more SAT Math options, but there are times when those options don't work or you decide that solving algebraically is the best approach. Consider all of your options on every question, and solve only when nothing else works or you are absolutely certain that solving is the best approach for you on that particular question. As always, remember that you are not in math class at school; algebra is often the last resort on the SAT.

POOD Point

The question numbers in this chapter, as in the previous chapters, represent where on a harder second module these questions are likely to appear. Many of the questions in this chapter would appear in the final third, so they are questions that the test-writers consider difficult. That's why some of the more efficient methods, such as PITA or using the built-in calculator, won't always work. However, sometimes those methods and tools *will* work, so learn the content that follows, but keep looking for ways to use what you've already learned in this book.

ALGEBRA AND GRAPHING

Some algebra questions on the SAT can be solved in multiple ways. Often, when there are one or two variables, PITA or Plugging In will be the best option. You saw examples of this in Chapter 22. When there are three variables, however, algebra is often the simplest and most efficient approach. If you need a refresher on basic algebra, refer to the *Digital SAT Premium Prep* book.

Try this example of a common type of three-variable algebra question.

---

7   🔖 Mark for Review

$$\frac{3a-1}{7b+2} = c$$

The given equation relates the distinct positive numbers a, b, and c. Which equation correctly expresses $7b + 2$ in terms of a and c?

(A) $7b + 2 = 3a - 1 - c$

(B) $7b + 2 = \dfrac{c}{3a-1}$

(C) $7b + 2 = \dfrac{3a-1}{c}$

(D) $7b + 2 = 3ac - c$

$$\frac{3a-1}{c} = 7b+2$$

Here's How to Ace It

The question asks for an equation in terms of specific variables. RTFQ and write down that the question asks for an equation that expresses $7b + 2$; hence, you want to solve for that expression instead of for any single variable. To begin to isolate $7b + 2$, multiply both sides of the equation by $7b + 2$ to get $3a - 1 = (c)(7b + 2)$. Because you're isolating $7b + 2$, don't distribute the c. Next, divide both sides of the equation by c to get $\frac{3a - 1}{c} = 7b + 2$. Flip the two sides of the equation to get $7b + 2 = \frac{3a - 1}{c}$. The correct answer is (C).

Plugging In would also have worked on the previous question: pick numbers for the two variables on the left side of the equation, solve for the variable on the right side of the equation, and then plug all three values into the answer choices and eliminate the three answers that don't work. On test day, you want to identify Plugging In and solving as options for a question like this, and then make an active, informed decision about which approach you want to take. Your goal is to make quick and confident decisions so you can start working on the question without having to sit there thinking about it for too long.

Exponents and Roots

Solving is also likely to be a better approach than Plugging In on questions about exponents and roots. The exponent rules tested on the SAT are covered in detail in the *Digital SAT Premium Prep* book, but here's an overview.

MADSPM

When the bases are the same,

- to **multiply** the quantities: keep the base and **add** the exponents.
- to **divide** the quantities: keep the base and **subtract** the exponents.
- to raise the quantity to another **power**: **multiply** the exponents.

If quantities with the same base and exponent are added or subtracted, just add or subtract the coefficients and do nothing to the base or exponent.

On harder exponent questions, the test-writers might go beyond the basics of MADSPM. Here are some special rules you should know.

Special Exponent Rules

- Any number (besides 0) to the exponent 0 is 1.
- Any number to the exponent 1 is itself.
- 1 to any exponent is 1.
- 0 to any exponent (besides 0) is 0.
- 0^0 is not tested on the SAT.
- In a fractional exponent, the numerator is the exponent and the denominator is the root.
- For negative exponents, calculate the positive exponent, and then take the reciprocal.

Try this exponent question.

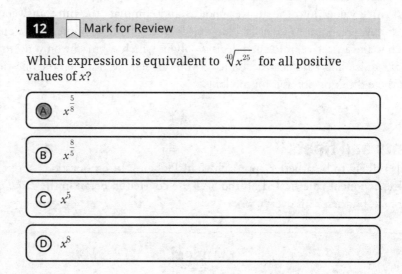

12 ☐ Mark for Review

Which expression is equivalent to $\sqrt[40]{x^{25}}$ for all positive values of x?

A) $x^{\frac{5}{8}}$

B) $x^{\frac{8}{5}}$

C) x^5

D) x^8

Here's How to Ace It

The question asks for an equivalent expression. There are variables in the answer choices, so plugging in with the help of the calculator is one option. Another option is to apply the exponent rules. In a fractional exponent, the numerator is the power and the denominator is the root. Rewrite the expression as $x^{\frac{25}{40}}$. The exponent is not an integer, so eliminate (C) and (D). The exponent is less than 1, so also eliminate (B). You just combined math knowledge (exponent rules) with a test-taking skill (POE) and got the question right quickly. The correct answer is (A).

On some exponent and root questions, you can also enter the expressions into the built-in calculator. The button you need isn't in an obvious place, so let's use the previous question to walk through how to do that. Open the built-in calculator and click the keyboard icon in the lower left. Click the *functions* key on the far right; this opens a new menu. Scroll to the bottom of that menu and click on the *n*th root button, which looks like this:

Enter 40 in the first space, and enter x^{25} under the root sign:

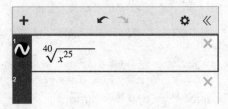

Enter the answer choices, either all at once in separate entry fields or one at a time in a single entry field, and look for the one that results in the same graph. Use whichever feature(s) of the built-in calculator work best for you—color coding, clicking on an entry field to focus on one graph at a time, or clicking the ⬛ button to the left of an entry field to hide that graph—to see that the graph of $x^{\frac{5}{8}}$ is the same as the graph of $\sqrt[40]{x^{25}}$, so (A) is correct.

In most cases, knowing and applying the exponent rules will get you the correct answer in the shortest amount of time, but it's good to know where the button for an *n*th root is in case you need it.

Linear Graphing

When an SAT Math question asks about the graph of a linear equation, the built-in calculator should be your first thought. For some questions, it is necessary to know the forms of linear equations and how to find the slope. In particular, knowing standard form is better than spending time converting standard form equations into slope-intercept form.

Here's what to know:

Linear Equations

Slope-intercept form	$y = mx + b$	slope = m
Standard form	$Ax + By = C$	slope = $-\dfrac{A}{B}$
Two points	(x_1, y_1) and (x_2, y_2)	slope = $\dfrac{y_2 - y_1}{x_2 - x_1}$

Here are two other facts about the slopes of lines that are likely to be tested on the SAT.

Parallel lines have the same slope and no solutions.
Perpendicular lines have negative reciprocal slopes and one solution.

Here's an example that uses several of these pieces of information.

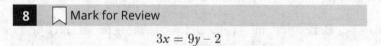

8   Mark for Review

$$3x = 9y - 2$$

Line *l* is defined by the given equation. If line *m* is perpendicular to line *l* in the *xy*-plane, what is the slope of line *m*?

$\boxed{-3}$

$$9y = 3x + 2$$
$$y = \frac{1}{3}x + \frac{2}{9}$$

Here's How to Ace It

The question asks for the slope of a line. The question states that *line m is perpendicular to line l*, which means they have slopes that are negative reciprocals of each other. The question gives the equation of line *l*, so find the slope of that line. The equation of line *l* is not in one of the familiar forms, so convert it into whichever form you prefer. To convert the equation of line *l* into slope-intercept form, add 2 to both sides of the equation to get $3x + 2 = 9y$, and then divide both sides of the equation by 9 to get $\dfrac{3}{9}x + \dfrac{2}{9} = y$, or

$\frac{1}{3}x + \frac{2}{9} = y$. Flip the two sides of the equation to get $y = \frac{1}{3}x + \frac{2}{9}$. In slope-intercept form, m is the slope, so the slope of line l is $\frac{1}{3}$. The slope of line m is the negative reciprocal of the slope of line l, so it is –3.

To convert the equation of line l into standard form, subtract $9y$ from both sides of the equation to get $3x - 9y = -2$. In standard form, the slope is $-\frac{A}{B}$, so the slope of line l is $-\frac{3}{-9}$, or $\frac{1}{3}$. The slope of line m is the negative reciprocal of the slope of line l, so it is –3.

Using either form of a linear equation, the correct answer is –3.

Knowing the forms of a linear equation can also help you recognize what a more challenging question is testing so you can start working on it faster. Take a look at the following example.

19 ☐ Mark for Review

x	$g(x)$
–6	172
–4	86
–2	0

The table shows three values of x and their corresponding values of $g(x)$. If function g is defined by $g(x) = cx + d$, where c and d are constants, what is the value of $c + d$?

(A) –129

(B) –86

(C) –45

(D) 43

$0 = -43(-2) + d$

$d = -86$

Here's How to Ace It

The question asks for the value of an expression based on information about a function. The function is a linear equation in slope-intercept form, which gives you a clue about where to start. Since c is the slope and d is the y-intercept in this function, solve for those two values and add them. Find the slope by using the formula $slope = \dfrac{y_2 - y_1}{x_2 - x_1}$. The table provides three pairs of x and $g(x)$ values, which represent three points on the line if the function were graphed. Any two points will work in the slope formula, so try the points with the smaller numbers. Plug $(-4, 86)$ and $(-2, 0)$ into the two-point slope formula to get $slope = \dfrac{86 - 0}{-4 - (-2)}$, which becomes $slope = \dfrac{86}{-2}$, or $slope = -43$. Thus, $c = -43$. That doesn't answer the final question, so keep working.

Next, solve for the y-intercept. Don't be tricked into thinking that $(-2, 0)$ is the y-intercept: it is the x-intercept. Look closely at the table: each time the x-value increases by 2, the y-value decreases by 86. Continuing this pattern, the next row in the table would have $x = 0$ and $y = -86$, so the y-intercept is -86, which means $d = -86$. If the pattern on a question like this isn't obvious or easy to calculate, you can also find the y-intercept by plugging the slope and the (x, y) coordinates of one of the points into the slope-intercept form of a linear equation and solving for b.

Finally, add the values of the two constants to get $c + d = -43 + (-86)$, which becomes $c + d = -43 - 86$, and then $c + d = -129$. The correct answer is (A).

Nonlinear Graphing

Graphs of quadratic equations are yet another great chance to use the built-in calculator. Once again, though, some questions call for knowledge of the underlying math. As with linear equations, it helps to know the forms of quadratic equations and what they tell you.

Quadratic Equations

- Standard form: $y = ax^2 + bx + c$

- Factored form: $y = a(x - m)(x - n)$
  In factored form, m and n are the solutions.

- Vertex form: $y = a(x - h)^2 + k$
  In vertex form, (h, k) is the coordinates of the vertex.

Here are some bonus hints that will come in handy when the built-in calculator isn't enough by itself.

More About Quadratic Equations

- In all three forms, the sign of a indicates direction: if a is positive, the quadratic opens upward; if a is negative, the quadratic opens downward.

- In standard form, the sum of the solutions equals $-\dfrac{b}{a}$.

- In standard form, the product of the solutions equals $\dfrac{c}{a}$.

- In vertex form, the vertex is (h, k).

- In standard form, the x-coordinate of the vertex can be found with the equation $h = -\dfrac{b}{2a}$.

- The axis of symmetry is a vertical line passing through the vertex. The x-coordinate of the axis of symmetry can be found with the $h = -\dfrac{b}{2a}$ equation or by finding the midpoint of two points with the same y-value.

Apply your knowledge of quadratics to the next two questions, and then read the explanations to see whether you found the most efficient approach.

15 🔖 Mark for Review

$$3x^2 - bx + 14$$

The given expression, where b is a constant, can be rewritten as $(px - r)(x - s)$, where p, r, and s are integer constants. Which of the following must be an integer?

(A) $\dfrac{b}{p}$

(B) $\dfrac{b}{r}$

(C) $\dfrac{14}{p}$

(D) $\dfrac{14}{r}$

22 🔖 Mark for Review

The quadratic function g is defined by $g(x) = ax^2 - 8x + c$, where a and c are constants. In the xy-plane, the graph of $y = g(x)$ is a parabola that opens upward. The vertex of g is at the point (h, k), where h and k are positive constants. If $g(-1) = g(5)$, which of the following must be true?

    I. $a \geq 1$
    II. $c < 1$

(handwritten) $a + 8 + c = 25 - 40 + c$
(handwritten) $2a = 48$ $a = 2$
(handwritten) $2 + 8 + c = 50 - 40 + c$
(handwritten) $10 + c$

(A) I only

(B) II only

(C) I and II

(D) Neither I nor II

Here's How to Ace #15

The question asks for an expression that must be an integer. The question provides a quadratic in both standard form, which is $ax^2 + bx + c$, and factored form, which is $a(x - m)(x - n)$. Use FOIL to expand the factored form expression into standard form: $(px - r)(x - s) = px^2 - psx - rx + rs$. Combine the middle terms to get $px^2 - (ps + r)x + rs$. Now set this equal to the standard form expression, $3x^2 - bx + 14$, and match up terms. It might make things clearer to write one expression above the other:

$$3x^2 - bx + 14$$
$$px^2 - (ps + r)x + rs$$

Therefore, $p = 3$, $b = (ps + r)$, and $rs = 14$. Examine the answer choices to see if any answers can be eliminated quickly. Eliminate (C) because $p = 3$ and $\frac{14}{3}$ is not an integer. Since b is the messiest term, save (A) and (B) for later and work with (D). Since $rs = 14$, $r = \frac{14}{s}$ and $s = \frac{14}{r}$. The question states that s is an integer, so any value that is equivalent to s will also be an integer. Thus, $\frac{14}{r}$ must be an integer. The correct answer is (D).

Here's How to Ace #22

The question asks for a true statement about a function. The question states that *the graph of y = g(x) is a parabola that opens upward*, and that the *vertex of g is at the point (h, k), where h and k are positive constants*. Apply your knowledge of parabolas and the forms of quadratic equations. When a quadratic is in standard form, $ax^2 + bx + c$, the sign of *a* indicates which way the parabola opens. Since this parabola opens upward, *a* must be positive, However, *a* could be a fraction between 0 and 1 or any number greater than or equal to 1, so this is not enough information to determine whether statement (I) must be true.

The question also states that $g(-1) = g(5)$, which means that, on the graph of the parabola, the point where $x = -1$ and the point where $x = 5$ have the same *y*-coordinate. It also means that the output value, $g(x)$, is equal for those two input values, *x*, so plug $x = -1$ and $x = 5$ into the function and set the results equal to each other: $a(-1)^2 - 8(-1) + c = a(5)^2 - 8(5) + c$. Simplify both sides of this equation to get $a + 8 + c = 25a - 40 + c$. Combine like terms to get $-24a = -48$; then divide both sides of the equation by -24 to get $a = 2$. This is greater than 1, so statement (I) must be true. Eliminate (B) and (D) because they do not include (I) as a true statement.

Keep using your SAT skills and tools. To check statement (II), plug in and use the built-in calculator. Plug $a = 2$ into the quadratic to get $2x^2 - 8x + c$. Enter this into the built-in calculator and click the slider tool for *c*. The question states that *k*, the *y*-coordinate of the vertex, is positive, so the vertex needs to be above the *x*-axis. Move the slider left and right to see that the vertex is above the *x*-axis only when *c* is greater than 8. When $c < 1$, the value of *k* is negative. Thus, statement (II) is not true. Eliminate (C) because it includes (II) as a true statement. The correct answer is (A).

Even using every tool in your toolkit, this was not a fast or easy question. Remember your POOD and pacing, and avoid getting stuck on a question like this. If you start it and realize how long it's going to take, use the mark for review tool to flag it to come back to later. When you come back, either finish working it or guess and go.

There's one more piece of information you might need for questions about quadratics. You saw in Chapter 24 how useful the built-in calculator is for questions that ask about the number of solutions. Occasionally, you might have to do the work by hand and use the discriminant. Here's how to use the discriminant to determine the number of solutions.

Number of Solutions

For a quadratic in the standard form $ax^2 + bx + c$, where *a, b,* and *c* are real numbers, the **discriminant** is $D = b^2 - 4ac$.

- If the discriminant is positive, the quadratic has two real solutions.
- If the discriminant equals zero, the quadratic has one real solution.
- If the discriminant is negative, the quadratic has no real solutions.

ADVANCED COORDINATE GEOMETRY

There is quite a bit of overlap on the SAT between algebra and coordinate geometry, as you saw in the previous section. This section covers three more coordinate geometry topics that may or may not require algebraic solving: translating graphs, circles in the coordinate plane, and graphs of higher-degree polynomials.

Translating Graphs

When a graph retains the same shape but moves within the coordinate plane, it has been translated. Know which math operation shifts a graph in each direction.

Rules for Translating Graphs

In relation to $f(x)$:

- $f(x) + k$ is shifted upward k units in the xy-plane.
- $f(x) - k$ is shifted downward k units in the xy-plane.
- $f(x + k)$ is shifted to the left k units in the xy-plane.
- $f(x - k)$ is shifted to the right k units in the xy-plane.

Apply these rules while working on the following question.

---

9 ☐ Mark for Review

$$p(x) = 4x^3$$

Function p is defined by the given equation. If the graph of function p is shifted up 3 units in the xy-plane to create the graph of $y = q(x)$, which of the following defines function q?

(A) $q(x) = p(x - 3)$

(B) $q(x) = p(x + 3)$

(C) $q(x) = p(x) - 3$

(D) $q(x) = p(x) + 3$

Here's How to Ace It

The question asks for the equation of a function that represents the translated graph of another function. When translating graphs, adding outside the parentheses shifts the graph up. Thus, adding 3 to function p will shift it up 3 units, which is function q. The equation in (D) adds 3 to $p(x)$, so it is correct.

Another method is to use the built-in calculator. Enter the $p(x)$ equation into the first entry field. Enter the answer choices, either all at once in separate entry fields or one at a time in a single entry field by modifying the equation as needed. Notice that you don't have to type $4x^3$ every time: the calculator automatically fills in what $p(x)$ equals because you entered the $p(x)$ equation first. If you enter all the answer choices at once, use the color coding or ![icon] button to see which graph is 3 units higher than the graph of $p(x)$. If you enter each answer choice one at a time, look at the two resulting graphs to see which way $p(x)$ was shifted.

A)
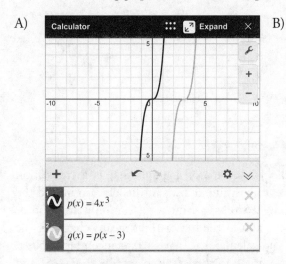

B)
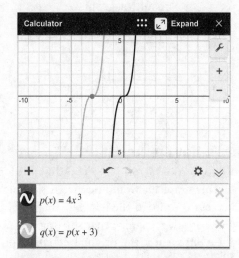

C)
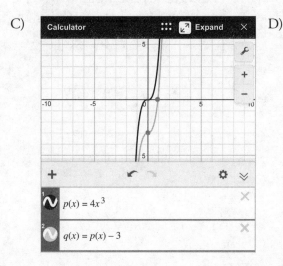

D)
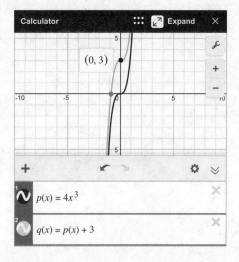

With (A), the graph moved to the right, not up; eliminate (A). With (B), the graph moved to the left; eliminate (B). With (C), the graph moved down; eliminate (C). With (D), the graph moved up; keep (D). Clicking on the gray dots can help, too: the y-intercept of $p(x)$ is (0, 0), and the y-intercept of the graph of the equation in (D) is (0, 3), so it is exactly 3 units higher, and (D) is correct.

Using either method, the correct answer is (D).

Things might get more complicated depending on the type of graph and the direction of the shift, and sometimes counting in a certain direction is not enough. The built-in calculator still helps, of course.

Here's a more difficult question about translating graphs.

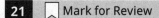

21   Mark for Review

The graph of the equation $3x + 4y = 15$ is translated 6 units to the left. What is the y-coordinate of the y-intercept of the resulting graph?

-0.15

Here's How to Ace It

The question asks for the y-coordinate of the y-intercept of a graph that is a translation of another graph. It would be nice if shifting a straight line 6 units to the left also moved the y-intercept 6 units to the left, but that's not how it works: a y-intercept can only move up or down. Instead, recognize that shifting a linear graph to the left or right means changing the x-value. First, enter the original equation on the calculator to have a reference graph. Next, recall that adding inside the parentheses shifts a graph to the left. Replace x with $(x + 6)$ and enter the equation again. Because you entered both equations, you can make sure you used the correct sign and confirm that the new line is to the left of the original line.

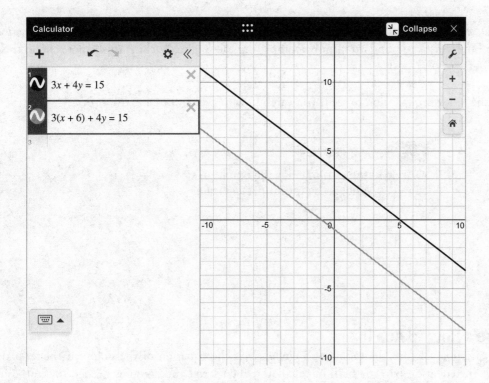

It is, so click on the second line or the second equation to bring back the gray dots, click on the gray dot at the y-intercept of the second line, and see that the coordinates are $(0, -0.75)$. Notice that this is *not* simply 6 units to the left of the y-intercept of the first graph. The question asks for the y-coordinate, which is -0.75. The fractional form, $-\dfrac{3}{4}$, would also be accepted as correct. The correct answer is -0.75 or an equivalent form.

Circles in the Coordinate Plane

After learning two forms of linear equations and three forms of quadratic equations, it may be a relief to find out that you need to know only one form of the equation of a circle in the coordinate plane. Here it is:

> The **standard form of a circle** is $(x - h)^2 + (y - k)^2 = r^2$, where (h, k) is the center and r is the radius.

If this were a math class at school, you would also need to know how to convert circle equations from other forms to standard form by completing the square. Luckily, this is not school: this is the SAT.

Try the following question to see if you catch how to avoid all that extra work.

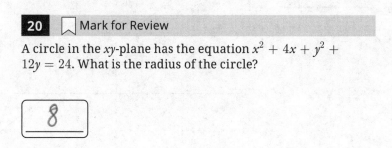

20   ▢ Mark for Review

A circle in the xy-plane has the equation $x^2 + 4x + y^2 + 12y = 24$. What is the radius of the circle?

[8]

Here's How to Ace It

The question asks for the radius of a circle given the equation of the graph in the xy-plane. Enter the equation into the built-in calculator; then scroll and zoom as needed to see the full circle. There are several gray dots on the graph; if they disappear, bring them back by clicking on the equation or on the circle itself. Four of them are where the circle intersects the x- and y-axes. Click on the other two dots, which are at the top and bottom of the circle and form the diameter. The points are (–2, 2) and (–2, –14).

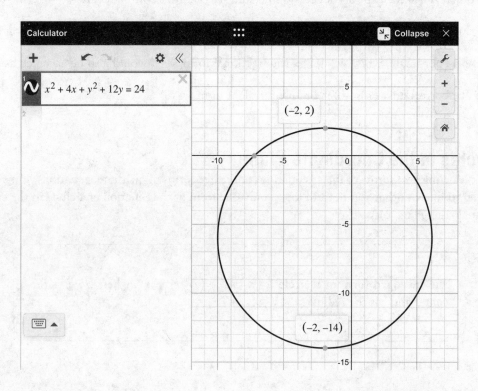

They have the same x-coordinate, so the distance between the two points, or the diameter, is the difference between the y-coordinates: $2 - (-14) = 16$. Before you type 16 in the fill-in box and cheerfully move to the next question, take a second to RTFQ: the question asks for the radius, not the diameter! The radius of a circle is half of the diameter, so the radius is 8. The correct answer is 8.

The built-in calculator made that much easier than #20 on the harder second module is supposed to be. The next example is about both circles and translating graphs. It's supposed to be another hard one, but using your skills and knowledge could make it a medium question in your *Personal* Order of Difficulty (POOD).

20   🔖 Mark for Review

$$(x + 3)^2 + y^2 = 9$$

The equation shown represents a circle in the xy-plane. A new circle is created by shifting the given circle up 4 units. Which of the following equations represents the new circle?

(A) $(x - 1)^2 + y^2 = 9$

(B) $(x + 3)^2 + (y - 4)^2 = 9$

(C) $(x + 3)^2 + (y + 4)^2 = 9$

(D) $(x + 7)^2 + y^2 = 9$

Here's How to Ace It

The question asks for the equation of a circle that has been translated from another circle in the xy-plane. All the equations are in standard form, so one option is to work with that and use POE. Shifting a circle does not affect the radius, and all the equations in the answer choices have 9 on the right side, so focus on the center. Moving a circle up or down does not change the x-value. Eliminate (A) and (D) because they change the $(x - h)^2$ piece from the original equation. To move a circle up or down, change the y-value. In the equation for the original circle, there are no parentheses on the y-term, so it is a simplified form of $(y - 0)$, making $k = 0$. Since the y-value of the center of the original circle is 0, the y-value of the center of a circle that is shifted up 4 units is $0 + 4 = 4$. Thus, the value of k in the equation for the new circle is 4, and $(y - k) = (y - 4)$. The term $(y - 4)^2$ must appear in the correct answer, so eliminate (C), which leaves (B) as the correct equation of the new circle.

Another option is to enter the equation of the original circle and the four equations in the answer choices into the built-in calculator, and see which circle is four units up from the original. This can help avoid the trouble you can get into with the signs on this question. As usual, you can use one entry field, change the equation, and evaluate the answers one at a time, or you can enter all four answer choices into separate entry fields. The latter makes a nice pattern, but either way you can tell that the graph of the equation in (B) is the original circle shifted up four units.

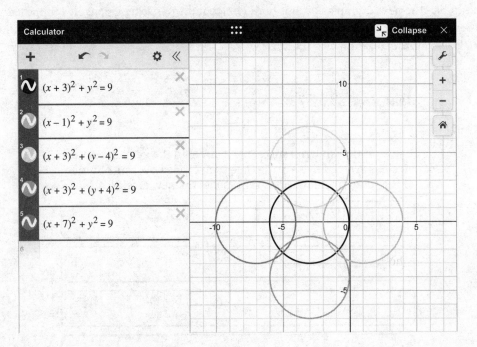

Using either method, the correct answer is (B).

Graphs of Higher-Degree Polynomials

Almost all the questions about graphs of equations on the SAT involve linear equations (straight lines) and quadratic equations (parabolas). Once in a while, there is a question about the graph of a higher-degree polynomial. This is an equation with an exponent greater than 2.

These graphs sometimes have a double root, meaning that you get one of the solutions twice when you solve algebraically. The graph will curve toward a point on the x-axis and then curve away in another direction. This also happens in a quadratic when the vertex is on the x-axis. No matter how strange the graph and the answer choices look, plugging in points from the graph and using the built-in calculator will get you the correct answer.

Here's what a question about a higher-degree polynomial might look like.

11 ⬚ Mark for Review

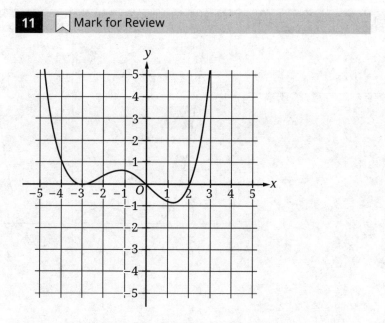

Which of the following could be the equation of the graph shown in the *xy*-plane?

Ⓐ $y = \frac{1}{20}x(x - 3)(x + 2)$

Ⓑ $y = \frac{1}{20}x(x - 3)(x + 2)^2$

Ⓒ $y = \frac{1}{20}x(x + 3)(x - 2)$

Ⓓ $y = \frac{1}{20}x(x + 3)^2(x - 2)$

Here's How to Ace It

The question asks for an equation that represents a graph. One option is to enter all four answer choice equations into the built-in calculator and see which one looks like the graph in the question. The equations are long, but if you're quick and careful entering them, that might be the most efficient way, and you will see that the graph in (D) is the correct graph.

Another option is to use points on the graph and POE. The first *x* in each equation represents the point at (0, 0). The graph also includes points at (2, 0) and (–3, 0), so the equation must include the factors $(x - 2)$ and $(x + 3)$. Eliminate (A) and (B) because they do not include those terms. At this point, you can enter the two remaining equations into the built-in calculator or use your knowledge of double roots. The graph curves toward (–3, 0), touches that point, and then curves away, so (–3, 0) is a double root. Thus, the correct equation must include $(x + 3)$ twice, or squared. Eliminate (C) because it includes this term only once. If you want to be absolutely sure, enter the equation in (D) into the built-in calculator. Scroll and zoom as needed to see that it is the graph in the question.

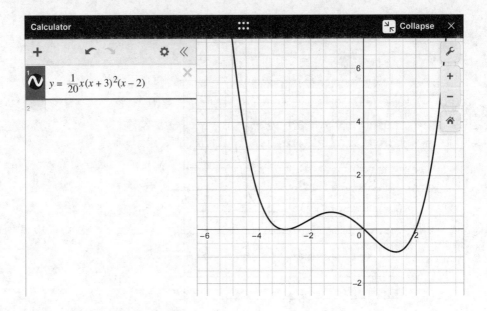

Using either the built-in calculator alone or a combination of plugging in, POE, and the built-in calculator, the correct answer is (D).

ADVANCED GEOMETRY AND TRIGONOMETRY

Many of the geometry and trig questions on the SAT cover the basics: angles, triangles, quadrilaterals, circles, area, volume, sine, cosine, and tangent. You can review that section of the *Digital SAT Premium Prep* book to make sure you're solid with the basics.

Keep in mind that you can open the reference sheet at any time to look up any formulas you may have forgotten, the ratios of the sides in the two special right triangles, and additional information about circles and triangles.

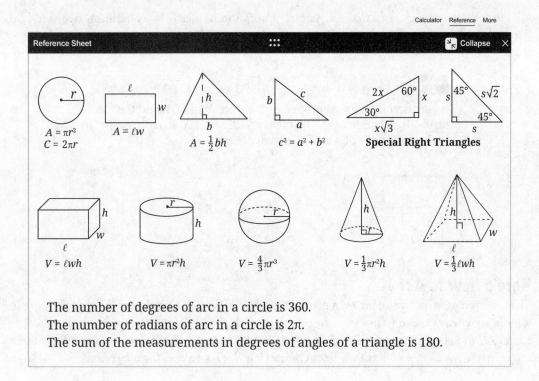

The number of degrees of arc in a circle is 360.

The number of radians of arc in a circle is 2π.

The sum of the measurements in degrees of angles of a triangle is 180.

It also helps to use a consistent approach on geometry questions. Here are those steps.

Geometry Basic Approach

1. **Draw a figure** on your scratch paper using the given figure (if there is one) and the information in the question.
2. **Label the figure** with any information given in the question. Sometimes you can plug in for parts of the figure as well.
3. **Write down formulas** that you might need for the question.
4. **Ballpark** if you're stuck or running short on time.

One way the test-writers can make a geometry question harder is by combining two standard shapes in one question. Here's an example.

18 🔖 Mark for Review

A certain circle has center O, and points R and S lie on the circle. In triangle ORS, the measure of angle ROS is 88°. What is the measure of angle RSO, in degrees?

Here's How to Ace It

The question asks for a measure on a geometric figure. There's no need to visualize the figure in your head when you can follow the first two steps of the basic approach. Draw a circle, label the center O, and then add points R and S on the circle far enough apart that OR and OS form an angle that looks close to 88°. Draw lines connecting R, O, and S to form a triangle.

The drawing should look something like this:

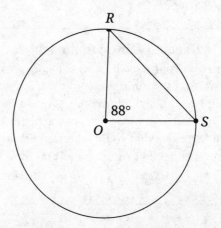

Since O is the center of the circle, OS is a radius and OR is a radius. Those are also two sides of the triangle, which means the angles opposite sides OS and OR have the same measure.

Label the figure with the new information, and it now looks like this:

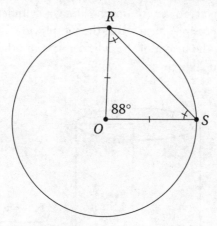

All triangles contain 180°, so the two equal angles add up to 180° − 88° = 92°. The question asks for the measure of one of those angles, *RSO*, which measures $\frac{92°}{2}$ = 46°. The correct answer is 46.

The previous question was about 2-dimensional shapes. Here's one in 3-D.

22 🔖 Mark for Review

A child makes a noisemaker by placing two identical blocks into a metal can. The can is a cylinder with a radius of 1.5 inches and a height of 4.5 inches, and the blocks are cubes with an edge length of 1.5 inches each. What is the volume of space in the metal can that is <u>not</u> taken up by the blocks, to the nearest cubic inch?

Ⓐ 7

Ⓑ 18

Ⓒ 25

Ⓓ 28

Here's How to Ace It

The question asks about the volume in a cylindrical metal can that is not filled by other geometric objects. Use the Geometry Basic Approach. Draw a cylinder and at least one cube on your scratch paper as best as possible. Next, label the figure with the information given. Label the radius of the cylinder 1.5, the height of the cylinder 4.5, and the edge of the cube 1.5. The drawing should look something like this:

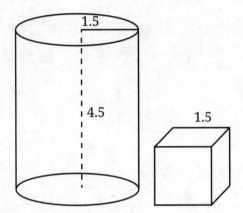

Next, write down the formulas you will need. The question is about volume, so write down the formulas for the volume of a cylinder and the volume of a cube. Look them up on the reference sheet if you don't have them memorized. The volume of a cylinder is $V = \pi r^2 h$. A cube is a rectangular prism in which the length, width, and height are all equal, so its volume is $V = s^3$. Plug the information given in the question and labeled on your figure into the volume formulas. The volume of the cylinder becomes $V = \pi(1.5)^2(4.5)$. Use a calculator to get $V \approx 31.81$ cubic inches. The volume of the cube becomes $V = (1.5)^3$, or $V = 3.375$ cubic inches. Don't forget that there are two cubes, so their total volume is 2(3.375), or 6.75 cubic inches.

Finally, you don't want all of that work to lead you to the wrong answer, so reread the final question. It asks for the volume in the cylindrical can that is <u>not</u> filled by the blocks. Subtract the combined volume of the two blocks from the volume of the can to get 31.81 − 6.75 = 25.06 cubic inches. Round to the nearest cubic inch to get 25 cubic inches. The correct answer is (C).

POOD Point

Was the previous question fun? Fast? Easy? Would it have been better to guess on it and go back to earlier questions that you skipped or marked for review? These are questions that you have to answer for yourself, but be sure to *ask* them. Don't just robotically do every question in order: that's what the test-writers want you to do. Instead, be an active test-taker and find the approach that works best for *you*.

Geometry on the Surface

Some SAT geometry questions are only superficially about geometry. They might describe a proportional relationship among parts of a figure or ask you to interpret something in a geometric context. Apply the Geometry Basic Approach as necessary, but recognize when setting up a proportion, using POE, or grabbing another tool from your SAT toolkit will help.

Try this example about interpretation.

---

14 ☐ Mark for Review

The volume of a cylinder can be modeled by the function $v(r) = 4r^3\pi$, in cubic centimeters (cm^3), when its radius is r cm and its height is 4 times its radius. Which of the following is the best interpretation of $v(8) = 2{,}048\pi$?

(A) When the radius of the cylinder is 8 cm, the height of the cylinder is $2{,}048\pi$ cm.

(B) When the radius of the cylinder is 8 cm, the volume of the cylinder is $2{,}048\pi$ cm^3.

(C) When the radius of the cylinder is 8 cm, the height of the cylinder is 10 cm.

(D) When the radius of the cylinder is 8 cm, the volume of the cylinder is 10 cm^3.

Here's How to Ace It

The question asks for the interpretation of an equation in the context of the volume of a geometric shape. Use Bite-Sized Pieces and POE to answer this question. Start by reading the final question, which asks for the best interpretation of the equation $v(8) = 2{,}048\pi$. The question states that $v(r)$ models the volume of the cylinder, so $v(8)$ must be a volume. Eliminate (A) and (C) because they refer to height, not volume. A volume of 10 is far too small if the radius is 8, so eliminate (D), which leaves (B) as the correct answer.

It is also possible to answer this question by plugging in. The question provides a value of 8 for r, so plug $r = 8$ into the function to get $v(8) = 4(8)^3\pi$, which becomes $v(8) = 4(512)\pi$, and then $v(8) = 2{,}048\pi$. Thus, when the radius is 8, the volume is $2{,}048\pi$, which matches (B).

Using either method, the correct answer is (B).

Similar and Congruent Triangles

Geometric proofs are *mostly* not tested on the SAT. The exception is similar and congruent triangles. For those questions, memorize the rules and follow the Geometry Basic Approach.

Two triangles are *similar* when at least **one** of the following is true:

- All three angles of the triangles are congruent (AAA).
- Pairs of sides of the triangles are in proportion, and the angle in between those sides is congruent (SAS).
- All three sides of one triangle are in proportion to the corresponding three sides of the other triangle (SSS).

Two triangles are *congruent* when at least **one** of the following is true:

- All three sides are equal (SSS).
- Two pairs of angles and the side between them are equal (ASA).
- Two pairs of sides and the angle between them are equal (SAS).
- Two pairs of angles and a side that *isn't* between them are equal (AAS).

Try the following example.

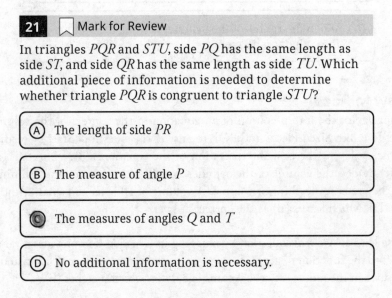

21 ☐ Mark for Review

In triangles *PQR* and *STU*, side *PQ* has the same length as side *ST*, and side *QR* has the same length as side *TU*. Which additional piece of information is needed to determine whether triangle *PQR* is congruent to triangle *STU*?

(A) The length of side *PR*

(B) The measure of angle *P*

(C) The measures of angles *Q* and *T*

(D) No additional information is necessary.

Here's How to Ace It

The question asks for information that will determine whether two triangles are congruent. Use the Geometry Basic Approach. Start by drawing two triangles on your scratch paper. Draw congruent triangles, but keep in mind that the question is about proving *whether* they are congruent, so they might not be. Congruent triangles have the same angle measures and the same side lengths, so draw two identical triangles. Be sure to match up the corresponding angles that are given in the question. Then label the figures with the given information. Mark sides *PQ* and *ST* as having the same length, and mark sides *QR* and *TU* as having the same length.

The drawing should look something like this.

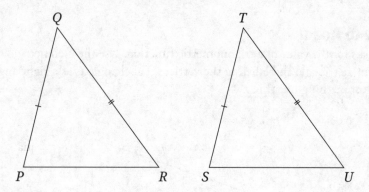

Without knowing anything about the third sides or any of the angles, it is not possible to determine whether the triangles are congruent, so eliminate (D). Choice (A) is not sufficient because knowing the length of side *PR* is not enough without also knowing the length of side *SU*; eliminate (A). Choice (B) gives only one angle in one triangle, so it is also not sufficient; eliminate (B). Choice (C) is sufficient because it allows you to test the side-angle-side (SAS) rule. If angle *Q* and angle *T* have the same measure, the triangles are congruent; if angle *Q* and angle *T* have different measures, the triangles are not congruent. The correct answer is (C).

Trig

Trigonometry questions on the SAT stick to the basics. If you have SOHCAHTOA memorized and take your time writing everything on your scratch paper, you will get trig questions right. Here's SOHCAHTOA in case you've forgotten it:

SOHCAHTOA

$$\sin = \frac{\text{opposite}}{\text{hypotenuse}} \qquad \cos = \frac{\text{adjacent}}{\text{hypotenuse}} \qquad \tan = \frac{\text{opposite}}{\text{adjacent}}$$

---

16 🔖 Mark for Review

In triangle ABC, $\sin(B) = \frac{70}{74}$. If angle C is a right angle, what is the value of $\sin(A)$?

Here's How to Ace It

The question asks for the value of a trigonometric function. Use the Geometry Basic Approach. Begin by drawing a triangle and labeling the vertices. Label angle C as a right angle. The drawing should look something like this:

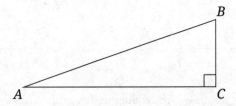

Next, write out SOHCAHTOA to remember the trig functions. The SOH part defines the sine as $\frac{opposite}{hypotenuse}$, and the question states that $\sin(B) = \frac{70}{74}$. Label the side opposite angle B, which is $\overline{AC}$, as 70 and the hypotenuse, which is $\overline{AB}$, as 74. To find the length of the third side, use the Pythagorean Theorem. You probably have this memorized, but it's on the reference sheet in case you forget: $a^2 + b^2 = c^2$. Plug in the known values to get $a^2 + 70^2 = 74^2$. Square the numbers to get $a^2 + 4,900 = 5,476$; then subtract 4,900 from both sides of the equation to get $a^2 = 576$. Take the positive square root of both sides of the equation to get $a = 24$. Label side $\overline{BC}$ as 24. With all three side lengths labeled, the drawing looks like this:

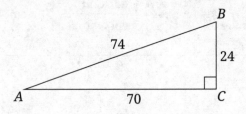

To find sin(*A*), use the SOH part of SOHCAHTOA again. The side opposite angle *A* is 24, and the hypotenuse is 74, so sin(*A*) = $\frac{24}{74}$. On fill-in questions there is room in the fill-in box for five characters when the answer is positive. This fraction fits, so don't bother reducing it. A fractional answer can also be entered as a decimal, with the decimal point counting as one of the five characters. In this case, $\frac{24}{74}$ ≈ 0.324324324, which is too long. Either stop when there's no more room and enter .3243 or round the last digit, which in this case also becomes .3243. It is allowed but not required to put a 0 in front of the decimal point, which would make the answer 0.324, but do not shorten it more than that. The correct answer is $\frac{24}{74}$ or equivalent forms.

There's one more handy trick to know for trig questions. In a right triangle, the two other angles (which are acute angles because they measure less than 90°) add up to 90°. The sine of one of the acute angles always equals the cosine of the other acute angle. Take another look at the triangle from the previous question to understand why.

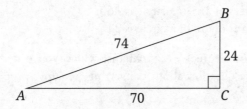

You already know that sin(*A*) = $\frac{24}{74}$ and sin(*B*) = $\frac{70}{74}$. Use the CAH part of SOHCAHTOA to find that cos(*A*) = $\frac{70}{74}$ and cos(*B*) = $\frac{24}{74}$. Since the side adjacent to one of the acute angles is the same as the side opposite the other acute angle, this will always be true. If an SAT question specifies that two angles add up to 90°, it's giving you a hint to apply this rule, and you might not even need to use the Pythagorean Theorem!

Radians

In your math classes at school, you are probably used to measuring the arcs of circles in radians, and you might have also encountered radians in calculus and physics. On the SAT, however, you are more likely to see an arc measured in degrees, and calculus and physics are nowhere to be found. When an arc measure is given in degrees, the arc measure is the same number of degrees as the central angle that defines it, like so:

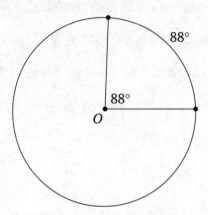

Radians are rarely tested on the SAT. When they are, you usually just need to convert radians to degrees or vice versa. The reference box provides all the information you need.

The number of degrees of arc in a circle is 360.
The number of radians of arc in a circle is 2π.

Thus, the conversion is 360 degrees = 2π radians, which you can reduce to 180 degrees = π radians. When you see a question about converting, set up a proportion and solve for the unknown value.

The following example complicates things by requiring an additional math operation.

17 ☐ Mark for Review

Angle A has a measure of $\frac{7\pi}{4}$ radians. Angle B has a measure that is $\frac{5\pi}{6}$ radians less than the measure of angle A. What is the measure of angle B, in <u>degrees</u>?

Ⓐ 150

Ⓑ 165

Ⓒ 315

Ⓓ 330

$$\frac{7\pi}{4} - \frac{5\pi}{6}$$

$$\frac{21\pi}{12} - \frac{10\pi}{12}$$

$$= \frac{11\pi}{12}$$

Here's How to Ace It

The question asks for the measure of an angle in degrees. Subtracting the fractions could get complicated with the different denominators. If you're comfortable working with fractions, go ahead and do that. The other option is to convert everything to degrees first. Set up a proportion for angle A: $\dfrac{180 \text{ degrees}}{\pi \text{ radians}} = \dfrac{x \text{ degrees}}{\dfrac{7\pi}{4} \text{ radians}}$. Cross-multiply to get $(180)\left(\dfrac{7\pi}{4}\right) = (\pi)(x)$, or $315\pi = \pi x$. Divide both sides of the equation by π to get $315 = x$. Thus, angle A measures $315°$. The question states that the *measure of angle B is*

$\dfrac{5\pi}{6}$ *radians less than the measure of angle A*, so convert $\dfrac{5\pi}{6}$ radians to degrees: $\dfrac{180 \text{ degrees}}{\pi \text{ radians}} =$

$\dfrac{x \text{ degrees}}{\dfrac{5\pi}{6} \text{ radians}}$. Cross-multiply to get $(180)\left(\dfrac{5\pi}{6}\right) = (\pi)(x)$, then $150\pi = \pi x$, and finally $150 = x$.

Thus, angle B measures $150°$ less than angle A, so angle B measures $315° - 150° = 165°$. The correct answer is (B).

Chapter 26
Use Everything

After working through the last few chapters, you now know some overall test-taking strategies, tactics that help you avoid trap answers and get questions right faster, lots of things the built-in calculator will do for you, and some of the more advanced or less common math topics. It's time to put everything together with a POOD review, a recap of how to recognize the best approach, and a comprehensive drill.

POOD REVIEW

Your personal order of difficulty (POOD) helps you decide what to do with a question within a few seconds so you can either start working on it or move to another question. Keep the following options in mind.

POOD and Pacing

- If the first step and each subsequent step are clear, Answer and Advance.
- If the first step is clear but a later step is confusing, Mark and Move.
- If the first step isn't clear now but might be later, skip for now.
- If the first step isn't clear and never will be, Guess and Go.

You did a POOD drill in Chapter 22 before you learned about all of the other options for approaching SAT Math questions. The drill is repeated below. Try the drill again, and then flip back to Chapter 22 to see whether your answers changed. Do some harder questions look easier now that you're an expert with POE, PITA, and Plugging In? Will the built-in calculator make a time-consuming question much more manageable? Are there math topics that you're still not completely comfortable with and want to save those questions for the end? Personal Order of Difficulty is just that, personal, but the skills you've acquired should help you approach the test your way, not the way the test-writers expect you to.

Look at the following 9 questions—all of which you worked through in the previous chapters—and then rank them based on your current POOD. Then compare the results to the same list you made in Chapter 22.

POOD Drill Revisited

7 ⬜ Mark for Review

$$\frac{3a-1}{7b+2}=c$$

The given equation relates the distinct positive numbers a, b, and c. Which equation correctly expresses $7b + 2$ in terms of a and c?

Ⓐ $7b + 2 = 3a - 1 - c$

Ⓑ $7b + 2 = \frac{c}{3a-1}$

Ⓒ $7b + 2 = \frac{3a-1}{c}$

Ⓓ $7b + 2 = 3ac - c$

9 ⬜ Mark for Review

The circumference of a circle is equal to twice its area. What is the area of the circle?

Ⓐ π

Ⓑ 2π

Ⓒ 4π

Ⓓ 16π

10 ⬜ Mark for Review

The function v models the value of a truck and is defined by $v(m) = 35{,}000(0.99)^m$, where m is the number of months after purchase. Which of the following best models the value of the truck y years after purchase?

Ⓐ $v(y) = 35{,}000(0.99)^{\frac{y}{12}}$

Ⓑ $v(y) = 35{,}000(0.99)^{12y}$

Ⓒ $v(y) = 35{,}000(12 \times 0.99)^{12y}$

Ⓓ $v(y) = (35{,}000 \times 12)(0.99)^{\frac{y}{12}}$

11 ⬜ Mark for Review

$$8|x-3| - 11|x-3| = -48$$

What is the negative solution to the given equation?

_____

12 Mark for Review

$$y = 4x^2 - 4x + 3$$
$$y = 3x + 2$$

At how many points do the graphs of the given equations intersect in the xy-plane?

- (A) 0
- (B) 1
- (C) 2
- (D) 3

14 Mark for Review

A certain amusement park sells two types of passes: half-day passes and all-day passes. The amusement park charges $40 for a half-day pass and $80 for an all-day pass. The amusement park sold a total of 70 passes one day for a total of $4,600. How many all-day passes did the amusement park sell?

19 Mark for Review

x	$g(x)$
-6	172
-4	86
-2	0

The table shows three values of x and their corresponding values of $g(x)$. If function g is defined by $g(x) = cx + d$, where c and d are constants, what is the value of $c + d$?

- (A) -129
- (B) -86
- (C) -45
- (D) 43

20 Mark for Review

$$(x + 3)^2 + y^2 = 9$$

The equation shown represents a circle in the xy-plane. A new circle is created by shifting the given circle up 4 units. Which of the following equations represents the new circle?

- (A) $(x - 1)^2 + y^2 = 9$
- (B) $(x + 3)^2 + (y - 4)^2 = 9$
- (C) $(x + 3)^2 + (y + 4)^2 = 9$
- (D) $(x + 7)^2 + y^2 = 9$

21 ☐ Mark for Review

In triangles PQR and STU, side PQ has the same length as side ST, and side QR has the same length as side TU. Which additional piece of information is needed to determine whether triangle PQR is congruent to triangle STU?

(A) The length of side PR

(B) The measure of angle P

(C) The measures of angles Q and T

(D) No additional information is necessary.

POOD RANKING

Question	My POOD Ranking
7	✍
9	✍
10	✍
11	✍
12	✍
14	✍
19	✍
20	✍
21	✍

QUESTION IDENTIFICATION

Part of the challenge of the SAT Math section—especially the harder second module—is pacing. Being able to look at a question, choose an approach, and start working as quickly as possible will help you get through the test faster without rushing. There are two places to look to identify the type of question and choose an approach.

How to Identify the Best Approach

- Use the Question—look for key words in the question stem, especially in the final question.
- Use the Answers—note the features of the answer choices, such as variables, words, or equations.

Here's an overview of the major tactics and tools and how to spot opportunities to use them.

Tactic/Tool	Question	Answers
Plugging In the Answers (PITA)	Asks for a specific value	Contain numbers in order or coordinates of points
Plugging In your own number	Asks about a relationship among values	Contain variables or unknowns
Bite-Sized Pieces and POE	Asks about representing a situation or interpreting something in context	Contain equations, expressions, inequalities, systems, or words
Built-in Calculator (can be combined with another tactic)	Involves graphs or something that could be graphed; asks for the number of solutions	Contain x- or y-values, coordinates, expressions, equations, or numbers of solutions
Solving	Nothing else works ☹	

In the following comprehensive drill, there is a space after each question for you to select your POOD choice, select the tactic you will use, and select whether you expect to use the calculator. It looks like this:

POOD	Tactic	Calculator
❏ Answer & Advance	❏ PITA	❏ Yes
❏ Mark & Move	❏ Plugging In	❏ No
❏ Skip for now	❏ Bite-Sized Pieces and POE	❏ Maybe
❏ Guess & Go	❏ Solving	

Don't spend too much time thinking before you start working: by the time test day comes around, you want to be making these decisions automatically. Plus, there might be more than one good way to approach a question; the goal is to identify the one that will be the most efficient and accurate for you.

Comprehensive Drill

For each of the following 10 questions, mark your decisions and answer the question. Come back to a question later if your initial POOD decision is to Mark & Move or Skip for now, and then either finish it or guess.

After you complete the entire drill, go to Chapter 27 to check your answers and read the explanations.

12 ☐ Mark for Review

The function f is defined as $f(x)$ equals 64% of x for all positive values of x. Which of the following could describe function f?

(A) Increasing linear

(B) Increasing exponential

(C) Decreasing linear

(D) Decreasing exponential

POOD	Tactic	Calculator
☐ Answer & Advance	☐ PITA	☐ Yes
☐ Mark & Move	☐ Plugging In	☐ No
☐ Skip for now	☐ Bite-Sized Pieces and POE	☐ Maybe
☐ Guess & Go	☐ Solving	

13 ☐ Mark for Review

The profit P, in dollars, made by selling x liters of a certain cleaning fluid is given by the function $P(x) = -3(x + 2)(x - 16)$, where $0 \leq x \leq 16$. Which of the following is the best interpretation of the positive x-intercept of the graph of $y = P(x)$ in the xy-plane?

(A) The maximum possible profit is $16.

(B) The maximum possible profit is $243.

(C) The profit when selling 0 liters of the cleaning fluid is 16 dollars.

(D) The profit when selling 16 liters of the cleaning fluid is 0 dollars.

POOD	Tactic	Calculator
☐ Answer & Advance	☐ PITA	☐ Yes
☐ Mark & Move	☐ Plugging In	☐ No
☐ Skip for now	☐ Bite-Sized Pieces and POE	☐ Maybe
☐ Guess & Go	☐ Solving	

14 | Mark for Review

The function p is defined by $p(x) = -3x^2 + 24x - 41$, and the function q is defined by $q(x) = p(x - 2)$. What is the value of x for the point at which $q(x)$ reaches its maximum?

(A) 2

(B) 4

(C) 6

(D) 7

POOD

❏ Answer & Advance

❏ Mark & Move

❏ Skip for now

❏ Guess & Go

Tactic

❏ PITA

❏ Plugging In

❏ Bite-Sized Pieces and POE

❏ Solving

Calculator

❏ Yes

❏ No

❏ Maybe

15 | Mark for Review

$$g(x) = (x - 8)(x - 7)(x - 4)$$

Function g is defined by the given equation. Function h is defined by $h(x) = g(x + 3)$. The graph of $y = h(x)$ in the xy-plane intersects the x-axis at three points. What is the sum of the x-coordinates of these three points?

(A) −28

(B) −16

(C) 10

(D) 28

POOD

❏ Answer & Advance

❏ Mark & Move

❏ Skip for now

❏ Guess & Go

Tactic

❏ PITA

❏ Plugging In

❏ Bite-Sized Pieces and POE

❏ Solving

Calculator

❏ Yes

❏ No

❏ Maybe

16 🔖 Mark for Review

A certain sequence has –12 as its first term. Each successive term is $\frac{1}{3}$ of the preceding term. The nth term of the sequence can be represented by which of the following expressions?

(A) $-12\left(\frac{1}{3}\right)^{n}$

(B) $-12\left(\frac{1}{3}\right)^{n-1}$

(C) $\frac{1}{3}(-12)^{n}$

(D) $\frac{1}{3}(-12)^{n-1}$

POOD

❏ Answer & Advance

❏ Mark & Move

❏ Skip for now

❏ Guess & Go

Tactic

❏ PITA

❏ Plugging In

❏ Bite-Sized Pieces and POE

❏ Solving

Calculator

❏ Yes

❏ No

❏ Maybe

17 🔖 Mark for Review

The function g is defined by $g(x) = 2(3)^{x}$. If $f(x) = g(x-3)$, which of the following equations defines function f?

(A) $f(x) = -6(-9)^{x}$

(B) $f(x) = -6(3)^{x}$

(C) $f(x) = \frac{1}{8}\left(\frac{1}{27}\right)^{x}$

(D) $f(x) = \frac{2}{27}(3)^{x}$

POOD

❏ Answer & Advance

❏ Mark & Move

❏ Skip for now

❏ Guess & Go

Tactic

❏ PITA

❏ Plugging In

❏ Bite-Sized Pieces and POE

❏ Solving

Calculator

❏ Yes

❏ No

❏ Maybe

18 ☐ Mark for Review

$$\sqrt[7]{2^{21}a^{35}} \cdot 3\sqrt[4]{6^4 a}$$

For values of $a > 1$, the given expression can be rewritten as ca^k, where c and k are positive constants. What is the value of $c - k$?

POOD

☐ Answer & Advance

☐ Mark & Move

☐ Skip for now

☐ Guess & Go

Tactic

☐ PITA

☐ Plugging In

☐ Bite-Sized Pieces and POE

☐ Solving

Calculator

☐ Yes

☐ No

☐ Maybe

19 ☐ Mark for Review

$$AB = 27$$
$$BC = 36$$
$$CA = 45$$

The lengths of the sides of right triangle ABC are given. Triangle ABC and triangle DEF are similar triangles, where A corresponds to D and C corresponds to F. What is the value of $\sin D$?

(A) $\frac{3}{5}$

(B) $\frac{3}{4}$

(C) $\frac{4}{5}$

(D) $\frac{4}{3}$

POOD

☐ Answer & Advance

☐ Mark & Move

☐ Skip for now

☐ Guess & Go

Tactic

☐ PITA

☐ Plugging In

☐ Bite-Sized Pieces and POE

☐ Solving

Calculator

☐ Yes

☐ No

☐ Maybe

20 ▢ Mark for Review

$$16x^2 + (4c + 4d)x + cd = 0$$

In the given equation, c and d are positive constants. If the sum of the solutions to the equation can be written as $k(c + d)$, where k is a constant, what is the value of k?

Ⓐ $-\dfrac{1}{16}$

Ⓑ $-\dfrac{1}{4}$

Ⓒ $\dfrac{1}{4}$

Ⓓ 4

POOD

❏ Answer & Advance

❏ Mark & Move

❏ Skip for now

❏ Guess & Go

Tactic

❏ PITA

❏ Plugging In

❏ Bite-Sized Pieces and POE

❏ Solving

Calculator

❏ Yes

❏ No

❏ Maybe

21 ▢ Mark for Review

$$p(x) = c^x + k$$
$$q(x) = p(x) + 8$$

Function p is defined as shown, where c and k are constants, and the sum of c and k is $-\dfrac{8}{5}$. If function q has a y-intercept of $\left(0, \dfrac{17}{5}\right)$ when graphed in the xy-plane, what is the value of c?

POOD

❏ Answer & Advance

❏ Mark & Move

❏ Skip for now

❏ Guess & Go

Tactic

❏ PITA

❏ Plugging In

❏ Bite-Sized Pieces and POE

❏ Solving

Calculator

❏ Yes

❏ No

❏ Maybe

Chapter 27
Math Drills:
Answers and
Explanations

CHAPTER 23: USE YOUR TPR MATH TACTICS

Use Your TPR Math Tactics Drill (Page 318)

7.   **A**   The question asks for the solution to a system of equations. The question asks for a specific point, and the answer choices contain points that could be a solution, so plug in the answers. Rewrite the answer choices on your scratch paper and label them "(x, y)." Pick one of the middle answers and try (C). You can start with either equation, but pick the one that will make the math easier. Even with the exponent, the first equation might be simpler. Plug $x = 3$ and $y = -1$ into the first equation to get $-1 = 3^2 + 2$, which becomes $-1 = 9 + 2$, and then $-1 = 11$. This is not true, so eliminate (C). Choice (D) will be even further off because squaring 11 will result in a large, positive number, so the right side of the equation cannot equal -3; eliminate (D). Try (B) next, and plug $x = -1$ and $y = 3$ into the first equation to get $3 = (-1)^2 + 2$, which becomes $3 = 1 + 2$, and then $3 = 3$. This is true, so try the same ordered pair in the second equation. Plug in $x = -1$ and $y = 3$ to get $3 + 2(-1) = 5$, which becomes $3 - 2 = 5$, and then $1 = 5$; eliminate (B). The only remaining answer is (A), so it must be correct.

       The built-in graphing calculator is also an excellent option for this question. Enter each equation into an entry field; then scroll and zoom as needed to find the point(s) of intersection. One of the nice things about the built-in calculator is that it will graph an equation in any form, so you don't need to rearrange the second equation. The graphs intersect at two points, $(1, 3)$ and $(-3, 11)$. Only the second point is in an answer choice, so (A) is correct.

       Once you become an expert with the built-in calculator, it will be an extremely efficient way to answer questions like this correctly. PITA is also efficient because you're just trying the numbers you see in the answer choices and doing arithmetic. Do you know what is NOT an efficient way to answer this question? Algebra. You would need to rearrange the second equation to set it equal to y, then set the two equations equal to each other, then combine like terms, then factor the resulting quadratic, and then set each factor equal to zero and solve. Notice that the answer choices use combinations of the same three numbers with varying signs, so you know that one small mistake will lead you directly to a trap answer. Algebra is the worst of the three options for this question, but it eventually gets you (A) as the correct answer.

       Using any method, the correct answer is (A).

13.   **D**   The question asks for a measure on a geometric figure. The question asks for a specific value, and the answer choices contain numbers in order, so plug in the answers. Rewrite the answers on your scratch paper and label them "l." Start with one of the middle numbers and try (B), 9. At this point, it will help to draw a rectangle on your scratch paper so you can label it and see what's going on. Opposite sides are equal in a rectangle, so label two sides as 9.

The drawing should look something like this:

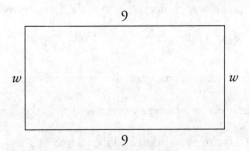

The perimeter of a geometric figure is the sum of its sides. For a rectangle, this can be written as $P = 2l + 2w$. Plug in the values for the perimeter and length to get $52 = 2(9) + 2w$, which becomes $52 = 18 + 2w$. Subtract 18 from both sides of the equation to get $34 = 2w$, and then divide both sides of the equation by 2 to get $17 = w$. Next, check whether this matches the other information in the question. The question states that the *value of l is 2 less than 6 times the value of w*. In this case, $w = 17$, so 6 times w is $(6)(17) = 102$, and two less is $102 - 2 = 100$. Thus, $l = 100$, which is definitely not the same as $l = 9$, the value that you plugged in. Eliminate (B).

The number you plugged in for l ended up being much smaller than the value of l after working the steps, so try a larger value for l, such as (D), 22. Label two sides of the rectangle as 22, and then plug $l = 22$ and $P = 52$ into the perimeter formula to get $52 = 2(22) + 2w$, which becomes $52 = 44 + 2w$. Subtract 44 from both sides of the equation to get $8 = 2w$, and then divide both sides of the equation by 2 to get $4 = w$. Find 6 times this value, which is $6(4) = 24$, and then subtract 2 to get $24 - 2 = 22$. Thus, $l = 22$, which is the same number you plugged in. Notice that (A) is the value of w, not the value of l. This is why you always label the answer choices: if you plug in for w instead of l, you will get the wrong answer. Once again, RTFQ avoids a trap answer! The correct answer is (D).

14.   **A**   The question asks for a change in value based on a formula. Since the question is about the relationship among variables, it's time to plug in. Since t is going to change, make it something simple like 2. Make a a multiple of 2, such as 4, to work well with the fraction. Now, solve for the lonely variable on the left side of the equation: $v = \frac{1}{2}(4)(2)^2$. This becomes $v = 2(4)$, and then $v = 8$.

Read more of the question to identify the next Bite-Sized Piece. The question asks about *the velocity of the object 2.5t seconds after it begins to accelerate*. You plugged in 2 for t the first time, so the new value of t is $2.5(2) = 5$. Plug $t = 5$ and $a = 4$ into the formula, and solve for v: $v = \frac{1}{2}(4)(5)^2$, which becomes $v = 2(25)$, and then $v = 50$.

Finally, find the ratio, but read carefully: the question asks for the ratio of the velocity after t seconds, which is 8, to the velocity after 2.5t seconds, which is 50. Ratios can be written as fractions, so this ratio is $\dfrac{8}{50}$. That isn't an answer choice, so reduce the fraction by dividing both the numerator and the denominator by 2 to get a ratio of $\dfrac{4}{25}$. The correct answer is (A).

19.　**C**　The question asks for an equation that models a specific situation. There are variables in the answer choices, so plug in. Choose a number that works well with the conditions of the question: since 150 is in the question, pick a factor or multiple of 150, such as 5. The question states that the dog eats *two cups of kibble three times per day for d days*, so when $d = 5$, the dog eats $(2)(3)(5) = 30$ cups of kibble. A large bag holds 150 cups, so $\dfrac{30 \text{ cups}}{150 \text{ cups}}$, or $\dfrac{1}{5}$ of a bag, is needed. Thus, when $d = 5$, $L = \dfrac{1}{5}$. Be careful not to write the fraction the other way: the dog is eating less than 1 large bag, not 5 large bags.

Plug these values into each answer choice, and eliminate any equations that are not true. Choice (A) becomes $\dfrac{1}{5} = 25(5)$, or $\dfrac{1}{5} = 125$; eliminate (A). The right side of the equation in (B) will be even larger, so also eliminate (B). Choice (C) becomes $\dfrac{1}{5} = \dfrac{5}{25}$, or $\dfrac{1}{5} = \dfrac{1}{5}$. This is true, so keep (C). Choice (D) will have a different result on the right side of the equation, so it won't work; eliminate (D). The correct answer is (C).

20.　**B**　The question asks for the table that contains values that are solutions to an inequality. There are numbers in the answer choices, but you can't plug in an entire table. Instead, let the answer choices help you decide where to start. If there were an x-value with four different y-values, you would almost certainly get the question right on your first attempt. That's not the case here, so start wherever you like. It wouldn't hurt to check $x = 1$ first because, if you're lucky and $y = 10$ is incorrect, you can eliminate three answers and be done. Plug $x = 1$ into the inequality to get $y < 6(1) + 7$, which becomes $y < 6 + 7$, and then $y < 13$. Thus, y cannot equal 13 when $x = 1$, so eliminate (A).

Compare the remaining answer choices: there are three different y-values when $x = -2$, so go there next. Plug $x = -2$ into the inequality to get $y < 6(-2) + 7$, which becomes $y < -12 + 7$, and then $y < -5$. Thus, y cannot equal -5 or -4, so eliminate (C) and (D), which leaves (B) as the correct answer. PITA and POE got you to the correct answer without having to try the third pair of values. The correct answer is (B).

21.　**B**　The question asks for solutions to an equation. A solution to an equation is a value of x that makes the equation true, so test each statement by substituting the given value for x. Be careful to plug in for x, not for c. Statement (I) has a number instead of a variable, so start there. Plug $x = -5$ into the equation to get $(-5 + c)(-5 + 5) = -5 + 5$. Simplify both sides of the equation to get $(-5 + c)(0) = 0$, and then $0 = 0$. This is true, so eliminate (A) and (D) because they do not include statement (I) as a solution to the equation.

Compare the remaining answer choices to see that it doesn't matter whether you try statement (II) or statement (III) next. If the one you try is a solution, eliminate the answer that does not have it; if it isn't a solution, eliminate the one that does have it. Statement (III) looks simpler, so plug $x = -c$ into the equation to get $(-c + c)(-c + 5) = -c + 5$. Simplify both sides of the equation to get $(0)(-c + 5) = -c + 5$, which becomes $0 = -c + 5$. Add c to both sides of the equation to get $c = 5$. Read carefully! The question states that $c < 4$. This probably seemed like unnecessary information at first, but it's important now. It means that c cannot be 5, so statement (III) is not a solution to the equation. Eliminate (C), which leaves (B) as the correct answer.

A question like this would likely be question 20 or 21 on the harder second module or question 22 on the first module, and it is by no means an easy question. However, by utilizing POE, a form of Plugging In, and, yes, a little algebra, you were able to keep working step by step and get it right. The correct answer is (B).

CHAPTER 24: USE THE BUILT-IN CALCULATOR

Use the Built-in Calculator Drill (Page 336)

14. **2** The question asks for a solution to an equation. Entering the square root symbol in the built-in calculator requires clicking open the keypad and finding the right button. To save some time, do a tiny bit of algebra first. Square both sides of the equation to remove the square root symbols and get $4x + 28 = (x + 4)^2$. Now enter this simpler equation in the built-in calculator, and then scroll and zoom as needed to find the positive solution. Click on the gray dot of the vertical line on the right to see that the coordinates are (2, 0). Thus, 2 is the positive solution to the equation. The correct answer is 2.

15. **B** The question asks for the value of a constant in a quadratic equation. The question asks for a specific value and the answer choices are numbers, so plug in the answers. Since the question is also about the number of solutions to an equation, use the built-in calculator. Enter the equation; if you leave out the "= 0" part, the slider tool will appear for b. Due to the size of the numbers in the answer choices, typing each value for b from the answer choices yourself will probably be easier than using the slider tool. Start with one of the middle numbers and try (B), 16. Enter $b = 16$ in the slider tool or replace b with 16 in the equation. The parabola is above the x-axis, meaning it has no solutions, so (B) is correct. If you had started with a different number, you would discover that, when $b = 36$ or $b = -36$, the vertex is on the x-axis, so the equation has one real solution. When $b = 324$, the graph crosses the x-axis twice, so there are two real solutions. When you use PITA, there is no need to try the other numbers once one of them works, so stop as soon as you try (B) and see that there are no real solutions. The correct answer is (B).

16. **19** The question asks for the value of a constant in a factor of a polynomial. This question is partly testing terminology: if the factor is $x - a$, the solution is a. Thus, the question is really asking for the greatest solution, or the greatest x-value when $y = 0$. Enter the expression in the built-in calculator. If the graphing area is at its default settings, you will see a narrow parabola and what looks like a straight line but actually isn't. There are gray dots at (0, 0) and (4, 0), so both 0 and 4 are solutions.

The equation has an x^4 term, however, so there should be at least one more solution somewhere. Zoom out to see whether a solution greater than 4 appears. You can use the minus button in the upper right to zoom out quickly and see that there is indeed another solution. Zoom back in as needed to see that this gray dot is at (19, 0), so 19 is the greatest solution and thus the greatest possible value of a. The correct answer is 19.

17. **D** The question asks for the value of an expression given a system of equations. Recognize immediately that this is a job for the built-in calculator, and then enter both equations. Scroll and zoom as needed to see the point of intersection, and then click on the gray dot to see that the coordinates of that point are (9, 16). Thus, $a = 9$, $b = 16$, and $a + b = 25$. There's no need for any messy and time-consuming algebra. The correct answer is (D).

19. **A** The question asks for the value of a constant in the solution to a quadratic. The question asks for a specific value and the answers contain numbers in order, so PITA is a good option. First, enter the quadratic into the built-in graphing calculator; then scroll and zoom as needed to find the solutions. Either enter the equation the way it is to see vertical lines at the solutions or leave out "= 0" to see a parabola. Either way, the coordinates of the solutions are (–3.732, 0) and (–0.268, 0). Write these down on your scratch paper to avoid having to look them up on the graph again.

Next, plug in each answer choice for c until one of them makes $-2 - \sqrt{c}$ equal one of the solutions. Start with one of the middle numbers and try (B), 4. Enter $-2 - \sqrt{4}$ into the built-in calculator or, because 4 is a perfect square, solve by hand to get -4. Neither of the solutions is an integer, so eliminate (B). The result was close to the solution -3.732, so the slightly smaller value in (A) might work. Enter $-2 - \sqrt{3}$ in the built-in calculator. If you entered the equation the first time, you can simply delete 4 and put 3 in its place. The result is -3.73205080757, which rounds to -3.732. This matches one of the solutions, so stop here. The correct answer is (A).

CHAPTER 26: USE EVERYTHING

Use Everything Comprehensive Drill (Page 376)

12. **A** The question asks for a description of a function based on a percent. You might think that you know the answer instinctively, but take your time and use all your tools to make sure you get the question right. First, compare the answer choices. Two choices say that the function is increasing, and two say it is decreasing. To determine whether the function is increasing or decreasing, one method is to graph it using the built-in calculator. The calculator automatically adds "of" after the percent sign, so translate "equals" as "=" and enter $f(x) = 64\% \ x$. The graph of this function is a line going up from left to right, so it is increasing. Eliminate (C) and (D) because they describe a decreasing function. Eliminate (B) because the graph is a straight line, not a curve like the graph of an exponential function would be. This leaves (A) as the correct answer.

Another option is to plug in increasing values for x and compare the corresponding values of $f(x)$. Plug in $x = 1$ to get $f(1) = \dfrac{64}{100}(1) = 0.64$. Plug in $x = 2$ to get

$f(2) = \dfrac{64}{100}(2) = 1.28$. Plug in $x = 3$ to get $f(3) = \dfrac{64}{100}(3) = 1.92$. The difference between $f(2)$ and $f(1)$ is $1.28 - 0.64 = 0.64$, and the difference between $f(3)$ and $f(2)$ is $1.92 - 1.28 = 0.64$. The values of $f(x)$ increase by the same amount each time, so the function represents a linear increase.

Using either method, the correct answer is (A).

13. **D** The question asks for the interpretation of a feature of a graph in context. Start by reading the final question, which asks for the best interpretation of the positive x-intercept of the graph. Enter the function into the built-in calculator; then scroll and zoom as needed to find the positive x-intercept. The coordinates of the point are $(16, 0)$. The question states that x is the number of liters and $P(x)$ is the profit in dollars, so the point $(16, 0)$ represents 16 liters and \$0 of profit. Eliminate (C) because it reverses these values. The maximum profit is the greatest value of $P(x)$, or y, which is represented by the vertex of the parabola. The question asks about an x-intercept, not the vertex, so eliminate (A) and (B). The correct answer is (D).

14. **C** The question asks for a value of x at which a function reaches its maximum. The question asks about the graph of a function that has been translated, or shifted, from the graph of the function given in the question. Enter both equations into the built-in calculator. Since one equation defines $p(x)$ and the other defines $q(x)$ in terms of $p(x)$, the calculator will graph both. A parabola reaches its minimum or maximum value at its vertex, so find the x-coordinate of the vertex of the translated function. Check which graph goes with which equation; then scroll and zoom as needed to find the gray dot at the vertex of the graph of $q(x)$. Click on the gray dot to see that the coordinates of the vertex are $(6, 7)$. The question asks for the value of x, which is 6, or (C).

Another approach is to find the vertex of function p and then apply the shift. Either use the built-in calculator or know that, when a quadratic is in standard form $ax^2 + bx + c$, the x-coordinate of the vertex can be found using the formula $h = -\dfrac{b}{2a}$. In this quadratic, $a = -3$ and $b = 24$, so the x-coordinate of the vertex is $-\dfrac{24}{2(-3)} = 4$. When graphs are transformed, or translated, subtracting inside the parentheses shifts the graph to the right. Thus, $x - 2$ shifts the graph two units to the right, which shifts the x-coordinate of the vertex from 4 to $4 + 2 = 6$, which is (C).

Using either method, the correct answer is (C).

15. **C** The question asks for the sum of constants given a function. One method is to use the built-in calculator. Enter both equations into the built-in calculator; then hide the graph of $g(x)$. Scroll and zoom as needed to see the gray dots that show the x-intercepts of $h(x)$. Click on the gray dots to see that the coordinates are $(1, 0)$, $(4, 0)$ and $(5, 0)$. The sum of the x-coordinates is $1 + 4 + 5 = 10$, making (C) correct.

It is also possible to solve using knowledge of the transformation of graphs. The x-intercepts of a quadratic are the values that give an output of 0. Function g is already factored, so set each factor equal to 0 and solve to find all of the *x*-intercepts. The *x*-intercepts of *g*(*x*) are (8, 0), (7, 0) and (4, 0). When graphs are transformed, or translated, adding inside the parentheses shifts the graph to the left. Thus, *x* + 3 shifts the graph three units to the left, which shifts the *x*-intercepts to (5, 0), (4, 0), and (1, 0). The *x*-coordinates of the *x*-intercepts of function *h* are 5, 4, and 1, so the sum is 5 + 4 + 1 = 10, making (C) correct.

Using either method, the correct answer is (C).

16. **B** The question asks for an expression in terms of specific variables. Since the question asks about the relationship between variables and there are variables in the answer choices, plug in. The question states that *n* represents the number of the term in the sequence and that the first term of the sequence is –12. Thus, when *n* = 1, the correct expression should equal –12. Plug *n* = 1 into the answer choices and eliminate any that do not equal –12. Choice (A) becomes $-12\left(\dfrac{1}{3}\right)^1$. Any number raised to the power of 1 is itself, so this becomes $-12\left(\dfrac{1}{3}\right)$, and then –4. This is not –12, so eliminate (A). Choice (B) becomes $-12\left(\dfrac{1}{3}\right)^{1-1}$, or $-12\left(\dfrac{1}{3}\right)^0$. Any number raised to the power of 0 is 1, so this becomes –12(1), or –12. This matches the value of the first term, so keep (B), but check the remaining answers. Choice (C) becomes $\dfrac{1}{3}(-12)^1$, or –4; eliminate (C). Choice (D) becomes $\dfrac{1}{3}(-12)^{1-1}$, or $\dfrac{1}{3}(-12)^0$, which becomes $\dfrac{1}{3}(1)$, and then $\dfrac{1}{3}$; eliminate (D). The correct answer is (B).

17. **D** The question asks for the equation that defines a function. One option is to use the built-in calculator. Enter the equations for *g*(*x*) and *f*(*x*), and then hide the graph of *g*(*x*) so it isn't a distraction. Then enter the equations in the answer choices to see which one generates the same graph as *f*(*x*) = *g*(*x* – 3). The equation in (D) works, so that is the correct answer.

There are variables in the answer choices, so another option is to plug in. Make *x* = 5 to avoid negative numbers. Since *f*(*x*) = *g*(*x* – 3), *f*(5) = *g*(5 – 3), or *f*(5) = *g*(2). Plug *x* = 2 into the *g* function to get *g*(2) = 2(3)², which becomes *g*(2) = 2(9), and then *g*(2) = 18. Since *g*(2) = 18, *f*(5) also equals 18. This is the target value; write it down and circle it. Now plug *x* = 5 into the answer choices and eliminate any that do not match the target value. Choice (A) becomes *f*(5) = –6(–9)⁵, or *f*(5) = –6(–59,049). This is far too large to equal 18, so eliminate (A). Choice (B) becomes –6(3)⁵, or *f*(5) = –6(243). This is negative, so eliminate (B). Choice (C) becomes $f(5) = \dfrac{1}{8}\left(\dfrac{1}{27}\right)^5$, or $f(5) = \dfrac{1}{8}\left(\dfrac{1}{14{,}348{,}907}\right)$. This is far too small; eliminate (C). Choice (D) becomes

$f(5) = \dfrac{2}{27}(3)^5$, or $f(5) = \dfrac{2}{27}(243)$, and then $f(5) = 18$. This matches the target value, so stop here and pick (D).

Using either method, the correct answer is (D).

18. $\dfrac{555}{4}$, **138.7, or 138.8**

The question asks for the value of an expression with two constants from an equation with exponents and roots. Apply the exponent rules and work in Bite-Sized Pieces. In a fractional exponent, the numerator is the power and the denominator is the root. A value without an exponent has an implied exponent of 1, so $a = a^1$. Rewrite the expression as $2^{\frac{21}{7}} a^{\frac{35}{7}} \cdot 3\left(6^{\frac{4}{4}} a^{\frac{1}{4}}\right)$. Simplify the fractional exponents to get $2^3 a^5 \cdot 3\left(6a^{\frac{1}{4}}\right)$, and then simplify further to get $8a^5 \cdot 18a^{\frac{1}{4}}$. Multiply the integers to get $(8)(18) = 144$. For the a-terms, apply the MADSPM rules. The MA part of the acronym indicates that Multiplying matching bases means to Add the exponents, so $\left(a^5\right)\left(a^{\frac{1}{4}}\right) = a^{\left(5 + \frac{1}{4}\right)}$. Use a common denominator to get $a^{\left(\frac{20}{4} + \frac{1}{4}\right)}$, and then $a^{\frac{21}{4}}$. The full expression is now $144a^{\frac{21}{4}}$. It is also possible to work with decimals instead of fractions, and that makes the expression $144a^{5.25}$.

The question states that the expression can be rewritten as cd^k, so $c = 144$ and $k = \dfrac{21}{4}$. Thus, $c - k = 144 - \dfrac{21}{4}$. Use a common denominator again to get $\dfrac{576}{4} - \dfrac{21}{4}$; then subtract the fractions to get $\dfrac{555}{4}$. The decimal form is $144 - 5.25 = 138.75$. This does not fit in the fill-in box, so either stop when there is no more room and enter 138.7 or round and enter 138.8. The correct answer is $\dfrac{555}{4}$ or an equivalent form.

19.   **C**   The question asks for the value of a trigonometric function. Use the Geometry Basic Approach. Start by drawing two right triangles that are similar to each other, meaning they have the same proportions but are different sizes. Be certain to match up the corresponding angles that are given in the question, and put the longest side opposite the right angle. Then label the sides of triangle ABC with the lengths given in the question. The drawing should look something like this:

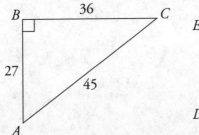
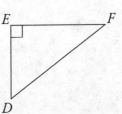

The question asks for the value of sin D. Because similar triangles have the same angle measures, the values of the trig functions for corresponding angles are equal. Angle D corresponds to angle A, so sin D = sin A. Use SOHCAHTOA to remember the trig functions, and find sin A. The SOH part of the acronym defines the sine as $\frac{opposite}{hypotenuse}$. The side opposite angle A is 36, and the hypotenuse is 45, so sin $A = \frac{36}{45}$. Therefore, sin D is also $\frac{36}{45}$. This is not one of the answer choices, so reduce the fraction by dividing both the numerator and denominator by 9 to get sin $A = \frac{4}{5}$. The correct answer is (C).

20. **B** The question asks for the value of a constant that is part of the sum of the solutions to a quadratic equation. It takes a lot of algebra to answer this question, but a shortcut is to recall that, when a quadratic is in standard form $ax^2 + bx + c$, the sum of the solutions is $-\frac{b}{a}$. In the given quadratic, $b = (4c + 4d)$ and $a = 16$, so the sum of the solutions is $-\frac{4c + 4d}{16}$. The question states that the sum of the solutions is $k(c + d)$, so set the two expressions that represent the sum of the solutions equal to each other to get $-\frac{4c + 4d}{16} = k(c + d)$. Factor the 4 in the numerator to get $-\frac{4(c + d)}{16} = k(c + d)$. Divide both sides of the equation by $(c + d)$ to get $-\frac{4(c + d)}{16(c + d)} = k$. Simplify the fraction on the left side of the equation to get $-\frac{1}{4} = k$. The correct answer is (B).

21. **4** The question asks for the value of a constant in a system of equations. The question gives a point on the graph of function q, so plug those values into the $q(x)$ equation, keeping in mind that $q(x) = y$. Plug in $x = 0$, $q(x) = \frac{17}{5}$, and $p(x) = c^x + k$, and the equation becomes $\frac{17}{5} = c^0 + k + 8$. Any value raised to the power of 0 equals 1, so the equation becomes $\frac{17}{5} = 1 + k + 8$, and then $\frac{17}{5} = 9 + k$. Use a common denominator of 5, write 9 as $\frac{45}{5}$, and then subtract $\frac{45}{5}$ from both sides of the equation to get $-\frac{28}{5} = k$. The question states that *the sum c and k is* $-\frac{8}{5}$, so set up an equation: $c + \left(-\frac{28}{5}\right) = -\frac{8}{5}$, which becomes $c - \frac{28}{5} = -\frac{8}{5}$. Add $\frac{28}{5}$ to both sides of the equation to get $c = \frac{20}{5}$, or $c = 4$. The correct answer is 4.

NOTES